THE POST-KEYNESIAN APPROACH TO ECONOMICS

NEW DIRECTIONS IN MODERN ECONOMICS
Series Editor: Malcolm C. Sawyer, Professor of Economics, University of Leeds

New Directions in Modern Economics presents a challenge to orthodox economic thinking. It focuses on new ideas emanating from radical traditions including post-Keynesian, Kaleckian, neo-Ricardian and Marxian. The books in the series do not adhere rigidly to any single school of thought but attempt to present a positive alternative to the conventional wisdom.

Post Keynesian Monetary Economics
New Approaches to Financial Modelling
Edited by Philip Arestis

Keynes's Principle of Effective Demand
Edward J. Amadeo

New Directions in Post-Keynesian Economics
Edited by John Pheby

Theory and Policy in Political Economy
Essays in Pricing, Distribution and Growth
Edited by Philip Arestis and Yiannis Kitromilides

Keynes's Third Alternative?
The Neo-Ricardian Keynesians and the Post Keynesians
Amitava Krishna Dutt and Edward J. Amadeo

Wages and Profits in the Capitalist Economy
The Impact of Monopolistic Power on Macroeconomic Performance in the USA and UK
Andrew Henley

Prices, Profits and Financial Structures
A Post-Keynesian Approach to Competition
Gökhan Çapoğlu

International Perspectives on Profitability and Accumulation
Edited by Fred Moseley and Edward N. Wolff

Mr Keynes and the Post Keynesians
Principles of Macroeconomics for a Monetary Production Economy
Fernando J. Cardim de Carvalho

The Economic Surplus in Advanced Economies
Edited by John B. Davis

Foundations of Post-Keynesian Economic Analysis
Marc Lavoie

The Post-Keynesian Approach to Economics
An Alternative Analysis of Economic Theory and Policy
Philip Arestis

THE POST-KEYNESIAN APPROACH TO ECONOMICS

An Alternative Analysis of Economic Theory and Policy

PHILIP ARESTIS
University of East London

Edward Elgar

© Philip Arestis 1992

All rights reserved. No part of this publication may be reproduced, stored in a retrieval system, or transmitted in any form or by any means, electronic, mechanical, photocopying, recording, or otherwise without the prior permission of the publisher.

Published by
Edward Elgar Publishing Limited
Gower House
Croft Road
Aldershot
Hants GU11 3HR
England

Edward Elgar Publishing Company
Old Post Road
Brookfield
Vermont 05036
USA

A CIP catalogue record for this book is available from the British Library

Library of Congress Cataloging-in-Publication Data
Arestis, Philip, 1941–
    The Post-Keynesian approach to economics: an alternative analysis of economic theory and policy/Philip Arestis.
    p. cm. — (New directions in modern economics)
    Includes bibliographical references and index.
    1. Neoclassical school of economics. 2. Keynesian economics. 3. Money. I. Title. II. Series: New directions in modern economics series.
HB98.2.A74 1992
330.15′7—dc20   92–6425
                                                                                                CIP

ISBN 1 85278 154 8

Printed by Bookcraft (Bath) Ltd

Contents

Preface   ix

1. **The Grand Neo-classical Synthesis**
   1.1 Introduction   1
   1.2 The micro and macro aspects of the GNS   1
   1.3 Economic policy analysis within the GNS   9
   1.4 Completing the GNS: the Phillips curve relationship   13
   1.5 The birth of rational expectations   21
   1.6 Concluding remarks   23

2. **Refinements of the GNS**
   2.1 Introduction   25
   2.2 New classical economics   27
   2.3 New neo-classical synthesis   30
   2.4 Open economy aspects   37
   2.5 The GNS growth model   43
   2.6 Business cycles   49
   2.7 Concluding remarks   57

3. **A Critique of GNS Economics**
   3.1 Introduction   60
   3.2 The atomistic, harmony and asocial nature of GNS   61
   3.3 Income distribution and the meaning of capital   65
   3.4 Rationality, optimization and equilibrium analysis   69
   3.5 Economic policy, rational expectations and market clearing   72
   3.6 Methodological problems   77
   3.7 Concluding remarks   85

4. Post-Keynesian Economics
   4.1 Introduction 86
   4.2 Prolegomena 88
   4.3 Methodological aspects and key features of post-Keynesian economics 94
   4.4 The constituent theoretical elements of post-Keynesian economics 101
   4.5 The post-Keynesian model 110
   4.6 Concluding remarks 115

5. Theories of Production, Investment and Distribution
   5.1 Introduction 116
   5.2 Production theory 117
   5.3 Theories of household and investment demand 122
   5.4 Distribution theory 133
   5.5 Concluding remarks 137

6. Theories of Prices and Pricing
   6.1 Introduction 139
   6.2 Kalecki's pricing theory 140
   6.3 Extensions of Kalecki's pricing theory 142
   6.4 Eichner's pricing theory 143
   6.5 Wood's pricing theory 154
   6.6 Inflation theory 159
   6.7 Concluding remarks 161

7. The Theory of Money Wage Determination
   7.1 Introduction 163
   7.2 'Target real wages' and 'wage-relativities' in wage determination 164
   7.3 Hysteresis effects 169
   7.4 Concluding remarks 177

8. The Theory of Money, Credit and Finance
   8.1 Introduction 179
   8.2 The endogeneity characteristic of money 180
   8.3 Money: residue not cause 182
   8.4 A model of money, credit and finance 186
   8.5 The post-Keynesian consensus on money, credit and finance 201
   8.6 Concluding remarks 203

Contents

9. Growth Dynamics and Business Cycles Theories
   9.1 Introduction ... 205
   9.2 Growth dynamics ... 205
   9.3 Business cycles ... 223
   9.4 Concluding remarks ... 239

10. Economic Policy Implications
    10.1 Introduction ... 240
    10.2 Obstacles to economic policy ... 242
    10.3 The closed economy case ... 254
    10.4 The open economy case ... 262
    10.5 Potential constraints ... 268
    10.6 Concluding remarks ... 270

Bibliography ... 273
Index ... 305

To Maro, Natalia and Stefan

Preface

Post-Keynesian economics is based on Keynes's ideas with the clear intent to extend them to their logical full development. As such it purports to complete the aborted Keynesian revolution in economics (Eichner and Kregel, 1975). Post-Keynesian economists view the 'grand neo-classical synthesis' (GNS for short) as fundamentally the neo-classical theory supplemented by a 'Keynesian' macroeconomics which is very different from Keynes's own ideas,[1] refined by its translation into mathematics by Hicks (1937) and Samuelson (1948). The GNS has been the dominant system of thought within the world of academic economics and, perhaps, within the world of most western governments, as is apparent from the theoretical content of their economic policies (but see Arestis, 1986b, for an exception in the case of Sweden).

For GNS, Say's Law provides a benchmark for economic systems of full employment. The GNS proponents argue that if Say's law does not hold, it is because of the existence of a number of rigidities. Thus, prices and wages are hypothesized as being rigid downwards, a liquidity trap in the demand for money and interest inelasticity of the investment relationship are the normal assumptions. Post-Keynesians insist that Say's law is refuted by the possibility of lack of aggregate demand in a monetary capitalist economy with or without any rigidities. Post-Keynesians do not dispute the existence of these rigidities; but even if they were removed, there would still not necessarily be full employment equilibrium. Even with flexible prices, sluggishly falling demand and prices reduce the flow of business income which may reduce expectations of further profits thereby causing less investment to be undertaken. The feedback on long-term expectations and the associated increase in bankruptcies pulls down prices and wages. With money wages falling, lower incomes ensue for precisely those people with the highest ratio of consumption to income. Thus, even if profit income increased equally to the decline in wages, consumer demand would decline. Flexible wages and prices by themselves will not, thus, drive the economy to full employment.

This book is concerned with the behaviour of advanced capitalist economies. Post-Keynesians argue that in such a system investment is not determined by saving.[2] Planned saving may differ from investment in the short run; and in the long run it is the level of saving – not investment – that adjusts with the possibility of the adjusted level being well below full employment. Investment is primarily an induced or derived demand from the expected growth in aggregate demand for goods and services. Firms make decisions on future investment plans on the basis of the relation between the trend in actual rates of capacity utilization and some desired rate of plant utilization, given expectations about the future growth of market demand and costs, and the expected profitability of various alternative investment projects. Given the state of external finance, firms choose a mark-up that might produce the required level of retained profits with which to finance the desired investment expenditure and persist with the implied price, allowing capacity utilization to vary with the level of demand around some average expected level associated with the chosen mark-up. External finance, however, is argued to be a subsidiary source of funds whereby the firm can satisfy the financial requirements of planned investment.[3] All these decisions are made with reference to the state of demand that experience suggests to firms as being reasonable. It follows that both the investment plans and the mark-up policy of the firm are influenced by the general state of business confidence. Investment plans and the size of the mark-up are inexorably linked through the demand for and supply of funds in the form of retained profits and external finance with which the firm finances proposed investment projects. In this sense the actual price is determined directly far less by current demand than by the mark-up which firms consider necessary to be able to increase their capacity sufficiently to meet the expected future level of demand. Clearly, the market structure thought to be prevalent in these circumstances is that of oligopoly. The typical firm is that of the megacorp (Eichner, 1976).

Investment is a primary determinant not only of output and employment but also of distribution. Post-Keynesians postulate that distribution depends on the rate of investment or accumulation: investment plans influence distribution through their impact on the mark-up, as mentioned earlier. Strictly, distribution depends on the mark-up. However, to the extent that the mark-up is determined by investment, then indirectly there is the link between distribution and investment, but not directly because this ignores any constraints on the ability of firms to increase the mark-up. The greater the rate of investment, and thus the more rapid the pace of economic expansion, the higher is the mark-up expected to be and the lower will be the relative share of income going to workers. Wages will need to be depressed, at least compared to profits, so that resources can be diverted from consumption into capital formation (unless, of course, there is excess capacity). Furthermore, if trade unions are to affect workers' share they must affect the mark-up. So if trade unions insist on workers obtaining a constant share of national income, any shift to a more rapid growth path will set off a wage–price spiral as trade unions first obtain higher wages to match the disproportionate increase in profits and then business firms insist on price increases to match the rise in unit labour costs. This process is accentuated by the capitalist insistence on a rate of accumulation without consulting the workers.

This book has two purposes: first, to argue that the GNS suffers from a number of weaknesses which render it inadequate as a body of thought which purports to analyse and explain real economic phenomena. We can summarize these problems as follows: the GNS was not really a synthesis of neo-classical with Keynesian ideas (as it purported to be) but merely the reassertion of the neo-classical framework with the addition of some Keynesian 'macro' terminology. The flavour of some of Keynes's specific policy recommendations was retained, but the essential *logic* of Keynes's economic theory was discarded. Thus the neo-classical synthesis clearly implied that the fundamental Keynesian revolution was aborted before it could establish roots in the economics profession (Eichner and Kregel, 1975). Essentially, then, the logic of the neo-classical synthesis is pre-Keynesian. This proposition entails further problems for GNS economics. These are: its unrealistic assumptions which purport to encapsulate how the real economy works; the inconsistency of GNS economics in terms of its attempts to combine the short-run Keynesian *disequilibrium* analysis with the long-run *equilibrium* neo-classical analysis (see, however, the relevant disclaimers by Swan, 1956, and Solow, 1956, about long-run equilibrium theory). We should also mention the failure of this economics to contribute to, or indeed, draw from 'social sciences'. So much so that it prompted Eichner (1983a) to argue that adherence to the principles of the GNS constitutes an epistomological 'obstacle', despite its formidable mathematical apparatus, which clearly implies that 'economics is not yet a science'.

The second purpose of the book is to attempt to put forward an alternative view emanating from the post-Keynesian tradition of economic thought. We hope to show that this approach provides a more fruitful and realistic starting point for economic analysis and study of a developed capitalist economy than the approach propounded by GNS. That post-Keynesian economics has become a serious challenge to GNS has been persuasively argued by Eichner and Kregel (1975) and Hamouda and Harcourt (1988). However, it should be pointed out at the same time that post-Keynesianism is not a homogeneous body of thought; indeed, it may sometimes appear that the proponents' only common focus is their dislike and rejection of the GNS (Harcourt, 1985; but see Hamouda and Harcourt, 1988, and Harcourt, 1989). None the less, there are some important characteristics and common elements which distinguish it from other schools of thought, especially from the GNS, and to which most, if not all, post-Keynesians would ascribe (Arestis and Skouras, 1985; Arestis, 1990).

It must be emphasized, though, that the non-homogeneity charge against post-Keynesian economics is also applicable in the case of the GNS economics. Non-homogeneity has different meanings with respect to different methodologies; but it is more damaging with respect to the GNS methodology which is based on classical logic and single axiomatic system. Whilst in post-Keynesian economics the common thread in the analysis may be the dislike and rejection of conventional economics, in the case of the GNS the common element springs from a shared view of its microeconomic foundations, and also from a strict adherence to a 'Newtonian atoms' view of economic agents. Indeed, authors working from a mainstream perspective have acknowledged this problem recently. Blanchard (1987) and Gordon (1990), for example, argue that in the case of recent developments within what we label below as the 'new neoclassical synthesis', there are theoretical explanations which are not always related. Mankiw (1988, 1990) argues in a very similar tone when reviewing recent developments in macroeconomics: the 'new classicals' and the 'new Keynesians', both being part of the GNS, are very far from moving 'towards a new consensus'. It is also worth mentioning Harcourt's (1989, p. 204) recent relevant remarks in this context: 'The attempt to confine Keynes's contributions within a small general equilibrium model allowed the neoclassical synthesis to occur.' And also the interpretation of Keynes's analysis offered by the neo-classical synthesis is viewed by post-Keynesians as 'illegitimate'. This charge was launched by Joan Robinson in particular, whose argument is summarized very colourfully by Harcourt (1989, p. 204) when he suggests that what neo-classical theorists 'saw as weaknesses were in fact strengths – to wit, a sense of time, of the structure of society and of economic life as a process'.

It should not, therefore, be surprising that we begin in the first two chapters with a comprehensive analysis of the GNS and its extensions, before we criticize it in Chapter 3. The rest of the book puts forward the alternative post-Keynesian economics; so that in Chapter 4 we offer an overview of post-Keynesianism emphasizing its methodology. Chapter 5 looks at production, aggregate demand and distribution. Chapter 6 is concerned with prices and pricing, and Chapter 7 concentrates on wage determination. Chapter 8 is on money, credit and finance and Chapter 9 deals with questions of growth dynamics and business cycles. Finally, Chapter 10 draws the policy conclusions of post-Keynesian economic analysis.

The book recognizes that whilst an established economics such as the GNS will show great tenacity in the face of an alternative such as the post-Keynesian theory put forward in this book, this latter has developed to such an extent that it must be seriously considered as a viable alternative. The book does not intend to erect a GNS strawperson, either, to be demolished and replaced by the post-Keynesian mould of thinking. The intention is rather to offer an exegesis of the GNS and a comprehensive critique of it. At the same time an attempt is made to put forward an alternative way of thinking about how the economy works and consider the extent to which it offers a more satisfactory way of understanding economic phenomena. We concur with J.K. Galbraith (1973, p. 1): 'I would judge as well as hope that the present attack will prove decisive. The established theory has reserves of strength. It sustains minor refinement which does not raise the question of overall validity or usefulness. It survives strongly in the textbooks although even in this stronghold one senses anxiety among the more progressive or commercially sensitive authors. Perhaps there are limits to what the young will accept.' It is hoped that this book will help to clarify the limits Galbraith refers to.

As will become obvious from what follows I owe a lot of the intellectual input to two very good friends and colleagues: the late Alfred Eichner, who introduced me to post-Keynesianism, and Malcolm Sawyer for stimulating my interest in this school of thought. Malcolm has read the entire manuscript and made numerous comments which he subsequently discussed with me very patiently. For these and other related discussions I am truly grateful. Vicky Chick, Sheila Dow, Geoff Harcourt and Tony Lawson are four more very good friends whose work has influenced my thinking on post-Keynesian economics. They have also been extremely helpful with their comments and suggestions on a number of aspects of the book. I also wish to thank Ciaran Driver (who has been very instrumental in and an excellent co-author of some of my post-Keynesian writings); George Hadjimatheou (with whom I have had numerous marathon conversations on post-Keynesian economics and economics in general, as well as on poetry!); Elias Karakitsos (with whom I have written so much about economics of the type that is not miles away from post-Keynesian economics); Peter Reynolds (who also helped me to redraft a much improved Figure 4.2); Andy Ross (who insisted so much on the usefulness of this book to students); and Frank Skuse (who so patiently made and discussed with me a number of points and observations). All read the whole manuscript and made a number of very useful comments and suggestions. Fred Lee, too, read parts of the book, and Donald Gillies patiently read parts of it and made helpful comments at very short notice. I would also like to express my special gratitude to Les Allen for his continous encouragement to write a book of this type. I am absolutely sure that it has been improved enormously as a result of their efforts, and in no way do I hold them responsible for any remaining errors or omissions. Marion Tighe typed a number of versions of this book; she and my personal assistant Pat Norris have been very tolerant of me during the long process of writing. I am grateful to both of them, as I am to Edward Elgar, Julie Leppard and Jo Rix who, as always, have been excellent commissioning editor, editor and editorial assistant respectively, as well as strong supporters throughout.

Finally, I would like to thank the following for special permission to draw on material I have published in their journals: the Association for Evolutionary Economics for work in the Journal of Economic Issues; M.E. Sharpe, Inc. for work in the Journal of Post Keynesian Economics; and the editor of the Review of Social Economy. Also, Blackwell Publishers, Cambridge University Press, Macmillan Press Limited, North Holland Publishing Company, M.E. Sharpe Inc., and Yale University Press for special permission to use diagrams from their publications as referred to in the text. This acknowledgement extends also to the authors of these publications.

Every effort has been made to trace all the copyright holders but if any have been inadvertently overlooked the author and the publishers will be pleased to make the necessary arrangements at the first opportunity.

NOTES

1. It should be added here that there are further differences between GNS and Keynes's ideas. The move from defining everything in *nominal* terms to *real* terms and the use of the price level rather than *wage units* (Weintraub, 1956) are differences of immense importance. Kregel (1976) analyses a number of methodological differences in this context. These include assumptions about uncertainty and its effects, rather than its existence or absence, and the concept of 'equilibrium'. In Keynes there are three models of 'equilibrium' (static, stationary and shifting), each taking successively more aspects of uncertainty into account in the model. Each model is applied to the same situation.
2. In other types of economies, for example Chick's (1986) first stage of banking, it is possible for saving to determine investment.
3. External finance is a very important ingredient of the analysis since without it there is the possibility of re-introducing Say's Law. As is clearly stated in the text, there is no intention to reintroduce Say's Law.

1. The Grand Neo-classical Synthesis

1.1 INTRODUCTION

The GNS model has its roots in the marginalist revolution of the 1870s. Its proponents claim that it is 'scientific', 'objective' and completely immune from any political persuasion. The 'scientific' standards of validation in the physical sciences are echoed and applied in economics. There exists a *positive* economics, quite separate from any normative considerations. Economics in this tradition is utterly free from historical peculiarities. The principles of economics are of a universal character and as such they are applicable to all forms of human societies and economies irrespective of history and social institutions. This ahistorical perspective enables this model to concentrate on one single case, the capitalist market economy. The GNS provides the intellectual justification for capitalism and operates as an apologetic for this system. Clearly, pre- and post-capitalist economies are ignored so that no attention is paid to stages of capitalism. A single view of capitalism is essentially adopted, that of perfect competition. Indeed, without the perfect competition assumption many of the crucial predictions, which form the ideological basis of *laissez-faire* capitalism, evaporate. There have been, none the less, developments of non-competitive models in GNS, though obviously the perfect-competition view still pervades most of the writing within GNS.

This chapter attempts to put forward and analyse the main ingredients of the GNS. Chapter 2 concentrates on attempts to further develop and refine it.

1.2 THE MICRO AND MACRO ASPECTS OF THE GNS

The GNS vision of economic behaviour is of choice-theoretic and market-theoretic fundamentals, with equilibrium being at the heart of analysis and with economic behaviour falling within the allocative mode of activity. Rational agents are assumed to trade stocks of commodities in the market place, which is supposed to be regulated by the price mechanism. In the absence of any structural, informational and other rigidities the price mechanism ensures a generalized market-clearing equilibrium. This is the very well known invisible-hand theorem. Divergences from a perfect allocative or full-employment equilibrium can only be due to a failure of one or more requirements of the invisible-hand theorem. Furthermore, the GNS is based on optimization behaviour by atomistic economic agents in perfectly competitive markets. This optimization behaviour is derived from utility maximization and profit maximization which are viewed as the main motives of individual economic units, both persons and firms. Aggregation of individual relationships thus derived produces the constituent elements of the macro aspects of the model.

Consequently, the starting point of GNS is the behaviour of the individual, and by summing up all individual functions macroeconomic theories of aggregate behaviour are derived. What is of paramount importance here is to point out that the sequence of events is from microeconomics to macroeconomics with no consideration of how the latter might affect the former. The constraints on individual behaviour that derive from the operation of the macroeconomic system as a whole are ignored. The question 'What is the macro foundations of microeconomics?' should, thus, be posed yet again (Crotty, 1980, p. 23). This is one aspect of the GNS that contributors such as, for example, Clower (1965) and Leijonhufvud (1968) focused upon. (More on all this in Chapter 2.) It is also very important to note at this juncture that aggregation is made possible through the assumption that all economic units can be accounted for by a 'representative' agent. The only distinction effectively employed is that between consumers and producers, but within these two categories all economic units are supposed to be homogeneous. All these features of GNS economics are taken directly from neo-classical price theory, with its roots firmly embedded in the 1870s marginalist revolution.

The nature of the behaviour of individual agents which underpins the observed aggregate relationships has produced interesting developments within the GNS. These have sought to overcome the micro–macro dichotomy which came about as a consequence of the emergence of macroeconomics. The choice-theoretic, market-theoretic and equilibrium-theoretic procedure which involved macro outcomes as a result of micro behaviour has given rise to a whole series of 'imperfectionist models' of macro misallocation whereby the micro–macro distinction has become less significant than previously. When we consider the aggregate relationships of the macro-economy of the GNS, we may refer to its *hydraulic* aspects (Coddington, 1976) which emerged especially from Hick's (1937) IS/LM interpretation of Keynes's (1936) *General Theory* – Harcourt (1989) suggests that both Harrod (1937) and Meade (1937) offered similar interpretations; see also Harcourt's (1969, 1984) contributions on the IS/LM theme. This interpretation focused on three relationships: the consumption (savings) function, the investment function and the demand-for-money relationship. The hydraulic aspects had three dimensions: the elucidation and elaboration of these three relationships; the extension of the IS/LM analysis to incorporate the issues of inflation, open economy as well as growth and business cycles; and thirdly, consideration of possible policy implications.

The aspects of GNS we have just briefly touched upon have been developed further and it is our intention to discuss them in Chapter 2. The rest of this chapter concentrates on the essentials of GNS which we sketch in the following set of equations:

$$E = C(Y - \bar{T}) + I(r) + \bar{G}, C_Y > 0, I_r < 0 \quad (1.1)$$
$$Y = E = Y^e \quad (1.2)$$
$$Y = Y(N), Y_N > 0, Y_{NN} < 0 \quad (1.3)$$
$$N^D = N^D(W/P), N^D_{W/P} < 0 \quad (1.4)$$
$$N^S = N^S(W/P), N^S_{W/P} > 0 \quad (1.5)$$
$$N^D = N^S = N^e \quad (1.6)$$
$$M^D = kPY + L(r), L_r < 0 \quad (1.7)$$
$$M^S = \bar{M}^S \quad (1.8)$$
$$\bar{M}^S = M^D = M^e \quad (1.9)$$

where a bar over a variable indicates exogeneity of that variable. The variables are defined as follows:

E = total expenditure
Y = aggregate income
C = consumption
T = taxes

I = investment
G = government expenditure
N = employment
W = wage rate
P = price level
M = money stock
k = the fraction of nominal income (PY) held in money
r = the rate of interest
e = superscript denoting 'equilibrium'.

Subscripts indicate first and second order partial derivatives. The variables are all in real terms with the exception of M and r which are in nominal terms.

The model comprises three markets and an aggregate production function − Equation (1.3) − which relates real income to employment. The three markets are: the goods market − Equations (1.1) and (1.2); the labour market − Equations (1.4)–(1.6); and the money market − Equations (1.7)–(1.9). We assume no foreign sector for the time being. When the above equations are graphed as linear relationships, with the exception of the production function which obeys the law of diminishing returns, that is to say $Y_{NN} < 0$, we arrive at the very well known diagram given in Figure 1.1 (see, for example, Blaug, 1976, p. 666; Harris, 1981, p. 166).

The IS curve is a locus of equilibrium points in the goods market when Equation (1.2) is satisfied. Differentiating totally Equations (1.1) and (1.2) and solving for (dr/dY) we have:

$$(dr/dY) = (1 - C_Y)/I_r < 0$$

which gives us the negative slope of the IS curve. Similarly the LM curve is a locus of equilibrium points in the money market when Equation (1.9) is satisfied. Differentiating totally Equations (1.7)–(1.9) and solving for (dr/dY) we obtain:

$$(dr/dY) = (-kP)/L_r > 0$$

which provides the positive slope of the LM curve. The production function (Equation 1.3) is the Y-relationship in Figure 1.1. The labour market is represented by N^S (the supply of labour) and N^D (the demand for labour); their interaction determines the equili-

Figure 1.1

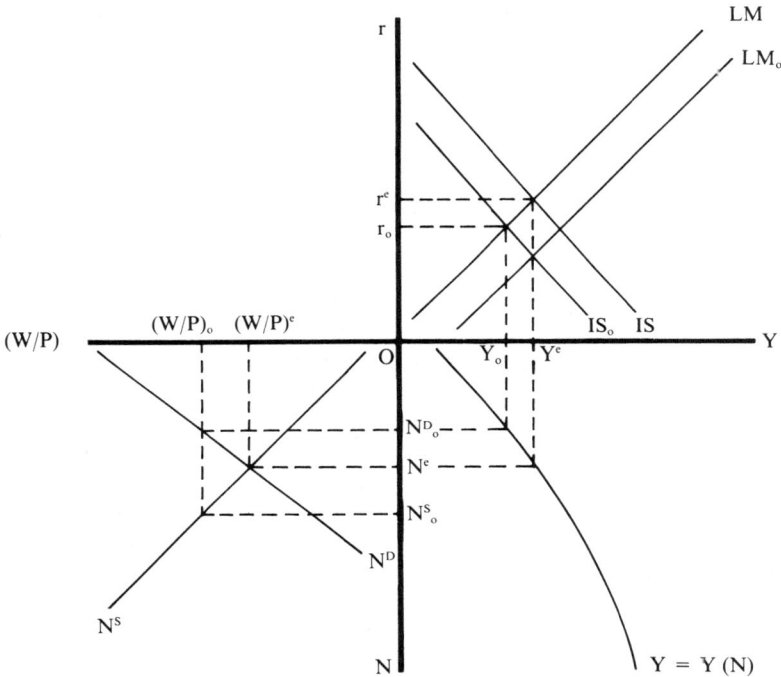

brium real wage $(W/P)^e$ and the equilibrium level of employment (N^e). With the latter determining Y^e – via the production function – at the intersection of the IS/LM relationships corresponding to an equilibrium rate of interest (r^e), the model is said to be at a full-employment equilibrium. Furthermore, this is shown to be a stable equilibrium. This can be demonstrated by assuming that because of lack of aggregate demand the IS (now IS_0) intersects the LM at Y_0. The resulting excess supply of labour $(N^S_0 - N^D_0)$ will cause wages and prices to fall by the same proportion. Falling prices shift the LM curve to LM_0 thus establishing Y^e. With high output, employment will be higher and the excess supply of labour disappears to give N^e and $(W/P)^e$.

The GNS does not, thus, differ very much from the pre-Keynesian neo-classical economics. For according to the latter, as employment decreases due to IS_0 producing $(W/P)_0$ real wage, it causes nominal wages to fall proportionately more than prices so that (W/P) falls to $(W/P)^e$ to clear the labour market with the goods market reverting back to Y^e equilibrium as a result of changes in the price level (LM shifts to LM_0). The latter postulate entails the main theoretical proposition of the school of thought that has come to be known as 'monetarism', while the assumptions of 'new classical' macroeconomics are also based on these principles although the emphasis is different. This school would stress the speed of adjustment in the various markets via the so-called 'market clearing' mechanism. It would not be an exaggeration to argue also that the ingredients of the 'rational expectations' school can be said to be based on this school of thought. (See Chapter 2 for more details on all this.) It is true to say that regardless of which of these schools of thought one subscribes to and despite differences in their internal mechanics, the implication is always the same, namely, that the economic system, left to its own devices, will always automatically tend to produce full employment (defined as that level of employment at which everyone has the best opportunity for employment subject to the physical and technological constraints of the real world). For the core of the economic philosophy to which these schools of thought adhere is basically that of *laissez-faire* economics as epitomized in the famous Walrasian general equilibrium model. The model asserts that 'market forces', in the absence of government interference, ensure that a capitalist economic system will always come to rest at full employment, with deviations from it being temporary and self-correcting. This means, of course, that markets behave like general equilibrium 'Walrasian markets' in that there is perfect competition, complete flexibility of wages and prices ensured by the existence of an auctioneer and the denial of the possibility of involuntary unemployment as an equilibrium phenomenon. It also means that there is a dichotomy between the real and monetary sectors of the economy, with relative prices being determined in the former (including the real rate of interest which influences real savings and investment and determines the composition of full-employment income), whilst the latter is concerned with the determination of the absolute price level within a quantity of money theoretic framework. The state protects the economic foundations of such a system; however, any overt state intervention in the economy or exercise of trade union power is condemned as causing rigidities in the system and, therefore, as a source of all disequilibrium phenomena.

The GNS proponents argue that Y_0 can be a level of output which can prevail for some time. This is attributed to rigidities in the system: a liquidity trap, an interest-inelastic investment and money-wage rigidity downwards can produce an under-full-employment level of output such as Y_0. What typically happens in the case of these rigidities is that the chain of events described above is broken somewhere along the line. When a liquidity trap prevails it is the demand for money that does the 'damage', in that given a low rate of interest and expectations of a higher interest rate economic agents will hold any amount of money available instead of spending it on bonds. Thus, the rate of interest cannot fall to induce a higher volume of investment. Similarly, if investment is unresponsive to interest rate changes, the falling rate of interest resulting from increases in the real money supply (itself due to falling prices) will simply fail to stimulate investment. Furthermore, if downward wage rigidity prevails, then again Y_0 can be sustained for some considerable length of time since, if wages do not fall as a result of unemployment, prices will not fall either and consequently the goods market will continue to produce Y_0.

An interesting defence of the automatic tendency towards the full-employment proposition, even with the assumption of rigidities other than prices, is the Pigou effect which introduces a real-wealth effect in the consumption function. This phenomenon is justified on the basis of the hypothesized utility-maximizing behaviour of individuals who are supposed to be choosing between present and future consumption. When this assumption is properly incorporated in the consumption function, Equation (1.1) can be re-written as:

$$E = C[(Y - \bar{T}), V/P] + I(r) + \bar{G} \qquad (1.1a)$$

where the partials are as before along with $C_{V/P} > 0$. V/P is real wealth where V stands for nominal wealth as the sum of money (M) and bonds (B), with all the other financial assets and physical assets being ignored as not changing in real value with P. The implication is that, given $C_{V/P} > 0$ and so long as wages and prices are flexible, there would be an automatic tendency toward full-employment equilibrium. In other words, falling prices, resulting from the excess supply of labour and consequent falling money-wages, shift the IS to the right up to the point where it intersects the LM at Y^e, thus making it possible to achieve full employment automatically.[2] Clearly, though, in the case of price rigidity the challenge of the Pigou effect is innocuous. The implications of the Pigou effect can be further qualified by referring to the following four arguments (by no means new to the literature): first, there is the interesting question of whether financial assets are components of net wealth. Secondly, there is the problem of expectations: to the extent that falling prices induce expectations of further declines in prices, current consumption could very well decrease, not increase. Thirdly, it might take an awfully long time for the Pigou effect to work. Fourthly, even if falling prices caused the IS curve to shift to the right, it may not produce full employment since not only may planned aggregate demand be influenced by real financial wealth but so may planned supply (this is usually justified by arguing that money balances should be treated as a factor of production). What this argument implies is that once Y^e is achieved, full-employment output will have increased so that Y^e now represents an under-full-employment situation.

When the GNS is couched in these terms, it is important to note Modigliani's (1944) early contribution to its development. This was that the GNS should only be considered as a partial-equilibrium explanation of the demand side, so that its analysis depends crucially on the assumption(s) made about the supply side of the economy. As demonstrated above, this assumption is in the form of money-wage rigidity, in which case involuntary unemployment turns out to be the result of supply maladjustment, not lack of aggregate demand. Consequently, GNS analysis adopts as its explanation of unemployment the pre-Keynesian thesis which emphasizes the nature and functioning of the labour market. It thus constitutes a departure from the Hicksian (1937) interpretation of Keynesian economics which views the determinants of aggregate demand as the major explanation of involuntary unemployment. The problem with this analysis is the assumption itself, in that no explicit choice-theoretic explanation is provided for wage rigidity. There were, of course, early attempts to elaborate upon the causes of wage rigidity. Money illusion, institutional and social restrictions, such as the impact of the monopoly power of trade unions on the downward flexibility of wages, are the most frequently cited suggestions. More recent and more formal developments within this tradition have relied upon these views as a basis for their excursion into this area. We discuss them in Chapter 2.

So, the importance of rigidities for GNS economics is that it can be demonstrated that unemployment can prevail for some time and, therefore, the argument that the economic system left to its own devices should always produce full-employment cannot be sustained any more. It follows from this, then, that economic policies become important and very much needed to help produce the required stabilization which should take the economy to the full-employment level of output.

1.3 ECONOMIC POLICY ANALYSIS WITHIN THE GNS

Discussions of economic policies within GNS usually focus on the sign and size of the various 'multipliers' which register the impact of a change in an exogenous variable on certain key endogenous variables. These 'multipliers' can be derived as follows: we may begin by totally differentiating Equations (1.1)–(1.9), substituting (1.1) into (1.2), (1.4) and (1.5) into (1.6), and (1.9) into (1.7) to give (in what follows we use C_Y instead of $C_{(Y-T)}$ for simplicity);

(i) $(1 - C_Y)dY - I_r\, dr + OdN + Od(W/P) = dG - C_Y\, dT$
(ii) $dY + Odr - Y_N\, dN + Od\,(W/P) = 0$
(iii) $OdY + Odr + OdN + (N^D_{W/P} - N^S_{W/P})d(W/P) = 0$
(iv) $kPdY + L_r\, dr + OdN + Od(W/P) = dM$

Next we solve for dY:

$$dY = [1 / [(1-C_Y) + (I_r/L_r)kP]]dG - [C_Y / [(1-C_Y) + (I_r/L_r)kP]]dT + [(1 / [(1-C_Y).(L_r/I_r) + kP]]dM \qquad (1.10)$$

from which:

$(dY/dG) = [1 / [(1-C_Y) + (I_r/L_r)kP]] > 0$ $\qquad$ (1.11)
$(dY/dT) = [-C_Y / [(1-C_Y) + (I_r/L_r)kP]] < 0$ $\qquad$ (1.12)
$(dY/dM) = [1 / [(1-C_Y).(L_r/I_r) + kP]] > 0$ $\qquad$ (1.13)

Depending now on the kind of rigidities that may exist different policies may have different impacts: consider the case where a liquidity trap exists (that is, $L_r = \infty$) or there is an interest-inelastic investment function (that is $I_r = 0$). In either case we get the following results:

$$(dY/dG) = 1/(1-C_Y),\ (dY/dT) = -C_Y/(1-C_Y),\ (dY/dM) = 0$$

If now it is assumed that it is the demand for money that is interest inelastic (that is $L_r = 0$) we get the opposite results where fiscal policies do not matter whilst monetary policy is effective, as can be shown from the expressions:

$$(dY/dG) = (dY/dT) = 0,\ (dY/dM) = (1/kP) > 0$$

The analysis so far has ignored what we labelled above 'wealth effects'. However, it is of paramount importance to explore the possibility of a wealth effect in the model as indicated in (1.1a) above. This is not difficult to do; (i)–(iv) would have to be rewritten as:

(i)' $\quad (1-C_Y)\,dY - I_r dr + OdN + Od(W/P) - C_{V/P}\,dV = dG - C_Y dT$

(ii)' $\quad dY + Odr - Y_N dN + Od(W/P) + OdV = 0$

(iii)' $\quad OdY + Odr + OdN + (N^D_{W/P} - N^S_{W/P})d(W/P) + OdV = 0$

(iv)' $\quad kPdY + L_r dr + OdN + Od(W/P) + OdV = dM$

(v) $\quad OdY + Odr + OdN + Od(W/P) + dV = dM + dB$

In fact, (v) can be expressed as $dV = dM + dB = dG - dT$ which is none other than the 'budget constraint'. It simply stipulates that any deficit in the government budget $(dG - dT)$ can be financed by printing new money (dM) and/or by borrowing (dB). Thus, any increase in government expenditure can be financed in three ways: raising taxes (dT), increasing the money supply (dM) and borrowing (dB). The way the deficit is financed can be very important. To show this we solve the system (i)' to (v) for dY to give us:

$$dY = [(I_r + L_r C_{V/P}) / [(1-C_Y)L_r + I_r kP]]dM + \\ [(L_r C_{V/P}) / [(1-C_Y)L_r + I_r kP]]dB + [L_r / [(1-C_Y)L_r + I_r kP]]dG \\ - [C_Y L_r / [(1-C_Y)L_r + I_r kP]]dT \qquad (1.14)$$

always subject to the 'budget constraint' $dG - dT = dM + dB$. We arrive at the following expressions:

(a) If $dG = dT$ (in which case $dM = dB = 0$) we have:

$$dY = [L_r(1-C_Y) / [(1-C_Y)L_r + I_r kP]]dG \text{ or}$$

$$(dY/dG) = [L_r(1-C_Y) / [1-C_Y)L_r + I_r kP]] > 0 \quad (1.15)$$

(b) If $dG = dB$ (in which case $dT = dM = 0$) then:

$$dY = [L_r(1+C_{V/P}) / [(1-C_Y) L_r + I_r kP]]dG \text{ or}$$

$$dY/dG = [L_r(1+C_{V/P}) / [1-C_Y) L_r + I_r kP]]dG > 0 \quad (1.16)$$

(c) If $dG = dM$ (in which case $dT = dB = 0$), we obtain:

$$dY = [L_r(1+C_{V/P})+I_r) / [(1-C_Y)L_r + I_r kP]] dG \text{ or}$$

$$(dY/dG) = [L_r(1+C_{V/P})+I_r) / (1-C_Y)L_r kP] > 0 \quad (1.17)$$

Clearly, the way deficits are financed does make a difference, as is indicated by Equations (1.15)–(1.17). This result highlights the importance of the budget constraint in policy analysis. The essence of this result does not change if a wealth effect is introduced in the demand for money. This can be shown by rewriting (1.7) above as:

$$M = kPY + L(r,V), \quad L_r < 0, \quad L_V > 0. \quad (1.7)'$$

We then make use of $(\dot{I})'-(v)$ as before:

(i)' $(1-C_Y) dY - I_r dr + OdN + Od(W/P) - C_{V/P}dV = dG - C_Y dT$

(ii)' $(1-C_Y)dY + Odr - Y_N dN + Od(W/P) + OdV = 0$

(iii)' $OdY + Odr + OdN + (N^D_{W/P} - N^S_{W/P})d(W/P) + OdV = 0$

(iv)' $kPdY + L_r dr + OdN + Od(W/P) + L_V dV = dM$

(v) $OdY + Odr + OdN + Od(W/P) + dV = dM + dB$

This system of equations can be solved as follows:

$$dY = [[I_r(1-L_V)+L_r C_{V/P}] / [(1-C_Y)L_r+I_r kP]]dM + [[L_r C_{V/P} - I_r L_V]/[(1-C_Y)L_r+I_r kP]]dB + [L_r / [(1-C_Y)L_r+I_r kP]]dG - [C_Y L_r / [(1-C_Y)L_r+I_r kP]]dT \quad (1.18)$$

Solving for (dY/dG) we may have the following cases:

(d) when dG = dT,

$$(dY/dG) = [L_r(1-C_Y) / [(1-C_Y)L_r + I_r kP]] > 0 \qquad (1.19)$$

and there is no change when compared to (a);

(e) when dG = dB,

$$(dY/dG) = [[L_r(1+C_{V/P}) - I_r L_V] / [(1-C_Y)L_r + kP]] \qquad (1.20)$$

which differs from (b) by the term $- I_r L_V$;

(f) when dG = dM,

$$(dY/dG) = [[L_r(1+C_{V/P}) + I_r(1-L_V)] / [(1-C_Y)L_r + I_r kP]] \qquad (1.21)$$

which differs from (c) above in that I_r is multiplied by $(1-L_V)$.

These results are very relevant, not just in terms of the discussion pursued so far but also of another related area, referred to in the literature as crowding out. More concretely, this is the proposition that increases in government expenditure unless accompanied by money creation will have very little, if any, impact on the level of economic activity as measured by the level of national income. The above analysis would suggest that although some crowding out may very well occur it cannot be complete; (dY/dG), in other words, is never equal to zero unless the demand for money is interest inelastic (that is, $L_r = 0$). Even in this case, (dY/dG) is not always zero, as can be ascertained from the results obtained above. We may note, however, that in the case of (e) and (f) if $L_r = 0$ then (dY/dG) < 0 so that 'super crowding out' occurs. Moreover, even if L_r is different from zero in (e) and (f), (dY/dG) can be positive, negative or zero, so that an increase in government expenditure need not expand demand.

An interesting critique of economic policy analysis of the type initiated in this section is rehearsed in Lucas (1976). The argument is that any such analysis based on the values of estimated multipliers is really of no help at all. This is so since the parameters of the model used to estimate the values of the multipliers are crucially based on historical data for periods during which the economic policy under scrutiny was not pursued. Since rational economic agents are expected to respond to changes in policy regimes, the parameters of the model are also bound to change. Consequently, economic policy prescriptions that rely heavily on historically estimated parameters are severely flawed, especially when the economic policy under investigation deviates substantially from previous policies. This contention has come to be known as the *Lucas Critique* despite the fact that it had been around as an argument well before Lucas (1976) – for example, in Keynes (1973). We return to the theoretical foundations of the contributions underpinning this critique in Chapter 2.

1.4 COMPLETING THE GNS: THE PHILLIPS CURVE RELATIONSHIP

Unlike Keynes's *General Theory*, the GNS as discussed so far is marred by a strict dichotomy between behaviour at full employment and behaviour at less than full employment (Lipsey, 1978, p. 49). At less than full employment the price level is assumed to be fixed and disturbances to the system are allowed to affect real income and employment; at full employment it is real variables which are assumed given, so that disturbances to the system affect the price level only. This dichotomy is removed through the incorporation of the famous Phillips curve relationship (Phillips, 1958; Lipsey, 1960). Consider Figure 1.2 where the symbols utilized are the ones we have already used, except $\dot{P}$ which stands for the proportional rate of change of prices over time and Y^* which refers to the level of income established by the IS/LM relationships without any reference to the determination of the price level. Y_f is that level of income where $\dot{P} = 0$ which could be the full-employment level of income. The line $OY_f\dot{P}'$ in the $\dot{P}Y$ plane shows the dichotomy referred to above: changes in the IS or LM which establish a level of income below the $Y_O^* = Y_f$ level imply no price changes, while changes which fix a level of income above $Y_O^* = Y_f$ imply price change only. The contribution of Phillips is to provide the relationship $\dot{P}_1'Y_f\dot{P}''$ so that any disturbance will have effects on both real and price variables. For if IS shifts to IS_1 following a disturbance, the resulting inflation ($\dot{P}_1$) causes LM to shift to LM_1 – the real quantity of money is lower – so that the economy comes to rest at $Y_O^* = Y_f$ with $\dot{P} = 0$. Similarly, if IS shifts leftwards – from the IS position – the fall in the

Figure 1.2

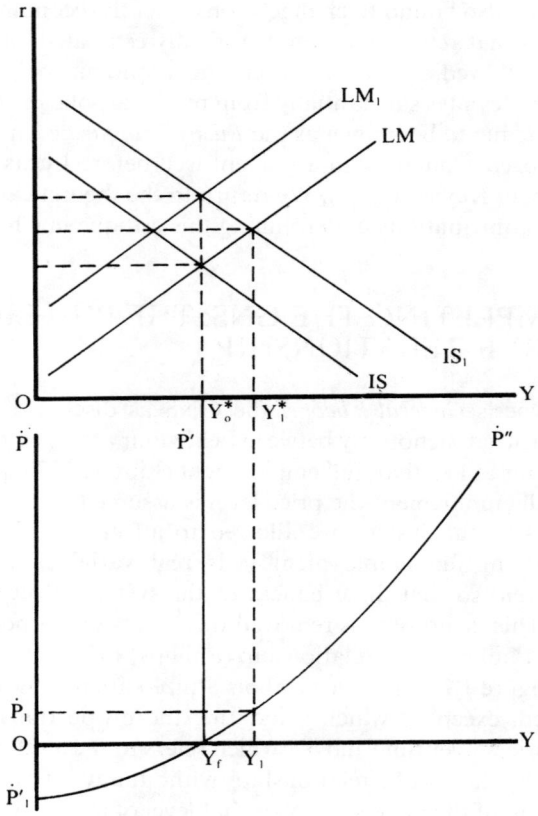

price level raises the real quantity of money and shifts the LM curve rightwards until again $Y_0^* = Y_f$ with $\dot{P} = 0$. Thus, 'the comparative statics of the macromodel closed by the Phillips curve are exactly those of the neo-classical model: there is a unique level of real income and a unique price level for any set of values of the parameters and the exogenous variables. What the Phillips curve does for the model is to provide a possible explanation absent from the dichotomised model, of the division of impact effects between real and monetary variables when the model is in disequilibrium' (Lipsey, 1978, p. 54).

Figure 1.3

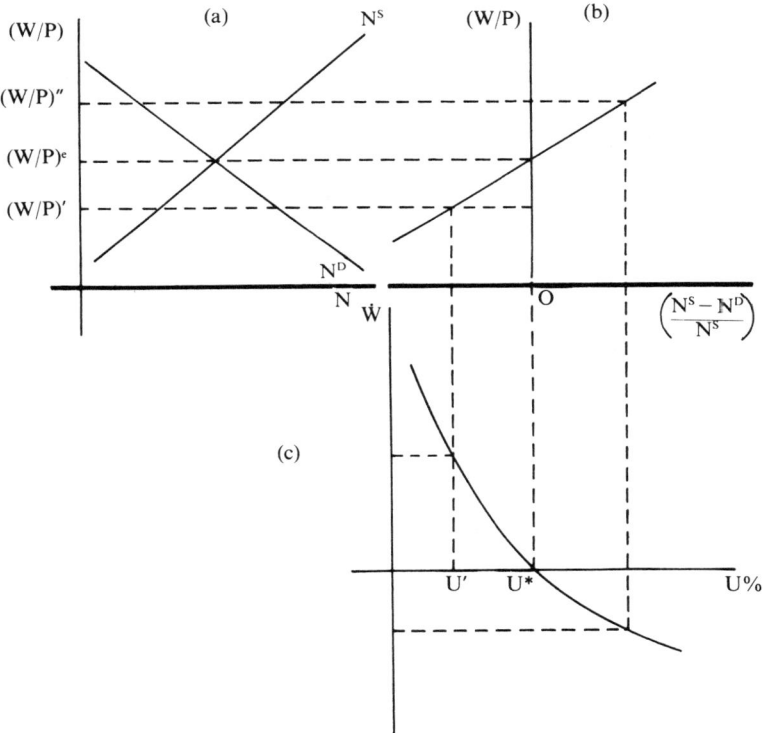

It is important to stress that the Phillips curve relationship was essentially an empirical discovery. Phillips (1958) carried out a statistical investigation of the relation between the rate of unemployment and the rate of money-wages in the UK over the period 1861–1957 with very little discussion of the theoretical underpinnings of this relationship. The theoretical justification for the observed Phillips relation was provided by Lipsey (1960) whose point of departure was a single 'typical' labour market, such as the one depicted in Figure 1.3a above where N^S is the supply of labour, N^D is the demand for labour, and (W/P) is the real wage. If the latter is below its equilibrium level, say at (W/P)', there is excess demand for labour; similarly, if it is above its equilibrium rate excess supply of labour ensues. This is depicted in Figure 1.3b, where the horizontal axis measures excess supply as a proportion of total labour supply. The problem with the latter ratio is that since there are no reliable data on the demand for labour, a testable relation based on the excess-supply proportion cannot be constructed. It is for this reason that Phillips and Lipsey used the unemployment rate as a proxy measure for the excess supply of labour. In Figure 1.3c, therefore, unemployment is used instead of $(N^S - N^D)/N^S$ on the horizontal axis. At point U* the going wage-rate in the market is the implied equilibrium wage-rate in Figure 1.3a; excess demand is zero. To the left of the point U* excess demand is positive and all unemployment is frictional; the wage rate is positive. To the right of point U* excess supply prevails and the wage rate is negative.

We thus have a negative relationship which is also non-linear; for the latter ingredient, though, an extra assumption is necessary, namely that changes in excess demand for labour are accompanied by diminishing marginal returns in reducing unemployment. It is clear, therefore, that the non-linear relationship in Figure 1.3c is firmly based on the proposition:

$$U = f[(N^S - N^D) / N^S] \qquad (1.22)$$

Aggregation over all markets will produce the macro Phillips curve which states that the rate of change in the money wage is high and positive when there is excess demand for labour, slow and negative when there is excess supply of labour. It thus clearly implies 'that lower unemployment can be purchased at the cost of higher inflation' (Tobin, 1972, p. 4). At U*, which is called the 'natural rate of unemployment', the rate of increase of money wages $\dot{W}$ would be zero. Furthermore, at a lower rate of unemployment, say point U', wages would rise and at an unemployment rate lower than U' the rate of increase of wages would still be higher. The policy implications of such a trade-off are clear enough. To the extent that there is such a trade-off between inflation and unemployment and a social welfare function could be chosen, then a point on the Phillips curve could be established which would represent an optimal combination available to policy makers. It ought to be pointed out at the outset that excess demand cannot be defined at all in markets where atomistic competition is not assumed (Sawyer, 1982a, p. 68). In the non-atomistic markets supply and demand functions cannot be defined; for example, under monopsony conditions quantity and price are not independent of each other for they are jointly determined by the monopsonist. Similarly, in the case of bilateral monopoly, price and quantity are determined by the joint interaction of both parties, so that demand and supply become meaningless. It has also been argued by Sawyer (1982a, pp. 70–4) that the mapping from excess demand for labour into unemployment is questionable.

Early empirical evidence seemed to suggest the existence of a short-run trade-off between wage inflation and unemployment; the evidence, though, for the existence of a long-run trade-off was rather inconclusive (Santomero and Seater, 1978, pp. 505–15). It was, in fact, demonstrated (Parkin *et al.*, 1976) that the Phillips–curve model retained its predictive capacity after 1967 only if expectations of price changes were included along with unemployment as an explanatory variable. But this then casts serious doubts on the existence of a long-run trade-off; for the expectations hypothesis denies the possibility of a non-vertical Phillips relationship in the long run.

The expectations hypothesis has, of course, been expounded by economists working within the neo-classical tradition (Friedman, 1968, 1975, 1977, and Phelps, 1968, are good examples). They argue that if policy makers attempt to sustain a level of unemployment below the natural rate they will, inevitably, plunge the economy into accelerating inflation, and into accelerating deflation if the target rate is greater than the natural rate. Now, the natural rate of unemployment is defined as follows: 'at any moment in time, there is some level of unemployment which has the property that it is consistent with equilibrium in the structure of real wage rates. The "natural rate of unemployment", in other words, is the level that would be ground out by the Walrasian system of general equilibrium equations, provided there is embedded in them the actual structural characteristics of the labour and commodity markets, including market imperfections, stochastic variability in demands and supplies, the cost of gathering information about job vacancies and labour availabilities, the cost of mobility and so on' (Friedman, 1968, p. 8).

This argument may be clarified by referring to Figure 1.4 where $\dot{P}^e$

Figure 1.4

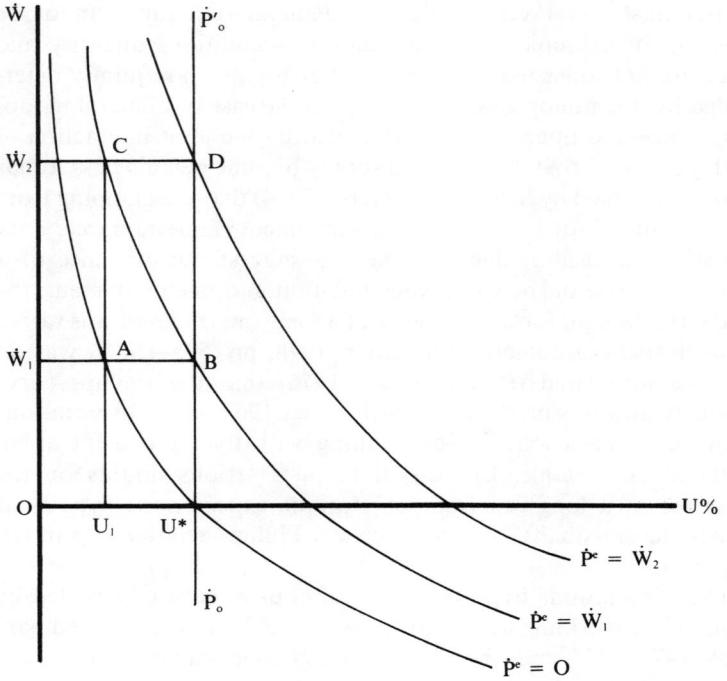

stands for the expected rate of change of prices, and U^* for the 'natural rate of unemployment'. When anticipated or expected rates of inflation are taken into consideration there is not one unique macro Phillips curve but instead a whole family of such curves with one curve for each expected rate of inflation. In Figure 1.4 three different trade-offs correspond to three different expected rates of inflation: $\dot{P}^e = O$ when no price expectations prevail, $\dot{P}^e = \dot{W}_1$ and $\dot{P}^e = \dot{W}_2$ when $\dot{W}_1$ and $\dot{W}_2$ inflation rates are anticipated, respectively.

Assume that the economy is at the natural rate of unemployment U^* and there is no inflation. If now the authorities reduced unemployment to U_1 by monetary expansion, then according to the Phillips-curve analysis a movement along the curve $\dot{P}^e = O$ would produce $\dot{W}_1$ rate of increase in money wages – there is therefore a clear trade-off between inflation and unemployment. As soon as inflation begins to become positive, however, individuals and firms would start to expect future price increases and would take price expectations into consideration when entering into new contracts. If a rate of increase in real wage of $\dot{W}_1$ is required, money wages would have to rise at a rate of $\dot{W}_1$ plus the expected rate of price inflation and the short-run Phillips curve would shift upwards. To the extent that the actual rate of inflation is fully anticipated in wage bargains, money wage rates would have to increase to $\dot{W}_2 = 2\dot{W}_1$ to maintain the real wage required to sustain a U_1 unemployment rate. If the authorities insist on maintaining the unemployment rate at U_1 through continuous monetary expansion, this process will continue, and the economy will eventually plunge into accelerating inflation (if U_1 were to the right of U^* the result would of course be accelerating deflation). In contrast, if the authorities do not insist on maintaining U_1, the rising price level would reduce the real value of the money supply and unemployment would start rising towards its natural rate U^*. And when the rate of increase of the money supply is the same as the actual and expected rates of inflation, unemployment would finally return to U^*. The economy would then arrive at point B on the new short-run Phillips curve $\dot{P}^e = \dot{W}_1$. Points like B and D trace the $\dot{P}_O \dot{P}_O{}'$ relationship, which is the long-run Phillips curve. In the long run there is no longer a trade-off; rather, the curve is vertical at U^*.

This theory can be expressed by the equation:

$$\dot{W} = f(U) + h\dot{P}^e \tag{1.23}$$

and for the 'natural-rate' hypothesis to hold the parameter h must be equal to unity. Thus the rate of change of money wages is determined by excess demand, proxied by the unemployment rate, plus the expected rate of inflation. When there is no excess demand the rate of increase of money wages would be equal to the expected rate of inflation; and when the latter is zero, wage inflation would also be zero. It follows that within this tradition inflation is caused by excess demand, which is mainly influenced by excessive monetary expansion and by expected inflation rates.

The above analysis depends, of course, on inflation being fully anticipated in the long run. When inflation is not fully anticipated, implying h < 1, the slope of the long-run Phillips curve would be steeper than that of the short-run curve, but it would be less than vertical; and in this case there would be a permanent trade-off between unemployment and inflation. The rationalization here of h being less than 1.0 has been attributed to 'money illusion' in the supply of labour (Tobin, 1967).

Clearly, the implications of the 'natural-rate' hypothesis for policy-makers are very strong indeed. First, inflationary policies which attempt to reduce unemployment below the equilibrium level (U*) will eventually result in accelerating inflation and continuous disequilibrium. Secondly, no trade-off exists in the long-run; but even in the short run 'Phillips-curves result from misinformation and suboptimal adjustment to economic realities' (Santomero and Seater, 1978, p. 525). Acceptance, therefore, of this hypothesis implies that policy-makers are faced with a severe reduction in their policy options. A major implication of this analysis for mainstream economic theory has been the realization of the lack of a rigorous microeconomic foundation of the theory of unemployment and inflation. This has led to the development of the so-called 'search theories' of unemployment, of which Phelps (1970) constitutes a representative approach.

Most of the 'search theories' make the assumption that all unemployment is 'search unemployment', with the individual being unable to work and search simultaneously, so that when the individual embarks on search s/he is necessarily unemployed. With the further assumption that the individual attempts to maximize the present value of lifetime income, the individual's problem is to decide how long to search, or equivalently to choose an 'optimal reservation' (or 'acceptance') wage. If an offer is below the reservation wage, it is rejected and search continues. If an offer is above the acceptance wage, it is accepted, employment begins and search ends. The reservation wage is seen as that wage which equates the marginal costs and gains from search. If it is also assumed that the individual's perception of the rate of inflation lags behind the actual rate, then a Phillips curve relationship emerges. An increase in the actual rate of inflation induces the individual to reduce search and become employed, because s/he receives unexpectedly high wage offers, and as a result unemployment falls. Once, however, the individual's perceived rate of inflation equals the actual rate, the individual will have reverted to the original level of search and employment will have gone to its original rate. Thus an anticipated increase in the rate of inflation reduces unemployment temporarily, but ultimately leaves it unchanged. The short-run Phillips curve is negatively sloped and the long-run curve is vertical; there is no trade-off in the long run. In this sense 'search theories' are part of the critique of the original Phillips curve. Its adoption by auction-market models with market-clearing outcomes reflects the belief in the efficiency of the price mechanism. This is made possible by the assumption of individual economic agents possessing sufficient price-adjustment information. Unemployment in this model is the result of economic agents having imperfect quantity-offer information so far as their labour supply decisions are concerned.

All these theories have come under severe attack. Perhaps the most important criticism derives from the inconsistency between search theory's implications and empirical observations. As Tobin (1972) pointed out, in search-theoretic explanations of the Phillips curve all unemployment is assumed to be voluntary, with the important phenomenon of layoffs completely ignored. Furthermore, they are based on the premise of 'clearing markets' and on the tendency of the economy to settle down at a full-employment equilibrium. This ignores any consideration of the institutional nature of the business sector, the segmentation of markets and the code of conduct of firms, that is, ideas propounded by non-neo-classical economists (for a guide see Eichner, 1979b; also Rowthorn, 1977). At the empirical level there is the problem of the numerical value of h, where the evidence is utterly inconclusive.[3] Furthermore, the natural-rate theories cannot explain why the economy since the Second World War has experienced long periods during which the actual rate of unemployment has been greater than the natural rate without accelerating deflations at the same time, as such theorists would have us believe. Similarly, for the 1950s and 1960s in particular, when unemployment was very low, there were substantial positive rates of inflation without there being signs of accelerating inflation.

1.5 THE BIRTH OF RATIONAL EXPECTATIONS

Whereas the theories just reviewed accept the possibility of a short-run Phillips curve but not a long-run one, there exists a more 'radical' school of thought, the so-called 'rational expectations' school, that flatly denies the existence of either a short-run or a long-run Phillips curve. The term 'rational expectations' was first introduced to the literature by Muth (1961), who argued 'that expectations, since they are informed predictions of future events, are essentially the same as the predictions of the relevant economic theory' (p. 316); (see also Sargent and Wallace, 1976). The 'rational expectations' school argues that since economic agents are rational, they are in a position to discern for themselves the 'correct theory' of what determines changes in the price level. All the determinants of inflation are known to, and understood by, the rational economic agents, who are supposed to have and to seek information up to the point where the expected marginal benefit is equal to the marginal cost of acquiring information, including information about the likely course of economic policy. Prediction errors could of course arise when the economy is subject to random shocks, or indeed because economic agents possess incomplete or limited information about the inflationary mechanism. This situation is unlikely to persist for long, however, for since economic agents are rational, they are capable of quickly incorporating new experiences and information into their expectations, which implies that systematic prediction errors are swiftly perceived and eradicated. As a result economic agents form their expectations with complete accuracy, in that their price expectations are the same as those implied by the actual inflation-generating mechanism. Price expectations are therefore unbiased and the economy will always rapidly return to its long-run steady-state equilibrium, which must imply that no short-run or long-run Phillips curve exists.

The policy implications of 'rational expectations' are clear. Rational economic agents can and do utilize the 'correct theory' to anticipate the impact of economic policies, so that when stabilization actions by the authorities occur they have no impact at all on real variables, since economic agents by making adjustments to nominal wages and prices will have neutralized in advance the effects of such actions. The only way policies can have even a short-run impact on real variables is for policy-makers to act in an unpredictable random fashion, in such a way that cannot be anticipated by rational economic agents.

We may refer to an example to clarify all these points. Suppose that the policy-makers announce their intention to increase the money stock, that economic agents are convinced that this increase will come about, and that the money stock does change eventually, as announced. Economic agents are supposed to react by increasing their price and wage expectations, in a way consistent with the price increases that are likely to come about from the monetary stimulus. Being rational, economic agents would actually correctly predict the price and wage changes induced by this policy and the result would be that real wages would not change, with neither employment nor output being affected. The increase in the money supply would only cause inflation. If, however, policy-makers act in an unpredictable manner, they could cause changes in the real variables. But in this case they could very well induce economic agents to over-estimate the inflationary impact of the policy action, so that producers may in the short run believe that the relative price of their product has fallen and workers perceive a decline in their real wage. As a result employment and production might actually decline. But this result would not be in the intended direction and, in any case, it would be short-lived, since rational economic agents adjust their expectations in the proper direction as new information is gathered.

1.6 CONCLUDING REMARKS

This chapter has put forward the main ingredients of the GNS. It has also discussed certain early developments of this school of thought which form the analytical basis for the more recent developments that have taken place within it.

One such development which we have discussed in this chapter is the hypothesis of rational expectations. When rational expectations prevail, stabilization policies are impotent, and even when they do affect real economic magnitudes not only is the impact of a short-run nature, but it may not be in the intended direction either. It is also important to emphasize that these results require not just the assumption of rational expectations but the additional one of 'market clearing'. These two assumptions are of paramount significance to the subsequent and more recent developments of the GNS and their importance will be highlighted further in Chapter 2.

NOTES

1. For an interesting survey of the literature, the reader is referred to Fischer (1988). Mankiw (1988) offers a survey of the literature from a critical perspective, followed by comments (Stein, 1988; Phelps, 1988).
2. It should be remembered that in the case considered in the text the LM could also be shown to shift to the right with a lower price level. But within a liquidity trap position, the LM is not affected. In the case of an interest-inelastic investment relationship, however, the LM does shift to the right.
3. The evidence ranges from the results provided by Solow (1969), who obtained an estimate for h of roughly 0.4, to the results of Saunders and Nobay (1972) and Parkin *et al.* (1976), who reported values for h which were close to 1.0. Cross and Laidler (1975), using data for 20 individual countries, found no evidence of a long-run trade-off for any country. Furthermore, according to Laidler and Parkin (1975), about half of the studies which employed the expectations hypothesis generated a coefficient on $\dot{P}^e$ significantly different from unity. We may also refer to Lipsey's (1978) observation that 'although inflationary expectations have undoubtedly adjusted to the more rapid rates of inflation in the seventies, even the most casual observation of the economy shows that we are a very long way from a fully anticipated inflation' (p. 66).

2. Refinements of the GNS

2.1 INTRODUCTION

A number of developments which have taken place recently constitute further explorations within the GNS. They are, in fact, refinements of the essential theme of GNS elaborated upon in Chapter 1. It is the purpose of this chapter to consider them. In order to appreciate fully the theoretical underpinnings of these refinements it will be helpful to introduce at this juncture the notions of aggregate demand and aggregate supply.

Consider Figure 2.1 where we reproduce Figure 1.1 and add another segment with price level (P) and real output (Y) as axes. We define the aggregate demand curve as the combination of the price level and real output at which the goods and money markets are in equilibrium. We can then assume different price levels and work out the corresponding equilibrium real income levels from segments (r,Y) and (N,Y). These different points trace in Figure 2.1 the relationship labelled AD. For example, price level P^e corresponds to $LM(P^e)$ and together with the IS they determine Y^e. Projecting Y^e via the production function into the (P,Y) segment, point (P^e, Y^e) is established. Next assume price level P_0'' ($> P^e$). $LM(P^e)$ shifts now to $LM(P_0'')$ with output being now Y_0 which as before is projected on the (P,Y) plane. A price level lower than P^e, say P_0', would establish Y_1 and thus another point on the (P,Y) segment. Joining all these points together we arrive at the relationship AD. It must be noted that the AD relationship is derived directly from the IS/LM framework as expounded above. It is, therefore, an equilibrium relationship in that every point along it represents simultaneous equilibrium in both the money and goods markets. Its position and slope are crucially determined by the factors which govern both IS and LM.

Similarly, the aggregate supply curve is defined as the combi-

Figure 2.1

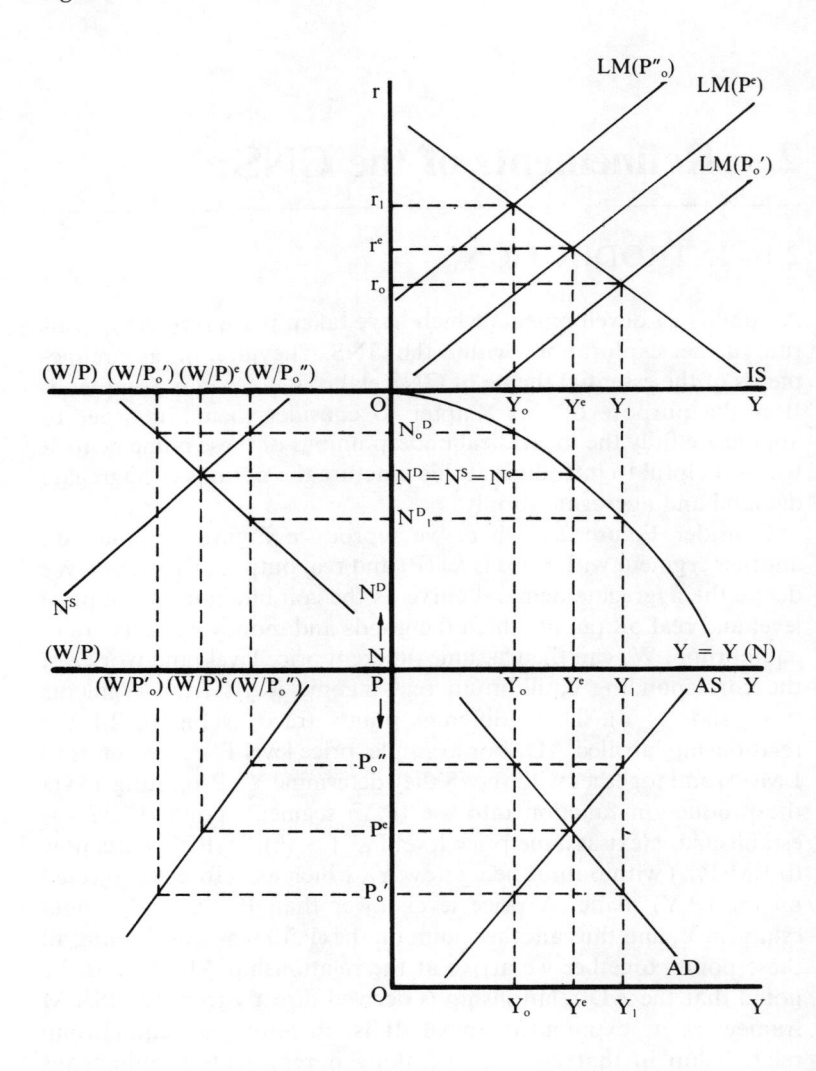

nation of output firms are willing to produce at different levels of prices. Returning to Figure 2.1 at P^e which is consistent with the labour market being at equilibrium, firms in the aggregate are willing to supply Y^e for a real wage $(W/P)^e$. We next assume that with given W, $P_O'' > P^e$ is established. (W/P_O'') will be, therefore, lower than $(W/P)^e$ so that the demand for labour increases to N^D_1 and via the production function a level of output Y_1 ($> Y^e$) ensues, so that point $P_O''Y_1$ in the (P,Y) segment results. If P_O' ($< P^e$) is the price level then the real wage is (W/P_O'), higher than $(W/P)^e$, with demand for labour N_O^D and Y_O level of output. Point $P_O' \; Y_O$ is now in order. Joining all these points we derive the AS relationship, which is upward-sloping. It is clear that its position and slope depend crucially on the demand for labour (N^D) relationship and thus on the productivity of labour (or the production function). AS is derived on the assumption of a given nominal wage rate. When the wage rate, and thus expectations of inflation, changes the whole AS relationship shifts. For example, if the wage rate increases the AS shifts to the left, showing that firms in the aggregate would be willing to offer a smaller amount of output for the same price level. At the point where the two relationships, AD and AS, intersect we have the simultaneous determination of the price level and real output.

Having explained the AD and AS relationships, we turn our attention to the refinements on GNS as mentioned above. We begin with the New Classical Economics.

2.2 NEW CLASSICAL ECONOMICS

The rational expectations assumption was quickly taken a step further along with the hypothesis of market clearing. These two assumptions are the theoretical backbone of what has come to be known as the *New Classical Economics*. We elaborate this refinement of the GNS with the help of Figure 2.2.

Figure 2.2 is reproduced from Figure 2.1 with one slight exception. We allow Y^e to be Y^N, where the latter corresponds to what we labelled above 'natural rate of unemployment' so that now Y^N would stand for 'natural rate of output'. We assume next that there is an increase in the money supply so that LM shifts to LM_O (the analysis would be exactly the same if the IS shifted to the right). In the (P,Y) plane AD shifts to AD_O so that output Y_1 is established.

Figure 2.2

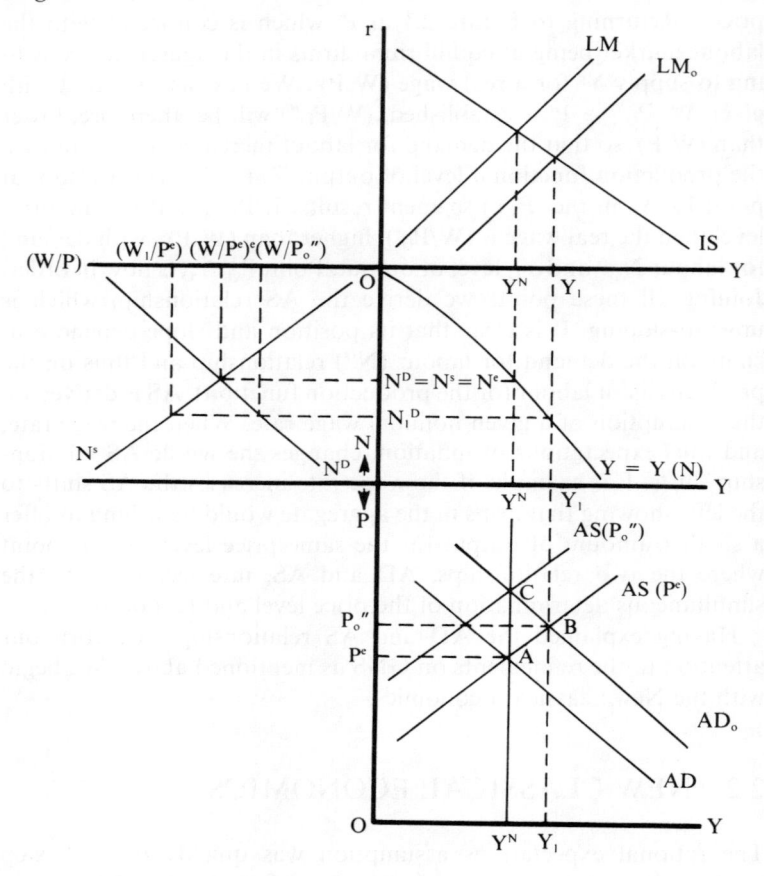

The new price level ($P_0'' > P^e$) reduces the actual real wage to (W/P_0'') and employment increases to N^D_1 which allows output to be Y_1. Workers, however, do not realize that the price level has now increased. This is an important assumption of the argument and it relies on the notion that firms have more-accurate information than workers. Firms are able to monitor prices in a way that workers have insufficient time and means to do; consequently, workers cannot notice immediately any price-level changes. To the extent that firms allow nominal wages to increase to, say, $W_1(> W)$, workers perceive of (W_1/P^e) as the real wage and are thus prepared to provide N^D_1 units of labour which allows Y_1 level of output to be maintained. Aggregate supply curve depends on the expected price level assumed in the case of AS(P^e) to be P^e. So long as P^e differs in the eyes of the workers from the actual price level P_O'', output could very well settle away from Y^N. This happens in the short term.

In the long term when workers realize that the actual price level has changed to P_O'' their expectations change to P_O'' and the aggregate supply curve will shift to AS (P_O''), with output returning to Y^N and the real wage returning to (W/P^e). So long as expectations are corrected, output can only be at Y^N. This is no more and no less than the *natural rate hypothesis* as expounded above. In the long run the supply curve is vertical at Y^N. To arrive at this result *two* basic assumptions are important: market clearing and imperfect information. We may now recall the assumption of *rational expectations* as defined above: that economic agents make the best forecasts they can, given the available data, and that forecasting errors can be made by economic agents but they are 'random' (that is, independent of previous errors). As such, forecasting errors do not follow a certain pattern and are unpredictable. If we abandon the assumption that workers are consistently slower in realizing price changes than producers and also retain the market-clearing hypothesis, we arrive at the New Classical model. An additional, and very important, assumption concerns the extent of available information. In particular, it is assumed that all economic agents have the same information as the government; they process it with the same economic model, which is the 'correct' one for the economy.

Returning to Figure 2.2, it is clear that if workers change their expectations about the price level from P^e to P_O'' as the AD shifts to AD_O, the aggregate supply will shift *pari passu* with the aggregate demand to become AS (P_O''). It follows that AS (P_O'') intersects AD_O at C, implying that even in the short term the supply curve would be a vertical relationship at Y^N. This analysis produces neatly what has come to be known as the 'Lucas supply function', that is:

$$Y = Y^N + h(P - P^e) \tag{2.1}$$

which suggests that actual output cannot deviate from the 'natural rate of output' unless there is a difference between actual price level and expected price level. It follows from this proposition that economic policies cannot affect real output in a regular and predictable way. The impact of predictable or announced change from policy-makers' past behaviour is immediately discounted by economic agents, who adjust their expectations of the price level to the actual price level so that in Equation (2.1) P cannot deviate systematically from P^e. Deviations of real from 'natural' output, therefore, cannot be sustained. Consequently, feedback rules whereby economic policies respond in a regular way to macroeconomic events (such as unemployment and inflation) are viewed as completely ineffective by the proponents of the New Classical model.[1]

Finally, there are two important points that ought to be made about the New Classical model. The first is that this model views firms as receiving information on prices but does not specify how prices change. It thus rules out imperfect competition where firms are price-makers. The second point is that the New Classical model attempts to bring back into the heart of economic analysis the invisible-hand assumption (see Chapter 1), removed from it, according to Leijonhufvud (1968), by Keynes (1936). For Leijonhufvud (1968) the central message of Keynes's *General Theory* is that the existing economic system is not in any significant way self-adjusting, which is tantamount to saying that the invisible-hand theorem disappears. The New Classical model, though, places the role of the auctioneer in the hands of economic agents, for the implication of the 'rational expectations' assumption is that economic agents know each others' aims and anticipate each others' actions (Buiter, 1980; Sawyer, 1982a). To appreciate this last point, though, we must turn to another type of refinement of GNS economics which we label as the *new neo-classical* synthesis.

2.3 NEW NEO-CLASSICAL SYNTHESIS

It was noted that GNS ignores the nature of the constraints on individual behaviour that emanate from the operation of the macroeconomic system as a whole. A further feature is the assumption that prices react to disequilibrium faster than quantities, especially when the Pigou effect is incorporated in the model. The alternative which has been considered by writers like Patinkin (1965), Clower (1965), Leijonhufvud (1968) and Barro and Grossman (1976), assumes that prices are inflexible relative to quantities, so that trade occurs at prices which do not correspond to full market-clearing, and individuals are faced with quantity constraints in product and/or labour markets.[2]

Furthermore, these contributors have attempted to get around yet another complication. In the analysis we have been conducting so far, economic agents are assumed to be moving along the demand curve. More concretely firms are always on their labour demand curve while workers can be off their labour supply curve. This asymmetry cannot really be justified and in addition it implies behaviour which cannot be defended empirically. This is the proposition that the movement along the labour demand curve implies countercyclical movements of the real wage rate when the opposite is observed. The new neo-classical synthesis attempts to overcome these problems by distinguishing between *notional* and *effective* labour demand and supply relationships, a device which also offers an analysis of the consequences of wage and price rigidity. It is recognized that labour and product contracts prevail which clearly stipulate wages and prices that are fixed in the short term. Similarly, there are also *pre-set* retail and wholesale prices not subject to contracts which are adjusted by mark-up pricing behaviour.[3] This dictates that the price is set as a mark-up over the average cost of raw materials and labour which guarantees a certain profit margin.

Consider Figure 2.3. The relationship N^S and N^D depict the *notional* supply and demand of labour equations. They are precisely the same relationships derived above. In the analysis initiated earlier, equilibrium is established at the point of intersection of the notional components. This, of course, assumes that firms can actually sell the output produced at this profit-maximization level of employment. If firms, however, find that they cannot sell the desired output, because say IS shifts to IS_O and AD to AD_O so that output is now at Y_O, their demand for labour will be subject to the constraint of actual supply (in addition to the constraints of the production function and prices) and they will be forced off their notional labour demand curve. Firms operate at the new point E_O with $(W/P)^e$ being the real wage rate which, as explained above, is fixed in the short run. They are thus off their notional labour demand curve (N^D) and find themselves on the *effective* labour demand curve. Consequently, at disequilibrium the *effective* demand for labour becomes $N_O E_O N_O' N_O''$. Clearly firms wish to employ N^e units of labour when the real wage is at $(W/P)^e$. But they cannot sell all the output the N^e units of labour

Figure 2.3

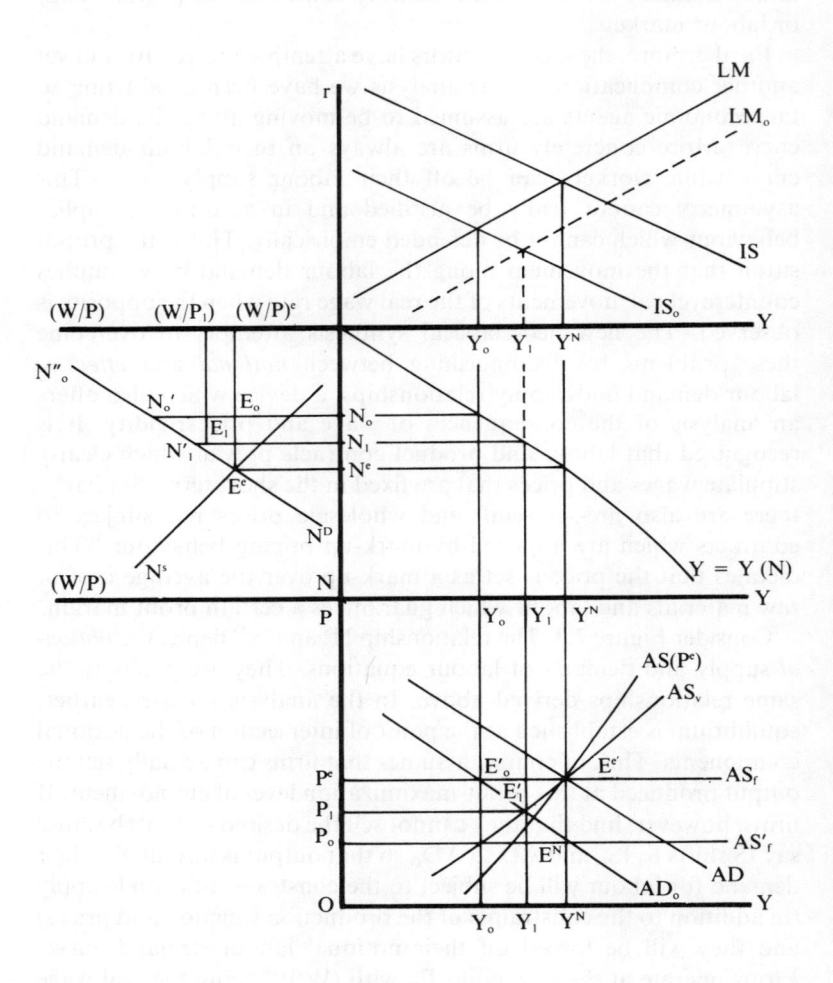

can produce; there is just not enough demand for it. The culprit is not the real wage any more, for it is fixed at $(W/P)^e$. It is, instead, the shift in aggregate demand along with the assumed fixed wages and prices that have caused unemployment.

In this non-market-clearing framework, unemployment is, quite obviously, involuntary. This is important because we can now redefine unemployment more precisely within the confines of this analysis as the excess of *notional* supply over *effective* demand; this amounts to the distance $E_O E^e$ ($= N_O N^e$). This way of defining involuntary unemployment makes it possible to have it occurring even at the 'equilibrium' real wage. It can be argued, therefore, that unemployment in this model is determined by the demand for output without being merely the effect of real wages being too high. The implied aggregate supply relationship must be horizontal at P^e – it is denoted in Figure 2.3 as $P^e AS_f$.

The analysis so far in this section has been conducted under the assumption that wages and prices are inflexible and therefore the burden of adjustment falls on quantities. It must be stressed, though, that the inflexibility under discussion is not complete in the sense that what is important in this context is that wages and prices do not adjust instantaneously to their equilibrium levels. It is precisely for this reason that notional and effective magnitudes differ, thus reinforcing the deviation of output, employment and other quantities from their full-employment equilibrium levels. Indeed, quantities are seen as adjusting more quickly than prices. But whether the burden of adjustment falls on quantities or on prices depends on the underlying theory of the dynamic adjustment of the system.

We may consider Figure 2.3 to illustrate the point. There is unemployment of the magnitude $N_O N^e$ and output is below the natural rate (Y^N). Firms and the unemployed must be unhappy with this situation since output is below its potential and unemployment prevails. So in the long run, the argument goes, new wage and price contracts will result with inevitably reduced W and P. The reduction in P will shift the AS_f to $P_O AS_f'$ with output eventually settling at E^N where output is again at its natural level. The $N_O N^e$ unemployment disappears with the effective demand for labour now being $N^e E^e N_O''$. This sequence of events, however, can take a long time. It is, thus, possible to explain on this view why wages and prices do not adjust instantaneously to a change in aggregate demand to clear the market – it can take a very long time indeed for the latter to materialize. It is, none the less, conceded that prices may change in the short term, even if the nominal wage rate is fixed. This, it is argued, can take place for two reasons: first, some prices may very well respond to changes in demand – the prices of some raw materials which are traded on auction markets can come under this rubric. Secondly, it is recognized that the mark-up for those firms that pursue this pricing behaviour may vary in the short run in response to changes in demand. When demand is high, firms may raise the mark-up and when demand is too low reduce it by offering discounts which would enable them to sell their excess inventories.

The implication of this analysis is that the short-run aggregate supply curve should be upward sloping. To illustrate consider Figure 2.3 again. With AD shifting to AD_O (as a result of a contractionary policy which shifts IS to IS_O) let us assume that whilst the nominal wage rate remains unchanged, the price level falls to P_1 which enables output to increase to Y_1 ($> Y_O$) – the lower price level shifts LM to LM_O, which makes sure that Y_1 is maintained; Y_1 is not on the AS (P^e) because firms are still off their notional demand for labour. The number of units of labour employed (N_1) is constrained by the level of output (Y_1); with a lower price level than previously, the real wage rate is now (W/P_1) [> ($W/P)^e$] and a new effective labour demand relationship is established, this being $N_1E_1N_1'N_O''$. Firms are still off their labour demand relationship and in terms of the (P,Y) plane, the economy is now at E_1', as opposed to point E_O', which implies the aggregate supply relationship AS_V, whose slope is positive but less than the slope of $AS(P^e)$. So long as AS_V is less steep than $AS(P^e)$, firms would be out of equilibrium in the short run. Note, however, that due to the flexibility of prices, unemployment now (N_1N^e) is lower than in the case where prices are inflexible (N_ON^e). In the long run the analysis is precisely the same as above in that nominal wages will fall too, so that the real wage drops to $(W/P)^e$ and output increases to its natural level (Y^N).

One important policy implication of this analysis is that when output is below its natural level, monetary and fiscal policies are recognized as being able to reduce this gap and take the economy to the Y^N level. Thus, the potency of economic policies is restored from its demise by the New Classical analysis. Policy, whether anticipated or unanticipated, can affect real output so long as policy changes were not anticipated and then discounted in all wage and price contracts currently in force. This is an important difference between the new neo-classical synthesis and the New Classical school of thought. But not the only one. In the New Classical model there is continuous market-clearing and economic agents are always on their demand and supply relationships. This feature can be contrasted to the augmented IS/LM scheme where workers can be off their labour supply curve with firms being always on their demand for labour relationship. In the new neo-classical synthesis markets do not clear and both firms and workers can be off their demand and supply curves. This is so since wage agreements and prices are renegotiated after a fixed period of time and some mark-up pricing behaviour is feasible which implies that prices are pre-set. But this approach is perfectly consistent with rational expectations, in that both firms and workers pay a lot of attention to the machinations of the policy-makers and that they learn quickly from past mistakes. Workers are not fooled in this model and could very well demand higher wage increases during inflationary periods along with contingency clauses in their contracts to protect their real wages from being eroded during the contract period.

It is worth mentioning here two relevant developments, both of which are perfectly consistent with 'rational' microeconomic behaviour, especially with that of profit maximization on the part of firms, and both attempt to deal with rigidities. The first concerns itself with the question of why firms resist real wage cuts. This is the efficiency wage theory based on the proposition that worker productivity depends on the level of the real wage. This is due to a number of reasons summarized by Gordon (1990, p. 1157): 'reduced shirking, lower turnover and training costs, the ability of high-wage firms to screen and obtain a higher-quality labour force, and improved morale and loyalty'. Clearly, in this case firms can conceivably pay a real wage rate above the market-clearing level. Similarly, firms would not be prepared to lower the wage rate to hire unemployed people who may be prepared to work for such a lower real wage. Firms would be afraid that such a reduction might reduce productivity by more than the gain from lower wages. The second development is based on nominal rigidities (Fischer, 1977; Taylor, 1980). Nominal wages are fixed over the life of the contract depending on expected prices and output. Price setting is according to the principle of mark-up over average wage rates. Any disturbances would then fall upon output over the contract period. At the next negotiation wages are supposed to adjust very rapidly. Prices, however, depend on wages established in the previous contract so that the output response to a disturbance can outlast the length of the contract.

The point remains, however, that the analysis pursued in this section is not concerned with the causes but rather the consequences of slow speeds of adjustment (Drazen, 1980). In this context it is very important to note that the analysis does not explain why prices and wages are slow to adjust. Just as in the case of wage rigidity discussed in Chapter 1, similarly here these are merely 'informal' explanations. They are based on 'informational' imperfections (Clower, 1965, Leijonhufvud, 1968) in the sense that the auctioneer is unable to pursue the tâtonnement process of adjustment. Consequently, it is imperfect information that causes the slowness of adjustment. The 'informal' nature of imperfections, however, has been taken a step further by a number of writers working within this perspective. The attempt here is to provide explicit choice-theoretic explanations of slow adjustments. In this spirit we may identify the following developments.

There is, to begin with, the imperfectionist approach which emphasizes macro-misallocations that emanate from the existence of imperfections in the allocative process. Failure to achieve allocative equilibrium is due to rational agents who do not possess sufficient information operating in atomistic markets. There is, then, the theory of conjectural equilibrium (Hahn, 1978; Negishi, 1979) which focuses on explaining why rational agents may find it optimal to opt for non-market-clearing prices and wages. An alternative theoretical construct maintains that economic agents behave in a non-rational manner at times or, indeed, they behave in a near-rational manner (Akerlof and Yellen, 1985a, 1985b, 1987). Other models emphasize the possibility of the existence of non-atomistic market structures (Hart, 1982) or the non-atomistic nature of the labour market (MacDonald and Solow, 1981; Oswald, 1986). An interesting contribution in this respect is Weitzman (1982) who ascribes macro-misallocation to the role of increasing returns to scale in forestalling the perfectly competitive, Pareto-optimal allocation. Finally, there is a class of models, labelled *contingency models* which focus their explanations on the existence of contingency plans arising from social norms of behaviour (see, for example, Akerlof, 1979; Mankiw, 1985; Summers, 1988).[4]

Finally, it is important to note that the developments we have been discussing in this section treat unemployment as a disequilibrium problem. Unemployment in this view is treated not as arising from one or more of the rigidities discussed earlier in Chapter 1 (downward wage rigidity, liquidity trap and interest-inelastic investment), but rather as a result of wages and prices not adjusting instantaneously to their equilibrium levels and also of quantities (effective demands and supplies) adjusting more quickly than prices. In doing so, the developments in question incorporate the nature of the constraints that individuals and firms are faced with and, thus, elaborate the underlying model of constrained optimization behind the GNS macroeconomics. The analysis is still 'choice-theoretic'; it is what Coddington (1976) refers to as 'reconstituted reductionism'.

2.4 OPEN ECONOMY ASPECTS

The analysis we have conducted so far and the observations we have made on the GNS are as pertinent in the case of 'open economies' as in the 'closed economies' case. Full coverage of these developments requires a full text by itself (see, for example, Morley, 1988). In this section we summarize the main features of this aspect of GNS.

We begin with the extension of the IS/LM closed economy framework with fixed prices to an open economy with different exchange rate regimes (Mundell, 1960, 1963; Fleming, 1962). We consider first an economy operating under a fixed exchange rate system. Consider Figure 2.4 where we superimpose on the IS and LM the BP curve. The BP curve traces different combinations of r and Y for which there is neither surplus nor deficit in the overall (capital and current) balance of payments. By construction, points above the BP curve represent points of surplus in the balance of payments, and those below are points of deficit. *Ceteris paribus*, then, above the BP relationship reserves will be increasing and will expand the money supply. Similarly, below the BP curve foreign reserves and the money supply will be falling. Its slope is greater than that of the LM curve in that it is assumed that for a given increase in the level of income a smaller increase in the rate of interest would be required to generate a capital account surplus to offset the deficit in the balance of payments emanating from the given increase in income. The increase in the rate of interest would be required to generate a capital account surplus to offset the deficit in the balance of payments emanating from the increase in income. The increase in the rate of interest just referred to would be smaller than the increase in the rate of interest required to restore equilibrium in the money market following the given increase in income. The slope of the BP curve

Figure 2.4

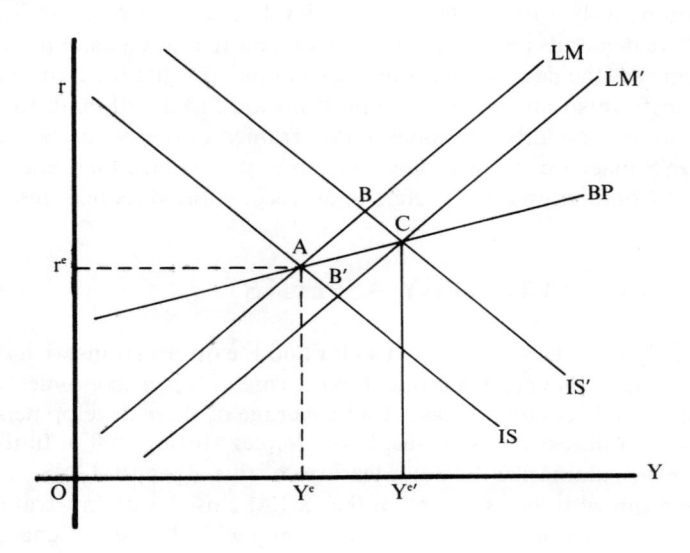

depends crucially on the degree of capital mobility and consequently on the degree of substitutability between domestic and foreign assets. Perfect capital mobility implies a horizontal BP curve while complete capital immobility is associated with a vertical BP curve.

In Figure 2.4 point (r^e, Y^e) is one of full equilibrium in that all three curves intersect at this point. Internal equilibrium coincides with balance of payments equilibrium. Consider next an expansive fiscal policy which shifts the IS curve to IS'. The shift moves the domestic economy to point B which lies above the BP curve and, consequently, is associated with a surplus in the balance of payments. The money supply increases (which is represented by a shift in the LM curve to LM') and the economy finds itself at point C with income at $Y^{e'}$, *mutatis mutandis*. If instead we assumed an expansionary monetary policy, the domestic economy would find itself at point B', below the BP curve with a deficit as a result. The deficit reduces the money supply and shifts the LM' to its original position.

We may now consider the case of a flexible exchange rate regime. When such a system is in operation it is changes in the exchange rate that restore overall equilibrium in the balance of payments, not changes in the reserves (as in the fixed exchange rate case). A surplus in the balance of payments appreciates the exchange rate which raises imports and reduces exports, thus removing the surplus. Similarly, a deficit in the balance of payments will depreciate the exchange rate and remove the deficit through exports rising and imports being squeezed. Capital flows are affected too. Arbitrageurs in the world markets move capital from one market to another in response to relative interest rate changes and expectations about exchange rate changes. If r_f is the foreign interest rate and s the *expected* proportionate depreciation of the exchange rate, then so long as $r - r_f > s$ arbitrageurs would be willing to hold domestic financial assets. The BP relationship, therefore, is expected to be affected by the interest rate differential $(r - r_f)$ and s. The analysis can be simplified at this stage, however, through the assumption that when r changes r_f does not follow suit and that s is so small as to be approximately zero.

With these assumptions the BP relationship can be interpreted as the locus of points that relate domestic interest rate and income, for a given exchange rate and foreign interest rate, which yield a zero *overall* balance of payments. Points above the BP represent *appreciation* whilst points below the BP display *depreciation* in relation to the exchange rate underlying BP itself. This means that a depreciation of the exchange rate would shift the BP to the right and an appreciation would shift it to the left of BP in Figure 2.4. It should also be stressed that the position of the IS relationship would be determined by the level of the exchange rate. An appreciation would shift it to the left (since exports would fall and imports rise) and a depreciation would shift it to the right (since exports would now increase and imports fall).

We may now examine the impact of fiscal and monetary policies under flexibile exchange rates. We employ Figure 2.5 for this purpose. An expansionary fiscal policy shifts the IS to IS' so that at a point B there is a surplus in the balance of payments which appreciates the exchange rate. The appreciation will displace BP to BP' and IS' to IS" so that final equilibrium occurs at C where a higher rate of interest and a higher level of income are established. Both 'internal' and 'external' equilibrium are attained again at this point.

The case of an expansionary monetary policy is depicted in Figure 2.6. The increase in the money supply produces a shift of the LM to LM'. The exchange rate now depreciates causing both the BP and IS

Figure 2.5

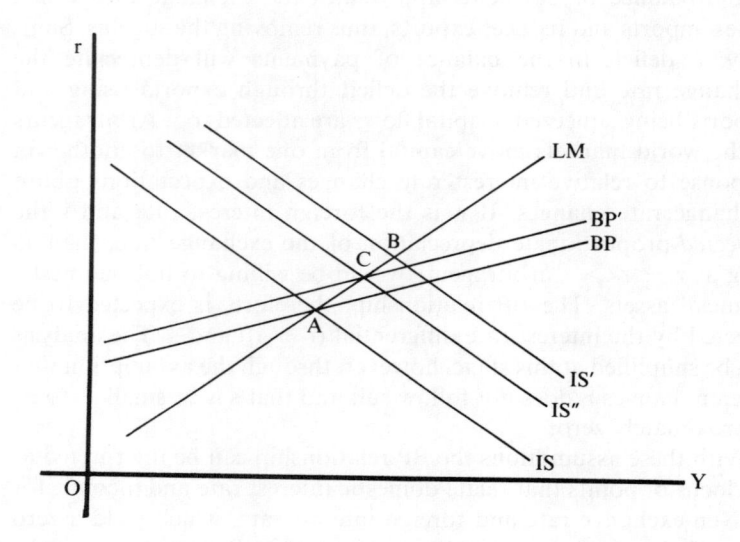

Figure 2.6

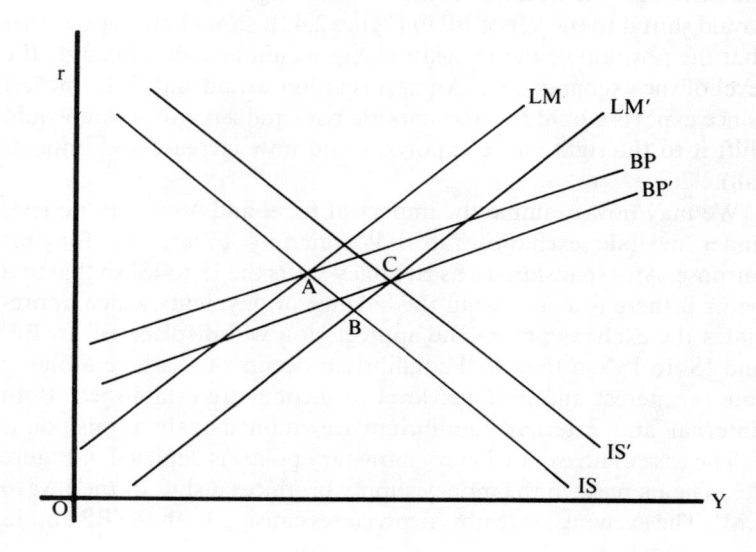

Figure 2.7

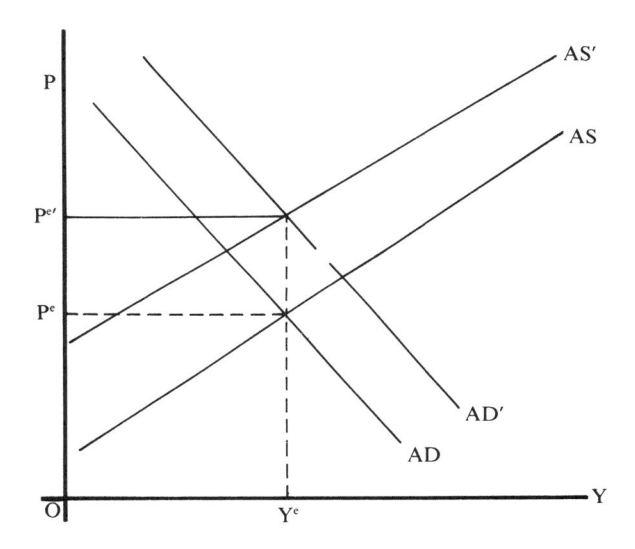

to shift to the right so that a new equilibrium point is established at C. A higher level of income is now associated with a lower rate of interest. Just as in the case of Figure 2.5, similarly here the change in the exchange rate affects the current account with the change in the rate of interest influencing the capital account. At point C in both figures overall payments balance prevails.

We turn our attention now to the 'current account monetary model' or 'international monetarist model' (Frankel and Johnson, 1976). This model assumes a stable 'domestic' and 'world' demand for money functions along with the 'purchasing power parity' proposition. With these two central assumptions, it is postulated that domestic monetary policy controls the domestic price level whilst the rate of growth in the domestic relative to the 'world' money supply determines the exchange rate. The 'purchasing power parity' clearly implies that domestic (P) and 'world' (P_w) price levels should be the same when expressed in equivalent currency units. If (ER) stands for the exchange rate (units of foreign currency per unit of domestic currency) we should then have: $P(ER) = P_w$. In Figure 2.7 equilibrium occurs at P^e given P_w (determined exogenously) and (ER) as

Figure 2.8

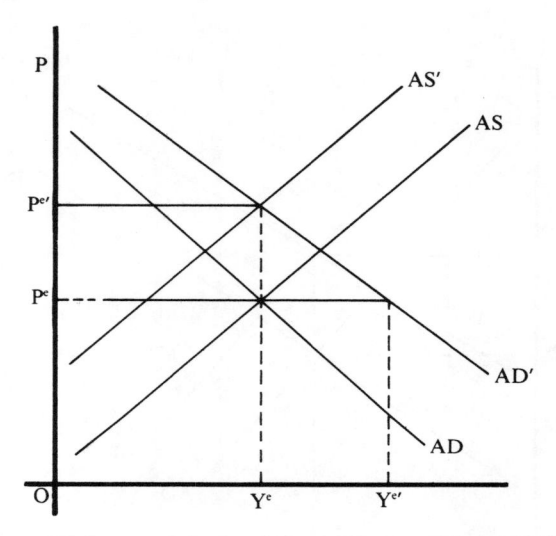

explained above. We assume that the money supply increases; this shifts the AD curve to AD′ and raises the price level. Agents now change their expectations about the new price level so that the AS curve shifts to AS′. Note that agents' expectations of the price level will adjust in proportion to the (expected) change in the money supply. Output does not change. The higher price level, however, will cause the exchange rate to depreciate so that 'purchasing power parity' is maintained. The amount of depreciation of the currency is precisely the same as the increase in the money supply.

There is also a 'capital account monetary model' (Dornbusch, 1976) which assumes 'sticky' goods prices in the short run but allows the money and foreign exchange markets to clear. The rational expectations hypothesis is also invoked to arrive at the prediction that monetary policy causes exchange rate 'overshooting' from its equilibrium but with output being unambiguously affected in the short run. However, money is neutral in the long run so that a stable demand for money and a firm grip over the money supply could control inflation. It is conceded, though, that tight monetary policy may be accompanied by short-run costs in the form of lower output.

Figure 2.8 shows what happens in the case of an increase in the money supply. AD shifts to AD' with income rising in the short run to $Y^{e'}$. But sooner or later prices begin to rise too and the exchange rate depreciates. In the short run (ER) falls faster than the rise in P so that $P(ER)/P_W$, the *real* exchange rate, falls which stimulates exports. The price level continues to rise. In the long run, however, when price expectations have adjusted in proportion to the increase in the money supply, AS shifts to AS'. In the long run there is no impact on output in this model either.

2.5 THE GNS GROWTH MODEL

So far we have been dealing with a static model and ignoring any growth dynamics. In this section we explore the conditions under which growth takes place and its determinants. We begin by enumerating the assumptions of this model. These are as follows: there is full employment and perfect competition. Capital and labour can be substituted for one another in the production process; in other words, any given level of output can be produced by an infinite number of combinations between capital and labour. Payments to factors of production are equal to their marginal products. A continuous, constant-returns-to-scale, aggregate production function is assumed.

We write this production function in general terms as:

$$Q = F(K, L) \tag{2.2}$$

where Q is aggregate output and K and L are capital and labour respectively. We can express the variables in (2.2) in per capita terms so that writing $k = (K/L)$ we have:

$$Q/L = f(k) \tag{2.3}$$

from which we derive the marginal product of capital as:

$$(dQ/dK) = f_k = r \tag{2.4}$$

where f_k denotes the partial derivative of the function with respect to k. It is equal to r, the rental rate of capital. Similarly, we derive the marginal product of labour:

$(dQ/dL) = f(k) - kf_k = w$ (2.5)

where w is the wage rate of labour.

Since factors are paid their marginal products, the sum of all payments to factors is:

$K.f_k + L[f(k) - Kf_k] = Lf(k) = Q$ (2.6)

which means that with constant returns to scale, output Q is exhausted by payments to the factors of production when they are paid their marginal products (Euler's theorem). Consider, now, the ratio of profits (π) to wages (W):

$(\pi/W) = (rK)/(wL) = k/(w/r)$ (2.7)

from which we can have:

$(\pi/Q) = (\pi/W) / (1 + \pi/W)$ (2.8)

that is the share of profits in output. When k changes, its influence on (π/Q), and thus (W/Q), depends heavily on the relative change of k to (w/r). That is, it depends on the elasticity of k with respect to (w/r), which is the elasticity of substitution between capital and labour. In the special case of this elasticity being equal to unity, we have the specific form known as the Cobb–Douglas production function:

$Q = AK^a L^{1-a}$ (2.9)

where A is merely a constant which usually stands for 'autonomous' growth factors; a and (1 − a) are the output elasticities of capital and labour which, when factors receive their marginal products, are the same as the respective relative shares of capital and labour in output. For output to be exhausted as in Euler's theorem, the production function must be such that the output elasticities sum to unity, so that constant returns to scale prevail. In (2.9) the parameters a and (1 − a) sum to unity (constant returns to scale) and also they are constant, thus ensuring that the elasticity of substitution is equal to unity. We utilize (2.9) for the rest of this section. We should stress at this stage that in neo-classical economics marginal productivity theory provides the crucial link from the production function to income distribution. The latter is determined by the elasticity of substitution between the two factors and technology.

We may now differentiate (2.9) totally to give us:

$$dQ = [a(Q/K)]dK + [(1-a)(Q/L)] dL$$

or

$$(dQ/Q) = a(dK/K) + (1 - a)(dL/L) \tag{2.10}$$

which suggests that the growth rate of output is a weighted average of the growth rates of capital and labour, where the weights are the respective shares.

The final assumptions are (a) that savings are proportional to output in the long run, in which case we can write:

$$S = sQ \tag{2.11}$$

and for simplicity (b) that the capital stock does not depreciate, in which case investment is simply the change in capital stock, that is:

$$I = dK \tag{2.12}$$

When the economy is at equilibrium we have:

$$S = I$$

or equivalently

$$sQ = dK \tag{2.13}$$

or, upon dividing through by K:

$$(dK/K) = s(Q/K) \tag{2.14}$$

which we graph on Figure 2.9 to give us the line labelled (dK/K).

Furthermore, if we substitute (2.13) into (2.10) we may arrive at:

$$(dQ/Q) = as(Q/K) + (1 - a)(dL/L)$$

and with the growth rate of labour taken as exogenous and equal, say, to n, we have:

Figure 2.9

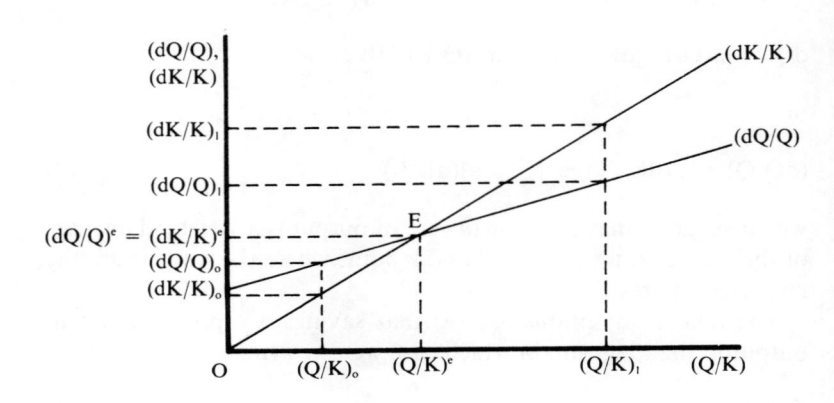

$$(dQ/Q) = as(Q/K) + (1 - a)n \qquad (2.15)$$

which suggests that the economy's growth rate is a function of the output/capital ratio (Q/K). We graph equation (2.15) on Figure 2.9 thus obtaining the line labelled (dQ/Q).

Figure 2.9 shows quite clearly that there can only be one equilibrium output–capital ratio and consequently only one equilibrium growth rate. Given the assumptions underpinning the two relationships in this figure, the equilibrium growth rate is established at E. Indeed, this is a stable equilibrium. For if (Q/K) were to be at $(Q/K)_o$ output would grow faster than capital and (Q/K) would grow towards E. Similarly, if (Q/K) were at $(Q/K)_1$, capital would be growing faster than output so that (Q/K) falls until $(Q/K)^e$ is established. Clearly, at the equilibrium point E we have that:

$$(dQ/Q)^e = (dK/K)^e = (dL/L) = n \qquad (2.16)$$

The growth rate of output is equal not just to the growth rate of capital but to the given growth rate of labour as well; that is to say,

Figure 2.10

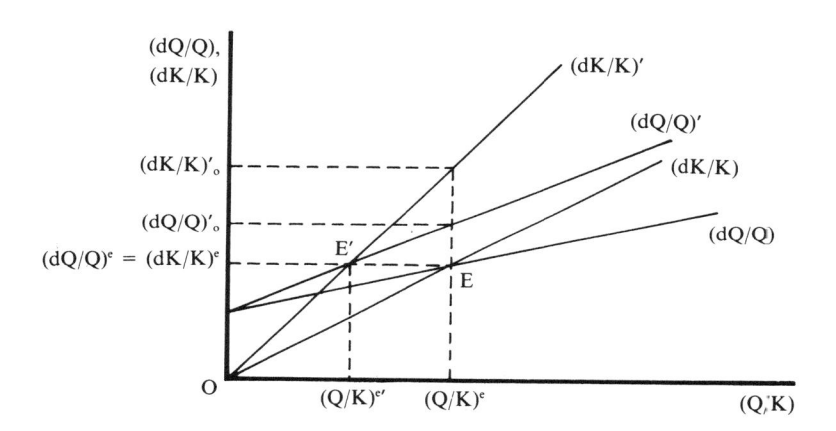

at E all the relevant variables grow at the same constant rate, namely the rate of growth of the labour force.

An interesting case arises when we allow s to vary. Let us examine this possibility by allowing s to increase and examine its impact on the growth rate. As s increases the two lines derived in Figure 2.9 shift as indicated in Figure 2.10. At $(Q/K)^e$ we have that $(dK/K)_0'' > (dQ/Q)_0'$ which causes (Q/K) to fall to $(Q/K)^{e'}$ where again the growth rate of output and capital are equal again. This occurs at point E' which provides the same equilibrium growth rates of output and capital at E. Thus, the long-run rate of growth of a GNS economy is n which is entirely independent of the proportion of income saved.

We now consider the effects of technical progress, which can be introduced in the Cobb–Douglas production function as follows:

$$Q = Ae^{\theta t}tK^aL^{1-a} \qquad (2.17)$$

where $Ae^{\theta t}$ is the index of technical change which grows at the rate θ. We may derive the expression for the marginal rate of substitution

(MRS), which is defined as the ratio of the marginal product of capital to the marginal product of labour, that is:

$$\text{MRS} = (dQ/dK) / (dQ/dL) = a(Q/K) / (1 - a)(Q/L)$$
$$= (a/1 - a)(L/K) \tag{2.18}$$

which implies that the MRS is completely independent of the rate of technical change (θ). Technical change raises the marginal product of both factors by exactly the same proportion thus leaving the MRS unchanged. We have, therefore, the case of 'neutral' technical progress.

Differentiating (2.17) with respect to time (t) and rearranging, we can arrive at the expression:

$$(1/Q)(dQ/dt) = \theta + a(1/K)(dK/dt) + (1 - a)(1/L)(dL/dt)$$

or, if the variables change instantaneously:

$$(dQ/Q) = \theta + a(dK/K) + (1 - a)n \tag{2.19}$$

This result indicates that the rate of technical change affects the rate of growth of output, independently of the rate of growth of capital and labour. We may also rewrite (2.17) as follows:

$$(dQ/Q) - n = \theta + a[(dK/K) - n] \tag{2.20}$$

Even if $dK/K = n$, the difference $[(dQ/Q) - n]$ would still be positive by an amount equal to θ.

The type of technical change hypothesized in this model is *disembodied*, in that it affects all capital equipment, both old and new. A common criticism of the model is that in the real world technical change is *embodied* in new capital equipment, with the old capital equipment not affected. But even when this modification is introduced, the key results of the GNS growth model do not appear to require substantial revision.

Let us summarize the key results of this growth model. There is always full employment, growth is determined by the supply side of the economy, distribution depends solely on technology and relative factor supplies, and there is absolutely no role for aggregate demand

– we note, in particular, the entire absence of an investment relationship. However, in terms of more recent developments these results may need some degree of modification. One may refer to what has been labelled as the 'new growth theory' (Romer, 1986; Baldwin, 1989), which emphasizes the role of economies of scale in the growth process. The basic assumption made is that of increasing returns which are largely due to technological progress and are external to the firm. The implications of this assumption in terms of steady-state properties are not different from the ones reached above when the output elasticity of capital is less than unity. But when this elasticity is unity, exogenous changes in the output–capital ratio will have an impact on the growth rate. Similarly, for a unitary output elasticity of capital, the savings ratio is expected to influence the growth rate. Savings, therefore, assume a more important role in growth process within the 'new' rather than the 'old' theory. But there is still the question of whether economies of scale are important at the economy-wide level (Baldwin, 1989, p. 257), and also the worry expressed by Solow (1991) who argues that the assumption of increasing returns, which is so central to the 'new growth theory', is extremely difficult to test in any case. Furthermore, the output elasticity of capital cannot be greater than unity if growth is not to be explosive. Not surprisingly, neo-classical economists insist that it cannot be equal to unity either.

2.6 BUSINESS CYCLES

Growth theory is essentially concerned with the explanation of continuous expansion in an economy's output over time. The study of the dynamics of income movements which display alternating periods of expansion and contraction is referred to as *business cycle theory*.

We begin this section with the multiplier-accelerator model, which may be stated in the following way (based on Samuelson, 1939):

$$Y_t = C_t + I_t \tag{2.21}$$

$$C_t = a + bY_{t-1} \tag{2.22}$$

$$I_t = v(Y_{t-1} - Y_{t-2}) \tag{2.23}$$

where all the variables are defined as above.

Equation (2.22), the consumption function, is the basis of the multiplier, where it is assumed that there is a one-period lag in response of consumption to income. Equation (2.23) is the accelerator principle, with v being the capital–output ratio. This principle relies on the notion that investment responds to changes in the level of income, where again it is assumed that there is a one-period response in investment following a change in the level of income.

The interaction of these two relationships can give rise to business cycles. This can be shown by solving (2.21) to (2.23) for Y_t to give:

$$Y_t = a + (b + v)Y_{t-1} - vY_{t-2} \qquad (2.24)$$

which can be expressed in terms of changes, or first differences, as follows:

$$\Delta Y_t = (b + v)\Delta Y_{t-1} - v\Delta Y_{t-2} \qquad (2.25)$$

So if income has remained unchanged in the recent past, then $\Delta Y_{t-1} = \Delta Y_{t-2} = 0$ and ΔY_t will also be zero. If now at period t_0 there is a change in autonomous demand, say by Δa, there will then be successive fluctuations in the level of income and this will create cycles.

The precise type of cyclical behaviour that can be arrived at depends crucially on the values of b and v, especially v. We may assume, to begin with, that v is zero and b is positive but less than unity. In this case there would be no cycle; we would simply have the usual multiplier process as shown in Figure 2.11 with income following the path $(Y_0 e_0 m_0)$.

If, on the other hand, v is positive and very large, income would explode upwards in response to a positive change in autonomous demand. In this case there would be no turning point since the large value of v simply swamps the multiplier, so that an explosive path for income ensues. This is also shown in Figure 2.11, with income following the path $(Y_0 e_0 e_0')$. The two cases we have just described are really extreme ones. For intermediate values of b and v cycles can result. For relatively high values for v and strictly positive fractional values for b, the resulting cycles are called anti-damped: the amplitude of the cycles becomes greater and greater through time (see Figure 2.12a). By contrast, relatively small values for v will produce damped cycles: the amplitude of these cycles becomes smaller and smaller as time goes by (see Figure 2.12b).

An intuitive explanation for the cyclical behaviour just alluded to may proceed along the following lines. The initial exogenous increase in demand sets off the multiplier and accelerator effects, which cause income to rise faster than it might without the accelerator effect because of induced investment. This change in income produces further changes in investment, which reinforce the increase in income through the multiplier effect. But as the latter effect weakens, the process just described comes to an end. Most important, aggregate demand is reduced as a result so that income begins to fall. The process is now reversed and the downswing is well on its way. When capacity is reduced to the required level, disinvestment ceases, which implies recovery of demand and income. The upswing phase begins.

Hicks (1949, 1950) pointed out that even the explosive cases could be made to produce business cycles only if a ceiling and a floor were introduced into the analysis precisely to contain explosiveness. His argument was based on the obvious fact that oscillations could not possibly be as infinitely large in the real world as implied by the multiplier–accelerator principle. To demonstrate, let us utilize the following equations which will build on (2.21)–(2.23) explained above, but adjusted to account for ceilings and floors.

Figure 2.11

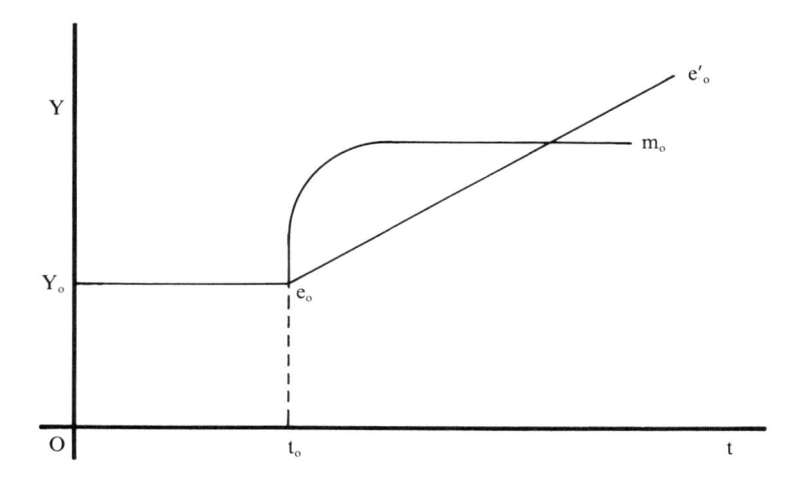

52   *The Post-Keynesian Approach to Economics*

Figure 2.12

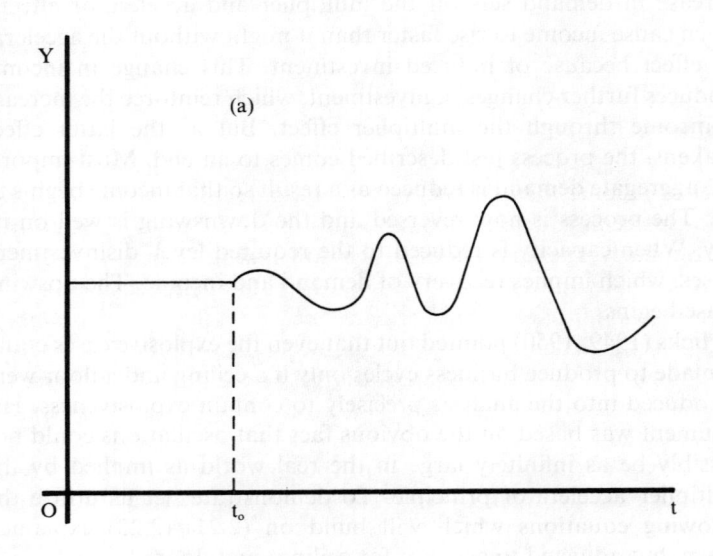

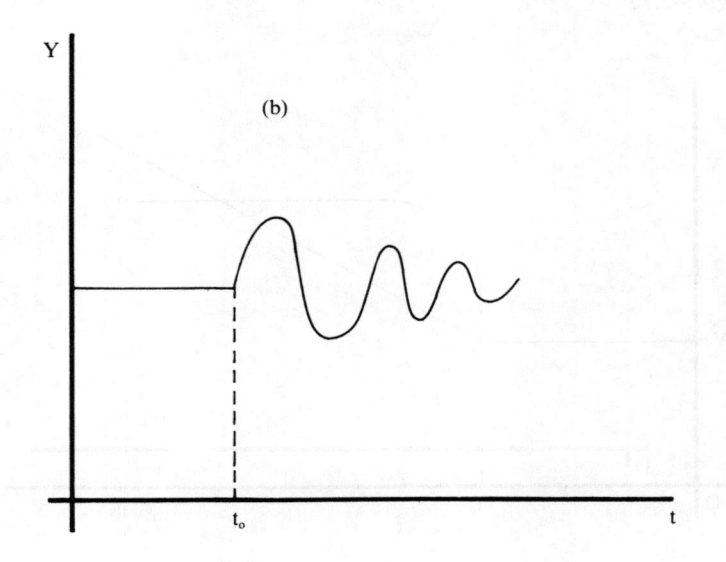

(a)

(b)

$Y_t = \text{Min} [Y_c, (C_t + I_t)]$ (2.26)
$C_t = a + bY_{t-1}$ (2.27)
$I_t = \text{Max} [I_f, [v(Y_{t-1} - Y_{t-2})]]$ (2.28)

Equation (2.26) simply suggests that there is a limit to the value income can take in the upswing. This is determined by the productive potential of the economy. There is, therefore, a ceiling to the level of income, denoted as Y_c. When aggregate demand is higher than this ceiling, actual income cannot be equal to $(C_t + I_t)$ but to Y_c. Similarly, there is a floor in the downswing. This is the limit to net disinvestment as determined by the rate of depreciation of the current capital stock. This floor to net investment is denoted in (2.28) as I_f. When the accelerator mechanism dictates a level of investment lower than I_f, then this level cannot be sustained and the accelerator analysis is ignored. Net investment will simply be given by I_f instead.

We may now elucidate this contribution with the help of Figure 2.13. The vertical axis is in logarithmic scale, so that the straight

Figure 2.13

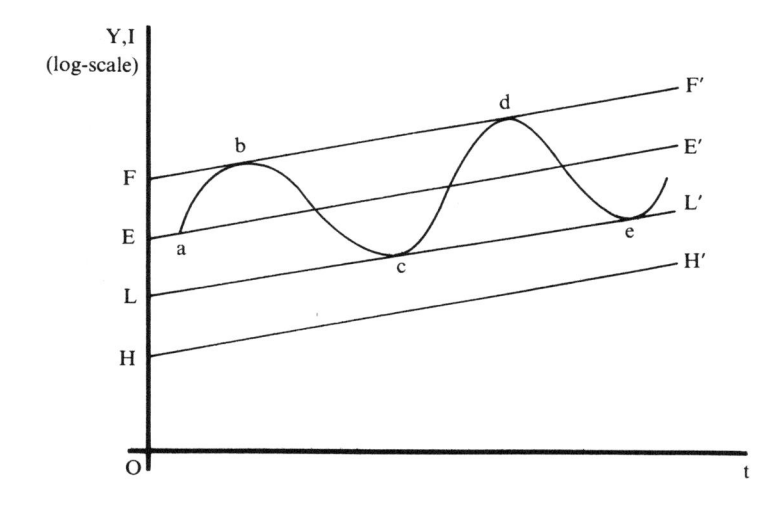

Source: Hicks (1949)

lines given in this figure indicate a constant percentage rate of growth for the variables in question. Line HH' indicates autonomous investment increasing at a constant rate; line LL' depicts autonomous investment plus its multiplier effect; if, in addition, the accelerator effect was added to LL' we arrive at EE'. Line FF' is the full-employment ceiling, which is assumed to be above the equilibrium path.

The economy has been in equilibrium and its level of output has been expanding along the EE' path. We assume that the economy is at point a, and that autonomous investment increases and then reverts to its previous path described by the line HH'. The multiplier will cause output to increase, which sets in motion the acceleration mechanism, and the economy is on its way towards FF'. When the ceiling FF' is reached, say at point b, output cannot expand any further. It will creep along the ceiling for a while and then bounce off in a downward direction. The downward movement is inevitable since the creeping along the ceiling is associated with a lower volume of induced investment than otherwise. The lag between reaching the ceiling and the reduction in investment determines how long the economy moves along the ceiling, after which the economy finds its way on to a downward track. Changes in output are now negative and the accelerator mechanism requires that induced investment declines. But in the downswing, unlike the upswing, the change in investment in any period is governed by depreciation only. Consequently the accelerator principle in the downswing becomes inoperative, so that the change in income is determined by the multiplier. The line LL', which is set by autonomous investment and its multiplier effects, imposes a limit to the falling income and thus becomes a floor. Once point c is reached, income cannot fall any further, as there is no excess capacity. Again the economy will creep along LL' for a while, which means that the multiplier process will be reversed. This will set in motion the accelerator mechanism. By this time the economy is well on its way into the upswing.

The 'business cycles' we have considered so far can be thought of as falling within the realm of the Neo-classical synthesis. A theory of cyclical behaviour can be derived from the New Classical economics also. We turn our attention to this business cycle theory next.

As explained and elaborated above the New Classical economics is based on three theoretical premises: market clearing (in a perfectly competitive environment), the Lucas 'supply function' and rational expectations. We begin our exploration into this theory of business cycles by pointing out that market clearing in a perfectly competitive environment implies that market-clearing prices are known to economic agents. And that the role of perfect competition in this model is to force economic agents to react quickly to price changes as they pursue their profit maximization objective.

The Lucas 'supply function' can be reproduced here, using lowercase letters to denote natural logarithms, as follows:

$$y_t = y^n_t + g(p_t - p^*_t) + e_t \qquad (2.29)$$

where in addition we have introduced e_t, which is a random error process. The rational expectations assumption comes on to the scene via the p_t^* variable, which is the price level under rational expectations conditional on information available at period $(t-1)$. In other words,

$$p^*_t = E_t(p_t/Z_{t-1}) \qquad (2.30)$$

where Z_{t-1} is the information set at $(t-1)$. Furthermore, if we let y^n_t be:

$$y^n_t = n_0 + n_1 t \qquad (2.31)$$

we have:

$$y^o_t = y_t - y^n_t \qquad (2.32)$$

where y^o_t stands for cyclical output at period t. The aim of business cycle theory in this context is to explain the deviations of output from the growing natural rate of growth. In other words, the aim is to explain cyclical changes in output.

Substituting (2.32) into (2.29) gives:

$$y^o_t = g(p_t - p^*_t) + e_t \qquad (2.33)$$

Since both terms on the right hand side are random processes under rational expectations, so is y^o_t a random process, which cannot form the basis for a business cycle theory. To overcome this Lucas (1975, 1977) and Sargent (1979) – see also Lucas and Sargent (1978) –

introduce a lagged cyclical output term in (2.33). This enables them to arrive at a propagation model which implies that shocks to the system have a persistent effect. This procedure transforms the random shocks into a cycle, as follows. The lagged cyclical output is added to (2.33) to give:[5]

$$y^o_t = g(p_t - p^*_t) + cy^o_{t-1} + e_t \tag{2.34}$$

Successive substitutions will result in:

$$y^o_t = g\sum_{i=0}^{\infty} c^i(p_{t-i} - p^*_{t-i}) + \sum_{i=0}^{\infty} c^i e_t. \tag{2.35}$$

where cyclical output is now a weighted average (with geometrically declining weights) of all past shocks. The effect of these shocks persists through time and can generate cycles within the confines of this theory.

The model relies for its explanation of business cycles on unanticipated price changes and on the persistence of price shocks on output. Unanticipated price increases, say, will induce increases in output if there is excess capacity or inventories will be reduced. If neither is possible, investment will be undertaken to increase productive capacity. An accelerator type of mechanism is invoked at this stage of the argument (Lucas, 1975, 1977). The importance of the accelerator mechanism is that it helps to explain the persistence of the effect of unanticipated price shocks.

The business cycle theory we have just touched upon does not give the government a major causal role in terms of generating cycles. (It is for this reason that the term 'real business cycles' is usually used to describe this theory.) The only exception, of course, is when the government produces random shocks in their pursuit of economic policies. By contrast, the 'political business cycle' theory (Nordhaus, 1975; MacRae, 1977, 1981; see also Kalecki, 1971a) gives the primary causal role to government behaviour. The objective function of the government and its implications for macroeconomic theory in general and business cycles in particular, are aspects at the heart of this approach. It is argued that the objective of utility maximization which depends crucially on being in office, is rigorously and vigorously pursued by the government in the form of vote maximization.

In this attempt the government causes a cycle in economic magnitudes where output, unemployment and inflation are the most obvious. The electorate is assumed to behave myopically in that current voting behaviour does not fully take into account past economic events. Only very recent economic performance is taken into consideration by the electorate. The same myopia is hypothesized in terms of future economic events. Most important, though, the electorate is viewed as being unable to foresee the impact of current economic policy on economic events in the next election period. Thus, economic agents do not vote strategically and are not rational in the Muth (1961) sense as this was explained in Chapter 1. Consequently, economic agents are not in a position to know the true, but intricate, workings and mechanisms of the economy. Business cycles, therefore, are created by the government through a process of 'fooling the electorate'. Manipulation of inflation and unemployment are initiated with the specific aim of winning votes, so that business cycles are generated fundamentally with respect to these two variables. As an election approaches, one should expect falling unemployment and rising inflation rates, with the opposite result following an election.[6] In this view, then, the government, in pursuing its own political objectives, creates an economic cycle within the electoral period. This theory ought to be contrasted with the analysis that assumes that the objective of government policy is to optimize general economic welfare, which entails active anticyclical economic policies.

2.7 CONCLUDING REMARKS

The various strands of thought within the GNS share a common 'vision' of how capitalism works. They differ over questions such as the interest-elasticity of the demand for money or the speed of adjustment of the economic system to the 'natural' rate of unemployment. These questions are thought to be resolvable by empirical observation and econometric estimation. They have policy implications, too. The relative importance attached to fiscal and monetary policies, whether governments should attempt to 'fine-tune' the economy and other related issues, are policy questions which have provoked debates, the outcome of which is of considerable significance for economic policy. A government persuaded by the argument that the economy is self-stabilizing would refrain from increasing aggregate demand via monetary or fiscal means during a recession, believing that such action was unnecessary or that it would have harmful inflationary effects. If such a belief is mistaken it clearly implies unnecessary misery in terms of unemployment and the loss of output which would result from foregoing expansionary policies during the recession. These differences notwithstanding, the various strands of thought considered so far have certain common features which enable us to suggest that they come under the GNS umbrella.

Whether the GNS is modelled as a 'closed' or an 'open' system makes very little difference to the underlying constrained-optimization feature which is essentially at the heart of this economics. This particular observation is of paramount importance because it indicates that the developments discussed in this chapter should be viewed as merely filling gaps in the GNS rather than constituting a fundamental departure from it. For these developments continue to rely heavily on the importance of deriving macroeconomic theories from the microeconomic principles of utility and profit maximization. Common to most, if not all, GNS theories is that they rest on the assumption of a perfectly competitive, atomistic model of a capitalist economy. The implication of this assumption is that a harmonious equilibrium, where the interests of various competing groups in the economy are reconciled, does prevail. By contrast, post-Keynesian analysis assumes economies characterized by oligopoly, imperfect competition and monopoly (see, for example, Kalecki, 1971a), and therefore it has no difficulty at all in recognizing and indeed incorporating the notion of *conflict* amongst competing groups, especially between capital and labour.

Furthermore, the developments discussed in this chapter are firmly based on the premise of 'equilibrium', with the presumption of stable relationships such as the consumption function, the demand for money and so on, just as in the case of the IS/LM apparatus. One other equally important feature commonly shared by the GNS strands, is their 'decidedly optimistic assessment of the efficiency of markets' (Bliss, 1983, p. 2). In the new classical case 'it is prices which change to produce market-clearing and equilibrium', and in the New Neo-classical synthesis view 'it is the rationing constraints of the fix-price equilibrium which ensure that no feasible gainful trade opportunity at the given price is left unexploited'

(Bliss, 1983, pp. 2–3). Clearly, there are differences between these developments and the analysis of GNS expounded in Chapter 1, including the degree of price flexibility, how long the time span of disequilibrium may last, the speed of adjustment of the economic system and the extent to which it responds to exogenous shocks by price or quantity adjustments. Incorporating these factors has led, further, to differences in policy recommendations. But even so, the point remains that these developments do not depart fundamentally from the GNS approach; they merely constitute an attempt to enhance its position.

NOTES

1. Sawyer (1984) argues persuasively that the Lucas supply function is not well-founded. It is marred by a number of problems, not least of which is that the various ways of deriving this function are inconsistent. Consequently, the implications and conclusions of the Lucas supply function analysis cannot be accepted.
2. The flexible-quantities assumption is not really terribly realistic, especially when the proposition that production takes time is admitted. In this case quantities of production can only be adjusted with a lag. On the other hand, when firms set prices they allow quantities traded to vary with stock variation.
3. We refer to Leijonhufvud's (1968) argument that in the absence of an auctioneer who bans disequilibrium trading, prices cannot adjust instantaneously.
4. It is impossible to account for all recent developments which attempt to explain slow wage and price adjustments. A whole book is required to cover them all. The interested reader might consult, for example, Adnett (1989). See also Chapter 6 below.
5. We may, of course, introduce a lagged output term in Equation (2.29) and arrive at exactly the same result.
6. This theory of political business cycles depends crucially on the notion that in the government's objective function the primary variable is the share of its votes. Frey and Schneider (1978a, 1978b, 1978c) have extended the model to account for a number of other variables, the most interesting and important being those that introduce ideological factors into the analysis.

3. A Critique of GNS Economics

3.1 INTRODUCTION

GNS economics has been severely criticized over a number of issues. In this chapter we attempt to bring together the various criticisms in a consistent way.

The emergence of GNS coincides with the development of its neo-classical arm which occurred towards the end of the nineteenth century. The challenge of the labour theory of value was serious enough to produce a new development in the 1870s which has come to be known as the *marginal utility analysis*. De Vroey (1975) interprets the transition from classical to neo-classical economics in terms of the radical conclusions the labour theory of value entailed. Such topics as transformation of the system and class interests, the heart of classical economics, did not feature at all in the new economics. In addition, the latter was very 'attractive' too, since it looked as scientific as natural sciences. Neo-classical economics has dominated economics ever since, even when Keynesian economics was supposed to have demonstrated the theoretical weakness of pre-Keynesian economics. The GNS has overshadowed all developments since the Second World War in a way that prompted the suggestion that over the more recent past this school of thought has been almost completely victorious (Startz, 1984). But as we have indicated above this school of thought is not immune from criticism. Kay (1984, p. 188), may have produced a very apt summary of the critique of GNS when he suggests that 'the individual intent on pursuing a career as economist has to be bright enough to understand the abstract ramifications of neo-classical theory and dumb enough to have faith in them'. This chapter attempts to clarify the issues Kay alludes to.

3.2 THE ATOMISTIC, HARMONY AND ASOCIAL NATURE OF GNS

The neo-classical micro-foundations which dominate the GNS were, in fact, influenced to a very large extent by the mechanistic view of the universe inspired by Newton's *Principia*. The assumption that 'effects can be clearly distinguished from, and are explained by, causes', coupled with the contention that 'material reality can be thought of as the interaction of internal atoms', constitute the heart of this mechanistic view. In neo-classical economics the 'cause and effect' principle is predominant with the *individual* being the analogue of the *atom* of Newtonian mechanics. It is precisely for this very reason that the postulate of 'reality' being the interaction of individuals whose natures are invariable and permanent, is of paramount importance within the confines of GNS. The implication here is that society is explained in terms of the individual rather than the individual in terms of society.

Newtonian mechanics gave the impetus to the proponents of GNS in the 1870s, whilst the early twentieth-century victory of *quantum mechanics* provided ammunition to its challengers with the proposition that 'all deterministic laws were merely limiting cases of a more fundamental stochastic substratum' (Mirowski, 1989, p. 227). The emergence of quantum mechanics, however, presented the GNS proponents with the opportunity to get away from an allegedly 'failed tradition', and proceed with the new stochastic and more relevant way of thinking. But the view that statistical laws of a stochastic economics were not in a position to achieve the status of statistical laws generated by the natural sciences, actually prevailed. For acceptance of the new concepts would have put the notion of 'the market as a natural organising force at risk' (Morowski, 1989, p. 235).

The GNS is characterized by its faith in the paramount role of the market. There are two types of individual actors: utility-maximizer households and profit-maximizer firms. They are separate from each other and interact through the market. All economic agents are ultimately subordinate to the constraints of the market. Their activities are essentially 'rational' in that they pursue them so that their own self-interest is maximized, whereby firms seek to maximize profits and households utility. In other words, firms and households seek to optimize, given the scarcity of resources and the unlimited number of needs. This notion of separate utility maximizers has been challenged by a number of economists, culminating in Preston's (1975) view that only very few, if any, of the elements of the relationship between real firms and their environments are, in fact, incorporated within the neo-classical framework. A relevant comment here may be made on the issue of rationality. Critics have argued that the notion is really empty and consequently unhelpful to economic analysis. Sen (1979) takes the view that it has too little structure, whilst Hirschman (1984) supports the proposition that if economic theory is to capture reality then rationality, being its basic concept, should be vested with a more complex structure. There is also here the question of the empirical existence of rationality where the central argument is that there exist several types of rationalities in real economies which may conflict with one another.

A closely related problem here is the assumption of a harmonious relationship between capitalists, landlords and workers in which each one makes a distinct contribution to production and receives an appropriate reward. This harmony-of-interest notion is part of the basic ideological stance of GNS, part of the hard core of the 'scientific research programme'. The attempt to construct a distribution theory which conforms to the harmony principle is the marginal productivity theory associated with the 'aggregate production function' (see Equation 1.3 above). Inputs are transformed into outputs through the 'aggregate production function' which determines the amount of output produced given the factor inputs of land, labour and capital with continuous substitution possibilities amongst them (the lack of substitution possibilities and also of a constant ratio between labour and output are not considered). It is assumed that the 'aggregate production function' exhibits constant returns to scale (so that the difficulties that arise without constant returns to scale are simply assumed away) and uniformly diminishing marginal products with respect to these three factors. These assumptions provide a unique equilibrium position where every factor receives its marginal product and, thus, every factor is rewarded according to its contribution to production at the margin. Under these conditions labour is treated as a passive economic agent. Indeed, the working class is supposed to be unable to raise their wages and improve their conditions, let alone control the production process; consequently, the working class should not and cannot attempt to improve its collective position by organizing itself at the economic level. Such organization will simply introduce rigidities and inefficiencies in the system even if one group of workers manages to improve their position, for this could only come about at the expense of other workers who would be forced to accept lower wages or else lose their jobs – there is, thus, a trade-off between unemployment and the real wage, the Phillips curve relationship. Thus, workers have no real need to organize themselves, for there is no need for the workers' class struggle (Rowthorn, 1974, p. 70).

Veblen (1898, p. 224) strongly attacked the 'harmony' assumption. He suggested, sarcastically, that it was 'the standpoint of ceremonial adequacy' and should be replaced with the more fruitful concept of 'cumulative causation' where the element of power struggle in the economy is at the forefront. More recently, Galbraith (1973, p. 2) has argued along similar lines that the neglect of the concept of power in GNS analysis is a fundamental weakness in that it 'destroys its relation with the real world'. Such neglect clearly implies inability to deal with and cure such problems as might arise from the so-called 'dynamic inefficiency' of capitalism (Lancaster, 1973). A very good example here is the 'wage earners' funds' arrangements legislated and introduced in Sweden in the early 1980s (Arestis, 1986b). In such a system, labour is involved as collective shareholders with capital. The assumption of 'conflict' is thus recognized and dealt with in some way, perhaps not wholly satisfactorily. This could lead to a situation where labour becomes increasingly a collective capitalist, thereby causing capitalists to feel more certain about labour's involvement. This state of affairs could conceivably result in higher investment activity. The kind of constraint to full employment that Kalecki (1943) was so adamant about, could thus be removed (Arestis, 1986b). But such an outcome could only materialize if the 'harmony' assumption is removed from GNS economics and replaced with the notion of 'conflict'.

A further implication of the neglect of 'power' is that the development of the modern corporation, what Eichner (1976) has labelled 'the megacorp', has not been considered seriously by the GNS exponents. Neither, for that matter, has the power of trade unions over markets been accounted for. This is an important omission since the power the megacorp and trade unions acquire over markets gives them a political character; and to deny this political character 'is not merely to avoid the reality. It is to disguise the reality' (Galbraith, 1973, p. 6). In the case of monetary and fiscal policies, the way they are pursued within the confines of GNS suggests that policies do not affect adversely the holders of power. It is essentially the weaker members of the economy who bear the consequences. Megacorps in particular can normally avoid the impact of monetary restraint since they have the ability to acquire the required finance. Similarly, fiscal policy is accommodated to the interests of the megacorp, in the form of tax concessions and other business benefits. In this sense, the role of the state is to serve the interests of the powerful, a state of affairs that ought to change. But it can only change when economics emancipates itself from the type of economic beliefs associated with GNS (Galbraith, 1973, p. 8).

Individuals are *asocial* within the GNS framework. Economic action, though, without the 'societal element' is, according to Polanyi (1957), 'bare bones' and unrealistic; it is, indeed, the cause of many misunderstandings in GNS economics. Not least is the undisputable proposition that such an approach to economic problems could not possibly account for women, trade unions, employers' organizations and similar institutions as distinct economic actors. As a result 'power' and thus 'role conflict', 'class struggle', 'negotiated order', 'relative deprivation' are the kind of concepts completely absent from GNS terminology.

Moreover, it is not just the individual who is taken to be asocial in GNS, but production too. The latter is not, therefore, seen as a social process but as a natural one, where the factors of production, labour, land and capital are combined to produce outputs of material and non-material goods (Rowthorn, 1974). The amounts of factors of production are given, and under conditions of atomistic and competitive conditions a set of relative prices is established which eliminates excess demands and supplies and thus produces full employment of all factors; market phenomena are consequently of primary importance. Now, the relative prices of factors of production, which follow closely their marginal products, determine the distribution of income always via the forces of demand and supply. It is, thus, not distribution of income between social classes that is at stake here, but between factor services through the determination of factor prices by demand and supply in the various atomistic markets. But even at the aggregate level it is the factors of production which are emphasized; there is, thus, a distinct difference between the analysis where classes of society are the backbone of distribution and the GNS where factors of production are the core of analysis.

3.3 INCOME DISTRIBUTION AND THE MEANING OF CAPITAL

If distribution is to be explained by the forces of supply and demand for factors of production, then the latter must have a measure. (This measure must also be homogeneous so that aggregation should be possible.) Land and labour present no problem in this respect since they have natural units, as, for example, land of a given quality and labour of given efficiency. However, the same cannot be said for capital as a factor of production (rather than as an amount of finance or the revenue of capitalists). Capital, being a produced means of production, requires inputs of labour and other means of production to become a factor. It has no natural unit that can be aggregated to give a quantity of a productive service which can then be used for the determination of its price. In other words, in order to provide a quantity of capital it must be first priced to yield its quantity. But the 'price' of the aggregate 'factor' capital will be affected by the distribution of income amongst factors. Thus, the aggregation of individual prices of capital to yield a unique measure of it cannot possibly be a fruitful way of doing so except in the highly special case when the capital/labour ratio is the same for all output produced. We should distinguish at this juncture between money and real forms of capital. Money capital does have a homogeneous unit, but in that form it is not productive. To be productive it must be transformed into produced means of production. But then the problem creeps in: in its productive form capital does not have a homogeneous unit.

So long as the capital stock is heterogeneous, its measurement requires knowledge of the relative values of individual goods. But then this could only be achieved if the price vector of the economy and the rate of profits were known. Consequently, aggregate capital, the production function and the marginal products of factors can only be defined when the rate of profit is given. They cannot be used to arrive at a theory of the rate of profit or distribution (Robinson, 1954). Clearly, then, when the assumption of homogeneity of capital is relaxed, a theory of the rate of profits is desperately needed. Two further problems, first recognized by Robinson (1954, 1956) as well as by Champernowne (1954) and developed by Sraffa (1960), also have to do with the homogeneity of capital.[1] The first criticism is that with heterogeneous capital, the relationship between the profit rate and the capital/labour ratio may not be negative as alleged by the GNS analysis, unless the capital-intensity in the production of different capital goods is the same. This is the famous *reswitching* phenomenon whereby an economy can move between techniques depending on the level of the rate of profit, so that at high and low levels of profit the same technique can conceivably be utilized, thus establishing the possibility of a non-negative relationship between the rate of profit and the capital–labour ratio. The second criticism is what has come to be known as the *Ruth Cohen Curiosum* (Robinson, 1956, pp. 109–10) or *capital-reversing*. This is when the value of capital moves in the same direction as the rate of profits. This can happen when the most profitable project is the one associated with a less capital-intensive, less productive technique accompanied by a low value of profit rates. Both the reswitching and capital-reversing problems contradict the generality and rigour of the GNS framework, thereby substantially weakening its robustness. For they clearly imply that the GNS proposition of an inverse relation between the profit rate and capital/labour ratio which relies on homogeneous capital is not generally valid. Even the GNS proponents conceded this point when they argued that reswitching was empirically unimportant rather than that it was theoretically impossible (see, for example, Stiglitz, 1974; Solow, 1975). Pasinetti (1966) argues that the GNS propositions can still be shown to be invalid without having to resort to the reswitching phenomenon.

It follows from this analysis that the distribution aspects of the GNS become invalid when the homogeneity of capital is dropped and it is assumed instead that capital is heterogeneous even for a competitive system. Thus, the GNS approach to distribution via a demand/supply framework suffers from this fundamental inconsistency which renders its distribution aspect problematic and thus unsatisfactory. And yet there is the view that distribution is of vital importance, since it is the subject-matter of economics. In this context it is worth referring to Ricardo who emphasized distributive shares in a growing economy. He identified three classes:

namely, the proprietor of the land, the owner of the stock of capital necess-

A Critique of GNS Economics

ary for its cultivation, and the labourers by whose industry it is cultivated. But in different stages of society . . . rent, profit, and wages, will be essentially different; depending mainly on the actual fertility of the soil, on the accumulation of capital and population, and on the skill, ingenuity, and instruments employed in agriculture. To determine the laws which regulate this distribution is the principal problem in Political Economy. (Ricardo, 1817, Preface)

In this view, then, if there is no satisfactory distribution theory there is no hope for serious economic analysis.

The GNS content of distribution theory is, of course, the marginal productivity theory. This theory purports to be 'applicable' to any factor of production, whether this is a trades union, a piece of capital equipment or land; it makes no difference at all! Income distribution will take place according to the value of the factor's marginal product. The theory is sufficiently general (Tobin, 1960). Clearly, by eliminating the need for separate theories to explain different factor shares, the theory has dangerously simplified the analysis of income distribution (Kaldor, 1960b). It also precludes the possibility of determining the values of the marginal product of each factor when the assumption of fixed technical coefficients (the factor proportion used in production) in multiple-plant operation is adopted. For it is impossible in this case to impute productivities by incremental analysis (Stigler, 1939, p. 309). Now, the assumption of fixed technical coefficients and the implied constancy of marginal costs was given strong empirical support as early as the 1930s (see references in Stigler, 1939, p. 322). Obviously, validation of the fixed factor proportions view discredits the marginal productivity theory.

But marginal productivity theory may not be sufficiently general, after all. For the theory is inconsistent with theories of firm behaviour other than perfect competition. In market structures other than perfect competition, prices are set by individual firms so that the profit margin, and consequently profit and wage shares, do not have any exact connection with the marginal productivity of factors. In particular, profits are linked with market power and not with production. These observations indicate that the marginal productivity theory is, in fact, extremely restrictive. It is only consistent with market situations which are very rare in the institutional set-up of twentieth-century economies. In a way this is not surprising, given that GNS economics is largely institution-free in that institutional arrangements are not important for the analysis of economic activity. Institutional arrangements are expected to have an impact on people's behaviour and they do introduce realism to the relevant assumptions. These are propositions, though, which are not considered important nor relevant by the GNS supporters. Related to these problems, there is the question of how advertising, research and development, invention and innovation are dealt with by the GNS. Advertising, of course, is viewed as ineffective in changing tastes. The theory cannot support the argument that advertising may be persuasive, for then it would be admitting that tastes can be moulded and utility functions can evolve over time. Both propositions would be unacceptble to the GNS proponents. Research and development, invention and innovation pose in a remarkable way the difficulties of maintaining the assumption of the decision-maker being fully informed and capable of possessing all relevant information. Again, the 'generality' characteristic of GNS economics is weakened considerably.

The aggregation used by GNS entails some interesting aspects, relevant to the above discussion. Income is treated as an aggregate, and whilst the distinction between wages and profits is not absent from the GNS analysis, once income is received its source becomes irrelevant (which is, of course, consistent with the neglect of any notion of class in this tradition). There is, therefore, no analysis of possible impacts on expenditure due to differences between the propensities to spend out of wages and out of profits. Similarly, the influence of profits on investment is not accounted for satisfactorily. The importance of profits is, thus, not fully appreciated by the GNS analysis; nor is saving by firms, which is largely their retained profits (Sawyer, 1982a). This neglect of profits may at first appear to be an unimportant element to worry about, but it has severe implications. An important implication is the one already mentioned in relation to the aggregation of income, that GNS is unable to consider seriously the distribution of income between profits and wages and thus the possibility of different propensities to save out of profits and out of wages. Another important implication is that GNS has very little to say on the mechanism whereby savings are channelled to firms from households. Within this economics, households are 'surplus units' and thus the source of savings utilized by firms which are typically 'deficit units', but no clear mechanism is postulated as to how this comes about.

3.4 RATIONALITY, OPTIMIZATION AND EQUILIBRIUM ANALYSIS

Optimizing rationality and the notion of equilibrium are at the heart of GNS, even though there have been attempts to show that rationality and optimization can be separated and that, in consumer theory in particular, it is optimization that is necessary rather than rationality (Chipman *et al.*, 1971). Furthermore, the assumption of imperfect information has been fundamental in certain recent developments within the GNS, as shown in Chapter 2. But here again optimization remains one of the most essential assumptions of the GNS.

Optimization, however, has been under attack by a number of economists. Shackle (1955, 1972) emphasizes the enormous difficulties of acquiring 'sufficient information' necessary for the optimization process. The uncertainty involved in making choices is another dimension in his argument which suggests that optimization is not possible. Similarly, Boulding (1956, p. 84) remarks that the information content of this procedure is such that it would require 'centuries of experience and enormous electronic calculators to perfect'. Leibenstein (1976, 1979) concurs, arguing that in the case of profit maximization there are 'X-inefficiencies' which GNS analysis does not account for. Hey (1979, p. 232) epitomizes these worries when he suggests that 'the optimisation problems that . . . agents are supposed to be solving . . . are so complicated . . . The "as if" methodology is stretched to breaking . . . Have we not gone wrong somewhere?' All these views point to a clear conclusion that economic agents should not be assumed to be optimizing.

Simon (1979, 1983, for example) and Cyert and March (1963) have suggested that the weight of uncertainty, the problems associated with complete knowledge and the limited computational capacity of economic agents are elements which indicate rejection of 'optimization'. They are, instead, in favour of 'bounded' rationality. The essence of bounded rationality is that although economic agents are supposed to be rational, their choices are made from a reduced set of possibilities, a subset of the total. Heiner (1983, 1986) proposes that there is a mismatch between the 'competence' of economic agents and the 'difficulty' in choosing amongst alternatives. This may very well arise from excess information that imposes severe burdens on economic agents. Arrow (1982) provides evidence, especially from financial markets, to show that situations of risk and uncertainty cannot be analysed and explained by either 'rational' or 'optimizing' behaviour. This and other evidence, ably summarized by Hodgson (1988, ch. 4), demonstrate the lack of empirical support for the 'rational optimization' principle, on top of the theoretical objections, some of which have been rehearsed above.

The GNS type of *logical equilibrium* analysis has been severely criticized for having very little meaning (see, for example, Kregel, 1973). To elaborate, let us remind ourselves that the problems of achieving equilibrium within GNS are bypassed by the method of comparative statics. It is clear from the analysis initiated in Chapters 1 and 2 that it normally begins with an equilibrium position and then assumes a change in an exogenous variable or parameter to arrive at a new stable equilibrium; it then merely compares the equilibrium points before and after the change. Indeterminate equilibrium situations are assumed away through the exclusion of interdependent utility and production functions. Stability of equilibrium is assumed through appropriate assumptions concerning the underlying relationships including the absence of ignorance and uncertainty (Blaug, 1978, p. 700). In other words, in this analysis each point in time is taken *de novo* to find the equilibrium point with little, if any, reference to the past and with perfect foresight as far as the future is concerned. Keynes (1973) was very categorical on the notion of equilibrium which he described, in a very well known passage, as 'one of these pretty, polite techniques which tries to deal with the present by abstracting from the fact that we know very little about the future' (p. 115). But surely, everything takes place at a point in *historical* time where the past has an undisputable impact on current actual economic conditions upon which the future exerts its impact through expectations, uncertainty and contracts made in money terms (Kregel, 1973; Kaldor, 1934).

Robinson (1980) draws the distinction between closed deterministic models, which operate in logical time, and open historical models, which operate in historical time, to launch her attack on the equilibrium technique. The closed deterministic case refers to models, such as those described in Chapters 1 and 2, which contain relationships in logical time without any reference to historical time and without a 'causation' mechanism embedded in them. These models are two-stage theoretical processes, comprising the first stage which concerns itself with building a closed deterministic equilibrium model, and subjecting it to empirical tests in the second stage – presumably the second stage is designed to examine whether the model in question adheres to the real world. But these models cannot analyse processes which are out of equilibrium. Disequilibrium dynamics are either merely assumed to produce stable outcomes – so a certain degree of 'faith' is resorted to – or an 'as if' methodological process is utilized. In the case of 'faith' in disequilibrium dynamics, there is no presumption that stable outcomes would ensue (Ingrao and Israel, 1965; Cohen, 1990). The 'as if' methodology (Friedman, 1953) requires the model to predict outcomes which are the same as those of the equilibrating process. Whether these outcomes are consistent with the results of an *actual* economic process is, in this view, of no consequence whatsoever. It is the predictive accuracy of the model that matters. Clearly, then, these two-stage models are incapable of explaining reality.

By contrast, open historical models, which require causal relations to be carefully specified, are designed to describe events in actual economies. These models are three-stage theoretical processes. There is the building of a closed deterministic equilibrium model: that is stage one; in stage two an historical and institutional context is embedded in it, thus creating an open historical model; the model is then exposed to empirical scrutiny, thus producing stage three. Stage two is, of course, what differentiates open from closed models. Robinson (1980, p. vii) describes it as 'an attempt to loosen [the stage 1 equilibrium model] up in form of approximation to make it useful for discussion of actual problems'. In such open historical models the concept of equilibrium is consistent with the analysis of real economies which is concerned with 'a sequence of events occurring in historical time'. Equilibrium models by their very nature simply cannot and do not describe the outcome of an actual economic process. Consequently, 'To make the argument applicable to actual situations, we have to leave equilibrium analysis and approach the problem in terms of a historical process, the system continually lurching from one out-of-equilibrium position to another' (Robinson, 1962a, pp. 6–7).

Furthermore, the mathematical generality and elegance which constitute important criteria for the GNS exponents when judging developments in economic theory are unsatisfactory and must be relinquished as such. Abstract theory is important when it purports to illuminate specific problems of real phenomena. But abstract theory must be judged in terms of its relevance and adequacy in providing satisfactory explanations of real economic phenomena and answers to real economic questions. Since a number of *critical* assumptions of GNS are unrealistic, they render it inadequate for the study of real economic systems. In this spirit we refer to another relevant problem with GNS which relates to the relationship between investment and savings decisions. Recall that within the GNS investment is assumed to be determined by savings at full employment. If *independent* investment functions are introduced,[2] there is the distinct possibility that *equilibrium growth* can only be achieved under highly restrictive assumptions, in which case explosive growth or stagnation become normal occurrences. Under these circumstances capital formation could very well be below the required amount for full employment and steady-state growth.

The work of Kaldor (1972, 1985) and Myrdal (1957) on the forces of 'cumulative causation' constitutes a serious challenge to GNS equilibrium analysis. Market forces in this view tend to enhance rather than diminish inequalities between regions. Trade operates in favour of the relatively richer and progressive regions and very much against the relatively poorer and less progressive regions. Similarly, large firms are cumulatively successful and small firms become increasingly threatened and tend to disappear (Myrdal, 1957). Cowling (1985) extends the ideas of cumulative causation to the political level to suggest that in addition to the size argument there is the organizational aspect of big business which can undermine democracy. Transnationalism and centripetal economic developments are two tendencies which can cause a vicious circle of relative decline with the inevitable result that whole communities can lose control over their affairs and thus their democracy. The usefulness of equilibrium analysis under conditions of cumulative causation is, thus, seriously undermined (Kaldor, 1972).

3.5 ECONOMIC POLICY, RATIONAL EXPECTATIONS AND MARKET CLEARING

The policy implications of GNS economics are framed in terms of an equilibrium analysis. As such they can be severely dubious for they may lead to profoundly and entirely misleading results. This can happen when the actual equilibrium is proved to be unstable (Blatt,

1983). The emphasis on equilibrium analysis, moreover, is really ill-focused, for the information required to provide answers to questions at hand is so enormous that severely restrictive assumptions are made to get around this problem. Blatt (1983) argues that models exist which purport to show that the necessary information content of GNS can easily be avoided by, for example, the Sraffian analysis (Sraffa, 1960) which, although not couched in dynamic terms, does provide solutions without requiring the severity of assumptions of the GNS type. And to quote Blatt (1983, p. 25): 'The information requirement of neoclassical theory is so enormous that it is hardly ever fulfilled even for the steady state . . . Sraffa's work shows that one can do with much less information and still obtain meaningful results about prices and rates of return.'

It may not be irrelevant at this juncture to refer to the 'new classical' arm of the GNS which, as noted above, through its emphasis on rational expectations and continuous market-clearing concludes that policy is ineffective. Despite the impact that this theoretical development has had on the economics profession, it suffers none the less from some severe problems. There is, to begin with, the evidence produced by Kahneman and Tversky (1979) which suggests that economic agents make systematic errors in their expectations. One may also refer to the repeated failures of rational expectations to perform satisfactorily in a quantitative sense. Joint tests of rational expectations with subsidiary hypotheses have produced inadequate empirical backing (Fischer, 1988). In view of all these findings, it can be argued that expectations are basically non-rational; that no costless procedure of gathering new information exists; that the private sector does not really acquire the same information as the authorities regarding the inflationary process; and that economic units do not really know enough about the operation of the economy and its structure, which, after all, is itself subject to unpredictable alterations (Friedman, 1979). The assumption that prices and the rate of inflation respond fully and immediately to anticipated policy changes implies complete denial of the possibility of prices being rigid and costly to adjust (Buiter, 1980). It also implies that workers always succeed in imposing their perceived adjustments of wages irrespective of market structures.

The possibility of divergent expectations creates further theoretical difficulties. Peel and Metcalf (1979) demonstrate that in a model with three groups – workers, managers and financiers – with different assumptions about expectation formation in each group, the policy implications of the 'rational expectations' model are undermined. More precisely, if one of these groups form their expectations 'non-rationally' or 'adaptively' and the other two groups are characterized by 'rational expectations', the model's behaviour is more like the 'adaptive expectations' than the 'rational expectations' case. Difficulties also arise when the information-processing ability of economic agents exhibits distinct differences. Haltiwanger and Waldman (1985) show that with heterogeneous economic agents, the 'sophisticated' or the 'naive' processors of information can conceivably have a disproportionate influence on the system. Not only does this result provide a further damaging indictment against *laissez-faire* propositions, but it also rehabilitates the possibility of 'less-rational' formation of expectations.

The requirements of perfect competition and information are as problematic. We need not expend a lot of effort to demonstrate the problems with the first assumption. Hahn (1991, p. 5), when discussing the 'fallacy of composition' as it relates to the demand for labour under conditions of perfect and imperfect competition, argues that 'There can be few economists who, in the privacy of their studies, believe the perfect competition assumption to be descriptively adequate. The question is whether this convenient assumption can lead to serious errors of analysis. I believe that it can.' In terms of the perfect information assumption, it is true to say that although information on prices is available with very short lags, markets do not behave in the way the model predicts. In real life there are long-term wage and price agreements which limit wage and price flexibility to a very large extent. These long-term contracts provide the justification of the argument that wages and prices are in fact rigid. But perhaps the most important of all criticisms is the one directed on the assumption of continuous market-clearing which implies that there can be no involuntary unemployment. Such an assumption, the critics have suggested, is unsatisfactory and bizarre. Markets simply do not clear instantaneously. The interwar period, and especially the 1930s, is used as evidence against this proposition. In the UK for almost the whole interwar period, unemployment was never below the 10 per cent mark; the USA and European experience of the same period were very similar to the UK's. More recently, and crucially since the late 1970s, the evidence, especially in Europe, tells pretty much the same story. It really is very difficult to marry these long periods of high unemployment with the continuous market-clearing assumption.

Furthermore,

> Not only are there sometimes many workers who cannot sell their labour, but also sometimes firms that complain that they 'cannot sell' their outputs or move their inventories. There are, especially during the recessions and depressions, complaints about 'surpluses', 'gluts', and 'buyers' markets', and not simply about 'low prices', and this terminology suggests that disequilibria exist. Recessions and depressions are not only or mainly periods of deflation, but also periods of reduced output and employment, and this also suggests that some firms and workers may be unable to trade at the going prices. It is presumably widespread perceptions of involuntary unemployment and other evidence of markets that do not clear that has kept so many economists from accepting the new equilibrium macroeconomics, with its emphasis that all workers and firms are able to make any sales or trades that they believe are in their interest. (Olson, 1984, p. 299)

But even when the GNS accepts the possibility of involuntary unemployment as demonstrated in the previous two chapters, an apparent inconsistency seems to creep in. The microeconomic foundation of such a proposition is not spelt out at all, although it is suggested that the principles of neo-classical microeconomics are adhered to. But then, how the utility and profit maximization assumptions can lead to involuntary unemployment, within the confines of this tradition, is a question without an answer. Consequently, there is no microeconomic basis for the contention of downward rigidity of wages and prices. And yet the neo-classical microeconomics is thought to provide such a basis. This inconsistency has prompted Olson (1984, p. 299) to argue that this type of economics is 'in the final analysis as unsatisfying as a murder mystery in which the victim is killed for no reason at all!'

It should also be mentioned at this stage that empirical support for the models referred to in this section is not as robust as is alleged by their proponents. The early result reached by Barro (1978) was very supportive of the thesis that only unanticipated changes in the money stock affected real magnitudes, that is output and employment. But later evidence, utilizing more-sophisticated econometric techniques provided by Gordon (1982) and Mishkin (1982, 1983), strongly supported the proposition that both unanticipated and anticipated changes in the money stock had a significant impact on output. The results produced by Barro and Hercowitz (1980) that 'the currently perceived money stock' appeared to affect output, provided further evidence against the proposition that only unanticipated changes in the money stock have real effects. Boschen and Grossman (1982) remarked that unanticipated components can only be regarded properly as the errors in the weekly published estimates of the money stock. These are implausibly small, however, to be used as the basis of a monetary explanation of the business cycle. They also demonstrated that monetary changes about which information had already been available had a strong impact on output changes. Laidler (1990) has argued recently that the initial Barro (1978) evidence was based on assumptions which were both implausible and contrary to what was implied by a wide variety of other studies. Laidler also argues that the experience of the 1980s, in particular, discredited new classical economics. Economic agents did not seem to react to widely and well-publicized anti-inflationary policies based on monetary contraction without causing in the process severely adverse consequences for real income and employment. Thus, new classical economics failed badly in its encounter with the USA and Canadian evidence on top of the theoretical problems alluded to above. One should add that the failure Laidler refers to is not confined to the experience of these two countries. It has been a worldwide failure.

A related problem is the statement by Mankiw (1988, p. 437) who, in reviewing the recent developments of new classical economics, remarks: 'The observation that recent developments have had little impact on applied macroeconomics is *prima facie* evidence that these developments are of little use to applied macroeconomists', and, we would add, to policy-makers. Another worry springs from the assumption that all economic agents are essentially aware of the underlying economic model so that they all know how the economy works. Hodgson (1988) has drawn from this the further implication that economists do not have much else to contribute to the vexed theme of how the economy works under this particular assumption – economic agents know it all! GNS proponents are, naturally, entitled to their views but, the same author argues, 'there is no such right to carry millions of non-economists into the mire of poverty and destitution as a consequence of ideas which are formally "interesting" but practically disastrous when applied to policy. The state of economic theory today would be farcical if it were not so tragic' (p. xii).

3.6 METHODOLOGICAL PROBLEMS

The methodology of the GNS, based essentially on Friedman's (1953) methodology, has been under attack. Not even attempts to redress it in Popperian clothes have made it immune from criticism, largely because the latter has had its problems, too. The essential problem with this approach is that it is theoretically incoherent and neither has it been applied properly by GNS proponents. This methodology relies heavily on the contention that theories are formulated in such a way as will generate predictions about economic phenomena. The 'realism' of assumptions is not important as, according to this view, assumptions can never be realistic. The fundamental criterion is the ability to predict. Thus, theories should be judged only by comparing predictions with experience (which is held to be the ultimate source of knowledge). In doing so, 'simplicity' and 'fruitfulness' should be further guiding criteria.

Friedman's views on methodology are consistent with the instrumentalist view (Boland, 1979, 1982) that theories cannot be false or true; they can be adequate or inadequate but can never be rejected empirically. Theories are merely tools, so that unrealism of assumptions should not be taken as devastating evidence against a theory. 'Unrealism' neither adds to nor detracts from the stature of a theory. Whether a theory is useful depends crucially on some instrumental criterion. Correct predictions should be the fundamental principle to validate theoretical frameworks.

This analysis indicates that the goal of science in the GNS view is prediction. Caldwell (1980) argues that philosophers of science have rejected this thesis, in that explanation rather than prediction is the goal of science. But this proposition is rather premature since the debate on this issue still continues. Be that as it may, instrumentalism has been decisively rejected by nearly everyone. Predictive instrumentalism is a version of empiricist epistemology. The main problem with this methodology is that 'observations' cannot be independent of the conceptual framework, the theoretical premiss and language of the researcher. Popper (1965) has remarked that acceptance of instrumentalism renders falsification of science impossible.

Popper's (1959, 1965) falsification principle shifts the focus of scientific investigation from *verification* to *refutation*. Whilst no amount of empirical evidence can verify a universal statement (for it is always possible that new evidence will appear to refute it), a finite amount of evidence can demonstrate that it is false. Consequently, for Popper it is the potential *falsifiability* upon which the progress of science depends. GNS methodologists have argued that the predictions of the GNS theory are both testable and have successfully survived attempts to falsify them. GNS is not only scientific but non-falsified too. The principle of 'correct predictions', not in the sense of confirming a theory but of failure to falsify it, is the essence of this reconstructed GNS methodology.

Once again, the realism of assumptions has no role to play in this methodology (but note that Popper has always advocated realism as well as falsifiability, though it is theoretically possible for someone to be an instrumentalist and a falsificationist). Another nagging worry with it is that it is never clear when falsification is thought to demolish a theory; especially worrying in this context is the existence of multiple criteria for a *good* theory (Kuhn, 1977). Yet another worry emanates from the Duhem–Quine thesis, which is that no hypothesis can ever be conclusively falsified. It is never clear if the main body of the theory has been subjected to falsification but that other auxiliary hypotheses may be lurking in the background. A single hypothesis cannot be falsified, simply because it is conjunctions of hypotheses that are put to the test. Consequently, even if falsification appears to be imminent, it is never obvious whether it is the main body of the theory that is falsified or its auxiliary hypotheses. A final comment on this methodology is that even in Popper there is a certain degree of empiricism. Falsification requires theories to be tested against the 'facts of observation'. Despite Popper's insistence that observations are theory-bound, this charge is serious enough since ultimately falsification depends decisively on empirical tests. But then falsification is impossible by the 'facts of observation' as they are tied to theoretical scrutiny. The thesis is incoherent!

Gillies (forthcoming) offers an interesting critique of the falsifiability proposition which enables him to suggest a new principle that relies on *confirmability*, or *corroborability*, rather than falsifiability. The approach is based on a distinction between two types of theory (or hypothesis, or law) – high-level theories and low-level theories. Low-level theories are falsifiable, so Popper's approach is retained for them. Examples are Kepler's laws in physics or the Phillips curve in economics. High-level theories, such as Newton's first law in physics or the labour theory of value in economics, are not falsifiable, but this does not necessarily mean that they are unscientific. A high-level theory is scientific if it is *confirmable*, that is, if it can acquire support from observations about the real world, following severe experimental testing. The more support a high-level theory enjoys, the higher the degree of confirmation it possesses. A high-level theory can never be proved to be true but it can be shown to be well-confirmed. In this view, therefore, not only is falsification retained but it is supplemented. Whilst confirmability is a definite improvement over pure falsifiability, it is not entirely immune from the criticisms expounded upon in this section. In particular, the question of how many 'successes' are required to confirm a high-level theory is a problem that cannot be easily tackled.

The methodological critique launched against the GNS mode of thought by Eichner (1983a, 1985), is as serious. He argues that GNS constitutes an 'epistemological obstacle', and since this mode of thought is predominant in economics, the implication is that 'economics is not yet a science' (a proposition to which Veblen, 1898, also addressed himself). Caldwell (1989), however, argues that Eichner's claim can be challenged on the crucial question of what constitutes 'real science'. To be able to appreciate these propositions fully we follow Eichner's (1983a) analysis and consider very briefly the 'epistemological rules of science' which can broadly come under two categories: necessary and sufficient conditions.

The necessary condition is actually a test of *coherence*. This test is set out to determine whether the conclusions reached follow logically from the assumptions made and, therefore, whether the theory in question is internally consistent. It is, thus, the logical consistency of the theory that is under scrutiny here, and it does not involve empirical investigation and analysis in any sense.

The sufficient condition refers to empirical tests; there are three such tests. The *correspondence test* purports to determine whether the conclusions of the theory can be empirically confirmed. Clearly, the more a theory corresponds to what is observed in the real world the more confidence one has that the theory corresponds to reality – Popper (1959) has argued particularly strongly in favour of this test. The *comprehensiveness test* can determine whether a theory is able to encapsulate all the phenomena under study. Again, it is clear that the more phenomena that can be accounted for, the more confidence one should have that the theory is comprehensive enough. This test thus checks the theory's conclusions against the real world to determine whether reality is fully explained, and consequently whether the theory is general enough rather than a special case of another theory. The *parsimony test* directs attention to the possibility of certain elements in the theory, especially assumptions, being unnecessary in terms of the theory being able to account for what can be empirically observed. It, therefore, helps to detect elements in the theory which ought to be dropped as being superfluous.

Eichner (1983a, 1985) examines whether these conditions are met in the case of GNS. In order to do this the basic theoretical elements of the GNS ought to be identified; it turns out that there are six such theoretical elements: (a) the indifference curves; (b) the isoquant curves; (c) the positively sloped supply curves; (d) the marginal physical product curves; (e) the IS/LM framework; and (f) the Phillips-curve relationship.

The indifference curves fail on the basis of both the correspondence test and the parsimony test. In terms of the correspondence test, the failure is due to the fact that it has been absolutely impossible to derive indifference curves empirically (Mishan, 1961; Blaug, 1980, ch. 6).[3] However, the argument has been put forward by the GNS proponents that since a negative coefficient can be derived in a demand equation, this can be construed as providing enough evidence for the empirical validity of indifference curves. There are three comments here: first, the negative coefficient is evidence of a negatively sloped demand curve, not of *convex* indifference curves. Secondly, the negative price coefficient can be interpreted in a simpler way as the result of household behaviour, whereby speculative inventories of consumer goods are changed in response to price changes around their 'normal' long-term values. Thirdly, in any case, empirical evidence on demand functions is irrelevant in terms of their acceptance. It is the character of the *introspection* of these relationships that is at stake, not their 'scientific success', which none the less ought not to be scorned (McCloskey, 1983, p. 512). It therefore follows that indifference curves are, in fact, superfluous and ought to be abandoned since they fail the parsimony test dismally.

The isoquant curves are equally suspect for the same reason, in that it has been impossible to derive them empirically. Furthermore, there is a body of empirical evidence, which contradicts the implication of isoquants, that factors can be employed in variable proportions in the production of given output. This evidence suggests, instead, that production requires fixed combinations of factors up to the point where a new plant or new equipment is employed when new fixed combinations of factors will be required and subsequently used. Clearly, the isoquant curves fail the correspondence test. They also fail the parsimony test since there are other explanations of production which do not require the assumption of variable factor proportions. One such explanation is the Leontief one, which is based on the premiss of fixed combinations of factors and it is predominant within the alternative economics we expound below.

Positively sloped supply curves are a short-run phenomenon and can be derived from the existence of the well-behaved GNS production function in the short run, allied to profit-maximizing behaviour. A number of comments are, then, pertinent. To begin with, we may reiterate the point that supply curves are only defined when firms are price-takers, though an output/price relationship may be derivable for specific demand shifts and for a price-making firm. We may also emphasize the contention that short-run profit maximization lacks precision; for example: what is the short run? how is profit defined? Kaldor (1975) makes the point that under conditions of increasing returns there occurs 'a process of polarization', what Myrdal (1939) and Young (1928) labelled as 'circular and cumulative causation'; that is, any change that may occur becomes 'progressive and cumulative' leading to disequilibrium situations with no hope at all of achieving 'Pareto-optimal full employment'. This process is responsible to a very large extent for the chronic 'rich and poor divide' both within and across countries. Furthermore, it is the case that the assumptions required for supply curves to have a positive slope are invalidated by empirical evidence (Blaug, 1980, ch. 7; Eichner, 1976, ch. 2). Firms, in the industrial sector at any rate, are price-setters with a long-run objective of survival and expansion rather than a short-run objective of profit maximization. Moreover, the available evidence seems to suggest that as output expands industrial firms do not experience higher unit costs (Johnston, 1960; Walters, 1963). There is no positively sloped supply curve: if anything, it is a perfectly elastic supply curve that would be more appropriate to the industrial sector. This latter conclusion receives further support by evidence suggesting that prices in the industrial sector are completely insensitive to demand conditions (Coutts et al., 1978; Eckstein and Fromm, 1968; Sawyer, 1983). Inevitably, the comprehensiveness test breaks down in the case of a positive supply curve.

The marginal physical product curves, which comprise the backbone of the 'marginal productivity' theory, fail all empirical tests. Our discussion above clearly indicates that it is fixed factor proportions that characterize the production process, not variable as required to make the 'marginal productivity' theory operational. Furthermore, the factor 'capital' cannot be determined, as we demonstrated above. It is, therefore, impossible to validate empirically a 'production function', aggregate or not, where 'capital' appears as one of the explanatory variables. Thus, the marginal physical product curves cannot possibly meet the correspondence test, or indeed any other empirical test (Blaug, 1980, ch. 9; Harcourt, 1972).

The four theoretical constructs we have just discussed comprise the microeconomic core of GNS which, in fact, purport to be empirical relationships. In line with Eichner (1983a, 1985), it has been argued that all four are 'metaphysical concepts without empirical foundation'. Dasgupta and Hahn (1985), however, have responded to Eichner's (1985) charge, arguing that GNS does not rely on marginal physical product curves nor on positively sloped supply curves. Substitution possibilities among factors of production is possible, as GNS empirical literature attests. Factors, therefore, can be employed in variable proportions, an isoquant requirement. They also argue that GNS consumer theory has developed 'empirically refutable propositions' (p. 590) which avoid the need to measure utility. Dasgupta and Hahn purport to have shown that Eichner's criticism of GNS is 'a remarkable exercise in imaginative writing' (p. 589). It is clear, though, from the above analysis that a lot more should be forthcoming from GNS proponents before Eichner's criticisms are answered.

The remaining two theoretical constructs of GNS constitute the macroeconomic core of it which is no less suspect on empirical grounds than the microeconomic one. We discuss the IS/LM framework of analysis first. This framework (see Figure 1.1) postulates that the rate of interest is the primary force behind the determinants of the level of economic activity as this is proxied by the level of national income. Changes in the rate of interest produce a new monetary equilibrium and a new level of income via the impact of the rate of interest on national income through investment.[4] However, the last proposition does not seem to have much empirical support since changes in the rate of interest produce only a very small, if any, movement in business investment (Nickell, 1978, pp. 299–300; Forman and Eichner, 1981, p. 123; Arestis *et al.*, 1985/6). The first proposition is also problematic in that it is normally assumed rather than justified. In fact, one can confidently argue that a 'monetary equilibrium' has not yet been properly defined for empirical purposes. It may very well be the case that 'monetary equilibrium' simply does not exist and that 'monetary disequilibrium' is more appropriate for both analysis and empirical investigation. In fact, what evidence does exist would seem to suggest that this is the case (Eichner, 1983a, p. 215). We should also refer to an early critique of the internal logic of the IS/LM framework, launched by Chick (1973). She shows that this apparatus produces an 'equilibrium solution' that depends on very special assumptions. It is shown that the 'equilibrium solution' is either transitory or consistent only with a stationary state, and also that the treatment of the implied bond market is fundamentally unsatisfactory, in that there is a conflict between stocks and flows.

Furthermore, Chick (1982) argues that there are further problems with the IS/LM model which emanate from Hicks's (1975, 1980/1) scrutiny of this framework. There is the problem of the incompatibility of Hicks's 'maintained method' (that is to say, the assumptions of the model are not to be challenged), essentially Walrasian, with the method of Keynes (assumptions need to be challenged). Another problem refers to the assumption of perfect foresight which is required to generate 'equilibrium' for money income. Also given that in the IS/LM apparatus there does not exist a supply dimension, the fix-price assumption is necessary too for the framework to produce a solution for output. Without either fix-price or the supply side the model does not determine output and employment (which is uniquely related to output in the short run). The model appears to have a relationship of very limited scope to *The General Theory*. This argument is reinforced when we turn our attention to policy questions and the use of 'equilibrium methods'. As Hicks (1980/1) correctly points out, policy prescription cannot take place without exploring the possiblity of policy changes. But this cannot happen under the assumption that the economy remains at 'its existing equilibrium'. However, should there be a change in policy, the model predicts that a new equilibrium will be reached in the future. Surely, though, 'there must necessarily be a stage before that equilibrium is reached. There must always be a problem of traverse. For the study of traverse, one has to have recourse to sequential methods of one kind or another' (Hicks, 1980/1, p. 154). These arguments raise the interesting question of the status of the IS/LM analysis and the concept of 'equilibrium', as a scheme of thought appropriate to account for reality. In any case, here again the correspondence as well as the coherence tests are not validated.

The Phillips curve relationship also fails the correspondence test. In this relationship it is the unemployment rate which is the predominant factor in determining wage inflation. However, it is clear that the unemployment rate does not perform satisfactorily from an empirical point of view. Moreover, it has already been demonstrated above that the Phillips curve relationship has proved to be unstable. In any case, unemployment may very well serve a completely different purpose than that hypothesized by the Phillips curve relationship. Unemployment, in this view, is seen to contain excessive wage claims and to put pressure on the labour force to work harder and enhance productivity (see, for example, Sawyer, 1989).[5]

Eichner (1983a) concludes that all these six elements which form the core of GNS ought to be purged if economics is to establish itself as a scientifically based discipline. An alternative to the GNS is, therefore, needed. This alternative should also attempt to avoid the fallacies from which GNS suffers: these are, according to Eichner, the solipsistic fallacy; the dualistic fallacy; and the Cartesian fallacy. The solipsistic fallacy concerns itself with the belief that the notion of 'external reality' does not enjoy separate existence and consequently the independence of 'external reality' and 'mind' is completely rejected. Thus, when economists construct models which have very little to do with reality and argue that what is required is to adhere to strictly internal consistency rather than 'external reality', they, in fact, engage in some form of solipsism. The dualistic fallacy involves the Thomastic synthesis of 'faith' and 'reason' which implies that there can be more than one 'external reality'. In a similar vein, GNS economics poses two separate realities: on the one hand, the reality the pre-Keynesian microeconomic theory is thought to describe, and on the other, the reality which the Keynesian macroeconomic theory is meant to explain. The Cartesian fallacy is the belief that knowledge external to the mind can only be derived by 'thought experiment' with no other experiment being conceivably able to confirm whatever is proposed. The implication here is that the axiomatic view is both necessary and sufficient for the acquisition of knowledge. The GNS proponents, by insisting that 'formal proofs' are both necessary and sufficient to establish the validity of any model, do effectively embrace the Cartesian fallacy.

3.7 CONCLUDING REMARKS

This chapter has put forward a number of the criticisms that have been launched on the GNS. There is one methodological critique that has been particularly emphasized, pinpointed by Eichner and other critics of the GNS: the amount of abstraction dictated by the excessive degree of mathematical formulations of the GNS theory. The simplifications required and, indeed, initiated are such that crucial aspects of economic reality are either ignored or distorted. Consequently, the actual nature of real economies is misunderstood and this can lead to serious errors in the conduct and implementation of economic policy. This charge clearly implies that 'theories should accurately represent economic reality' (Caldwell, 1989, p. 54). Post-Keynesian economics may very well be in a better position to incorporate this methodological claim. The rest of the book will attempt to show that it does.

NOTES

1. Harcourt (1976) refers to this problem as the 'climax' of the capital controversy. See also Harcourt (1969, 1972) for a lucid account of the debate, and Dobb (1973, ch. 9).
2. Haache (1979) demonstrates how this can be done by referring to Kaldor (1957, 1961) and Kaldor and Mirrlees (1962) growth models and the independent investment functions utilized in them.
3. In line with Gillies's (forthcoming) thesis, indifference curves might be considered as high-level theoretical assumptions which are not empirically falsifiable, but which are, none the less, part of a theory which is overall confirmed. The key question in this thesis is whether GNS explains a large number of facts without resorting to too many (*ad hoc*) assumptions. It clearly does not.
4. We should sharply distinguish at this juncture, between the investment relationship which is essentially a function of the rate of interest, that is to say, $I = I(r)$, and the equilibrium outcome in the IS/LM framework that involves the rate of interest and the level of income.
5. In the thesis put forward by Gillies (forthcoming), the relevant argument is that since the Phillips curve relationship is viewed as low-level theory, it is thought to be empirical but it has been falsified.

4. Post-Keynesian Economics

4.1 INTRODUCTION

This chapter attempts to identify and analyse briefly the major characteristics of post-Keynesian economics. In doing so we hope to show that post-Keynesian economics does in fact constitute a new approach to our understanding of economic phenomena.

There are themes which are clearly identified as post-Keynesian. It is really for this reason that its boundaries have not been precisely defined, if boundaries can ever be (Dow, 1990b). This is partly because post-Keynesianism as a school of thought is a fairly recent development, although the ideas which are classified as post-Keynesian have a long history. There is not a single model which can be taken to represent the post-Keynesian approach (Harcourt, 1985, 1989; Moore, 1988), but then, of course, there is not really a single model that encapsulates orthodox approaches, as was shown in Chapters 1 and 2. This could very well explain to some extent why post-Keynesian economists have not yet managed to be persuasive enough (Arestis, 1990), although a number of other reasons suggest themselves. These additional reasons are: that the economic issues with which post-Keynesians are concerned are controversial; that there is substantial diversity in their theoretical premises; that there are ideological objections to post-Keynesianism which emanate from the orthodox character of the economics profession; and that post-Keynesians tend to define their programme as a reaction to neo-classical economics (Hamouda and Harcourt, 1988; Lavoie, 1992).

Yet there is another dimension to this argument, in that there are different 'approaches' comprising post-Keynesian economics which differ in terms of method and economic features subsumed in their models. This should not be surprising nor be taken as by any means unhealthy, for a relatively new approach needs to have divergences and disagreements within its ranks. Nor should it be surprising to find that post-Keynesian methodology has been described as a 'horses for courses' approach (Hamouda and Harcourt, 1988), and in terms of its mode of thought as 'Babylonian' (Dow, 1985, 1990a), which is tantamount to saying that it is a holistic and non-dualistic rather than a reductionist or an atomistic approach. It is a unified methodology, not a collection of different ones, or is not necessarily so. The implication here is that acceptance of such a position would be consistent with the argument that the Lakatosian criteria for evaluating a research programme with its associated hard cores and protective belts may not be applicable.[1]

The post-Keynesian school of thought represents a positive statement of methodology, ideology and content. It is also true to say that post-Keynesians are united not just by their critical attitude to neo-classical economics, but more importantly by their attempt to provide an alternative approach to that of orthodox economics. There is a difficulty with this effort, though, which arises when a synthesis is aimed at ascertaining whether a coherent post-Keynesian model can emerge. For there is the view that since there is no uniform way of tackling all issues in economics, any attempt to synthesize must be a misplaced exercise (Robinson, 1979). This is especially so within post-Keynesian economics, where its various strands of thought differ from one another in that they deal with different issues and often enough with different levels of abstraction at the analytical level (Hamouda and Harcourt, 1988, p. 25). Coherence, however, prevails within the strands identified as post-Keynesian. It is, in fact, the vision and the underlying framework, which positively embraces a diversity of methods, that lends coherence to post-Keynesianism. Indeed, post-Keynesians have endeavoured to provide a coherent mode of thought. Brown (1981) claims to have been able to identify a post-Keynesian research programme, whilst Lavoie (1992) offers an interesting synthesis of post-Keynesianism and neo-Ricardianism to produce a post-classical *modus operandi*. Eichner (1987) and Arestis (1989) offer a synthesis of a number of strands within post-Keynesian economics which is amenable to both theoretical and empirical investigation (see also Rowthorn, 1981; Schefold, 1985).

The contributions just referred to may be thought of as springing from Robinson (1956, 1962a) and Pasinetti (1974, 1981). Eichner and Kregel (1975) argue along similar lines and suggest that the main aim of post-Keynesian economics is to complete the unfinished Keynesian revolution. It is an attempt at a generalization of the *General Theory* (Eichner and Kregel, 1975, p. 1293; Robinson, 1952). It is for this very reason that the *principle of effective demand* is the backbone of post-Keynesianism, as it was in Keynes's *General Theory* (1936). There is the convincing argument, though, that this principle had been discovered well before Keynes by Michal Kalecki (see, for example, the introduction to Kalecki, 1971a). There are differences in the two approaches and Sawyer (1982a, 1982b, 1985) enumerates the most important ones. Nevertheless, there are common elements between Kalecki's path-breaking work and the position adopted by post-Keynesian economics. In what follows we adhere to both Kalecki (1971a) and Keynes (1936).

Our main preoccupation in the rest of the book will be with a post-Keynesian model which, although it does not encompass all the 'approaches' that comprise the post-Keynesian school of thought, incorporates none the less the main elements of the fundamental strands within post-Keynesianism. This approach is not inconsistent with the 'horses for courses' approach, but it goes beyond it, in that it provides a coherent framework to explain post-Keynesian economics. To hazard a guess about future developments within post-Keynesian literature, it would be that a coherent core will be identified which will form the basis for theoretical and empirical explorations. This eventuality need not be inconsistent with the 'horses for courses' or the Babylonian approaches referred to above.

We begin with a general statement of post-Keynesian economics. This is followed by an exploration of the main methodological and, then, theoretical issues of post-Keynesian economics, which enables us to put together the key theoretical features of post-Keynesianism to form a coherent model, a task which is undertaken in the final section of this chapter.

4.2 PROLEGOMENA

There are a number of propositions which all post-Keynesians accept. Sawyer (1989) concurs with Davidson (1981) on the following three: (i) the economy is a historical process, (ii) in an uncertain world, expectations have a significant and unavoidable impact on economic events, (iii) institutions, economic and political, are of paramount importance in shaping economic events. Furthermore, realism is a further important element, along with the observation that post-Keynesian economics is based on the premiss that capitalism is a class-divided society.

Post-Keynesians view economics as an integral part of the social sciences, concerned with people organized in groups to satisfy their material needs. The focus of analysis is on the behaviour of these groups in historical time where the past is immutable and the future is uncertain and unknowable; both past and future have a critical role to play in influencing the present. When economics is studied in this way, it is paramount that the institutional framework within which the economic groups operate be spelt out clearly.

Perhaps the most important of these institutions is the large corporation or megacorp. This is the dominant institution in the technically more advanced, oligopolistic sector of the economy. Pricing is linked to investment behaviour, with prices set to provide sufficient retained earnings to enable megacorps to finance their planned investment. Some post-Keynesian writers have argued that there is also a 'neo-classical' proprietorship (non-oligopolistic) sector of the economy, which is the type of firm emphasized in the more conventional textbooks. (Kalecki, 1971a, pioneered this thesis; see also, amongst others, Eichner, 1976, 1987.) Whilst it is true to say that there are small firms, it is doubtful if even they behave as 'perfectly competitive' firms in the neo-classical sense, being more akin to what Kalecki described as 'pure imperfect competition'. Be that as it may, the production subsystem of the economy is essentially dominated by the megacorp.

On the other side of industry there are the trade unions with a substantial proportion of workers belonging to them. Trade unions bargain with employers over conditions of employment in general but wages in particular. There is a conflict of interest here, not harmony, so that the distribution between wages and profits is determined to a very large extent by the real wage demands of labour and the profit objectives of firms. In fact, workers bargain over money wages, the acceptable level obviously being determined by a real wage target, information on immediate past inflation and expectation as to future inflation. Workers are handicapped in this process because the achieved real wage can only be known after the event as a function of capitalist pricing decisions. The distribution which results is effectively determined by these pricing decisions and not by the wage bargaining process itself, unless it can be shown that the degree of monopoly or megacorp power is somehow reduced in the process. The realities of what has just been said prompted Galbraith (1978) to argue that they amount to 'the decline of the market' as the mode of economic organization. Once this is recognized, 'Then one addresses oneself to considering how the resulting economic performance can be made socially acceptable to as many people as possible. That is my view as to what post-Keynesian economics is about' (p. 11).

The economic activities of the groups considered so far, however, are influenced by the actions of the central government. This is the institution which is vested with the power to pursue Keynesian contracyclical policies in an attempt to reduce the amplitude of the cyclical behaviour of capitalist economies. This institution is also able to create money, though the bulk of the money in use in modern economies is credit money, created by the banking system, which is able to do so because the central bank is a lender of last resort (Kaldor, 1980, 1982). Finally, there is the international economy with its own institutions which interact with national institutions.

The emergence of the post-Keynesian paradigm has been helped by the development of the *system* or *cybernetic* framework. In this scheme, the economy is modelled as a group of dynamic subsystems. Each one of them interacts with all the other subsystems, influencing them and being influenced by them. In this way, the economic system is part of several societal systems, each with its own particular dynamics. The conception of economics in this system is no longer the study of how scarce resources are allocated to finite needs. It is, instead, the study of how actual economic systems are able to expand their outputs over time by producing and distributing the resulting social surplus. The expansion path is uneven and likely to change the very nature of economic systems in unprecedented ways, so that economic processes are viewed as erratic. Clearly, post-Keynesian analysis is concerned with an 'economics without equilibrium', an alternative to the equilibrium solutions of GNS, which 'looks upon the economy as a continually evolving system whose path cannot be predicted any more than the evolution of an ecological system in biology' (Kaldor, 1985, p. 12).

We shall comment on four further characteristics of the economic system that post-Keynesian analysis emphasizes. The first is the existence of *uncertainty*, in that the future is unknown and unknowable so that economic agents' expectations can be easily frustrated. Uncertainty is endemic in the real world (Bharadwaj, 1983), and as such is one of the central elements of post-Keynesian analysis (Davidson, 1988b). It has also been argued that uncertainty is structural in nature (Roncaglia, 1978). Market forces cannot account for the unknowability and unpredictability of the future and so can only disseminate incomplete, even misleading, information. The prices of goods and services today cannot tell buyers or sellers what the consequences of their collective actions will be on prices tomorrow. In an uncertain world all they can do is assume that if they have been happy with their actions in the past they are likely to be so in the future. 'Knowledge' of the future can only be formed indirectly from past events. Such 'knowledge' of the future can be ascertained with probability and not with risk certainty. But the conditions under which such a probability can be quantified are rarely met in everyday life, so that in general terms probabilities of this type cannot be arrived at. And to quote Keynes (1973, pp. 113–14): 'By uncertain knowledge . . . I do not mean merely to distinguish what is known for certain from what is only probable . . . About these matters there is no scientific basis to form any calculable probability whatever. We simply do not know.' Uncertainty is, of course, related to the notions of irreversible time, that production takes time, that economic agents enter into commitments well before outcomes can be predicted and, inevitably, that uncertainty is the *sine qua non* of the existence of money.

With the future uncertain, the final stage of the uneven process of expansion cannot be deduced; but the process of expansion can be carefully and intelligently analysed. The world is nonergodic: 'past observations do not produce knowledge about current and/or future events, while current observations of events provide no statistically reliable unbiased estimates about future time and/or space averages' (Davidson, 1988a, p. 180, fn. 1). In the presence of uncertainty as distinct from risk, past and current events do not provide a statistical guide to knowledge about future outcomes (Hicks, 1982). Knight (1921, pp. 232–3) is very categorical on this point, which he puts succinctly as follows:

The practical difference between the two categories, risk and uncertainty, is that in the former the distribution of the outcome in a group of instances is known (either from calculation *a priori* or from statistics of past experience), while in the case of uncertainty this is not true, the reason being in general that it is impossible to form a group of instances, because the situation dealt with is in a high degree unique. (See also Keynes, 1937)

Whilst decisions about the future are made all the time, there is absolutely no guarantee that these decisions will turn out to be the right ones, and it may be difficult to judge whether such decisions were right. Consequently, as the future unfolds and becomes the present, continued adjustments must be made. This process proceeds indefinitely without equilibrium ever being achieved, let alone maintained. Thus, history matters (Robinson, 1974).

This takes us to the second characteristic: the existence of *irreversible time*, where economic agents enter into commitments well before outcomes can be predicted. Keynes (1923, p. 33) is very specific on this point:

During the lengthy process of production the business world is incurring outgoings in terms of money – paying out in money for wages and other expenses of production – in the expectation of recouping this outlay by disposing of the product for money at a later date.

Historical time is sharply distinguished from logical time, which is rejected in post-Keynesian economics. Logical time is closely related to rationality and logical calculus, which are two of the essential characteristics of GNS economics. Problems associated with historical time are consequently assumed away by this mode of thought. Uncertainty is reduced to risk which can be calculated by recourse to the calculus of probability, in which case history becomes logical time. Then the real economy tends to a long-period position which is stable in that there is no tendency to drift away from it; indeed, if for some reason the system found itself away from this 'equilibrium' position, forces would be generated to take it back to long-period 'equilibrium'. Hicks (1982, p. 291) argues that this type of steady-state economics 'has encouraged economists to waste their time upon constructions that are often of great intellectual complexity but which are so much out of time, and out of history, as to be practically futile and indeed misleading'. Clearly then, these central concepts of GNS are completely inappropriate for an analysis which relies heavily on historical time.

The third characteristic, which is closely related to the second, is that economic agents commit themselves to contracts which are denominated in money, so that money and contracts are 'intimately and inevitably related' (Davidson, 1978, p. 148). This characteristic is pervasive, since money 'comes into existence along with debts, which are contracts for deferred payment, and price lists, which are offers of contracts for sale or purchase' (Keynes, 1930, p. 13). In this sense, the importance of money is that it is a link between the past and the present and also between the present and the future (Keynes, 1936, p. 294), with the past given and unchangeable and the future uncertain and unknowable (Moore, 1979a, p. 121). It is precisely the uncertainty inherent in historical time which is both the necessary and the sufficient condition for the existence of money. (Sardoni, 1987, draws out the similarities and differences between Keynes and Marx on this and other issues.) There would be no need for it in a stochastic, stationary and ergodic world (see also Rogers, 1989). The emphasis on the contractual relationship of modern money to debts leads quite neatly to the proposition that, today, money is credit driven and demand determined. Once this premiss is accepted it follows logically that the supply of and demand for money are interdependent. This is so since the supply of credit essentially depends upon its demand. It is, indeed, the determinants of the latter that can be said to influence the flow of credit, and thus money, in a particular period of time. The bulk of the demand for credit is for production. Production costs are incurred and paid for *before* revenues from sales materialize. The need to bridge this gap, to satisfy the working capital requirements of the industrial and commercial companies (what Keynes, 1937, labelled as the finance motive), is met by bank borrowing in addition to any internally generated funds. The amount of borrowing needed to bridge this gap is crucially determined by the total wage bill, the raw-material and tax-payments bills and other variables, such as unexpected changes in borrowing needs. Consequently, industrial and commercial companies borrow in expectation of higher future sales revenues to finance higher *current* production and distribution costs. So long as these companies can produce sound and adequate collateral, commercial banks will supply the amount of credit requested by them.

Whenever businessmen wish to invest, bankers will accommodate their demand for funds for credit-worthy projects at interest rates based on markup over the central bank's supply price of reserves. It is the endogenous nature of credit money that permits investment expenditures to be carried out independently of the current saving flows ... investment determines savings, rather than the reverse. (Moore, 1988, p. 376)

It is in this sense that money in modern capitalist economies is credit driven and demand determined; central banks cannot have a firm grip over its quantity. They can only control the supply price of credit money via the discount rate, which is under the authorities' direct control.

The fourth characteristic of post-Keynesian economics is the unique role accorded to labour and labour markets. In the post-Keynesian view, there is not a labour market in the real world in the way envisaged by neo-classical economics, where wages are just one set of many prices determined by 'market forces' in a general equilibrium framework. Instead, wages 'emerge as the result of a bilateral administered pricing process between employers and employees. Nominal labour contracts are agreed upon and then prevail over some future period' (Moore, 1988, p. 379). The process whereby these agreements materialize is governed by a 'conflict' of interests between employers and employees. Wage determination is crucially influenced not just by economics but also by a host of other factors, including political, historical, sociological and psychological forces. With money wages thus determined, it is prices that adjust to money wages, not the other way round. The mark-up hypothesis is invoked by post-Keynesians, so that in effect real wages are determined not just in labour markets but in product markets as well (Kalecki, 1969). It is, thus, conceivable that higher wages are accompanied by additional demand for labour, not less. There is no functional relationship between the two variables, simply because wages and employment are determined by independent variables (see also Riach, 1981).

4.3 METHODOLOGICAL ASPECTS AND KEY FEATURES OF POST-KEYNESIAN ECONOMICS

There are certain methodological premises to which all post-Keynesians claim to adhere. The most important of these is that a free-market economic process is inherently unstable and generates forces from within the system that are responsible for the instability and fluctuations in economic activity. Theories, then, should represent economic reality as accurately as possible. Post-Keynesian theory is very much based on this premiss and has as its primary objective an explanation of the real world as observed (Eichner and Kregel, 1975, p. 1309). Post-Keynesianism is thus very much at home with recent developments in the philosophy of language which emphasize this particular aspect. When it comes to the relevant criteria for theory adequacy, this approach highlights the ability of the theory to account for and explain successfully economic reality so that 'the success with which that theory as a whole captures reality can be explained in terms of the referential capacity of its key concepts and expressions' (Davies, 1989, pp. 424–5).[2] Consequently, post-Keynesian theory is context-specific and as such it requires continuous and repeated reappraisal of its uses in view of current developments (Dow, 1988, p. 15). To do so, post-Keynesian theory begins with observation (Dow, 1985, p. 76) and proceeds to build upon 'realistic abstractions' rather than 'imaginary models' (Rogers, 1989, pp. 189–92). Dow (1985, 1990a) discusses the 'Babylonian' approach referred to above, in the context of the arguments just touched upon. This approach is an attempt to theorize about a complex reality in an essentially *open system*, and posits that the study of economic phenomena may require many different, equally valid, approaches to understand the same phenomenon. More specifically, the 'Babylonian' approach is seen as constructing theory in a non-dualistic manner which does not require thought to be organized in 'all-encompassing mutually-exclusive' categories where the principle of 'the excluded middle' prevails. 'Babylonian' thought accepts that knowledge is endemically incomplete so that a large intermediate category exists of things which are 'believed to be known, subject to uncertainty of various degrees which are generally non-quantifiable' (Dow, 1990a, p. 148). Keynes's theory of uncertainty and investment behaviour is thought to be a very good example of the 'Babylonian' mode of analysis.

An emphasis on *realism* is also an essential characteristic of post-Keynesian economics. The issue here is a debate between critical realist and positivist positions within philosophy and methodology. The realist views the economy and society as an open system; the positivist views it as closed. The criterion for describing any system as open or closed is the occurrence of constant conjunctions of actual events – the ubiquity of constant conjunctions being a key element of positivist philosophy. For the realist, in contrast, the world in general is open, and constancy, or relative endurability, lies at the level of underlying causes (Lawson, 1989a, 1989b, 1990, 1993).

Reality, on this view, consists not only of 'events in, and states of affairs of, the world, and of our experiences of them, but also of the generative structures and causal mechanisms that govern the events that we experience' (Lawson, 1990, pp. 1–2). From this perspective a constant conjunction of events can usually only be expected (and outside astronomy is indeed only found) in a situation of experimental control, wherein a non-empirical mechanism may, through human intervention, be isolated and thereby empirically identified. Such a situation, of course, is quite unavailable in the social sphere (see Lawson, 1990; this is the best reference on the issues touched upon here).

One important implication of the realist position is that explanation rather than prediction is recognized as the relevant criterion of theory assessment (although there are economists – Caldwell, 1989, for example – who have argued that post-Keynesians should pay more attention to prediction). Post-Keynesian theory, in other words, looks to a theory's ability or power to explain and illuminate a range of empirical phenomena as its generic criterion of theory adequacy (Lawson, 1989a, 1989b, 1990, 1993). Keynes (1973, pp. 296–7) argues along similar lines:

> Economics is a science of thinking in terms of models joined to the art of choosing models which are relevant to the contemporary world. It is compelled to be this, because, unlike the typical natural science, the material to which it is applied is, in too many respects, not homogeneous through time. The object of a model is to segregate the semi-permanent or relatively constant factors from those which are transitory or fluctuating so as to develop a logical way of thinking about the latter, and of understanding the time consequences to which they give rise in particular cases.

This discussion leads to the question of the relevance of econometric modelling. From the realist perspective it is no wonder that 'In the main, econometricians appear to be continually puzzling over why it is that presumed identified empirical regularities, or "estimated relationships" always "break down" as soon as new observations become available (Lawson, 1990, p. 3; see also 1989b). Realists do recognize the existence of stylized facts – interpreted as rough and ready generalizations. But these are viewed as marking situations in which non-empirical mechanisms partially reveal themselves – dominating other causal mechanisms for a region of time and/or space (Lawson, 1989a). Thus, although falling leaves are governed not only by gravitational forces but by aerodynamic, thermal, inertial and other forces, most leaves do fall to the ground. Stylized facts, then, provide the starting point of analysis, the entry point for the search for causal mechanisms (Lawson, 1989a). If econometrics is to have any role, according to this perspective, then it is in identifying the phenomena from which realist research is to take off. The aim though can never be to generalize, or render precise, any rough empirical pattern, but to move to an understanding of the underlying causal mechanisms that give rise to it (Lawson, 1989a, 1989b, 1990, 1993). The 'observations' necessary for this analysis are regarded by post-Keynesians as containing both objective and subjective elements (Dow, 1985, p. 77). A certain degree of objectivity is present when 'facts' are observed, whilst the grouping of 'facts' for purposes of theoretical analysis entails some degree of subjectivity. But even observation is selective. We all have our 'blind spots'.

A further methodological premiss is that an organic, rather than atomistic, approach to economic processes is more relevant and appropriate. Post-Keynesians see individuals as social rather than atomistic beings. This proposition necessitates concern with economic institutions, especially when we come to the vital questions of production and distribution, and the causes and consequences of structural change which become key issues. The major concern of production analysis is with the causes of the growth of output and resources rather than with the allocation of existing resources. Given the 'reserve army of unemployed' and the possibility of increasing the rate of capacity utilization, the principle of scarcity is de-emphasized within this framework of thought. The theories of imperfect competition embedded in post-Keynesian analysis predict excess capacity and hence no scarcity of resources (at least of capital equipment) – although it should be said that where models predict the existence of excess capacity, for example as an entry barrier, then this in itself is fulfilling a need in that it provides a service.

Post-Keynesian analysis recognizes the possibility of 'insufficient demand' rather than concentrating on scarcity of resources, so that 'effective demand' assumes a central position. The role of exchange is such that individual choice is limited, for it is determined by income, class and the technical conditions of production rather than by relative prices. Consumer choice is based on lexicographic ordering, that is to say, on a hierarchy of needs (Robinson, 1956, ch. 34; Pasinetti, 1981, p. 75). This ordering is based on the notion that different goods satisfy different needs so that goods can be grouped according to the needs they satisfy. In other words, lexicographic ordering means that non-numerical criteria are employed to arrange goods into categories with an appropriate taxonomy. Just as there are rules for arranging words in a *lexicon*, similarly in this case there are rules which help to ascertain the listing of goods into categories where the order of listing is crucially determined by the degree of their importance (Eichner, 1987). Substitution effects may only take place within groups, so these effects are neither dominant nor even prevalent. Consequently, the demand for goods depends on the social and income class of consumers. Income and not substitution effects, along with income distribution amongst social classes, are the objects of analysis.

In the sphere of production, monopolies and oligopolies assume socio-political as much as economic power in product markets, which gives them the prerogative to administer prices. This capacity relative to the power over input costs, especially wage costs, determines the surplus which monopolies and oligopolies can muster. It is this surplus which, when translated into investment, provides the engine for growth. The extent to which the surplus is translated into investment depends on effective demand and expectations. These are long-term expectations about the health of product markets, and short-term expectations that relate to the prices of financial assets. These prices are essentially determined by social relations, themselves influenced by the relative power of financial institutions. It is important to stress at this stage that within post-Keynesian economic analysis, institutional structure and industrial organization are by no means fixed. They are continuously evolving and influencing the historical development of economies, themselves being the main objects of analysis. They play a vital role in terms of the determination of income distribution, the level and composition of output, the generation of surplus and its translation into vital investment.

Turning to individual behaviour, in the post-Keynesian approach individuals are not assumed to be omniscient. They are seen as being able to acquire information but their capacity to do so is limited.

Individuals rely on group behaviour and conventions. They are not assumed to optimize. Procedures and rules are set by those individuals or groups which possess power, obtained by their place in the social or economic hierarchy, that allows them to impose their values upon the rest. Individuals as decision-makers are assumed to suffer from 'bounded rationality', in that 'their mental capacities prevent them from seeing problems in all their complexity and working out solutions to them' (Earl, 1989, pp. 165–6). Bounded rationality, however, is the outcome of uncertainty, another important ingredient of post-Keynesian economics discussed earlier, which is viewed as an element of the general environment where the systematic processes of production and accumulation interact and operate (Eatwell, 1983, p. 127).

In post-Keynesian economic analysis the emphasis is on change over time. In such a framework growth and dynamics are its central parts, so that the explanation of the erratic nature of the expansion path of a capitalist economy becomes the main focus of analysis. There is no attempt to associate mathematical determinism of models with causality in the explanation of erratic economic processes; nor is there any consideration as to whether economic processes would ever reach a Pareto-optimal point. On the contrary, post-Keynesian analysis attempts to explain the actual level of economic activity as well as movements in economic processes by placing particular emphasis on the endogenous nature of the erratic expansion path of a free enterprise economy. The driving force behind the erratic expansion path of the economic system is seen to be *investment*.[3]

The tradition of post-Keynesian economics reflects its focus on the classical economists, Keynes and Kalecki. It is possible to identify three approaches in this tradition (Hamouda and Harcourt, 1988, elaborate extensively on this). There is the approach that stresses uncertainty, the full integration of money with the rest of the analysis, the centrality of the money-wage and the stock/flow interrelationship in capital accumulation. This approach has its roots in *The Treatise on Money* and *The General Theory* and was influenced by Marshall. Another approach, essentially Kaleckian, emphasizes the role of effective demand failures, but is based on a 'social class' perspective rather than on a Newtonian 'atomistic' one. It adapts Marx's reproduction scheme to tackle the realization problem where social relations are essential to the analysis of dynamic processes. Not unexpectedly, this approach incorporates the contributions of Joan Robinson and her followers. These two approaches are concerned with, and highlight, economic problems and phenomena through a short-term focus. The third approach concentrates on and provides an explanation of long-period levels of prices, income and employment. It encompasses Sraffa's contribution along with Keynes's effective demand in a way that rejects the proposition that supply and demand determine price and, also, the Keynesian analysis of the demand for assets, essentially Chapter 17 of Keynes's *General Theory* (1936).

We would add a further approach within post-Keynesianism. This is the one which is rooted firmly in the institutionalist tradition of Veblen (1899) and others. It is orientated to process and evolution and is thus dynamic. It emphasizes the structure of power in an economic system. The economy is not just the atomistic 'market mechanism' but the institutional and organizational structure of the larger economy, which is the main mechanism whereby resources are allocated (Samuels, 1987). Institutionalism demonstrates that economic performance should be judged according to emerging societal values, in which case the economy becomes a 'valuation mechanism'. An interdisciplinary approach is pursued along with a detailed and painstaking study of institutions and their evolution. It is argued that the institutionalist approach provides a very important link in post-Keynesian analysis (Hodgson, 1988). This relates to the contention that in Keynes (1936) and in post-Keynesianism expectations are exogenous. Although there is a rich analysis of the effects of expectations about the future on present economic behaviour, there appears to be very little on the determinants of these expectations (Champernowne, 1963). Hodgson (1988) suggests that a post-Keynesian framework based on the institutionalist approach fills this gap. An endogenous theory of expectations formation which draws on 'a functional and historical study of political and economic institutions' (Hodgson, 1988, pp. 33–4) provides the link referred to above. Arestis and Eichner (1988) argue along similar lines in their analysis of monetary phenomena.[4]

We do not intend to elucidate these approaches here. What we propose to do instead is to draw on these contributions in an attempt to provide a coherent post-Keynesian mode of thought.

4.4 THE CONSTITUENT THEORETICAL ELEMENTS OF POST-KEYNESIAN ECONOMICS

The discussion so far in this chapter demonstrates that post-Keynesian economics is a general theory of capitalism. The class division characteristic of capitalism depends on the ownership of the means of production. Workers, who do not own any means of production (see however Pasinetti, 1962, and Chapter 5 below), are obliged to work for the capitalist class, who are the principal owners of the means of production. Such an economy produces a surplus of output which is the source of profit income. The latter is a residual accruing to the capitalist class which owns the means of production. The existence of this surplus is an important source of conflict between social classes. It is clear, therefore, that post-Keynesian economics does not rely on 'harmony' among economic agents in its explanation of how capitalism works, but on conflict. This approach, therefore, comes much closer to capturing the essence of a capitalist economy, and it can serve as the theoretical basis for a more 'realistic' approach to the study of economics and the design of human institutions. Post-Keynesian analysis firmly embraces the view that 'the institutional framework of a social system is a basic element of its economic dynamics' (Kalecki, 1970, p. 311). The analysis below is very much in this spirit.

In an attempt to highlight these propositions we refer to Figure 4.1, where the post-Keynesian circular flow is depicted. The social pyramid is particularly emphasized in this approach. The triangle includes the capitalist class, workers and unemployed workers. The arrows in the triangle convey the notion that some upward and downward mobility is possible. Wage income accrues to the working class and profit to the capitalist class. Workers' expenditure is entirely on necessities, and capitalist expenditure is on both luxuries and necessities, but part of capitalist income is saved. Savings are channelled to firms (so that along with their retained earnings they are able to invest) through financial markets. Workers typically do not save in this particular model, capitalists being the only savers. Firms provide consumer goods and services through the goods market. Revenues from these transactions are channelled to firms which enable them to carry on with production and capital accumulation.

The model underpinning Figure 4.1 entails essentially the follow-

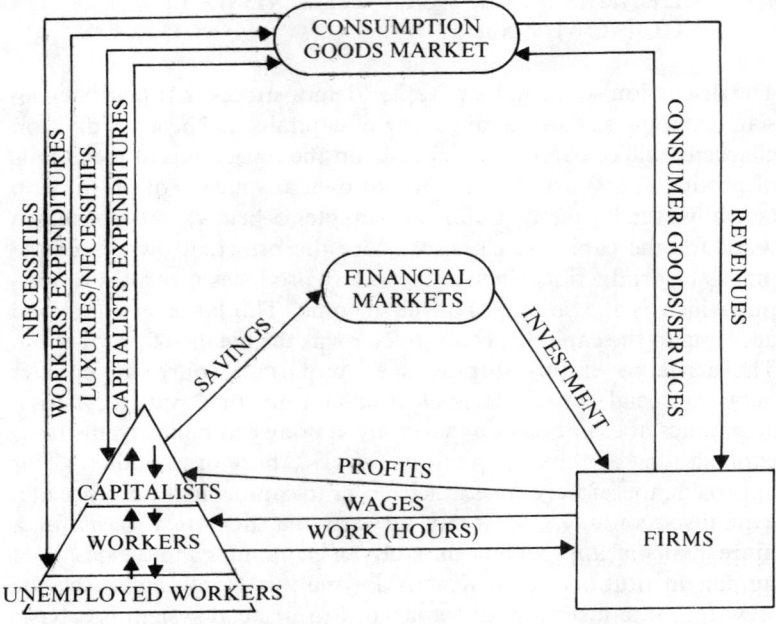

Figure 4.1 Post-Keynesian circular flow

[Figure: Circular flow diagram showing CONSUMPTION GOODS MARKET at top, FINANCIAL MARKETS in center, FIRMS on right, and a triangle on the left containing CAPITALISTS, WORKERS, and UNEMPLOYED WORKERS. Flows include NECESSITIES, WORKERS' EXPENDITURES, LUXURIES/NECESSITIES, CAPITALISTS' EXPENDITURES from the triangle up to the consumption goods market; SAVINGS from triangle to financial markets; INVESTMENT from financial markets to firms; CONSUMER GOODS/SERVICES and REVENUES between firms and consumption goods market; PROFITS, WAGES, WORK (HOURS) between firms and the workers/capitalists triangle.]

Source: As adapted from Hollis and Nell (1975) by Lichtenstein (1983, p. 19).

ing theories. The first is the theory of *value and pricing*. Value is based on technical, that is, objective, conditions of production (the way production is organized, its input and cost requirements, types of technology used, the productivity of labour and capital, the latter's availability and so on). The value of a commodity is directly linked to the way it is produced – not to utility as in the GNS world. Commodities are produced by the application of human labour under certain technical conditions. It follows that income paid out to economic agents who do not physically participate in production is residual income. Wage income is not residual; profit income is. Output is thus produced by one class of society so that social relationships are of paramount importance in production.[5] One social dimension of production which ought to be emphasized at this juncture is the *power relationship* involved in production between the representatives of capital and workers (as well as between workers) – in other words, between those who manage and those who are managed. Non-working classes share the output produced by the working classes, and yet it is capital which hires labour and thus the former has a considerable degree of control over the latter – an inherent facet of capitalism. In this power relationship, capital's interests are, at one level, served by lower wages and higher productivity. We must bear in mind, however, the question of effective demand and the ability of capital to realize the value of output, so the relationship is more complicated than it appears on the surface. Individual capitalists have an interest in lower wages, although for the capitalist class as a whole this may be detrimental to their interests. But higher productivity involves higher intensity of work, *ceteris paribus*. It is, thus, possible to argue that lower wages and higher productivity benefit capital but harm labour. Class relationships cannot be harmonious, as they are purported to be in the GNS world; 'class conflict' is at the heart of the analysis.

Modern capitalist economies are dominated by large corporations. This 'corporate revolution' has produced the notion of the 'megacorp' and the 'oligopolistic' sector. As a result, there has occurred a new class of 'professionally trained managers and executives' who are at the centre of decision-making. As such, it is to this group, and to the owners of capital who lie behind this 'managerial class', that the residual income flows when in the past it was the capitalist class that were the recipients of this type of income (Eichner, 1987). Furthermore, the emergence of the oligopolistic sector has meant that the megacorp has replaced the neo-classical type of firm and has become the dominant form of enterprise in modern advanced industrial societies. The pricing behaviour of the megacorps is simply to add a certain percentage mark-up on their unit cost of production at a normal level of capacity utilization. The mark-up is determined by the needs of the megacorps to finance their investment plans, tempered by the exact extent of their market power (Eichner, 1976; see also Wood, 1975). It follows from this analysis that pricing theory is inevitably and inextricably linked to the theory of *investment* and *class conflict*.

Investment in the post-Keynesian tradition is essentially determined by expected profitability. The latter in its turn depends on the marginal efficiency of investment which gives rise to an interest-elastic investment relationship; profitability also depends on the expected growth of sales. However, post-Keynesian analysis recognizes that volatile expectations and firms' 'animal spirits' render the ranking of investment projects according to their marginal efficiencies of investment inappropriate. Furthermore, to the extent that firms use barriers to entry in their sector to stave off competition and to entrench an existing market position, investment decisions in this respect may not be related to any 'rational' profit calculation. Consequently, interest rates would have no role to play in the circumstances just considered, which suggests that they must be viewed as unimportant, within a range, as a determinant of investment. The expected growth of sales is thought to be a more serious explanatory variable. This is so since this variable influences investment behaviour on new plant and equipment. And this type of investment is thought to be by far the most important part of total investment. But again, the pervasive nature of expectations under uncertainty plays a vital role in the capital accumulation process.

Investment in its turn is the most important variable in *distribution theory*. This theory recognizes that national income is divided into total wage income (wages and salaries which workers receive for their labour services) and total profits (capitalists' income earned through the ownership of the means of production), just as is shown in Figure 4.1. It is also assumed that marginal propensities to consume out of wages and profits differ, from which the very wellknown proposition follows that on a steady-state growth path the shares of profits and wages are related to the marginal propensities to consume but also, most importantly, to the ratio of investment to income. Consequently, distribution of income in post-Keynesian analysis is treated as a variable directly linked to the rate of economic expansion for a given degree of monopoly that allows control over pricing (Eichner and Kregel, 1975, p. 1296). Pasinetti (1974, p. 113) has shown, in fact, that control over the rate of investment implies control over distribution and the rate of profit. Distribution and investment, now, are the fundamental features of *growth dynamics*.

Growth dynamics is at the heart of post-Keynesian analysis, a feature which emanates from its dynamic nature and concern with an economic system that is expanding over time. The dynamic element is derived from Harrod's (1939, 1948) fundamental equation for the rate of growth of national income which is equivalent to the ratio of average propensity to save to the capital/output ratio. This expression is modified to take account of the contention that the average propensity to save is affected by income distribution, since the propensities to save out of profits and wages differ. This approach requires two types of analysis: long-run and short-run. The long-run analysis concerns itself with the 'secular' or 'trend' developments of the economy. The short-run analysis attempts to explain the 'cyclical behaviour' of the economy, which can only be understood in relation to the 'secular' developments from which it represents a deviation. Post-Keynesian analysis concerns itself with the study of both of these phenomena. In doing so, it recognizes that trend and cycle are in fact interdependent (Goodwin, 1967; Kalecki, 1971a), with the study of the two comprising what Eichner (1987) has labelled, 'the economy's macrodynamic behaviour'.

The long-run analysis is concerned with the determination of the warranted rate of growth, and therefore the conditions required for a steady rate of expansion. Post-Keynesian analysis is also concerned with comparison and analysis of different growth paths, with the relationship between actual and warranted growth paths and with their determinants. The short-term analysis focuses on the forces that operate to divert the economy from its warranted growth path. In what follows we try to account for both analyses. We do this by specifying variables in terms of the difference between the actual and the secular rates of growth (denoted by an asterisk*). Hence, we distinguish between short-term influences which are concerned with deviations from trend, and long-term influences which affect the trend. In this way we distinguish between the factors which determine the cyclical behaviour of the economy and those which determine the secular growth rate with the further aim of bringing them together in a coherent manner within the confines of a macro-economic model. The decomposition of each variable into a *cyclical component* and a *trend component* can then be used to reconcile the short-run analysis with the long-run analysis within post-Keynesian economics. Such an approach has been initiated by Robinson (1956, 1962a) and further argued by others (see mainly Eichner and Kregel, 1975; Goodwin, 1967; Eichner, 1987).

There is one aspect of this analysis which needs to be clarified. It concerns the terms 'run' and 'period', which are not synonymous nor is there a direct correspondence between them. 'Period' refers to states of 'equilibrium' while 'run' is about 'processes of motion'. Short-period and long-period 'equilibrium' can be defined independently of short run and long run. Short run and long run refer to movements towards 'equilibrium' which must take place in historical time. Robinson (1956, p. 180) is very clear on the difference:

Long-period changes are going on in short-period situations. Changes in output, employment and prices, taking place with a given stock of capital, are short-period changes; while changes in the stock of capital, the labour force and the techniques of production are long-term changes . . . A given short-period situation contains within itself a tendency to long-period change.

This distinction is apparent in both GNS and post-Keynesian economics, and Carvalho (1984/5) gives a number of examples to clarify the point. In the GNS framework, if a process of short-run 'noise-removal' is to exist and enough time is allowed for necessary changes to take place, full long-run 'equilibrium' can be attained. There is no reason, of course, to expect convergence to equilibrium. Arrow and Hahn (1971) have actually shown that the conditions for convergence are very difficult to satisfy even under the most simplified assumptions of pure exchange economies. In Sraffa (1960), production prices are long-run equilibrium prices. They are a centre of gravity around which market prices fluctuate (Garegnani, 1978, 1979; Eatwell, 1983; Harcourt, ed., 1977). There is here the idea of a process whereby production prices emerge, towards which market prices converge. Competition ensures that the long-run equilibrium position is achieved when capitalists earn the uniform rate of profit. There is a short run as a result of 'accidents' or 'noises'. But this is of 'minor' concern because it lacks 'determinateness' and it is, thus, ignored. Further examples where the notion of 'gravity centres' is utilized are Kaldor (1970b) and Pasinetti (1970, 1981). They base their analysis on Harrod's (1939) growth model to show that changes in income distribution produce convergence between 'warranted' and 'natural' growth rates. For Pasinetti (1970, 1981), short run is synonymous with 'transitory' factors just as in Garegnani (1978, 1979), so that the process of actually getting to the long run is of no consequence. Kalecki (1971a), by contrast, does not view long run as a gravity centre. Long and short runs are inseparable, in the sense that 'the long run trend is but a slowly changing component of a chain of short run situations; it has no independent entity' (Kalecki, 1971a, p. 165).

These examples clearly portray the notion of 'long-run' analysis in which there is a definite duration aspect. 'Long-period' analysis, by contrast, is not characterized by any duration aspects (Carvalho, 1990). In this sense, long period describes a state of full *atemporal* 'equilibrium' which can very well exist without there being a corresponding long-run 'equilibrium' process. A good example to make the point is Marshall (1920) who changed the meaning of market and production prices, referred to above, into short-period and long-period equilibrium prices (Bharadwaj, 1978). In this way, prices become 'amenable to analysis' (Carvalho, 1990): demand factors determine value in the short period, with costs of production being essentially the determinant of long-period prices. There is no actual process involved in this example. Nor is there a description of the dynamics of change that take us from the short-period to the long-period situation. Long-period values are established in the long run, and they are those which 'economic factors would bring about if the general conditions of life were stationary for a run of time long enough to enable them all to work out their full effect' (Marshall, 1920, p. 289). There are ample examples of these differences in Keynes (1936), and Carvalho (1984/5, 1990) has analysed them superbly. There is, however, an important difference between short and long periods emanating from Keynes. This is that 'the short-period framework includes the data of the actual environment where agents act, while the long-period situation has no such "reality". They do not relate in the same way to actual processes that are to take place in definite "runs" of time' (Carvalho, 1990, p. 285). Clearly, in this framework a long-period analysis as a centre of gravitation does not have a place.

We return to the cyclical behaviour of the economy and the related problem of explaining its turning points. This particular focus directs attention to the *business cycles* aspect of post-Keynesian economics. The fundamental starting point of post-Keynesian business cycles theory is that cycles are viewed as an inherent aspect of capitalist economies. Business cycles are thus depicted as being an endogenous phenomenon caused by the normal functioning of the capitalist economic system (Kaldor, 1940; Kalecki, 1971a, ch. 11; Goodwin, 1967). Exogenous shocks, such as technological innovations, oil price changes and so on, can spark off cyclical fluctuations, but they simply accentuate an underlying, endogenously embedded instability. This instability arises from the motive of producers and financial investors alike to accumulate wealth for its own sake. It is, therefore, not surprising to find that investment and expectations are at the heart of post-Keynesian business cycle theory.

To demonstrate, let us assume that the economy is on the upswing of the cycle. Expectations of returns on investment and profits are optimistic, so demand for lending is high with commercial banks being more willing to lend than otherwise. Investment is boosted substantially and the economy is on an upward growth path. Improved profitability, however, carries the seeds of its own destruction by engendering a too-vigorous expansion of output and employment, thus reducing the reserve army of labour and strengthening labour's bargaining power. It has been observed (Sherman, 1987, for example) that profitability rises in the initial stages of the upswing but tends to fall in the later phases, with real wage increases occurring at the top of the cycle (see also Sawyer, 1989, ch. 12). It is inferred that higher real wages reduce actual, and thus expected, profitability, which discourages investment. As expansion comes to an end the process goes into reverse. This is characterized by lower-than-expected returns and high interest costs, so that profits and investment take a further turn for the worse. Markets become less active and the economy is well on its way to the downswing. At the bottom of the cycle the reserve army of labour is weakened substantially, real wages are squeezed and profitability begins to recover. As it does so, expected profitability and investment are enhanced sufficiently to produce an end to the downswing and the beginnings of the expansion phase, as explained above. This short excursion into the mechanics of the turning points of the economy's cyclical behaviour clearly shows that the search for profits by both producers and financial investors, and the degree of willingness to undertake investment opportunities to make it possible in an uncertain world, are the main causes of business cycles in post-Keynesian analysis.

The 'class conflict' element is particularly highlighted in the *wage determination* theory, where bargaining in the labour market is the kernel of this analysis. Unionized or non-unionized workers have drives and aspirations as well as economic and political power which are described in terms of a *target-relative real wage*. Deviations of actual real wages from the desired level affect the level of money wage demands, thereby causing an upward pressure on money wages if the desired level is less than the actual. Similarly, there would be a downward pressure on money wages when the real wage exceeds the target-relative real wage. Expectations of price inflation over the contract period, the rate of change of unemployment seen as a proxy for the speed of expansion or contraction of 'the reserve army of unemployed', and the workers' position in the income distribution relative to other groups are further variables that are thought to be important determinants of nominal wages. Now, the rate of wage inflation relative to productivity along with that of prices of imports and raw materials are taken to be the most vital determinants of price inflation. Clearly, the theory of inflation advanced by post-Keynesians belongs squarely in the 'conflict theory' framework, reflecting the struggle of labour for its income share.

The final key theoretical proposition underpinning our model relates to its *monetary aspects*. Money is viewed as essentially endogenous in a credit money economy. Its behaviour is governed by the portfolio needs of firms, persons, governments and financial institutions. Money responds mainly to the behaviour of private economic agents rather than to the behaviour of the monetary authorities. The emphasis, then, in post-Keynesian monetary analysis is on credit rather than on money in enabling spending units to bridge any gap between their desired level of spending and the current rate of cash flow. Money, therefore, is completely integrated within production and exchange, so that attempts to curtail the required flow of money will produce severe cutbacks in production. The monetary authorities, though, should aim to create financial stability, something which is important in discouraging funds being devoted to speculation rather than to productive activity. However, when speculation causes liquidity to increase excessively, direct credit controls should be used to curb it.

Furthermore, the monetary authorities can control the discount rate, changes in which influence the market interest rate via a markup. It is, therefore, apparent that Kalecki's (1971a) theory of markup pricing as applied to interest rate determination is relevant in this regard. Consequently, it is the rate of interest that is the control variable in this approach. In addition, the discount rate, as determined by the monetary authorities, affects the exchange rate. This link brings to the fore the *foreign sector* aspects of the economic system. These aspects are incorporated into the analysis through the current and capital accounts of the balance of payments, where the exchange rate influences, and is influenced by, the state of both accounts. A novel feature of the imports element of the current account is the hypothesis of different marginal propensities to import out of workers' income and out of the income of capitalists (Arestis and Driver, 1987). This is a result of the proposition that there are different savings and consumption propensities out of wages and profits. Finally, there are the government activities which are captured by two variables: taxes and government expenditures. They are both endogenized in that they are related to the level of economic activity as this is proxied by the level of national income.

4.5 THE POST-KEYNESIAN MODEL

When all these theoretical constructs are brought together we arrive at the full model summarized in Table 4.1. The model is conveniently divided, for the purposes of this book, into six blocks.[6] Blocks I and II comprise the real segment of the economy in Table 4.1. These are equations (1)–(7), where equations (1)–(5) comprising block I, with (6) and (7) constituting Block II. In these two blocks, as well as in the whole model, the most important variable which is responsible for the cyclical behaviour of the economy is discretionary expenditure. Discretionary expenditure has two important characteristics: it is postponable and it is usually partly externally financed. Investment (both public and private), consumer durables expenditure and expenditure on exports are the constituent elements of discretionary expenditure. This variable is determined in block I in both nominal (E) and real (DE) terms and it appears in every sector – where the following sectors are assumed: personal sector, industrial and commercial companies (ICCs), public corporations, general government and the foreign sector. Block III – Equations (8) and (9) – is concerned with the determination of 'discretionary funds' (F), which is another crucial variable defined as the difference between income received and non-discretionary expenditure by any sector. The ratio of sectoral discretionary expenditure to sectoral discretionary funds, which measures exposure to external financing, is an important determinant of a number of variables in our model. The ratio is expected to have a negative impact on

Table 4.1

Block I

(1) $DE^* = \sum_{i=1}^{n} DE_i^*$

(2) $DE_i^* = DE_i^*[\underset{-}{[(Y-T)_{wi}^*/(Y-T)_{ci}^*]}, \underset{+}{(Y^e{}^*)}, \underset{+}{(E_i,^*/F_i^*)}, \underset{-}{R^*}, \underset{+}{\Delta LP_i^*}]$

(3) $E_i^* = DE_i^* + P^*$

(4) $E^* = \sum_{i=1}^{n} E_i^*$

(5) $NDE^* = Y^* - DE^*$

Block II

(6) $Y^* = Y^*[\underset{+}{DE^*}, \underset{+}{(E^*/F^*)}]$

(7) $EMP^* = EMP^* \underset{+}{(Y^*)}$

Block III

(8) $F^* = \sum_{i=1}^{n} F_i^*$

(9) $F_i^* = F_i^*(\underset{+}{Y_i^*}, \underset{+}{P^*}, \underset{+}{W^*}, \underset{-}{T_i^*})$

Block IV

(10) $\dot{P}^* = \dot{P}^*(\underset{+}{\dot{W}^*}, \underset{-}{PR\dot{O}D^*}, \underset{+}{\dot{P}_{RM}^*})$

(11) $\dot{P}_{RM}^* = \dot{P}_{RM}^* (\underset{-}{ER^*}, \underset{+}{WT^*})$

(12) $\dot{W}^* = W^*[\underset{+}{[(W/P)^d - (W/P)_{t-1}]}, \underset{+}{(W^* - P^*)}, \underset{-}{\Delta U^*}, \underset{+}{\pi^*}, \underset{-}{H_i^*}]$

Block V

(13) $\Delta M^* = \Delta TD^* + \Delta SD_i^* + \Delta GDC^*$

(14) $\Delta TD^* = \Delta BLP_i^* + \Delta BLG^* + \Delta BLOS^* - \Delta SD_i^* - \Delta DBD^*$

(15) $\Delta SD_i^* = \Delta SD_i^*[\underset{+}{\Delta Y_i^*}, \underset{-}{\Delta R^*}, \underset{+}{(E_i^*/F_i^*)}]$

(16) $\Delta BLP_i^* = \Delta BLP_i^*[\underset{+}{\Delta Y_i^*}, \underset{-}{\Delta R^*}, \underset{+}{(E_i^*/F_i^*)}, \underset{-}{X_i}]$

(17) $\Delta LP_i^* = \Delta BLP_i^* + \Delta OLP_i^*$

(18) $\Delta BLG^* = PSBR^* + \Delta EF^* - \Delta BC^*$

(19) $PSBR^* = G^* - T^* - OGR^*$

(20) $G^* = G^* \underset{-}{(Y^*)}$

(21) $T^* = T^*(Y^*)$
$+$

(22) $\Delta R^* = \Delta R^*(\Delta r^*, \Delta EF^*, \Delta BC^*)$
$+ \quad - \quad +$

Block VI

(23) $\Delta EF^* = CB^* + \Delta KM^* - \Delta OEF^*$

(24) $CB^* = CB^*[[(Y-T)_{wi}^*/(Y-T)_{ci}^*], Y^*, WT^*, (P/P_w \cdot ER)^*]$
$\phantom{CB^* = CB^*[[(Y-T)_{wi}^*/(Y-T)_{ci}^*],}- \quad\quad - \quad + \quad\quad -$

(25) $\Delta KM^* = \Delta KM^*[(R/R_f)^*, ER^*]$
$+ \quad\quad +$

(26) $ER^* = ER^*[(R/R_f)^*, CB^*, \Delta KM^*]$
$+ \quad\quad + \quad +$

Glossary of variables

DE	=	discretionary expenditure in real terms
Y	=	real national output
T	=	taxes
$(Y-T)_w$	=	disposable income of workers
$(Y-T)_c$	=	disposable income of capitalists
E	=	discretionary expenditure in nominal terms
F	=	discretionary funds in nominal terms
R	=	long-term rate of interest
LP	=	total lending to the public
P	=	domestic prices
$\dot{P}$	=	inflation rate
NDE	=	non-discretionary expenditure
EMP	=	employment
$\dot{W}$	=	money wage rate
PROD	=	productivity
$\dot{P}_{RM}$	=	rate of change of prices of raw materials
H_i	=	stands for various other variables
TD	=	time deposits
BLP	=	bank lending to the public
BLG	=	bank lending to the government
BLOS	=	bank lending to the overseas sector
SD	=	sight deposits
OBD	=	other bank deposits (including non-deposit liabilities)
PSBR	=	public sector borrowing requirement
EF	=	external financing
ΔBC	=	sales of government debt to the non-bank public (including currency)
M	=	money stock
GDC	=	public sector deposits (including currency)
G	=	government expenditure
OGR	=	other government revenue
OLP	=	other lending to the public
r	=	short term rate of interest
KM	=	capital movements
OEF	=	other external financing
X_i	=	policy variables which can affect credit directly
CB	=	current balance
WT	=	world trade
P_w	=	world prices
ER	=	exchange rate
R_f	=	foreign rate of interest
Δ	=	'changes in'
e	=	superscript which stands for 'expected' magnitudes
*	=	denotes that variable is specified in terms of the difference between actual and secular rates of growth

The signs under variables indicate the signs of partial derivatives.

discretionary expenditure in Block I, given targets of indebtedness, and a positive effect on national output in Block II since it enhances the multiplier effects if the source of funding is external debt. Similar effects prevail in the credit segment. Block IV – Equations (10) and (11) – comprise the distribution segment of the model; and Equations (13)–(22), Block V, describe the credit segment. Finally, the foreign sector, Block VI, comprises equations (23)–(26), where we stress the distribution variable in Equation (24), which emanates from its appearance in the imports equation as 'a distribution of income' variable referred to above. For more details on the six blocks see Arestis *et al.* (1985/6) and Arestis (1986a; 1989); Chapters 5–9 below provide the background analysis and full justification of all these relationships.

In Figure 4.2 we show the interrelationships between the six blocks that comprise the whole model. Block I determines the strategic variable 'discretionary expenditure' both in real and nominal terms. The interaction of Blocks I and III determines the ratio of discretionary expenditures to discretionary funds (E^*/F^*) variable, which feeds into Block I (as explained above). It also feeds into Block II where output and employment are determined, with the ratio (E^*/F^*) influencing output in addition to the impact of discretionary expenditures in real terms $(DE)^*$ on the same variable. (E^*/F^*) along with real output $(Y)^*$ play an important role in Block V in terms of determining one of the central variables of this block, this being the flow of total lending to the public $(\Delta LP)^*$. The other important variable of this block is the long-term rate of interest $(R)^*$ which is partly influenced by the actions of the monetary authorities and partly by changes in the external financing $(\Delta EF)^*$, itself being one of the variables determined in Block VI. Both $(\Delta LP)^*$ and $(R)^*$ feed into Block I. In addition $(R)^*$ and $(Y)^*$ constitute important links between Blocks V and I as well as I and VI respectively In Block VI three variables are determined: the exchange rate $(ER)^*$, the current balance $(CB)^*$, and $(\Delta EF)^*$. The third variable feeds into Block V while $(CB)^*$ feeds into Block I. Furthermore $(ER)^*$ influences $(CB)^*$ via exports and thus $(DE)^*$ in Block I; $(ER)^*$ also affects directly the prices of raw materials $(\dot{P}_{RM})^*$ in Block IV which are an important determinant of the inflation rate and, via the latter, also affects wages. Both wages and prices feed into three blocks: I, III and IV.

Figure 4.2 Flow diagram of a post-Keynesian model

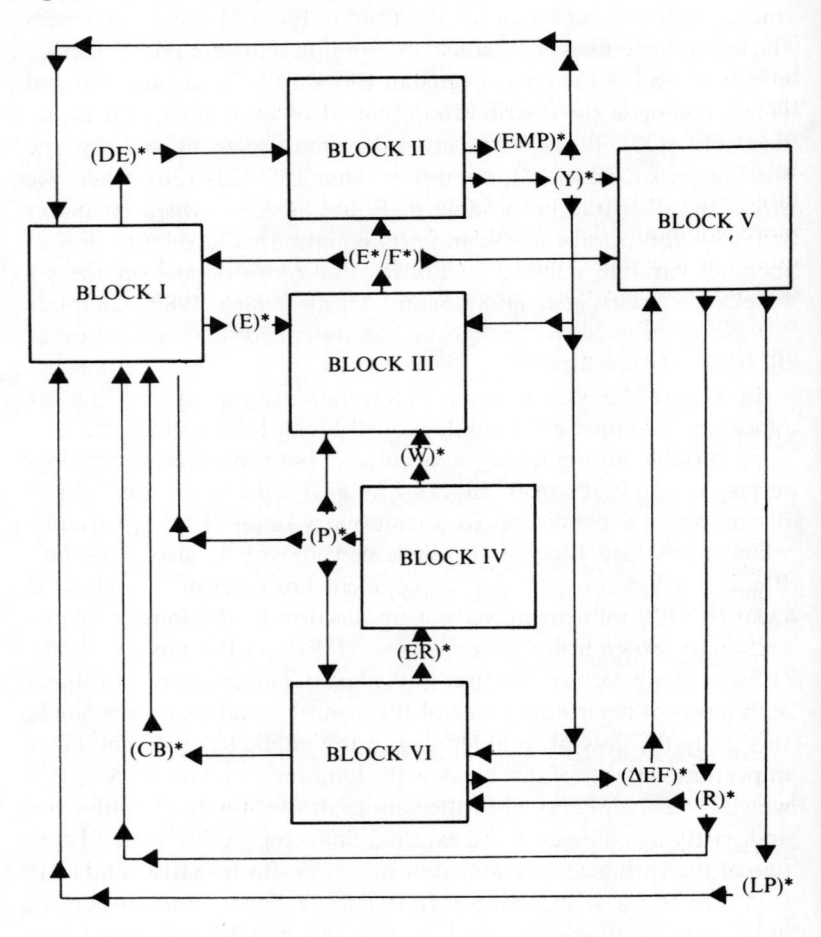

4.6 CONCLUDING REMARKS

The constituent elements of the post-Keynesian mode of thought have been identified and discussed in this chapter. This has given us the opportunity to elaborate at length on the methodological aspects of post-Keynesianism too. All these elements have been put together to give us the model reported in Table 4.1. The relationships in this table need to be discussed, explained and justified at substantially more length and detail, and the economic policy implications of the model as a whole should be ascertained. The next six chapters are designed to deal with precisely these matters. We begin in Chapter 5 with the relationships that arise from the theories of production, investment and distribution.

NOTES

1. There is the argument that even the neo-classical methodology cannot be Lakatosian. But see Lavoie (1992) who summarizes this argument neatly and goes on to argue that essentially the core of neo-classical economics is Walrasian economics, whilst the less theoretically rigorous but quantitatively biased aspects of it comprise its protective belt (see also Brown, 1981).
2. Davies (1989, p. 425) argues that the recent philosophical developments referred to in the text imply that 'the key concepts and expressions of General Equilibrium Theory fail to identify actual objects in economic reality, such that the theory as a whole cannot be said to be representationally adequate'. Also, that 'Axiomatic General Equilibrium Theory is then, as many have suspected, simply unrealistic' (p. 437). It is the case, however, that the proponents of general equilibrium theory have argued that they never meant the theory to be so (see, for example, Arrow and Hahn, 1971).
3. See Brown (1981) for a comprehensive analysis and comparison of post-Keynesian and neo-classical views on the points touched upon in the text.
4. There are, in fact, many ways of classifying post-Keynesian thought (see, for example, Reynolds, 1987). Indeed, there are contributions by economists who do not fall into any of the approaches discussed in the text. For example, Kaldor, Pasinetti, Goodwin, Godley, Tarshis and others referred to in Hamouda and Harcourt (1988, pp. 19–24) belong in this category and yet their thinking has been of immense importance in the development of post-Keynesianism.
5. Social classes and social relations are particularly emphasized by post-Keynesian analysis. In this respect there is an interesting and important contrast between orthodox economics and post-Keynesian economics. Orthodox economics attempts to show that markets allocate scarce resources according to relative efficiency, whilst post-Keynesian economics sets out to demonstrate that markets distribute income according to relative power (Nell, 1980, p. 26).
6. This model has been empirically estimated and used for policy analysis with revealing and interesting results. The details are to be found in Arestis (1989).

5. Theories of Production, Investment and Distribution

5.1 INTRODUCTION

The analysis in Chapter 4 shows that although post-Keynesian economics is primarily macroeconomic in its orientation, there is at the same time a solid microeconomic foundation. The microeconomics that underpins the macroeconomic aspects of this mode of thought is essentially pricing. We argued in Chapter 4 that pricing in post-Keynesian economics is very much influenced by factors and conditions that prevail in the production sphere, and that pricing is linked to investment and distribution. The purpose of the present chapter is to amplify and elucidate the production, investment and distribution aspects. Pricing is the subject-matter of Chapter 6.

We begin with the important question of how much will be produced not just by the whole of the economy, but also by each industry. We propose to tackle this question by resorting to the input–output model which is characterized by the assumption that inputs can be used only in fixed proportions to each other in production. It is the model that has come to be labelled the 'fixed-coefficient' model. It is also termed the Leontief model, following the attempts by Leontief (1951) to formulate it in both theoretical and empirical terms. This model belongs to the more general category of fixed-coefficient models of production which have their roots firmly embedded in the *tableau économique* of François Quesnay. It is also related to Sraffa's (1960) fixed-coefficient model and to Pasinetti's (1981) input–output model, both of which highlight issues of distribution and growth. In this sense the post-Keynesian approach to production is very much within the classical rather than the GNS tradition.

The discussion in this chapter, therefore, commences with production theory, followed by investment and distribution, before we turn our attention to pricing theories in the next chapter.

5.2 PRODUCTION THEORY

The Leontief model consists of n industries (with n being greater than 2), each producing intermediate and/or final output as shown in Table 5.1 (which is reproduced here from Eichner, 1983b). In this table p_i is the price of the ith good produced; a_{ij} is a technical coefficient defined as q_{ij}/Q_j where q_{ij} is the quantity of the ith industry's output used as an input in the jth industry and Q_j is the total output produced in the jth industry. So for example $a_{1,2}$ is the amount of output produced by industry 1 and is used as an input to industry 2's production. Similarly, coefficient $a_{2,1}$ indicates the amount of output produced by industry 2 and required as an input in the production of good 1. X_i represents what is termed final output, as distinct from the intermediate output. It is, in other words, the output which goes to meet final demand, rather than being utilized by other industries as input to their production. w is the money wage rate; l_j is the jth industry's labour technical coefficient defined as the quantity of labour in manhours used in the jth industry relative to the output of the jth industry; L is the total quantity of labour in manhours; π_j is the residual, or margin above costs, earned in the jth industry and π is the total residual.

The technical coefficients a_{ij} for each industry indicate each industry's technology in terms of input requirements from other industries. In terms of Table 5.1 configuration of labour inputs, it is assumed that labour requirements are of one type only. This assumption can, of course, be relaxed to account for different types or skills of labour, in which case w would differ among the various groups of workers. In the value added box of Table 5.1 there is also the residual income for each industry (π_j). We emphasize that it is not possible to reduce the residual income row to a set of technical coefficients. This is so since residual income cannot be expressed as the 'return on capital' because the concept of aggregate capital is meaningless (see section 3.3 above for the details). Consequently, it is not possible to specify a quantity of 'capital' used by each industry, and a price received by that input. This particular point reflects

Table 5.1 The Leontief production model

The Leontief production model consists of n sectors, or industries, each producing intermediate and/or final output as follows:

	Value of intermediate output $\hat{P}AQ$					Value of final output $\hat{P}X$	Value of total output $\hat{P}Q$
Value of intermediate output $\hat{P}AQ$	$p_1 a_{1 \cdot 1} Q_1$	$+ p_1 a_{1 \cdot 2} Q_2$	$+ p_1 a_{1 \cdot 3} Q_3$	$+ \ldots$	$+ p_1 a_{1 \cdot n} Q_n$	$+ p_1 X_1$	$= p_1 Q_1$
	$+ p_2 a_{2 \cdot 1} Q_1$	$+ p_2 a_{2 \cdot 2} Q_2$	$+ p_2 a_{2 \cdot 3} Q_3$	$+ \ldots$	$+ p_2 a_{2 \cdot n} Q_n$	$+ p_2 X_2$	$= p_2 Q_2$
	$+ p_3 a_{3 \cdot 1} Q_1$	$+ p_3 a_{3 \cdot 2} Q_2$	$+ p_3 a_{3 \cdot 3} Q_3$	$+ \ldots$	$+ p_3 a_{3 \cdot n} Q_n$	$+ p_3 X_3$	$= p_3 Q_3$
	$\cdot$	$\cdot$	$\cdot$		$\cdot$	$\cdot$	$\cdot$
	$+ p_n a_{n \cdot 1} Q_1$	$+ p_n a_{n \cdot 2} Q_2$	$+ p_n a_{n \cdot 3} Q_3$	$+ \ldots$	$+ p_n a_{n \cdot n} Q_n$	$+ p_n X_n$	$= p_n Q_n$
	$+$	$+$	$+$		$+$	$=$	$=$
Value added $\hat{V}Q$	$w l_1 Q_1$	$+ w l_2 Q_2$	$+ w l_3 Q_3$	$+ \ldots$	$+ w l_n Q_n$	wL	
	$+ \pi_1$	$+ \pi_2$	$+ \pi_3$	$+ \ldots$	$+ \pi_n$	$+ \pi$	
	$=$	$=$	$=$		$=$	$=$	
Value of all inputs $\hat{P}Q$	$p_1 Q_1$	$+ p_2 Q_2$	$+ p_3 Q_3$	$\ldots$	$+ p_n Q_n$		$= \hat{P}Q$

Source: Eichner (1983b).

the critique launched against the GNS production function as discussed in Chapter 3.

These coefficients are taken as fixed, implying that certain quantities of labour and material inputs are required to produce given quantities of output. The state of technology is, therefore, very much taken as given, and embodied in the specific capital inputs used in production. Assuming, furthermore, that there is sufficient supply of inputs available in these fixed combinations, it follows that post-Keynesian production theory is consistent with both fixed technical coefficients and constant returns to scale.

The Leontief model can be solved in the following two ways: first, given that total output is equal to intermediate output plus final output we can write in matrix form:

$$\hat{P}AQ + \hat{P}X = \hat{P}Q \tag{5.1}$$

where

$$\hat{P} = \begin{bmatrix} P_1 & O & O & \ldots & O \\ O & P_2 & O & \ldots & O \\ O & O & P_3 & \ldots & O \\ \cdot & \cdot & \cdot & & \cdot \\ \cdot & \cdot & \cdot & & \cdot \\ \cdot & \cdot & \cdot & & \cdot \\ O & O & O & \ldots & P_n \end{bmatrix}$$

is a diagonal matrix with the elements along the main diagonal being the prices in each industry;

$$A = \begin{bmatrix} a_{11} & a_{12} & a_{13} & \ldots & a_{1n} \\ a_{21} & a_{22} & a_{23} & \ldots & a_{2n} \\ a_{31} & a_{32} & a_{33} & \ldots & a_{3n} \\ \cdot & \cdot & \cdot & & \cdot \\ \cdot & \cdot & \cdot & & \cdot \\ \cdot & \cdot & \cdot & & \cdot \\ a_{n1} & a_{n2} & a_{n3} & \ldots & a_{nn} \end{bmatrix}$$

is the matrix of coefficients;

$$Q = \begin{bmatrix} Q_1 \\ Q_2 \\ Q_3 \\ \cdot \\ \cdot \\ \cdot \\ Q_n \end{bmatrix}$$

is the vector of total industry output; and

$$X = \begin{bmatrix} X_1 \\ X_2 \\ X_3 \\ \cdot \\ \cdot \\ \cdot \\ X_n \end{bmatrix}$$

is the vector of final output.

Pre-multiplying through expression 5.1 by the inverse of P gives:

$$AQ + X = Q$$

from which:

$$Q = (I - A)^{-1} X \tag{5.2}$$

where I is an $n \times n$ unit matrix and $(I - A)^{-1}$ is the Leontief inverse. Equation (5.2), now, determines the output of each of the industries which comprise the production system.

Secondly, given that value added ($\hat{V}Q$) is equal to the value of total output produced ($\hat{P}Q$) less the value of all the inputs obtained from other industries ($\hat{P}AQ$) we have:

$$\hat{V}Q = \hat{P}Q - \hat{P}AQ \tag{5.3}$$

where $\hat{V} = wL_n + \pi$ with w being a scalar and L_n and π being row vectors of labour inputs and residual income earned by each industry respectively, both per unit of output produced. Noting that

$$\hat{V} = \begin{bmatrix} V_1 & O & O & \ldots & O \\ O & V_2 & O & \ldots & O \\ O & O & V_3 & \ldots & O \\ \cdot & \cdot & \cdot & & \cdot \\ \cdot & \cdot & \cdot & & \cdot \\ \cdot & \cdot & \cdot & & \cdot \\ \cdot & \cdot & \cdot & & \cdot \\ O & O & O & \ldots & V_n \end{bmatrix}$$

we may proceed to multiply (5.3) by the inverse of Q so that

$$\hat{V} = \hat{P} - \hat{P}A$$

from which

$$\hat{P} = (I - A)^{-1} \hat{V} \tag{5.4}$$

Equation (5.4) provides the solution for the set of relative prices that must be charged if the production system is to cover all the costs of production. Equation 5.4, in other words, specifies a value condition which must hold in the long run. It does not represent the set of prices that will actually prevail. It must be emphasized at this juncture that the simultaneous solution of Equations 5.2 and 5.4 (as part of the model that depicts the production system) would give us both P and Q. This simultaneous solution presupposes, of course, that the Leontief inverse $(I - A)^{-1}$ can be determined empirically, along with the composition of final demand (X), the wage rate and the residual income for each industry (π).

The matrix of technical coefficients (A) is a key parameter in the post-Keynesian production system. By contrast, these technical coefficients do not assume the same importance within GNS economics. Quantity produced and prices charged are crucially determined by demand and supply functions in each industry. Furthermore, the isoquants ensure substitutability between any two inputs of production, with the proviso that factors are imperfect substitutes; that is, there is a diminishing marginal rate of technical substitution. So the requirement of diminishing returns is ensured. In the Leontief production, no factor substitution is possible: output requires factors in given combinations determined by technology embodied in capital. In addition, constant returns to scale are assumed. This assumption is vital if the coefficients of matrix A are to be taken as given.

The Leontief model has been extended in a number of ways. There is Sraffa's (1960) reformulation of it for theoretical purposes. This produces the important proposition that distribution of income can be treated independently of prices, and leads to the conclusion that distribution need not be tied to the labour theory of value. In this reformulation, economic analysis based on surplus and exploitation can avoid the labour theory of value and rely instead on Sraffa's prices of production. There is also Pasinetti's (1981) construction of a vertically integrated version of the Leontief model with labour as the only input. Technical progress is included in the model too, thus making it possible to examine its impact on productivity, defined as output per worker over time. Leontief *et al.* (1978) extended the model still further to account for natural resources in addition to labour as the inputs to production on a global scale. They are thus able to examine the terms of trade between primary producers and industrial countries.

It is this type of production theory which underlies Block II of the model propounded in this book. This block explains the growth of aggregate output and employment. In doing so it assumes fixed technical coefficients in production so that cyclical movement of aggregate employment depends entirely on the cyclical movement of aggregate output (Equation 7). Also, final demand is assumed to depend critically on the demand for durable goods. This part of final demand along with investment and other similar components are what we have labelled above as 'discretionary expenditure' (DE), a variable which is the moving force of aggregate demand and thus output (Equation 6). What has to be determined at this stage, therefore, is (DE). The analysis pursued for this purpose constitutes the theories of household demand and investment to which we now turn our attention.

5.3 THEORIES OF HOUSEHOLD AND INVESTMENT DEMAND

Discretionary expenditure, essentially durables and investment expenditure (and exports in the case of open economies), possesses three characteristics which make it particularly important and relevant to the macrodynamic behaviour of the economy: its partial dependence on external finance; its postponability; and its supply enhancing effects (Eichner, 1987, pp. 98–106).

When households and firms decide to undertake these types of expenditure, they have the option of acting upon them immediately or postponing such decisions for a more appropriate occasion or, indeed, indefinitely. This discretionary ability extended to economic agents in relation to these forms of expenditure makes their decisions problematical enough from the point of view of the circular flow of funds to require a careful analysis. The external financeability of these expenditures emanates from the durable nature of what is intended to be bought. Even in those cases when internal funds are the fundamental source of finance, the availability of external finance is important in that it brings into the circular flow of funds items which are created in other sectors and may remain unstable otherwise. The supply-enhancing effects are clear enough. The expenditure in question enhances the economy's aggregate supply and thus its growth potential (Harrod, 1939, 1948).

Just as we define discretionary expenditure in this way, we may similarly define discretionary funds as the difference between any sector's income received and its non-discretionary expenditure. Clearly, the latter is defined as expenditure on non-durable goods and services. When these magnitudes are defined in this way, they are obviously wider in their meaning than the conventional 'investment' and 'saving' terms. So that the very well known notion of *ex ante* 'macro-equilibrium', investment = saving, should now be redefined to read: discretionary expenditures = discretionary funds in the aggregate. When the current rate of cash inflow in a sector exceeds the current rate of cash outflow, there will be an increase in the stock of financial assets held by that sector. A shortfall of inflow relative to outflow results in a fall in the stock of financial assets. It is, thus, the flow of discretionary funds relative to the flow of discretionary expenditures in nominal terms that ultimately must determine whether a sector's stock of financial assets would be increasing or falling. If there is an excess of discretionary expenditures to discretionary funds then the sector faces several alternatives: it can liquidate its financial assets, create new liabilities, reduce its level of discretionary expenditure, or enact a combination of all three. Consequently, an excess of discretionary funds relative to discretionary expenditures will lead to the acquisition of new financial assets, liquidation of liabilities, or an increase in discretionary expenditure.

The rest of this section concentrates on theories of household demand and investment. We begin with household demand.

5.3.1 Household Demand Theory

The post-Keynesian theory of household demand begins with the fundamental assumption that in an economic system it is the income effects rather than the substitution effects which are more important. This proposition reflects two important considerations. First, purchases of various consumption goods are thought to serve different physical needs so that substitution can only take place within extremely narrow subcategories. Secondly, substitution possibilities are very much limited by social convention and acquired tastes. In this way the institutionalist argument that consumer preferences are socially conditioned, rather than being innate at birth and thus given, is adhered to. Household expenditure is assumed to follow a lexicographic ordering. Just as there are rules for ordering words in a dictionary, so in the case of household expenditure the grouping of goods into categories follows similar rules. Just as there are rules which stipulate how words beginning with the letter P are grouped separately from words beginning with the letter A, there are rules which group items of goods into different categories. Just as there are rules which group words further – for example, those whose second letter is A are separated from words whose second letter is B – similarly there are further groupings within the already identified groups of goods. Essentially, what is proposed here is that goods are grouped into major categories of consumption along with nested sets of sub-groupings. This lexicographic ordering is crucially influenced by social conventions, habits and acquired tastes. The importance of these influences in determining the groupings and sub-groupings is absolutely fundamental.

It is recognized that there are two rules adopted by households when deciding upon consumption patterns. The first is that households continue to maintain consumption patterns already established. However, as new information flows in the form of new consumption goods or as households' circumstances change, consumption patterns are liable to be modified. This is very similar to Duesenberry's (1949) 'relative income' hypothesis which views consumption as a function of current in relation to previous peak income, and may also depend on the distribution of income. Consumers attempt to maintain previously attained levels when current income levels fall, and adjust fully upwards their consumption when income surpasses previous peak levels. Consumption is thus analysed in relation to social norms in the form of past consumption habits or peer group consumption levels. The second rule concerns itself with the way modifications in consumption patterns take place. When changes of this type occur and confront households with multiple choices, they transform these into discrete choices thus enabling them to arrive at consumption patterns with single items which can meet their needs.

The household behaviour just portrayed is determined by a number of factors. These include not just advertising and other forms of social conditioning but the growth of income levels within each of the social classes, as well as the credit that households can obtain. The growth of income enables households to enhance their relative lifestyle in society (although it is conceivable that people in particular groups can become *absolutely* better off and *relatively* worse off). Households are assumed to have an order of priority in terms of the goods they can buy when their income increases. This order of priority reflects both households' objective material needs and the type of social conditioning they have been subjected to. This theory of household expenditure is reflected in the equations of Block I which explain the durable goods part of discretionary expenditure. It is, in fact, hypothesized that the income and price elasticities for the various types of consumer durables determine the *trend* growth rate. The cyclical behaviour of durables depends heavily on the variables in Equation (2), especially on the income distribution variable, $[(Y - T)^*_{wi} / (Y - T)^*_{ci}]$, as well as the ratio (E_i^*/F_i^*) and $(\Delta LP)_i^*$. There is, in fact, a large literature on the disaggregation of income either by functional category or by income bracket in a consumption function (for example, Arestis and Driver, 1980). One school (Kaldor, 1956; Pasinetti, 1962) draws on the views of classical economists who see workers as too poor and landlords as too profligate to save, so that the bulk of saving is done by capitalists out of their profits. Another school emphasizes the differing variability of types of income. The greater variation in incomes of the non-wage category means that a larger cushion of assets is required than with the wage category where incomes are more stable. This argument is reinforced if the non-wage category includes economic units who are risk averters and if their future knowledge of capital markets is not perfect (Burmeister and Taubman, 1969).

In addition to the distribution income variable, the ratio (E_i^*/F_i^*) influences household demand in pretty much the way described above. This variable can be thought of as registering the need to satisfy unanticipated changes in household demand for durables. The variable $(\Delta LP)^*$, changes in total lending to the public, can be hypothesized as capturing the need for external financing of durable purchases. In this sense this variable, too, should be construed as accounting for unexpected changes in household demand. The rest of the explanatory variables in the household demand relationship can, then, be thought of as capturing expected changes in household demand.

5.3.2 Investment Theory

Shackle (1970) argues fervently that the investment decision is a 'crucial decision' in that it is impossible to repeat it; added to which, its sequel cannot be generalized, given the complexity that underpins this type of exercise. For it is true that

Decision is choice in face of a lack of sufficient knowledge, and so the study of decision is the study of conjectural appraisal and assessment. The *investment decision*, the choice of the character, scale and timing of durable productive facilities to be acquired, necessarily shares this character of the management of uncertainty. (Shackle, 1970, p. 77)

The importance of uncertainty in investment decisions is explicitly recognized in this book and in what follows in this section in particular. The theoretical aspects of investment decisions are very much within the spirit of the household demand theory in as much as expected income effects are believed to outweigh substitution effects. Expected income is considered to be the most important variable with the interest rate effect viewed as of secondary importance. To demonstrate, we rely heavily on the two theoretical positions on which post-Keynesian investment theory is based. Keynes's investment function as in the *General Theory* is one, with Kalecki's (1971, ch. 10) model of investment being the other.

The Keynesian investment function depends crucially on the notion of the 'marginal efficiency of capital' (MEC) or what was subsequently termed the 'marginal efficiency of investment' (MEI).[1] Investment is expected to yield a stream of net returns in the future. One can calculate the *present value* of the future returns, where the discount rate is taken to be the market rate of interest. Scrap value, if any, is added and discounted appropriately. In this way we obtain the current value of the investment to be compared to its supply price or replacement costs. Alternatively, we may use the MEI as the discount rate, instead of the market rate of interest, which we may define as the prospective rate of return on investment. We should then try to establish that value for MEI for which the value of investment is equal to its supply price. Keynes's argument was that firms calculate the MEIs for each of the different investment projects, so that on this basis all projects are ranked in descending order depending on their prospective rate of return. Given the current rate of interest, a comparison of it with the MEIs would determine the current level of investment. Variations in the market rate of interest should then cause the level of investment to vary, so that the current rate of interest is expected to be inversely related to the level of investment.

Keynes (1936, p. 136) warns us that the MEI should not be confused with the *current* yield of investment or, indeed, with the GNS notion of the *physical* productivity of capital. MEI is related to the *expectation* of investment yields. For it is the *perspective* yield of investment that gives rise to the notion of MEI. The dependence of MEI on expected yields is of paramount importance since it is responsible for the violent fluctuations observed in it. So much so, Keynes (1936, ch. 22) argues, that business cycles can be described and analysed by resorting to the behaviour of the MEI in relation to the rate of interest. It is also important to emphasize another aspect of the MEI: it is through this particular variable in Keynes's model that expectations of the future affect the present. Thus, Keynes's investment theory contains the crucial idea that decisions relating to this magnitude are governed by the expected *profitability* of investment (Asimakopulos, 1971; Shapiro, 1977).

Clearly, the calculation of MEI depends crucially on the values assigned to the stream of expected net returns of investment. These values, however, cannot be known with certainty. They are highly uncertain. Keynes argued that calculation of these returns depends heavily on firms' state of expectations and, indeed, confidence about the future. But, Keynes (1936) maintains, there is very little, if anything at all, that can be said *a priori* about the state of confidence. One should rely on observations of the actual behaviour of markets and on business psychology. *Convention* has been highlighted in *The General Theory*. Essentially, convention relies on the assumption that the 'existing state of affairs' does not normally change. Naturally, changes can and do take place. The existing market valuation is assumed to be 'uniquely correct' given our current knowledge; changes can only take place in relation to modifications to this body of knowledge. We may also note at this juncture that Keynes does not have much faith in the rate of interest to stimulate investment 'continuously'. It is the state of confidence and thus expectations that is recognized by Keynes as being the most decisive and dominant factor affecting investment decisions. To be sure, Keynes's uncertainty that surrounds investment decisions does not have anything to do with its 'physical product'. It is, instead, concerned with the realization of the *value* of the product of investment due to the possibility of prices changing between the time when capital equipment is installed and the time when it begins to deliver its products. Expectations, therefore, in investment analysis are necessary from the point of view of treating the result of investment as *profits* rather than as physical goods. Investment, then, is the result of the 'animal spirits' of entrepreneurs (Keynes, 1936, pp. 161–2).

In this sense, then, the expected net returns may be assigned notional probabilities. Optimistic assessments of the future by firms imply higher values for the probabilities and pessimistic values for the lower probabilities, so that as expectations change the MEIs change and thus the investment relationship shifts over time. As firms' perceptions of the future direction of the economy change, the investment relationship changes too. The point ought to be made that the probabilities required to account for expected net returns cannot be assigned any values in an actuarial sense. This is because there is no past experience relevant to the future which can be used to gauge these probabilities, so that they cannot be determined by firms prior to the events. The MEI relationship is, then, very unstable and as such could not possibly be predicted in advance. This type of uncertainty surrounding investment decisions is, therefore, very much different from the risk of certain insurable events occurring, for which actuarial probabilities can actually be calculated.

This way of analysing Keynes's investment relationship draws on Chapters 11 and 12 of *The General Theory*. It is of paramount importance to remind ourselves of the significance of these two chapters, not just from the point of view of investment but also of the suggestion that Keynes's contribution was not so much to put forward a new way of how the economy works as to demolish a model of his own construction. The investment relationship as exemplified in these two chapters is

Theories of Production, Investment and Distribution 129

an excellent example of this latter approach. Shackle (1967, p. 130) makes the point very well when he argues:

> Chapter 11 shows us the arithmetic of the marginal efficiency of capital and its relation with the interest rates, a matter for actuaries and slide-rules. Chapter 12 reveals the hollowness of all this. The material for the slide-rules is absent, or arbitrary. Investment is an *irrational* activity, or a non-rational one. Surmise and assumption about what is happening or about to happen are themselves the *source* of these happenings, men make history in seeking to apprehend it.

Another relevant observation, especially on Chapter 11, is that the argument there is incoherent and illegitimate (Asimakopulos, 1982, 1983, 1988). This is so because of the use in a single function of the two notions of (a) the *ex ante* prospective yields, and (b) the *ex post* notion of higher capital equipment prices when investment is higher. These two elements should be treated as separate relationships, just as in Kalecki (1971a) who argues that Keynes's investment relationship is unsatisfactory, in that a matter which is essentially dynamic is tackled through a basically static approach.

This takes us conveniently to Kalecki's theory of investment, which is not necessarily different from Keynes's. It can be viewed as an attempt to improve upon Keynes's MEI theory in that in Kalecki's model the factors which cause the MEI relationship to shift are identified. Kalecki's basic premiss is that investment depends on the level of profits relative to capital as well as on the rate of interest. This is not a very different proposition from Keynes's once we recognize that the rate of return in Kalecki is calculated at the aggregate level rather than at Keynes's firm level, and that the size of capital stock is relevant to investment decisions in a way that it is not in Keynes's model.

There are now two different ways in which the level of profits affects investment. First, profits are seen as a source of funds which enables investment to be undertaken. Obviously, then, retained profits along with funds set aside for depreciation purposes assume a very significant role in the investment decision process. The larger retained profits and depreciation allowances are, the greater the ability of firms to proceed with the capital expenditure programmes. External sources of funds are also viewed as being important, but because of the principle of increasing risk[2] the level of investment is still constrained by available internal funds.

The second way in which profits affect investment is in terms of the indication they provide as to whether firms' expectations about the future are likely to materialize. It is, therefore, changes in the level of profits that are important here. Rising profits signal healthy future economic conditions, which are likely to make firms adopt a more optimistic stance and thus proceed with their investment plans. Falling profits indicate to firms deteriorating economic conditions. Firms become pessimistic and are more reluctant to go ahead with planned investment. Therefore, the direction of change in profits is the main cause of shifts in the MEI.

Kalecki also considers the possibility of interest-elasticity of the investment relationship. He maintains that whilst it is plausible to argue that the rate of interest is relevant to long-term investment decisions, it changes very little; a proposition which was apt when Kalecki was writing but may not be quite true any more. But most importantly, given that internal financing out of profits is more prevalent than external financing, interest rate changes assume less significance than otherwise. Also changes in interest rates are seen as following the same pattern as changes in the profit rate – that is to say, rising in the boom and falling in the slump – so that their effects are incorporated in profit rate movement.

Besides the level of profits and the direction of change in profits, Kalecki argues that the degree of utilization of the existing capital stock is a significant contributory factor in explaining investment. Underutilized capacity encourages firms to cut back on their capital expenditure, and a period of cumulative decline is expected to ensue. Similarly, when demand increases relative to capacity it puts pressure on the existing capital stock, encouraging firms to be more adventurous in their investment decisions. A period of cumulative expansion is now predicted to follow.

The impact of the determinants of investment within this theoretical framework is subject to a certain time-lag. Actual investment materializes well after the decision has been taken to undertake the investment. This lagged effect is responsible for introducing a dynamic element in investment behaviour. A further dynamic element is introduced in Kalecki's model in the case of inventory investment where the 'acceleration principle' (see Chapter 2) is invoked. It is hypothesized that the rate of change in output or the volume of sales influences inventory investment positively. But again, Kalecki is very much concerned with the lags involved between cause and effect. Increases in output and sales do not cause an immediate increase in inventories. Only after some time has elapsed would expenditure on inventory investment increase.

Decreases in the level of output and sales would cause inventories to be curtailed after some time. The time-lag in both these cases is justified on the ground that firms wait to ascertain whether the change in output is permanent or not before they proceed to make the necessary adjustments. It is also pertinent to say that the relationship between changes in output and changes in inventories differs between commodities.

We return to Kalecki's investment model in Chapter 9 when we discuss his theory of business cycles. As we argue there, investment behaviour is crucial to the understanding of the cyclical behaviour of a capitalist system within the confines of this model. We should comment here, however, on an interesting development of Kalecki's investment theory which has been initiated by Steindl (1952, 1979).[3] Steindl's argument is that increases in concentration lead to higher mark-ups, and with profits determined by past investment decisions, a slow-down in capacity utilization ensues which increases excess capacity. This process affects investment decisions adversely since firms are fearful of increasing excess capacity. The economy, therefore, tends to stagnate – this is Steindl's 'maturity thesis'. Furthermore, utilizing the distinction between investment financed out of internally generated funds and investment financed out of 'outside savings', Steindl defines the 'gearing ratio' as the ratio of total investment to that financed by internally generated funds. The gearing ratio affects investment in that if there are no sufficient internal funds to maintain the desired level of the gearing ratio, total investment declines, leading to further increases in this ratio. Also, as the proportion of 'outside savings' increases relative to 'business savings', it tends to reinforce the maturity thesis, since in Steindl's (1982) argument the constraint of the gearing ratio does not allow full utilization of the higher 'outside savings', thus leading the ratio to increase further and exacerbating the decline in investment.

Investment in the post-Keynesian tradition is very much influenced by the theories we have just considered, especially by Kalecki's. It is thus argued that investment is determined by expected profitability. But it is recognized that whilst it is *expected* profitability that induces capital accumulation, *realized* investment creates the profitability which makes investment possible, partly through internally generated funds. Expected profitability is essentially influenced by two sets of factors. One is the expected rate of return on investment, or what is termed the MEI, which, as demonstrated earlier in this section, can give rise to an investment relationship that is sensitive to fluctuations in interest rates. The other is the expected growth of sales.

The MEI determinant is more important to that category of investment expenditure which is designed to enable the megacorp to reduce costs, differentiate its product more sharply, erect higher barriers to entry, and/or create a more favourable public image. Indeed, this grouping would include the purchase of cost-reducing equipment and the initial expansion into a new industry. It is precisely the ranking of investment projects which fall into this category, in the descending order of their expected return over cost, that makes it possible to show the amount of investment that can be profitably undertaken which will vary as the MEI itself varies. As shown above, it is this proposition that can give rise to a downward-sloping investment schedule that is sensitive to interest rate fluctuations.

Most investment, however, falls into another category where investment expenditure is undertaken specifically to maintain, if not enhance, the existing market share within each of the industries to which the megacorp belongs. This second category consists entirely of investment expenditure on new plant and equipment and is intended to provide the megacorp with sufficient capacity to meet whatever demand is likely to manifest itself for its various products. Since it is designed specifically to meet fluctuations in demand, the key determinant for this type of investment is, quite obviously, the expected growth rate of industry sales which we proxy here with the expected growth of income (Y^e).

It follows, therefore, that since the latter category of investment accounts for most of total investment expenditure, the expected growth rate of industry and thus Y^e is by far its most important determinant. Interest rates account for only a small part of the total variation in investment expenditure. It is precisely for this reason that we argue that in a post-Keynesian aggregate investment function it is income effects that are prominent rather than substitution effects. It is also important to note that the pervasive nature of expectations under uncertainty is very much taken on board and emphasized in post-Keynesian theory of investment. Uncertainty influences entrepreneurs' animal spirits, that is to say, what Keynes labelled as profit expectations of the business community, and plays a vitally important part in the capital accumulation process. So much so that the volatility of expectations under uncertainty is thought to lead to structural breaks and crises.

Another determinant of investment is the pace of technical change. There is, however, a two-way relationship here. On the one hand, technical change stimulates *net* investment. In this sense, technical change can be thought of as affecting profitability and capacity utilization and thus opening up new opportunities for firms. Clearly, these opportunities would not be forthcoming otherwise. On the other hand, the implementation of technical change requires only gross investment so that the new capital equipment would facilitate the application of new technology. Consequently, faster technical change can only come about if a higher rate of investment expenditure is undertaken. If firms are reluctant to invest, the pace of technical progress will, inevitably, slow down. Investment depends on expectations of growth, profitability, capacity utilization and confidence. Consequently, the health of the economic environment should be expected to influence the effective rate of technical progress through investment. Very obviously, then, the rate of technical progress within post-Keynesian economic analysis is endogenous rather than exogenous.[4]

We conclude this section by saying that out of all the variables which are thought to be significant in the determination of discretionary expenditure in Block I, the most important is the cyclical movement of aggregate output. With discretionary expenditures thus determined, the foundation is laid for explaining, via the multiplier effect, the growth of output and employment in Block II. The two blocks, therefore, give rise to a combined multiplier/accelerator process which forms the basis of the cyclical movements of the economy. Central to this process is, of course, the rate at which capital accumulation takes place. Capital accumulation determines, in addition to the cyclical fluctuations in economic activity, the secular growth of the economy and the resulting distribution of income. The post-Keynesian theory of growth and distribution is thus fundamentally linked to capital accumulation.

We look into the issue of distribution of income next, leaving growth, both secular and cyclical, as the subject-matter of Chapter 9.

5.4 DISTRIBUTION THEORY

It is clear from the post-Keynesian analysis we have been conducting that income (Y) could be written as follows:

$$Y = W + \pi \qquad (5.5)$$

which states that national income is divided into wage income (W) and profit income (π). We can also write Y as:

$$Y = C_w + C_c + I \qquad (5.6)$$

where C_w = consumption of workers, C_c = consumption of capitalists and I = investment. The following assumptions may be invoked:

$$C_w = c_w W \tag{5.7}$$

$$C_c = c_c \pi \tag{5.8}$$

that is to say, workers' consumption is proportional to wages and capitalists' consumption is proportional to profits. Investment can be treated as fully exogenous for the purposes of this analysis. We may now manipulate Equations (5.5)–(5.8) by substituting (5.7) and (5.8) into (5.5) to arrive at:

$$Y = c_w W + c_c \pi + I$$

and from (5.5) since $W = Y - \pi$, straight substitution would give us:

$$Y = c_w (Y - \pi) + c_c \pi + I$$

from which

$$(1 - c_w)Y = (c_c - c_w) \pi + I \tag{5.9}$$

Furthermore, solving for (π/Y) we can obtain:

$$(\pi/Y) = - [(1 - c_w)/(c_w - c_c)] + [1/(c_w - c_c)] (I/Y) \tag{5.10}$$

If we assume that $c_w = 1$ and $c_c = 0$ we derive the result:

$$(\pi/Y) = (I/Y) \tag{5.11}$$

Equation (5.10) demonstrates, and (5.11) makes neater, the proposition that at steady state the greater the rate of economic expansion as a result of a higher level of investment, the greater the share of profits and the lower the share going to workers.

Allowing now for the possibility of some fraction of profits spent on consumption goods, we derive:

$$(\pi/Y) = 1/(1 - c_c) (I/Y) \tag{5.12}$$

which suggests that (π/Y) in (5.12) is greater than this ratio in (5.11).

Furthermore, if capitalists spend half of their income on consumption, their share of the national income will be twice as high as it would be with $c_c = 0$. Clearly, in the case of (5.12), (π/Y) is determined by the ratio (I/Y) and the propensity to consume out of profits. Indeed, it is the case that where the share of profits to income (π/Y) is greater, the greater is the marginal propensity to consume of the capitalist class and the greater the share of investment to income.

This conclusion is still applicable when we work with the profit rate (π/K) – where K is capital – instead. We may go back to Equation (5.9) and divide through by K to derive:

$$(1 - c_w)(Y/K) = (c_c - c_w)(\pi/K) + (I/K) \qquad (5.13)$$

and upon rearranging we can have

$$(\pi/K) = [1/(c_w - c_c)](I/K) - [(1 - c_w)/(c_w - c_c)](Y/K) \qquad (5.14)$$

where the rate of profit depends on c_w and c_c and also on the ratios (I/K) and (Y/K). Assuming that $c_w = 1$ we may have:

$$(\pi/K) = [1/(1 - c_c)](I/K) \qquad (5.15)$$

where the rate of profit now depends on c_c and (I/K) only.

Following Pasinetti (1962) we modify assumptions (5.7) and (5.8) to account for the possibility of workers undertaking savings. To do this they must accumulate and thus acquire wealth and consequently receive profits. We may, therefore, modify (5.7) and write:

$$C_w = c_w'(W + \pi_w) \qquad (5.16)$$

where π_w is profits of the workers. Furthermore, (5.8) ought to be rewritten as:

$$C_c = c_c' \pi_c \qquad (5.17)$$

where, now, π_c is profits of capitalists.
Similarly, (5.5) becomes:

$$Y = W + \pi_w + \pi_c \qquad (5.18)$$

so that utilizing (5.16)–(5.18), we can arrive at

$$(\pi_c/Y) = - [(1 - c_w')/(c_w' - c_c')] + [1/(c_w' - c_c')](I/Y) \qquad (5.19)$$

which is the same as (5.10) except that π_c replaces π, c_w' replaces c_w and c_c' replaces c_c.

It can also be shown that the rate of profit under these circumstances will be:

$$(\pi/K) = G_n/(1 - c_c') \qquad (5.20)$$

where G_n is the natural growth rate (see Chapter 9). Once again, (5.20) is a statement of a relationship that must hold if the economy is assumed to be on its steady-state growth path.

The share of profits will be:

$$(\pi/Y) = (1/1 - c_c') (I/Y) \qquad (5.21)$$

In both case the c_w' and the ratio (Y/K) are completely absent. Whatever modifications are introduced, (π/K) and (π/Y) would always depend on c_c, suggesting, of course, that the profit share and rate of profit depend on the consumption/saving behaviour of those who live off capital. Most importantly, though, both (π/K) and (π/Y) do not depend on the marginal propensity to consume out of workers' income. This conclusion has come to be known as the *Pasinetti paradox*.

We may now account for the existence of what we referred to above as 'large corporations' or, what amounts to the same thing, 'megacorps' and their mark-up pricing behaviour. In this case the propensity to consume out of profits becomes the propensity to consume of the megacorp. What is interesting about this extension is that the conclusions reached above in this section are still applicable. Thus, the higher the level of investment that the megacorp undertakes, the higher will be its share of the national income. And if there is consumption out of the megacorp's profits, the megacorp's relative share will be even higher. The key to this type of behaviour on the part of the megacorp is, of course, its pricing policy, an aspect which we shall explore in the next chapter. Here we only need to note the compatibility between this analysis and Kregel's (1971) contribution. The analysis conducted in this section suggests that for the megacorp to increase its savings, the margin above costs need only be raised, holding the dividend rate constant. When the latter is allowed to vary, with the margin above costs being held constant, we then have the explanation put forward by

Kregel (1971), that the lower the dividend rate the higher will be the megacorp (π/Y) ratio. Consequently, the two explanations *complement* each other.

Equations (8) and (9) in Table 4.1 incorporate the theory of income distribution, where the cyclical movement of the discretionary funds of the various sectors is explained. With discretionary funds (F) determined in Block III and discretionary expenditure in nominal terms (E) in Block I, the ratio (E/F) for each sector is also determined. There are two effects emanating from the operation of this ratio. There is the cash-flow feedback effect which stimulates the economy when E > F, whilst when E < F the opposite happens. There is also the monetary effect which arises from the fact that any difference between E and F will have to be financed in some way or other. It is, in fact, the need to raise finance that leads to the post-Keynesian theory of prices and pricing.

5.5 CONCLUDING REMARKS

We explored in this chapter post-Keynesian production theory, theories of household and investment demand and distribution theory. Central to production theory is the fixed coefficient model which enables us to suggest that the growth of employment is determined by the growth of aggregate output. The moving force of the latter is aggregate demand or, more concretely, discretionary expenditure. Household and investment demand were therefore considered where investment plays another important role through its effect on distribution. Keynes's and Kalecki's theories of investment provide the essential theoretical elements of post-Keynesian investment theory. The role of capital accumulation in post-Keynesian economics is crucial. It determines not just secular and cyclical developments in the economy, but also distribution of income and wealth. Post-Keynesian theory of distribution was reviewed in this chapter and a number of assumptions considered to demonstrate the link just referred to.

The fixed-coefficient model solves for both quantities produced and prices charged. But these prices are long-period prices and have nothing to say about the process of price formation or, as we call it in the next chapter, pricing. This is precisely the subject-matter of Chapter 6, to which we turn our attention next.

NOTES

1. The distinction between MEC and MEI can be very important because MEC can be thought of as referring to the *long-period* returns on investment and the MEI to *short-period* returns. This can come about when short-period returns on investment deviate from long-period returns due, for example, to the *temporarily* higher cost of capital goods which may come about when current demand for investment goods cannot be satisfied by available capacity. This argument assumes full capacity so that to the extent to which firms, especially oligopolistic industries, maintain excess capacity the distinction between MEC and MEI is blurred. We shall utilize MEI throughout in what follows.
2. The principle of increasing risk refers to the greater risk of a profit short fall to a firm with a high gearing ratio (external borrowing/total capital employed) than to a low-geared firm. Kalecki (1954, pp. 91–5) used this principle to argue that, effectively, smaller firms face discrimination in the market for borrowing precisely because they have a smaller capital base.
3. Another interesting development that emanates from Kalecki's and Keynes's theory of investment is Robinson's (1962a) contribution discussed in Chapter 9 below.
4. The reader is referred to Sawyer (1989, ch. 12) and the references therein for more details on the observations made in the text. Salter (1960) is another important contribution that should also be referred to at this stage.

6. Theories of Prices and Pricing

6.1 INTRODUCTION

The Leontief model produces a price vector or set of relative prices which can be interpreted as a set of cost-of-production prices. These are the prices which must prevail in the long period if the costs of production are to be covered. This configuration of prices which satisfies some economy-level, steady-state conditions, generates a theory of prices without being concerned with the process of price formation. This price solution requires that the wage rate and the labour coefficients for each industry are specified. With the wage rate determined as hinted in section 4.2 and fully elaborated below (see Chapter 7), and the labour coefficients taken as given, the price solution depends on the residual income or the mark-up set in each industry. Such concern with the process of price formation, or how prices are determined at the level of firm or industry, gives rise to the notion of pricing. The relevant pricing theory proposed here is firmly based on the notion that the mark-up is determined by the financial needs of firms relative to the monopoly power they can exercise. It is, in fact, the theory of pricing as espoused by Eichner (1973, 1976) and Wood (1975) – but see also Harcourt and Kenyon (1976) – which we adopt as comprising our micro-foundations of post-Keynesian economics. These theories are not, of course, the only post-Keynesian pricing theories. Most, if not all, of these theories are essentially based on Kalecki (1954) in that they recognize that all markets are not perfectly competitive and that there is a distinction between sectors where price changes are 'cost-determined' and where they are 'demand-determined'. Furthermore, they all postulate that prices of finished goods are determined by a mark-up on some measure of unit costs. We begin with Kalecki's pricing model.

6.2 KALECKI'S PRICING THEORY

In Kalecki (1954), average variable costs are thought to remain constant until full capacity is reached, an assumption supported by empirical evidence. It is also assumed that excess capacity exists so that prices are determined by a mark-up on average costs. It is recognized that once full capacity is reached, demand may very well have a role to play, but this is considered to be highly exceptional. Firms are further assumed to pay attention to the prices of other firms producing similar products. We could then write:

$$p = mu + n\bar{p} \tag{6.1}$$

as the firm's pricing equation, where p = firm's price, u = average variable costs, $\bar{p}$ = the weighted average price of all the other firms in the industry producing similar products; m and n are parameters which reflect the firm's degree of monopoly. These parameters are determined by factors such as degree of industrial concentration, trade union influence, and the importance of fixed costs in relation to variable costs, although the influence of the latter factor is rather unclear in that 'The degree of monopoly may but need not necessarily increase as a result of a rise in overheads in relation to prime-costs' (Kalecki, 1954, p. 18).

Moving from the individual firm to the industry as a whole, we may consider the general case where m and n differ between firms. Kalecki (1954) employs the notion of the representative firm which enables him to write:

$$\bar{p} = \bar{m}\bar{u}/(1-\bar{n}) \tag{6.2}$$

where $\bar{p}$ and $\bar{u}$ are average price and average variable costs for the industry as a whole, and $\bar{m}$ and $\bar{n}$ are weighted averages of an individual firm's pricing parameters.

If we define $\beta = \bar{m}/1-\bar{n}$ we have:

$$\bar{p} = \beta\bar{u} \tag{6.3}$$

which is the industry pricing equation. Prices are thus determined by a mark-up on variable costs with the mark-up determined by 'the degree of monopoly', which is a shorthand for the set of environmental/institutional factors referred to above.

Theories of Prices and Pricing

One important aspect of Kalecki's pricing theory is that it is linked to distribution. Consider the pricing equation just derived with the following economy-wide identities:

$$Y_v = W + F + \pi \qquad (6.4)$$

where Y_v is value added, W is the wage bill, F is fixed costs and π is profits. Also,

$$pX = Y_v + TM \qquad (6.5)$$

where p is price, X is volume of gross output, and TM is total spending on materials.

Returning to the pricing relationship $p = \beta u$ we note that $u = (W + TM)/X$ so that

$$p = \beta[(W + TM)/X] \qquad (6.6)$$

and multiplying both sides by X we obtain:

$$pX = \beta(W + TM) \qquad (6.7)$$

Combining this equation with (6.5) we have:

$Y_v + TM = \beta(W + TM)$, or

$$Y_v = \beta W + (\beta - 1)TM \qquad (6.8)$$

from which:

$$(Y_v/W) = \beta + (\beta - 1)(TM/W) \qquad (6.9)$$

and if we let $j = TM/W$ and reverse the equation we arrive at:

$$(W/Y_v) = 1/[\beta + (\beta - 1)j] \qquad (6.10)$$

which is the share of wages to income. This is related to β and j. Furthermore,

$$(Y_v - \pi)/Y_v = 1/[\beta + (\beta - 1)j], \text{ or}$$

$$(\pi/Y_v) = 1 - 1/[\beta + (\beta - 1)j] \qquad (6.11)$$

which is the share of profits to income, obviously related to β and j. It follows that distribution is related crucially to j and the mark-up, and thus to the degree of monopoly. It is important to note at this juncture that in terms of the pricing relationship, $p = \beta u$, Kalecki did not provide a formal theory to explain β.

6.3 EXTENSIONS OF KALECKI'S PRICING THEORY

A number of contributions have sought to fill the gap left by Kalecki, and have taken the form of extending his pricing model. There are two of these we particularly wish to mention at this juncture. The first is Asimakopulos (1975) who assumed complete vertical integration in industry so that there are no raw-material inputs. Labour costs (W) are thus the only variable cost. His pricing equation is thereby given by:

$$p = (1 + n)(W/a) \qquad (6.12)$$

where n is the mark-up and a is the average output per unit of labour. The main feature of this extension is that there is a price leader who sets the price, and also that the mark-up over unit variable costs, which reflects the degree of monopoly, is designed to cover both fixed costs and an expected rate of return, or profit, on investment. One important implication of this analysis is that a relationship is established between pricing and investment and thus between pricing and the rate of growth of firms or the rate of growth of the economy.

The second extension is the contribution by Cowling (1982; see also Cowling and Waterson, 1976) which we view as an important attempt in this respect. In this pricing model the industry consists of a number of firms each pursuing independent *profit maximization* but the expected reactions of each firm's rivals are taken into account. The model predicts a relationship between mark-ups and the industry price elasticity of demand (e_d), industrial concentration as measured by the Herfindahl index (H) as well as expected responses by firms to output changes by rivals (b) – where the assumption is made that individual firms' bs are all the same. Denoting the ratio $(pX - MC)/pX$ by h, where pX stands for total receipts and MC for marginal costs for the industry as a whole, we can write the relevant formula as:

$$h = (1/e_d)[-b + (b-1)H] \qquad (6.13)$$

Clearly, the excess of receipts over marginal costs for the industry is inversely related to the absolute value of the industry price elasticity of demand but directly related to the level of industry concentration. It is also affected by the reaction coefficient b. Short-run fluctuations in price are not expected to occur from the three sources, e_d, H and b, identified above; it is cost changes that produce short-run price variations. It follows that the model is perfectly consistent with Kalecki's view that short-run price changes in manufacturing industries are essentially due to cost factors (as reflected in h) rather than to variables emanating from demand.

An interesting ingredient of Cowling's model is that profit maximization is reintroduced into the analysis with some force. Eichner's pricing theory does not entail such a characteristic. Another important ingredient of Cowling's model is that investment in excess capacity is considered to act as an effective barrier to entry. As will be shown shortly, Eichner's megacorp price leader is constrained by the threat of entry. We may now move on to discuss this pricing model that we view as crucial to the development of post-Keynesian pricing theory. We also view it as an attempt to provide a consistent explanation of the mark-up and fill the gap referred to above which Kalecki left unexplained.

6.4 EICHNER'S PRICING THEORY

In Eichner's (1973, 1976) theory, the large corporations, the 'megacorps', are typically price setters. There is some degree of interdependence between firms in an industry so that firms operate a system of price leadership. The price leader sets a price to yield a target rate of return sufficient to finance the investment plans necessary to meet the firm's growth maximization objective. Given the price structure within the industry, price leadership is consistent with all prices changing in step, preserving relativities. It is thus recognized that the majority of the funds to finance investment are generated internally and come out of undistributed profits. In fact, post-Keynesian analysis pays particular attention to the megacorp and views it as the representative firm in the mature capitalist economies. We shall therefore focus on the megacorp in this section.

There are three important characteristics of the megacorp. The first is that there is the separation of management from ownership. The actual power of decision-making rests, in fact, with management. Owners are essentially interested in the size of the dividend. Management is loyal to the megacorp as a permanent institution and not to the owners *per se*. Therefore, the goal of management is not to maximize profits but to *survive* and *grow* to the full extent permitted by external circumstances. If, then, the megacorp is to maximize its long-term *rate of growth*, it should aim at maximizing the secular growth rate of the cash flowing into the megacorp over and above current expenses – the so-called 'corporate levy' (Eichner, 1973, 1976). In pursuing a growth-maximizing strategy, the megacorp will attempt to maintain, if not actually to increase, its market share while simultaneously acting to minimize its cost of production (which will enable the megacorp to increase its cash flow given unchanged market share). It will also try to expand into newer, more rapidly growing industries, while simultaneously withdrawing from any older, relatively stagnant industries.

This shift in emphasis from short-run to long-run maximization has certain interesting implications. It is absolved from the serious shortcomings of the conventional theory of a *short time* horizon assumed in price determination. For since pricing decisions have implications beyond the current accounting period, the time horizon of the pricing theory under discussion extends well within a *long time* pattern. Also, the Chamberlin–Robinson model of price determination under non-competitive conditions is made irrelevant, because the behavioural rule of equating marginal cost to marginal revenue is no longer applicable. The equality of marginal revenue and marginal cost can only occur when the elasticity of demand is greater than one (for otherwise marginal revenue is less than zero and with marginal costs being positive equality cannot occur); and yet it appears that empirical evidence shows that megacorps operate in the inelastic portion of their demand curve (Eichner, 1976). A further implication is that since the firm is presumed to have an extended time horizon going beyond the current accounting period, the pricing decision can no longer be separated from investment planning as in the case of the conventional theory of the firm. The analysis concerns itself with the recognition that the primary means which such a firm has for financing the investment it wishes to undertake is the net revenue earned from the sale of its product. Due to its market power, the megacorp is presumed able to increase the margin above costs in order to obtain more internally generated funds, that is, a larger cash flow to finance its intended investment expenditures.

The second characteristic of the megacorp is its multi-plant operation, and thus the existence of a divisible capital stock with fixed factor coefficients. The implication of this particular assumption is that cost curves do not have the usual U-shape emphasized in the GNS analysis, instead they are as depicted in Figure 6.1. The megacorp faces constant average costs over the relevant range of output, with costs increasing once full capacity operation is reached. Two important propositions follow from this: first, an increase in the demand for the firm's product will not raise its price. It is, thus, the firm's supply curve which is perfectly elastic (in the short run) and not the demand curve, as assumed in the GNS-type models. Secondly, profits are an increasing function of the rate of capacity utilization or the level of demand. This is clearly so since an increase in the latter will imply lower average fixed costs so that average total costs fall and, with an unchanged price, the gap between average total revenue and average total costs grows.

The third characteristic is that the megacorp is part of an oligopolistic industry. It is thus not a price-taker. It *sets* a price and accommodates whatever quantity the market will absorb. In the oligopolistic industry firms act together since they are fully aware of their interdependence through their 'price leader' who acts as the surrogate for its fellow oligopolists (this firm is usually the one with the largest share of the market and/or the lowest costs of production). In terms of Figure 6.1, what this means is the indeterminacy of the price, unless of course output expands over the 100 per cent mark. But a determinate solution can be arrived at when the pricing decision in an oligopolistic industry is linked to the accumulation process. More specifically, megacorps, through their price leader, are assumed to change their prices to generate funds internally for investment. This is what Eichner (1976) has labelled 'the required corporate levy (RCL)', which he defines as 'the amount of funds available to the megacorp from internal sources to finance invest-

Figure 6.1

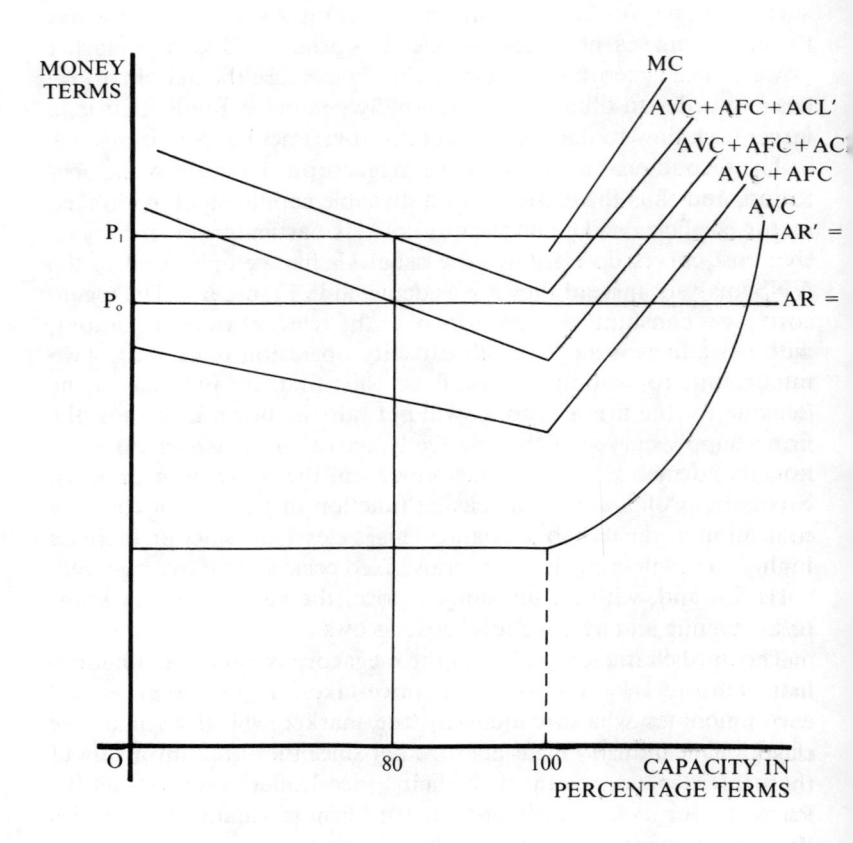

Source: Eichner (1976)

ment expenditures' (p. 61). We thus have a pricing model based on a mark-up over costs. The formula suggested by Eichner (1976) to determine the absolute price level (P) is:

$$P = AVC + [(TFC + RCL)/ENRQ] \qquad (6.14)$$

where AVC = average variable costs (essentially, the sum of average wage and raw material costs); TFC = total fixed costs (Eichner includes the dividend paid to equity share holders in the definition of fixed costs but excludes the expenditure undertaken to enhance the megacorp's long-run market position); RCL = required corporate levy; ENRQ = expected normal rate of output. So in Figure 6.1 the AVC + AFC should be AVC + AFC + ACL as the appropriate cost curve. This leads to price P_o in Figure 6.1. In other words, the megacorp does not operate at 100 per cent capacity or 'engineer-rated capacity', in Eichner's (1976) words, but at less, at what is labelled as 'standard operating ratio', this being the level at which firms expect to operate their plant – what we call ENRQ. The price leader estimates the ENRQ and then adds a mark-up to average variable costs that will be just sufficient to cover fixed costs and the corporate levy if the plant is to be operated at the expected level. In Figure 6.1 ENRQ will be 80 per cent and price P_o.

However, when considering the pricing policy of the megacorp posed in this way there are three constraints on the ability of the megacorp to raise additional funds through price manipulation. The first is the *substitution effect* – the resulting loss/gain to the megacorp's sales when prices increase/decrease. Clearly, the higher the elasticity of demand, the higher the loss of an increase in price and thus the lower the volume of internally created funds for investment. Price increases generate funds, due to the inelasticity of demand, but do so at a decreasing rate. So raising the price now causes the flow of funds to increase in the immediate future. However, offset against this is the longer-term consequences to the firm of a price rise as the shift of consumers takes place under the substitution effect. Consequently, the flow of funds will initially be positive, followed by a series of increasingly negative terms. This allows the cost of generating the initial increase to be expressed as the rate of discount that gives the estimated flow a present value of zero. This is referred to as the implicit interest rate (R_s) which is expected to be a function of the elasticity of demand.

The second constraint is the *entry factor*, which is the possibility of new firms entering the industry as the price increases – with existing firms suffering a decline in their sales. However, this too takes time, and initially the firm will earn increased funds as the result of the increase in price. Once entry materializes, market shares will fall and the initial positive change to funds will become negative. The effect is to generate a time pattern of flows, whereupon an implicit interest rate (R_e) can again be calculated which is also expected to be a function of the elasticity of demand.

The third constraint is the possibility of *meaningful government intervention*, which could conceivably place an upper limit on the ability of firms to raise prices. This may take a variety of forms, from special taxation through regulation of industries to outright nationalization. The megacorp's monopoly power is thus limited by government with the risk of such intervention being clearly determined by the magnitude of price changes. It is perhaps safe to assume, however, that the implicit interest costs will generally rule out excessive price increases before they reach a stage at which government intervention is likely (Eichner, 1976).

These three constraints give rise to a supply curve for internally generated funds. First of all, by taking the two implicit costs together, the firm is able to undertake a comparison between the projected return on investment and the implicit cost of generating funds internally in deciding its investment level and therefore the required price increase. So by combining R_s and R_e we may derive R_I which may be viewed as the implicit interest rate on the additional investment funds generated internally through a percentage increase in price mark-up (m). In Figure 6.2 we show in quadrant IV that as m increases, R_I is expected to increase, but there is a limit (m_x) dictated by the fear of meaningful government intervention. The curve OR_I is drawn in such a way as to show that as m increases there is a larger substitution effect and a greater probability of entry so that we expect increasingly higher values for R_I; and after some point, R_I must begin to rise at a faster rate than m. In quadrant II we show the relationship between m and internally generated funds, this being the curve OAF. The substitution effect and the entry factor imply that the slope of OAF must be less than the straight line OA – operative in the absence of these two effects. Given OR_I, OAF and the 45° line in quadrant III, OS in quadrant I is derived, which is the supply curve of *internally generated investment funds*. It shows the

Figure 6.2

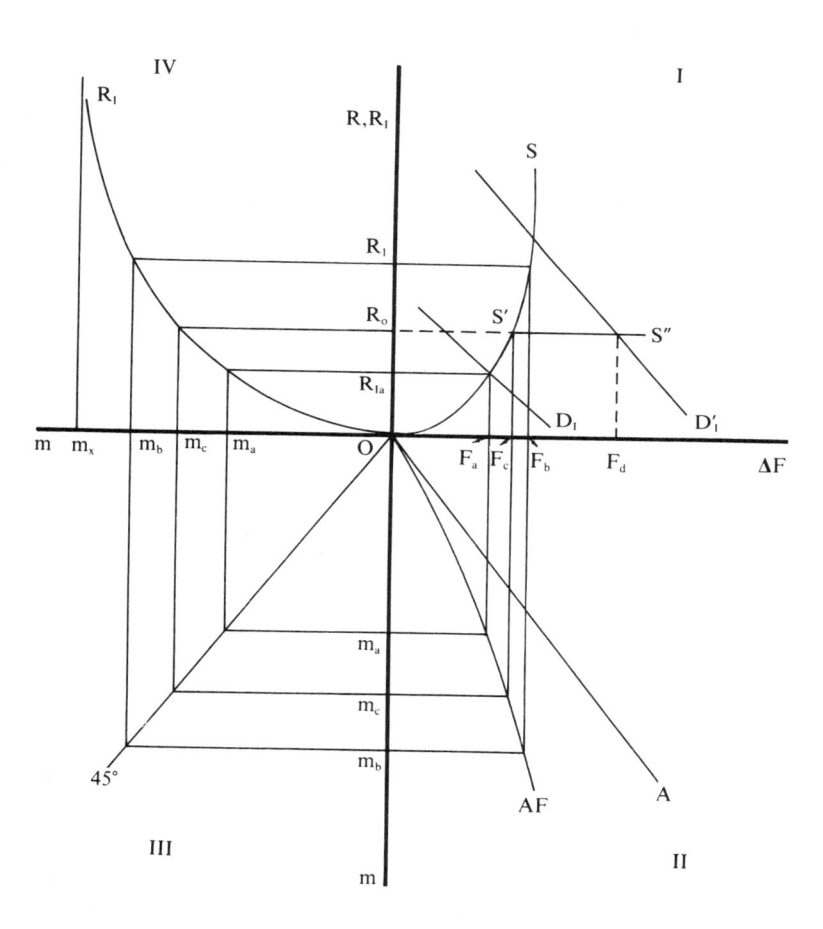

Source: Adapted from Eichner (1973)

various amounts of investment funds internally generated which correspond to different implicit interest rates, R_I. OS in conjunction with the other parts of Figure 6.2 can be defined as the locus of all possible combinations of R_I and ΔF as m varies. The slope of the supply of the internal funds relationship depends on the elasticity of demand for the industry's product, barriers to entry and government intervention. Thus, the more elastic the demand for the megacorp's product, the higher the barriers to entry; and the less likely the government is to intervene, the steeper the OS curve will be.

The interesting question, however, is that of price determination. To show this we need to consider the total supply of funds for investment (internal and external) and the demand for investment funds. Given the market rate of interest, say R_o, then so long as R_I is lower than R_o the supply of investment funds will be OS', and when R_I is higher than R_o, the possibility of obtaining external finance exists so that the supply for external funds becomes S'S''. In other words, the total supply of investment funds becomes OS'S''. There is also a downward-sloping demand for investment schedule (D_I), which is the usual Keynesian *marginal efficiency of investment* (MEI) schedule. It is worth mentioning here the contribution by Harcourt and Kenyon (1976) where a demand for investment schedule is derived that does not emanate from MEI considerations. In this pricing model the decision to invest depends on the relationship between price and expected marginal cost for new plant and the relationship between price and expected marginal costs for existing plant. The method and cost of finance are equally important in their model, and a relationship is derived between price and funds available for investment.[1]

The point of intersection of the S and D_I curves – in terms of Figure 6.2 at F_a – determines the amount of additional investment funds consistent with the megacorp's long-run market position, with m_a being the required change in price to achieve it. Similarly, when D'_I is the prevailing MEI schedule F_d funds will be required, this being OF_c internally created at a required change in price m_c, and F_cF_d will be sought from external sources. Given, now, the required change in price along with the prevailing price, say P_o in Figure 6.1, one can determine the new price, say at P_1. The price P_o is determined by the equality of the average revenue obtained during the previous time period, with the average variable costs plus the average expected fixed costs and the average cash flow required to finance the level of investment. It is the price which, during the previous time period, the megacorp must have announced and then tried to maintain. The price announced by the megacorp in the following period as a result of the change in the rate of planned investment and hence the rate of cash flow required is P_1, which is determined by the equality of the *new* average revenue (AR') with the average variable costs plus the average expected fixed costs and the *new* average required corporate levy. It thus follows that, under the conditions described here, price is determined whereby the level of planned investment, the sources of finance for that investment and the mark-up are all jointly determined by the marginal efficiency of investment funds relative to the marginal supply cost of those funds.

There is a very important implication here that is worth commenting upon relating to the source of finance for investment. The GNS theory of the firm considers the source of funds as completely irrelevant. This is because this theory emphasizes the opportunity cost of own funds, assumed equal to the market rate of interest, which is also the cost of borrowed funds. Thus, while for the GNS theory of the firm the source of finance for investment is something of little or no importance (see, for example, Modigliani and Miller, 1958), post-Keynesian analysis explicitly considers the source of finance for investment (see also Duesenberry, 1958). As we have just seen, this has considerable implications for economic analysis.

It has been argued (Reynolds, 1989) that Eichner's model provides microeconomic underpinnings to Kalecki's analysis which are closer to the spirit of Kalecki's own work than those provided by the Cowling model considered above. On the other hand, the Cowling model, more than the Eichner model, can be said to highlight the importance of market structure, thus providing more rigorous underpinnings to the notion of 'the degree of monopoly'. However, a closer examination of the Eichner model reveals that the substitution effect and the entry factor provide the link between the degree of monopoly and the mark-up. A higher degree of monopoly implies a weak substitution effect and low entry threat so that the implicit interest rate associated with a given mark-up will be relatively lower. Mark-ups will, therefore, inevitably be higher, causing a higher proportion of investment funds to be generated in the form of internal funds. This is clearly shown in Figure 6.3. A higher degree of monopoly *shifts* the R_I relationship to the left (R'_I) and the OS to

152   The Post-Keynesian Approach to Economics

Figure 6.3

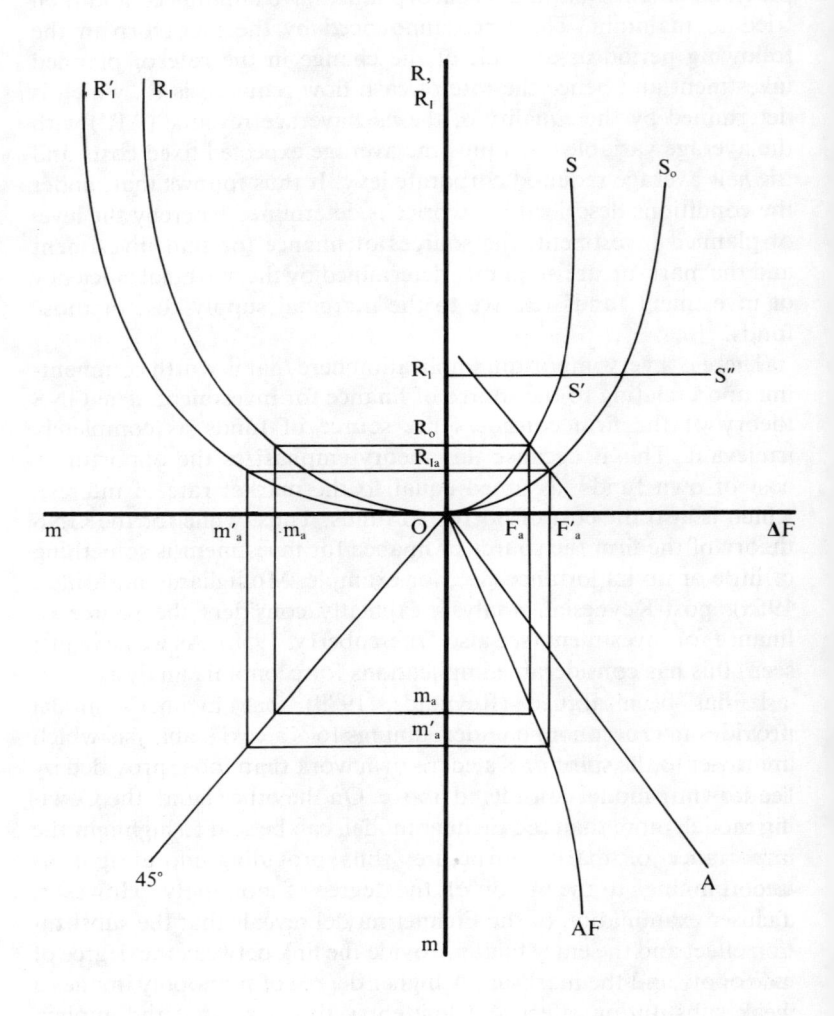

OS_o. The mark-up is now higher ($m_a' > m_a$) and internally generated funds are consequently $F_a' > F_a$.

Eichner's model does not incorporate *class struggle* and therefore cannot be construed as being as comprehensive as Kalecki's. After all, Kalecki (1954, p. 17) argued that an important cause of change in the degree of monopoly was 'the significance of the power of trade unions', as it provides the channel whereby labour may affect its share of output. Kalecki (1971b) demonstrated that changes in money wages would be reflected wholly as changes in the mark-up, so that class struggle finds expression not in the process of wage setting but in mark-up determination. Such an effect does not appear in Eichner's model, but as Reynolds (1989) has correctly noted, such an effect can easily be incorporated in it. This would take the form of an additional cost associated with increases in the mark-up and thus included in the implicit interest rate. Consequently, the presence of powerful trade unions may act as a further constraint on raising investment funds via the corporate levy, the rationale being that as the mark-up is raised beyond a certain level it could very well trigger militant action by trade unions. Unions may feel that since the firm is achieving high profit rates, they too deserve a higher share. In this way an explicit role for class struggle is introduced in Eichner's model, just as in Kalecki's (1971b) contribution.

The Eichner model has been analysed under the important assumption that the price leader anticipates that the other firms will follow any changes in the price with probability of 1.0. If we were to remove this assumption and propounded instead that the price leader is uncertain about the precise probability attached to other firms following any change in the price, we would then have an additional constraint on the mark-up. This constraint can be accounted for in two ways: it can be treated as a further additional factor constraining the mark-up and incorporated in the implicit interest rate. It could also be included in the substitution effect as an additional element. In this case the substitution effect would have to be redefined to include the possibility of the price leader losing sales to other firms in the industry. But regardless of how this additional element is treated, the essence of it all is that uncertainty provides an interesting dimension to post-Keynesian pricing which can be taken on board in the way we have just indicated. (See Reynolds, 1989, for a further elaboration of this point.)

There are two further criticisms of Eichner's pricing theory. The first is concerned with the independence of the demand and supply functions in quadrant I. The megacorp's investment plans are based upon its projection of sales growth and the demand for capacity that this implies. In quadrant IV the whole basis of the implicit cost of generating funds is that the price rise slows down future sales growth, which allows the construction of the implicit interest rate. But that must affect the corporate levy as well, since the anticipated lower sales growth will trim the megacorp's investment demand. The demand and supply functions in the model are thus interdependent (Hazeldine, 1974; Robinson, 1974; Marris, 1977). Eichner (1974) responded by suggesting that the effect referred to is likely to be unimportant. The second criticism is that whilst Eichner's pricing theory does not ignore the financial side of company affairs, the treatment is none the less limited. Firms switch to external finance when the market rate of interest equals the implicit internal interest cost, and all further funds are acquired in this way. The implication is that external funds are borrowed rather than raised through new equity finance, and no account is taken of the consequences for the firm's gearing and level of financial risk.

Wood (1975) attempts to build a model which takes much more explicit account of the financial side. It is interesting to explore this contribution at some length, given that the broad objective of this model is the same as Eichner's: the gist of the approach is to establish the size of the target mark-up. As in the case of Eichner's model, similarly here it is the firm's investment requirements that determine target profits and thus the mark-up. In this sense Wood casts his model as an explanation of target profits at normal long-run capacity and utilization level.

6.5 WOOD'S PRICING THEORY

Wood develops a theory of long-run[2] profits couched in terms of profit margin and profit share rather than profit rate – thus the need for valuation of capital is entirely avoided. This analysis is based on the assumption that the objective of the firm is the growth of sales revenue, so that it is the size of the firm which becomes the primary objective. For this, investment is needed, the main source of investment funds being retained profits. Thus, firms have investment

Theories of Prices and Pricing

requirements which determine target profits, with the further implication that current investment is related to current profits.

We may begin to explore Wood's model with the following defintions: the gross retention ratio, ϕ, is defined as retained earnings plus depreciation to profits. The external finance ratio, x, is the ratio of new borrowing plus share issues to investment. The financial asset ration, f, is defined as the ratio of financial asset acquisition to investment. Using these expressions we may also define: total capital spending as being equal to $(1 + f)I$, where I stands for investment in real terms; amount of investment funded externally as being equal to xI; and the rest of outlay which must be funded internally which is $(1 + f - x)I = \phi\pi$, so that solving for π we have:

$$\pi = (1 + f - x)I/\phi \qquad (6.15)$$

which gives the level of profits that would be needed to finance any given level of investment for particular values of ϕ, x and f.

As mentioned above, the basic goal of the firm is to cause its sales revenue to grow as fast as possible; but there are constraints to this objective. These concern the growth of demand, capacity and finance. The first two constraints are combined in what is called an *opportunity frontier*, leaving the third constraint to define the *finance frontier*. The two frontiers are then combined to determine the long-run profit margin. In deriving the *opportunity frontier*, the fundamental problem is to enquire into firms' opportunities to invest. In doing so, firms have a set of possible strategies, each strategy being associated with a particular level of average profit margin, a particular growth rate of sales and a particular level of investment. These three elements can be combined to form the *opportunity frontier*. In the process of doing so we find that there are two trade-offs. The first is between demand growth and profit margins. These two can conceivably move together, but beyond a certain point if firms try to increase demand, lower profit margins may very well result. This trade-off depends essentially on the relative selling efficiency and cost efficiency of the firm; and both depend on the quality of management. The position of the demand–profit margin trade-off depends on the amount of investment undertaken by the firm. For any given demand–profit margin trade-off, extra investment will increase profits and lower investment will reduce it. Once the frontier is reached, however, there is a second trade-off, this time between the demand–profit margin and the desire on the part of the firm to keep down the level of investment expenditure. These two trade-offs can now be combined to give us the *opportunity frontier*. We can utilize the following expression to make the point:

$$\pi_m \leq \mu(g, k) \tag{6.16}$$

where π_m = the profit margin, defined as the ratio of profits (π) to sales revenue (SR); g = proportional growth of sales; k = investment coefficient, defined as the ratio of the amount of investment required to the absolute change in sales. It should be noted that (6.16) specifies the maximum profit margin that can be achieved for a particular growth rate of sales and investment coefficient. It should also be emphasized that the partial derivative of the function with respect to g is negative whilst that with respect to k is positive.

We may now proceed to derive the *finance frontier*. This shows the minimum level of profits needed to finance a given level of investment, and can be achieved by referring back to (6.15) from which we can have:

$$\pi \geq [(1 + f - x)I]/\phi \tag{6.17}$$

Dividing through by SR and reminding ourselves that (I/SR) = gk and that (π/SR) = π_m, we have:

$$\pi_m \geq [(1 + f - x)/\phi]gk \tag{6.18}$$

which gives us the minimum profit margin necessary to provide finance for a particular sales growth rate and investment coefficient.

The analysis so far has produced the two frontiers: (6.15) being the *opportunity frontier* and (6.17) the *finance frontier*. We may now bring them together to determine π_m. This is undertaken in Figure 6.4 where the two frontiers are drawn for a given value of k, this being k_1. The object of the exercise is, of course, to maximize g subject to the two frontiers. The emerging profit margin decision is, in fact, a resolution of two conflicting pressures: the first is that competition encourages the lowest possible profit margin as this tends to maximize the rate of growth of sales. The second is that finance encourages the highest possible margin as this enables finan-

Figure 6.4

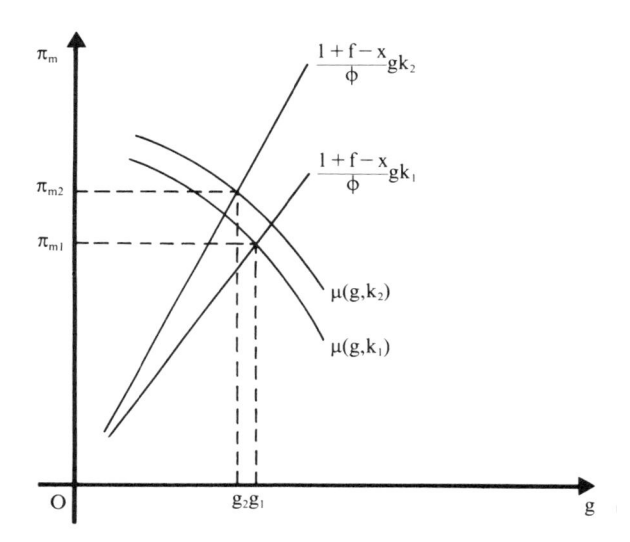

(Figure: axes with π_m vertical, g horizontal. Curves labeled $\frac{1+f-x}{\phi}gk_2$, $\frac{1+f-x}{\phi}gk_1$, $\mu(g,k_2)$, $\mu(g,k_1)$. Dashed lines from π_{m2}, π_{m1} to points above g_2, g_1 on the horizontal axis.)

Source: Adapted from Wood (1975).

cially viable growth in capacity to take place. In Figure 6.4 the resolution occurs at the point (π_{m1}, g_1). This, however, assumes that k is constant. If we now allow k to change, say to $k_2 > k_1$, then both relationships will shift as indicated in Figure 6.4. The *opportunity frontier* shifts to the right, since a higher k lowers unit cost and thus allows higher profit margins for given growth rates. The *finance frontier* also shifts but to the left (with its slope increasing too) because investment needs increase and would have to be financed out of a higher profit margin now that k is greater. These changes produce a new point of intersection, this being (π_{m2}, g_2), which raises the required profit margin unambiguously, whilst the effect on g is ambiguous (for it depends on the relative shift of the two frontiers).

In Figure 6.5 we illustrate this point by referring to eight values for k. What happens in this case is that as k increases from k_1 to k_2, g increases too. But as k moves beyond k_4, g falls. The heavy line in Figure 6.5 gives us the points that relate values of the profit margin and the rate of growth of sales associated with each value of k. There

Figure 6.5

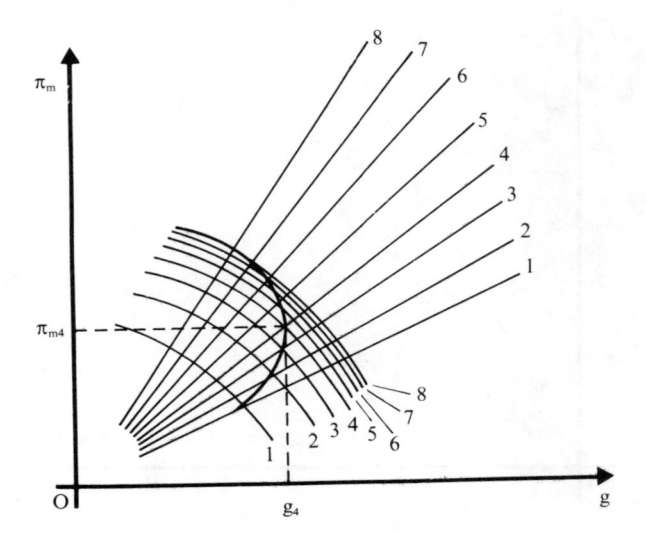

Source: Adapted from Wood (1975).

is a maximum at g_4 for k_4 which is the investment coefficient the firm would select. The required profit margin is inevitably π_{m4}.

There are important differences between Eichner's and Wood's pricing models. One difference is Wood's move away from the conventional MEI approach. Another is his departure from the assumption of unlimited availability of finance, and his explicit modelling of the financial constraints on the firm in a way that is consistent with Kalecki's (1954) principle of increasing risk. But both Eichner's and Wood's contributions are *Golden Age*, logical-time type of models, unlike the analysis of Harcourt and Kenyon (1976) which is conducted in historical time. In this sense, the Harcourt and Kenyon model is much more in the spirit of post-Keynesian analysis in general and pricing in particular.[3] Furthermore, both Eichner's and Wood's models emphasize the internal structure of firms rather than the institutional structures of the economy (see Çapoğlu, 1991, for more details on this issue). In particular, the financial sector and its relationship to the industrial sector is not considered in view of the focus on internal finance. The importance of the institutional structure of the economy is, however, recognized by post-Keynesian literature. For example, Harris (1978, p. 288) concludes by reminding us that:

> The profit-retention or pay-out policies of the firm and size of its mark-up or profit margin require theoretical treatment consistent with the position of the firm within the overall economic structure. For the individual firm, these relations govern its internal savings. Beyond this, the problem of savings for the firm becomes a matter of its access to finance, so that the structure and operation of the financial system have to be introduced.

6.6 INFLATION THEORY

Despite the differences just referred to between Eichner's and Wood's pricing models, there is an important common thread between them, and indeed with Kalecki's original theory in terms of the degree of monopoly. This thread is that prices are determined, at least in a significant proportion of the economy, by a process of mark-up on costs. In determining the price, firms take the unit costs as given, even though this level of unit costs is influenced by firms through their investment activities. The price will remain constant in the medium to longer term despite demand variations, so that realized profit may vary from planned profit. However, whenever unit costs change, price will be affected in line with those changes because the target variable which firms pursue is the mark-up, not the price itself. We can, therefore, write:

$$P = (1 + m)[WL + (P_{RM})(RM)] \qquad (6.19)$$

where the constant mark-up is on unit costs in terms of labour costs (WL) and costs of raw materials $(P_{RM})(RM)$ (see for example, Arestis, 1986a). The variables have the meaning given to them above, with the exception of L which stands for labour requirement per unit of output, and RM which is raw materials requirement. Expressing (6.19) in 'rate of change' terms, we have:

$$\dot{P} = m_1\dot{W} + m_2\dot{L} + m_3\dot{P}_{RM} + m_4(\dot{R}M) \qquad (6.20)$$

where the effect on prices of changes in the cost elements are assumed to be different. If we let the last term have a value of zero, noting that the percentage change in labour requirement is the inverse of the percentage change in output per head, it follows that:

$$\dot{P} = m_1\dot{W} - m_2(\text{PROD}) + m_3\dot{P}_{RM} \tag{6.21}$$

where PROD measures productivity of labour. Equation (6.21) suggests that the effect of the markup on $\dot{P}$ is assymetrical with respect to its sign: increases in wages or material prices will be passed on more completely through increased prices than will productivity rises into reduced prices (Arestis, 1986a). It should be emphasized that Equation (6.21) holds under the post-Keynesian assumption of spare capacity and unemployment. If either of these does not hold, then demand factors will affect the mark-up, and hence prices and inflation, as there will be problems in expanding output in line with demand. Only under these circumstances is demand a direct influence on the level of prices and inflation. Furthermore, we follow Arestis (1986a) and assume that the variable $\dot{P}_{RM}$ is related to the exchange rate (ER) and world trade (WT), so that,

$$\dot{P}_{RM} = p_0(\text{WT}) - p_1(\text{ER}) \tag{6.22}$$

When in Equations (6.21) and (6.22) the variables are taken as deviations from their trend values, and the two equations are written in an implicit form, we arrive at Equations (10) and (11) of Table 4.1. These equations, along with whatever assumptions are made about the determination of wages, provide a theory of inflation. Post-Keynesian economists emphasize, however, the importance of $\dot{W}$ in the inflationary process. It is the rate of change of nominal money wages relative to productivity, which is recognized to be the most important variable in the determination of the rate of inflation. But as will become clearer in the discussion of wage determination, price and wage changes are inextricably linked, so that there is a mutually reinforcing process of price and wage changes built in to the economic system. It is therefore paramount that the determination of $\dot{W}$ is investigated, a task that we undertake in the next chapter.

6.7 CONCLUDING REMARKS

One of the central features of the post-Keynesian models of price determination is that for a given level of unit costs, the higher the level of investment, the higher the price level desired by firms. Pricing, therefore, in post-Keynesian analysis is closely linked to investment. So in an economy which has a high growth rate, with firms having ambitious investment programmes, there will be stronger upward pressure on prices than in an economy which is growing more slowly or stagnating. The growth process carries with it inflationary pressures, even if the economy is operating at less than full capacity levels.

Inflationary pressures are captured in this framework by the interaction of price and wage changes. The analysis as espoused in this chapter is very much within the realm of the particular theoretical premiss which underpins Equations (10) and (11) of Table 4.1. Prices are determined according to a mark-up setting, which is imposed on money wages and prices of raw materials. Material prices are crucially influenced by the exchange rate and the volume of world trade, whereby the latter is expected to dominate given the prominence of income effects over substitution effects, as explained above. The next logical step in our analysis is how the other variable in Equation (10) is determined. This leads us neatly to the discussion of Equation (12), that is the money-wage determination, thus completing the analysis of Block IV. We move on to discuss this issue in Chapter 7.

NOTES

1. The contribution by Harcourt and Kenyon (1976) differs from the other pricing models in an important way. Three fundamental decisions relating to pricing and investment are considered: the amount and type of investment; the choice of technique; and the method and cost of finance. When these decisions are considered a unique solution is established for the mark-up and for the level of investment expenditure. The difference between this contribution and the others referred to in the text accounts for only a subset of these three decisions.
2. Long run in this model is defined as a 3–5 year period, with the short term being a month-to-month period but subject to decisions made in the context of long-run goals. In the short run, capacity is assumed to be fixed with the long run allowing a variable capacity. Profit targets are linked to long-run strategy but there must be also a short-run financial strategy to accommodate imbalances between short-run profits and investment needs.
3. It is worth mentioning at this juncture that the Harcourt and Kenyon (1976)

theoretical framework is, as the authors clearly suggest, essentially an extension of Salter's (1960) pioneering work.

7. The Theory of Money Wage Determination

7.1 INTRODUCTION

The post-Keynesian money wage determination theory is firmly based on conflict theory. The essence of this analysis is that wage rate determination is seen as the outcome of a bargaining process which is treated as an expression of conflict over relative income shares. In an open economy the conflict does not express itself solely between workers and capitalists. It incorporates conflict between workers and workers, capitalists and capitalists and domestic workers and capitalists on the one hand and foreign suppliers on the other. All these aspects are considered in Block IV of the model.

In this section we concentrate on Equation (12), where the money wage aspirations of workers are accounted for, both in terms of the conflict between workers and employers and the struggle of workers to maintain differentials via the 'target real wage' component. In this view the aspirations of workers and their economic and political power are highly relevant to the determination of money wages. In this sense the analysis conducted in this section follows the contributions of Rowthorn (1977), Sawyer (1986), Arestis (1986a), Arestis and Skott (forthcoming), amongst others. There is another important element in this theoretical framework. This is wage relativities, an aspect which plays a key role in Keynes's explanation of the observed stickiness of money wages. Wage relativities have also been prominent in the work of Hicks (1974), Trevethick (1976b), Wood (1978), Paldam (1989), Bhaskar (1990), Skott (1991), Arestis and Skott (forthcoming), and others.

These two theoretical elements are, in fact, complementary. The division between profit and wages can sit comfortably in the Keynesian view of wage relativities whilst the 'target real wage' component can be extended to include distributional conflict from the point of view of not just the functional distribution between wages and profits but wage relativities as well. There is still a further element to be considered in this section. This is the recognition of the existence of significant hysteresis effects. Hysteresis means 'that which comes after' and demonstrates that a change in economic magnitudes 'so displaces its equilibrium point that the new one cannot be reached from the old one by infinitesimal steps' (Schumpeter, 1934, p. 64; see also Cross, 1988). Wage and profit aspirations of different groups can be expected to depend on past distributional outcomes and it is this feature that may introduce a significant element of inertia into the system. In this sense we follow Arestis and Skott (forthcoming) who introduce hysteresis effects in a model based on wage relativities and 'target real wages'. We begin the analysis with the latter ingredients of the post-Keynesian theory of wage determination, leaving the analysis on hysteresis until later.

7.2 'TARGET REAL WAGES' AND 'WAGE RELATIVITIES' IN WAGE DETERMINATION

The theoretical framework considered in this section relies heavily on the premiss that workers, whether unionized or, indeed, ununionized, bargain for a 'target real wage'. It is of paramount importance to stress at the outset that the existence of trade unions modifies the aspirations of workers but does not change the essence of the analysis. So much so that Routh (1980, p. 203) argued: 'it is a mistake to imagine that there is a sharp division between unionised and ununionised workers, for trade unions cannot do much more than institutionalise and direct drives and aspirations that are already present in the individual workers'. It is true, though, that 'unions protect individual workers against arbitrary acts; they give collections of workers more control over their own destiny than they would have as individuals and present the possibility of pursuing social ends that might not otherwise be attainable' (ibid.). Hicks (1974, 1975) argues along similar lines: that workers' perception of 'fair wages' embodies not just a comparison with other workers' earnings but also with their own past experience. It is precisely this perception that makes workers resist reductions in both the level and growth of the purchasing power of the wages they have come to enjoy.

The wage formation hypothesis which we are concerned with here, treats the determination of wages as the result of a bargaining process between unions and employers. Trade unions attempt to obtain a target level of real wages (net of tax), although, of course, negotiations centre around gross money wages. At each negotiation, therefore, trade unions attempt to bargain for a level of money wages, which accounts for inflation and tax changes (direct taxes including national insurance contributions) since the previous settlement. There are, in fact, three objectives: maintenance of current real wage; the attainment of a target real wage; and restoration of wage differentials.

Maintaining the current real wage is the starting point in wage negotiations. Wage-earners inevitably compare their own current position with their past experience where wages are concerned. They resist any deterioration in the purchasing power of their wages, even a reduction in its growth, which presumably they have been used to (Hicks, 1975). Wage negotiations, then, begin by unions trying to uprate current money wages in view of differences between expected prices at the time of negotiations and prices that existed at the previous settlement. Full compensation for price changes need not come about at current negotiations. For example, when there are positive changes in prices, then the real wage will be lower at the next round of negotiations if full compensation is not achieved. The gap between target and actual real wage will be larger, and the unions will be pushing for a greater wage increase at the next round of negotiations.

The desire of unions to close any gap between a target real wage and a current real wage is the next objective we consider.[1] Clearly, the larger the gap between the target and the current real wage, the harder the unions will push to close it. The coefficient that relates this gap with the nominal wage indicates the degree of militancy of the workers and the unions. The relationship is symmetrical in that the intensity of the attempt to close the gap is the same for both negative and positive discrepancies between target and actual real wage rates. There is a problem here, though, in that the unions are unlikely to attempt to negotiate for real wage declines when the target real wage is below the current actual real wage. One might wish to impose a restriction of unity on this term, so that real-wage declines are precluded from being aimed at. But this problem can only be resolved once the question of the determination of target real wage is examined, an aspect which we discuss below.

The third objective referred to above is the restoration of wage differentials relative to other comparable groups. It was, in fact, Keynes (1936, p. 14) who suggested that workers care about both their position in the relative wage structure and the real wage rate. Keynes's wage-relativities argument relies on the assumption that workers resist reductions in their wage rates because it would imply a decrease in their relative wage. The implication of this proposition is, then, that money wage rates are historically given and workers' concern over wage relativities does not allow wage rates to fall, even under conditions of unemployment. This assumption is premissed on the notion that each group of workers expects the average nominal wage of other groups to remain unchanged. But there is absolutely no justification for the suggestion that the average nominal wage cannot change. We can argue that in this particular case workers would resist attempts to reduce their wage increase below the expected average rate. The latter becomes a benchmark below which it becomes very difficult, if not impossible, to force wage changes.[2] We may also refer to Wood (1978) who argues that there are two types of pressure operating to determine wage formation: 'normative pressures', which arise from prevailing views of what is a 'fair wage' and from pay norms; and 'anomic pressures', which emanate from labour shortages and other competitive influences. In fact, Wood's arguments can be construed as providing a general theoretical framework, with Keynes's concern over wage relativities being viewed as a special case (Skott, 1991).[3]

We may, therefore, write our wage equation as follows:

$$W_t = g[(W/P)_{t-1}, P^e_t, [(W/P)^d_t - (W/P)_{t-1}], (W^e/P^e)_t] \qquad (7.1)$$

where the variables are as before with the exception of $(W/P)^d$ which is the target or desired real wage. We also note that all the partial derivatives in (7.1) are positive. The first two terms on the right-hand side of (7.1) stand for the first objective, the second for the 'target real wage' hypothesis itself, and the third proxies the wage-relativities aspect of the theory.

There are certain caveats to expression (7.1). The state of the labour market or, to put it rather differently, the size of the reserve army of unemployed as proxied by the change in the level of unemployment, may condition the extent of the ability of the unions to press their claims. In this context the real benefits of unemployed workers ought to be another variable that should appear in expression (7.1) above. The state of the labour market may also condition the willingness of firms to satisfy wage demands. In other words, there is the question here of whether firms are able to grant wage demands when they are put to them. This can reasonably be accounted for by expected profitability, in as much as the higher the predicted profitability the more willing and able firms will be to satisfy wage demands and the less willing and able when the reverse is true.

Yet another caveat to expression (7.1) concerns the crucial question of the determination of the desired real wage. Sawyer (1982a, pp. 111–12) suggests a number of alternative mechanisms in an attempt to explain how the desired real wage is set. The most frequently discussed view is the one which proposes that the target real wage can be taken as being the previously achieved peak real wage. Not only do unions strive to maintain wages but they seek to regain previously attained real wage levels. In this case the target real wage cannot be viewed as a policy instrument. It is seen instead as the outcome of a decision-making process on the part of the unions.

Another view emphasizes the costs associated with a desired real wage, for example, costs of strikes in the pursuit of the desired real wage and the costs required for the maintenance of the achieved real wage. These costs can be assumed to increase *pari passu* with the target real wage. There are, furthermore, costs required to organize strikes and other forms of militancy by the unions. A very important cost in this respect is that associated with the discontent of the membership when the target real wage is underachieved.

Still another view sees the desired real wage as the outcome of a maximization problem. What is maximized in this case is the union's utility function, with the real wage and unemployment being its main arguments, subject to the constraints presented by the employers. This maximization procedure produces the target real wage which establishes the long-run position of the economy on the real wage–unemployment trade-off with which employers confront unions.

We take the view that a more appropriate mechanism to adopt for the purposes of this book may be the one that suggests that the target real wage is predetermined. This relies heavily on the premiss that the target real wage is generated by the expectations and aspirations of unions and workers in general. Furthermore, it can be argued that these considerations depend on a host of other factors such as, for example, the militancy of the unions and their members, beliefs about profits and profit motives and how acceptable they are in a social context, and views about how dependent investment, output and employment are on profits. Bowles (1985, p. 23) comes very near to suggesting precisely the same story when he argues that in deriving the relationship for the intensity of work a number of factors should be taken into account: 'the worker's sense of commitment, injustice, resentment, deference, patriotism, or whatever may affect the difficulty or ease of extracting labour from labour power'. It clearly follows, then, that under these types of consideration, the target real wage would be exogenously determined by social, political and economic factors.

A related contribution worth exploring at this stage is Rowthorn's (1977) model which is based on conflict over income-relative shares. Taxes, the terms of trade, expectations and money register their impact via the struggle between workers and capitalists. Workers negotiate on a firm-by-firm basis, causing a 'negotiated wage share' to be established and by implication a 'negotiated profit share'. If subsequent decisions imply different wage and profit shares, conflict occurs due to the 'aspiration gap' generated, which depends on the power wielded by workers in labour markets and firms in product markets. 'Unanticipated' nominal wage and price adjustments ensue which depend on the 'aspiration gap' and the speed of adjustment of wages and prices. From the point of view of the objective of this chapter, Rowthorn's model entails similar characteristics to the 'target real wage' hypothesis advanced above.

We may, now, combine these ideas with (7.1) to arrive at:

$$W_t = h[(W/P)_{t-1}, P^e_t, [(W/P)^d_t - (W/P)_{t-1}], (W^e/P^e)_t, \Delta U_t, (W^e_u/P^e)_t, \pi^e_t] \quad (7.2)$$

where in addition to the variables defined above, ΔU stands for changes in the level of unemployment, W_u is unemployment benefits and π^e is expected profitability.

All the partial derivatives are greater than zero, with the exception of that of the variable (W^e/P^e) which is negative. It is instructive to note at this stage that the role of unemployment in this relationship

The Theory of Money Wage Determination

is to reconcile the various claims on income, and thus conflict over distribution, as well as pressures emanating from stochastic shocks in disaggregated labour markets such as labour shortages and other competitive influences. If we assume that Equation (7.2) is additively separable and log-linear we have:

$$w_t = h_1(w_{t-1} - p_{t-1}) + h_2 p^e_t + h_3 \ln[(W/P)^d_t - (W/P)_{t-1}] + h_4(w^e_t - p^e_t) - h_5 \Delta u_t + h_6(w^e_{ut} - p^e_t) + h_7 \pi_t \qquad (7.3)$$

where lower-case letters stand for logarithms, for example $w_t = \ln W_t$. Assuming $h_2 = 1$, Equation (6.3) implies:

$$w_t - w^e_t = h_1(w_{t-1} - p_{t-1}) + h_3 \ln[(W/P)^d_t - (W/P)_{t-1}] + (h_4 - 1)(w^e_t - p^e_t) - h_5 \Delta u_t + h_6(w^e_{ut} - p^e_t) + h_7 \pi^e_t \qquad (7.4)$$

Adopting the following simple expectation hypothesis:

$$w^e_t - w_t = w_t - w_{t-1} = \dot{w}_t$$
$$p^e_t - p_t = p_t - p_{t-1} = \dot{p}_t$$
$$w^e_{ut} - w_{ut} = w_{ut} - w_{ut-1} = \dot{w}_t$$
$$\pi^e_t - \pi_t = \pi_t - \pi_{t-1} = \dot{\pi}_t$$

the following expression can be arrived at:

$$\Delta \dot{w}_t = (h_1 - 1)(\dot{w}_{t-1} - \dot{p}_{t-1}) + (h_1 - 1)(w_{t-2} - p_{t-2}) + (h_4 - 1)(\dot{w}_t - \dot{p}_t) + (h_4 - 1)(w_t - p_t) + h_3 \ln[(W/P)^d_t - (W/P)_{t-1}] - h_5 \Delta u_t + h_6(\dot{w}_{ut} - \dot{p}_t) + h_6(w_{ut} - p_t) + h_7 \dot{\pi}_t + h_7 \pi_t \qquad (7.5)$$

The endogenous formation of wage aspirations which is firmly embedded in the model we have just postulated is a natural source of hysteresis. There are, however, other types of hysteresis effects which are compatible with the analysis initiated in this section. We turn our attention to these effects next.

7.3 HYSTERESIS EFFECTS

Hysteresis, which was defined in section 7.1, is based on the notion that the equilibrium rate of unemployment is a consequence of past actual rates of unemployment, so that a rise in unemployment may increase the equilibrium rate, if not permanently then at least for a considerable period (Cross and Allen, 1988). In other words, the equilibrium rate of unemployment is path-dependent. The policy implications are important: when governments pursue policies which affect unemployment, they also have an impact on the rate of sustainable unemployment at which the economy can operate. Not only do economic policies influence unemployment, but also determine the path of the equilibrium rate of unemployment.

There are three *main* hypotheses advanced to explain the hysteresis effect. The first distinguishes between long-term and short-term unemployed and assumes that the long-term unemployed exert little pressure on wages. It is labelled as the *duration theory* (Layard and Nickell, 1986). The second is based on the distinction between insiders and outsiders and is called the *membership theory* (Lindbeck and Snower, 1986; Blanchard and Summers, 1987a). Wage-setting in this view is determined by workers in the firm (insiders) rather than by the unemployed (outsiders). The third hypothesis is based on the role of capacity scrapping (Sneessens and Dreze, 1986; Soskice and Carlin, 1989; Carlin and Soskice, 1990), and is appropriately labelled the *capacity scrapping theory*. We elaborate on all three theoretical versions of hysteresis, beginning with the duration theory.

7.3.1 Duration Theory

The *duration* theory stresses the negative effects of duration of unemployment and subsequent effective labour supply (Hargreaves-Heap, 1980; Clark and Summers, 1982; Nickell, 1990). There are three main types of duration effect: deterioration of skills; the perception of firms on productivity differences between long-term and short-term unemployed; and changes in motivation or search behaviour (Blanchard and Diamond, 1990).

Prolonged unemployment decreases human capital and weakens the work habits of the unemployed, thus creating a less-skilled labour force. Deterioration of human capital is caused either by a loss of previously acquired skills or by a failure of the unemployed to acquire new ones. As a result, productivity of the long-term unemployed declines and they may become unemployable at the common wage or at their reservation wage. This may affect the relation between unemployment and wages in two ways. First, the unemployed risk becoming unemployable so that the longer unemployment persists the less the pressure it exerts on wages. Secondly, at high and persistent unemployment rates the proportion of long-term unemployed increases, so that the effective excess supply of labour declines. Consequently, any downward pressure on wages emanating from unemployment is substantially reduced.

The second aspect of *duration* theory emphasizes firms' perceptions of the difference between long-term and short-term unemployed. It is based on the assumption that there is a negative relationship between productivity and duration of unemployment, so that firms rank workers on the premiss that the probability of re-employment decreases with duration (Toetsch, 1988). As a result the relationship between wages and unemployment is affected in the following way. High unemployment is of little concern to those who are currently employed, because they know that if they become unemployed their chances of re-employment are much better than those who have been unemployed for a longer period. It follows that since firms take unemployment duration as an indication of the quality of the worker, increases in unemployment have a strong effect on wages initially, but eventually, as unemployment persists, effective excess supply of labour comprises only short-term unemployed.

The third candidate contributing to the explanation of duration effects is search behaviour and search intensity of the unemployed. As unemployment persists, more and more workers give up effective search, thus excluding themselves from the labour supply. Also, there may be a change in 'taste' from work towards leisure, so that during the time of unemployment workers get used to the new situation and reduce their search intensity. The implication is that as unemployment persists and search intensity weakens, effective excess supply is reduced and the relationship between wages and long-run unemployment becomes tenuous.

Duration theories commonly stress the fact that the pressure the unemployed may exert on wages declines with the duration of unemployment. This contention entails an important implication. Any decrease in unemployment causes the proportion of long-term unemployed to rise. Falling unemployment reduces the downward pressure on wages, because the proportion of less-easily employable workers is higher. In the long run, however, the level of long-term unemployed falls in tandem with the level of unemployed. Consequently, the dynamic relationship between unemployment and wages seems to be highly nonlinear (Nickell, 1987; see also Blanchard and Diamond, 1990).

Criticisms of these variants of the *duration* theory frequently concentrate on the lack of substantial and unanimous empirical support. Doubts are also expressed on the notion that losses of human capital may be a significant reason for the persistence of unemployment. Studies on the composition of unemployed (for example, Hughes and Hutchinson, 1988) conclude that it is mainly unskilled workers that suffer from unemployment. The loss of skill in this group may be small and only modest retraining would be required to reintegrate these workers into the productive process. The argument that long-term unemployment changes the work ethic gets some support from empirical research (Clark and Summers, 1982). But there does not seem to be microeconomic evidence for the ranking process of the firm or the search behaviour of the unemployed (Stanton, 1988).

7.3.2 Membership Theory

Turning now to the *membership* variant of hysteresis, we find that the emphasis in this case is on the relation between employment status and membership of the group of insiders, the employed (Blanchard and Summers, 1987a, 1987b; Lindbeck and Snower, 1987). The analysis in this case focuses on the behaviour of, and the relationship between, insiders and outsiders and their impact on wage-setting.

The main idea is that insiders manage to prevent downward adjustment of wages even in periods of high unemployment. This proposition depends crucially on insiders having some degree of monopoly power within the firm in the wage-setting process and relies on the reluctance of the firm to bargain with outsiders. There is, however, the interesting question of why involuntarily unemployed workers do not try to underbid employees. The proponents suggest that it is costly, due to high turnover costs (Lindbeck and Snower, 1986), for the firm to exchange their trained staff (insiders) for unemployed (outsiders). As insiders are assumed to have a certain degree of monopoly power, they are expected to raise the cost of turnover in wage negotiations, so it would be expensive for the firm to take on new employees. Furthermore, the higher the turnover costs the less attractive it is for outsiders to underbid. In other words, the reservation wage of outsiders has to be lower than the wage of insiders minus the turnover costs of insiders. The latter are interested in raising their turnover costs and, knowing that they may lose their insider status if they become unemployed, they will set wages at such a level as will make sure that they remain employed. Involuntary unemployment, then, arises out of the conflict between insiders and outsiders.

The *pure membership* model suggests that factors inside the firm – for example, profits, productivity, competitiveness, firm-specific skills of workers, forms of unions in the firm – are far more important in wage determination than factors like regional unemployment and wage levels or even aggregate unemployment. It also suggests that if insiders do not care about the unemployed and if they can set wages unilaterally, the level of unemployment does not play any role in wage determination (Blanchard and Summers, 1987a), and outsiders have no influence on wage determination. There are, however, two channels through which outsiders may influence wage-setting. First, since high unemployment rates mean worse re-employment chances, insiders take this consideration into account and put more emphasis on employment maintenance than on higher wages. Secondly, high unemployment rates and a high wage differential between employed and unemployed strengthen the bargaining power of the firm. If the wage differential is great enough, it may become more attractive for a firm to replace either part of or all its insiders, though in both cases high turnover costs will result (Lindbeck and Snower, 1986). There are further problems with this theory. The assumption that the workers who care about wages and job security set the level of unemployment precisely at the current level, is problematic in that it may very well be that it is aggregate unemployment, rather than industry-specific unemployment, that affects wages. Also, if wages are set at that level of unemployment which is exactly the current level, then employment should fall steadily in response to the high level of turnover observed in industry. The theory does not have an explanation for this occurrence, nor does it offer an explanation of the fact that sustained employment over long periods is bound to affect employment ultimately (see Arestis and Biefang-Frisancho Mariscal, 1991, and references therein).

7.3.3 Capacity Scrapping Theory

The *capacity scrapping* theory is the third explanation of hysteresis effects. It emphasizes the impact that aggregate demand has on capacity utilization and thus on investment. We follow Carlin and Soskice (1990) in our attempt to demonstrate its main ingredients and assume, to begin with, that aggregate demand falls. As it falls, lower rates of capacity utilization ensue which induce a slower rate of investment, and with capacity scrapping taking place, a smaller size of capital stock is inevitable. This now causes rates of capacity utilization to rise, and when they reach high levels they may very well produce higher prices and wider profit margins. When this happens, equilibrium unemployment increases as prices respond to the shortage of capacity, so that high rates of capacity utilization are accompanied by higher rates of actual and equilibrium unemployment. The theory predicts that capacity utilization is bound to return to its 'normal' rate which establishes a 'unique' long-run equilibrium rate of unemployment. The argument is symmetrical with respect to changes in aggregate demand. Higher aggregate demand is seen as raising levels of capacity utilization and investment, and thus lowering the equilibrium rate of unemployment. This symmetry in terms of the impact of changes in the direction of aggregate is, in fact, common to all three hypotheses discussed in this section. The *capacity scrapping* hypothesis, however, has not generally attracted much attention because of insufficient theoretical and empirical backing (Blanchard and Summers, 1987b).

The analysis in this section has clearly shown that *duration* theories emphasize the idea that the unemployed lose their influence on wage-setting with the passage of time, while *membership* theories stress that only insiders, frequently identified with the employed, determine the wage level. If we allow for the fact that the recently unemployed still belong to the group of insiders and that outsiders are those unemployed for a long time, elements of both theories are combined. In this case we may define wages as a decreasing function of both the level and the rate of change of unemployment. We may also split the rate of change of unemployment into different components, exhibiting features of theories of *membership* as well as ideas of *duration* theories. We can summarize all these influences under the single variable H and introduce it in (7.5). If next we take the variables as deviations from their trends we can arrive at Equation (12) of Table 4.1.

Before we move on to the next topic in our analysis, there are certain pertinent comments which relate to the discussion in this chapter and also to certain theoretical aspects discussed in Chapter 2. We begin with the observation that although the ideas of the hysteresis hypotheses have been promulgated by GNS economists, they are, none the less, strongly consistent with post-Keynesian analysis, as this section has attempted to show. This is an area in economic analysis which provides that rare 'common meeting-ground' for GNS, post-Keynesian and, indeed, radical economists. Another such topic is the efficiency wage theory (Gordon, 1990), touched upon in Chapter 2. In terms of this theory it is essentially the policy implications which have been emphasized by the post-Keynesian camp. Bowles *et al.* (1984) have propounded these ideas, and their policy proposals impinge upon raising the minimum wage. Such policy action should be expected to produce increases in productivity and growth, given the theoretical propositions of the efficiency wage hypothesis. This analysis assumes, of course, that the current wage is below the 'optimum' efficiency wage.

The GNS wage-efficiency model, along with the hysteresis hypotheses, makes the assumption that firms pay wages in excess of market-clearing. The efficiency-wage hypothesis views firms as setting wages above the market-clearing level in order to motivate employees and thus retain them or, indeed, to recruit new ones. One version of this theory adopts the distinction between the perceived 'fair' wage (with firm profitability being an important determinant of it) and the market-clearing wage, so that when the former is greater than the latter, employees are expected to reduce their work effort. (It is worth noting the similarity with the target real wage hypothesis analysed above.) Firms may very well respond by increasing the actual real wage above its market-clearing level.[4] In the hysteresis hypotheses, wage determination is the result of bargaining between insiders and employers so that wages above the clearing level arise from the bargaining power of insiders generated by turnover (hiring, training and firing) costs, as well as costs which emanate from insiders withholding effort and harassing new recruits (Lindbeck and Snower, 1988). This power is at its greatest when employees act collectively, including threats of industrial action (the similarity here with the target real wage hypothesis is, again, unmistakable). Consequently, these hypotheses assume that the actual wage is at the optimum efficiency-wage level. It thus follows that there is an important difference between the theories in the method of wage determination. The efficiency-wage and hysteresis models are based on the principle that wage determination is the result of an optimization process. By contrast, post-Keynesian analysis emphasizes conflict in wage bargaining and thus in wage determination. As such it does not depend on optimization principles at all. This is an interesting comparison and points to the observation that the discussion in this section indicates quite clearly that although the post-Keynesian arguments are different from those of the GNS models of wage determination, there are at the same time important similarities.

The argument posed by Bowles *et al.* (1984) relies crucially on the relationship between wage levels and productivity performance. The causation is, of course, from wages to productivity, so that higher wages cause greater productivity. Enhanced productivity boosts the economy towards full employment and full-capacity utilization. The really interesting question, though, is why the causation runs in this way. Following Bowles *et al.* (1984), an important contributory factor is that higher wages are associated with increased worker motivation. Productivity is much influenced by the amount of effort and, perhaps more importantly, by the quality of work. High wages and good working conditions are very significant prerequisites in terms of attracting high-quality labour. Also, high wages force firms to modernize their capital equipment and this is expected to enhance productivity. Similarly, greater equality of wages amongst workers can contribute to healthier productivity, again because it improves worker motivation. Furthermore, there are the beneficial effects from a higher aggregate demand for goods and services emanating from higher wages which help to push the economy to full-capacity utilization and sustain it once it is achieved.

Naturally, there is the problem that higher wages might reduce the expected rate of profit and reduce investment. But what is important in this context is that the profit rate is influenced by the real unit cost of labour, not the absolute level of real wages. And whilst higher real wages *per se* should imply higher real unit labour costs, the increased productivity thereby caused guarantees lower real unit labour costs. However, at full capacity persistent increases in wages could very well increase real unit labour costs and thus depress investment. But in the case of open economies, wage increases can improve competitiveness if productivity increases and/or the exchange rate depreciates sufficiently.

Needless to say, when the effects just referred to operate together, their impact is much stronger than when they are considered in isolation. Furthermore, problems like racism and sexism can be tackled by the wage-led productivity strategy. These problems do not stem just from discrimination but also from low-wage employment of these groups of people. A wage-led strategy should obviously not be expected to solve the roots of these problems, but it provides the basis for a more egalitarian economic system. It is in this very sense that the wage-led productivity growth strategy is at the heart of the analysis of Bowles *et al.* (1984), and is very consistent with our own analysis.

7.4 CONCLUDING REMARKS

This chapter has dealt with the post-Keynesian theory of money wage determination. We have demonstrated that conflict theory lies at its heart. Bargaining between workers and employers and workers' struggle to achieve and maintain their desired real wage along with their relative position in the wage structure constitute the two theoretical arms of the post-Keynesian theory of wage determination. In addition, hysteresis effects also have an important role to play in this theoretical framework. We discuss three dimensions of hysteresis in wage determination, and argue that they are consistent with the approach adopted for the purposes of the analysis in this book. As such, these elements have been incorporated in the relationship we derived to describe the process of wage determination in post-Keynesian economics.

With the discussion of the wage determination now in place, the justification of most of the relationships summarized in Table 4.1 is nearly ready. What is left to complete the model is the discussion of the credit and monetary sector. Chapter 8 attempts to examine these aspects at some length. It concentrates on the financial and monetary dimensions of post-Keynesian economics which are viewed as an integral part of the analysis. This endeavour gives us the opportunity to introduce further elements to our excursion into post-Keynesian economics, which assume relevance and crucial significance in open economies.

NOTES

1. The concept of a 'target real wage' plays a very important role in the Cambridge Economic Policy Group's macroeconomic model (see Cripps and Godley, 1976).
2. Trevithick (1976a, 1976b) rehearses Keynes's argument and generalizes it in an environment where wages are expected to grow at a non-zero rate. Tobin (1972), too, emphasizes workers' concern with relative wages and the inflationary bias due to multiple labour markets as the non-linear relationship between aggregate demand and wage rate.
3. Routh (1980), Hicks (1975), Kaldor (1976) and Paldam (1989), *inter alia*, offer arguments which are in a similar vein to Wood's (1978).
4. An interesting policy implication of the wage efficiency models discussed in the text is that lump-sum subsidies for each worker employed, financed by a tax on the wage bill in the same market, should reduce unemployment. This is because subsidies in this case act as a deterrent to firms' attempts to raise wages. This would be a form of tax-based incomes policy of the type discussed later in the book (see Chapter 10).

8. The Theory of Money, Credit and Finance

8.1 INTRODUCTION

The purpose of this chapter is to identify the main elements of what constitutes post-Keynesian monetary theory. It is concerned with both the monetary aspects (Block V) and open economy aspects (Block VI) of post-Keynesian economics. We argue that these two facets are so interrelated that it is necessary to discuss them together. They rely on a model which is based on the UK monetary framework. It is none the less general enough, so far as its theoretical basis is concerned, to include most of the constituent elements of post-Keynesian theory of money, credit and finance. In doing so we recognize that the choice of model to be used depends very much on the problem at hand.

Post-Keynesian monetary analysis adopts the thesis that no general model can resolve all economic problems for all times and all situations. Particular attention is therefore paid to monetary institutions as they operate and evolve in the UK, in an attempt to highlight the emphasis put by post-Keynesians on this evolutionary aspect. Institutional developments, however, reflect fundamental characteristics of money, since the institutions of money and of banking are inextricably related to each other. The most important characteristic in this respect is that money is credit-driven. Another characteristic which we highlight in this chapter is that money is also demand-determined. The result is that money is best viewed as endogenous rather than as an exogenous magnitude.

Keynes (1936) ignored the endogeneity aspect of money, or at least he seemed oblivious to it (Goodhart, 1983), by assuming money to be completely exogenous, fully controlled by the monetary authority. The analysis in this chapter, therefore, can be seen as a step towards satisfying one of the important aims of post-Keynesian economics which is, as Joan Robinson (1962a, for example) insisted, to complete the unfinished *General Theory*. But Moore (1984) has shown that whilst Keynes in the *General Theory* treated the supply of money as exogenous, in his earlier writings, especially in the *Treatise* (Keynes, 1930), he did in fact recognize the endogenous nature of the money supply process. The underlying mechanism propounded was via the demand for bank credit to finance working capital requirements.

8.2 THE ENDOGENEITY CHARACTERISTIC OF MONEY

Money comes into existence in three ways. The first arises because production takes time and the purchase of inputs has to be financed prior to the sale of the output. Money necessarily comes into existence at the same time as debt (Davidson, 1978). In a *dynamic monetary production economy* credit is generated to facilitate production and other activities, such as purchase of durables. Thus, 'credit-granting' institutions, especially the banking ones, are of paramount importance and therefore the way they operate must be carefully analysed. It is none the less recognized that whilst productive credit is the normal case, there exists the possibility of credit misallocation. This anomaly occurs when credit is utilized for non-productive purposes, as, for example, when credit is channelled to speculation due to uncertainty. This, along with the inability of firms to repay loans when banks unsuccessfully indulge in risky ventures, forms the basis of financial crises.[1]

The second way money is introduced into the system is via fiscal and open-market operations initiated by the monetary authorities. There is, however, a fundamental asymmetry here. Monetary authorities are generally able to increase the money supply on their own initiative except in conditions of severe and extreme slump when economic agents would not wish to hold any extra money injected into the system, occasions when monetary authorities may really wish to increase the money supply. They are not, however, able to initiate a reduction in the money supply, except in periods of slump when economic agents would be favourably disposed towards destroying money, circumstances in which the monetary authorities may be reluctant to take such action.

The third way is overseas flows which can be responsible for the creation or destruction of money in an open economy. In general terms a balance of payments surplus enhances money creation and a deficit destroys it. Dow (1986/7) argues that the degree of openness of an economy and the distinction between fixed and flexible exchange rates are important considerations in terms of the demand and supply of finance and money. But not all foreign transactions have a definite impact on the money supply. The crucial criterion here is whether the government acquires or supplies domestic currency in the process. When the government supplies domestic currency there is money creation, and there is money destruction when the government acquires it. Thus, for example, transactions involving overseas lending to the public sector in foreign currencies do not have an impact on domestic money.

It ought to be emphasized that the two latter ways by which money can enter the economic system may not have a direct effect on the creation of money. Once it is recognized that money is determined by the decisions of economic agents and not by the monetary authorities, that is to say money is endogenously determined, any money creation emanating from fiscal or debt management operations initiated by the authorities and/or from favourable balance of payments, can be compensated by an equivalent reduction in commercial bank credit brought about by the actions of private economic agents. It clearly follows that the government may not be able to create or destroy money directly. What it can do instead is to redistribute money amongst different groups of economic agents. This can happen when governments in their attempts to increase/reduce money set in motion the destruction/creation of bank credit by group(s) of economic agents. To the extent that the latter group(s) are different from those initially receiving/destroying money following the government initiatives, redistribution of money between these groups takes place.

This analysis, however, should be qualified in two important respects. Chick (1983, and especially 1986) demonstrates that there are several stages of banking development, and it is only in some of them that money can be said to have the characteristics attributed to it above. Five stages of banking are identified: stage 1 is characterized by a large number of banks with their liabilities not being widely used as means of payments. In stage 2 the number of banks is smaller but their size is bigger compared to those in stage 1. Deposits are used as transactions balances and the 'bank deposit multiplier' becomes relevant. This becomes even more relevant in stage 3 where interbank lending mechanisms become more prevalent. Stages 4 and 5 are the two relevant stages for the analysis pursued in this chapter. In stage 4 the central bank accepts full responsibility for the stability of the system so that the principle of lender-of-last-resort is firmly adhered to. In stage 5 banks seek lending opportunities which they try to balance by attracting deposits. This 'liability management' activity is an important recent development and will be discussed further below.

The second qualification is that there may very well be a difference in behaviour between large companies and persons. Large companies operate in relatively 'perfect' financial and credit markets and the above analysis would be more apt in their case. For persons, however, financial and credit markets are imperfect, so that any excess/deficiency of money would not lead to credit market operations as depicted above. Rather, any excess/deficiency would be adjusted through changes in purchases/sales of assets, but not necessarily changes in credit behaviour (Goodhart, 1989). It has actually been shown (Arestis *et al.*, 1992) that this distinction has become particularly pronounced in the UK since the early 1980s. Such difference in behaviour between large companies and persons is accounted for in what follows.

8.3 MONEY: RESIDUE NOT CAUSE

The emphasis in post-Keynesian monetary theory is on credit rather than on money in enabling spending units to bridge any gap between their desired level of discretionary spending and the current rate of cash flow. Money is viewed as essentially endogenous in a credit money economy responding to changes in the behaviour of private economic units rather than, in the main, to the behaviour of the monetary authorities. Money is an output of the system with its endogenous behaviour governed by the borrowing needs of firms, households and the government and the portfolio behaviour of financial institutions and of the personal sector.

The underlying theory here is that money is the result of credit flows in a dynamic monetized production economy (Eichner and Kregel, 1975). When entrepreneurs expand their production they must increase their wage bills as well as their other outlays. Production takes time; until, therefore, the output is sold and consequently cash begins to flow in, entrepreneurs will require more loans to bridge this gap. Commercial banks will satisfy this demand for loans, bringing about an increase in deposits with the banks. Variations in the supply of money are therefore caused by fluctuations in prices and quantities of production instead of the reverse. It can thus be argued that:

> a marked rise in the level of activity is likely to be preceded by an increase in the supply of money (if M is widely defined) because a rise in the wage bill and in borrowing for working capital is likely to precede an increase in the value of output appearing in the statistics. Or that a fall in activity sharp enough to cause losses deprives the banks of credit-worthy borrowers and brings a contraction in their position. (Robinson, 1970, p. 510)

In all these, the leading role is essentially played by entrepreneurs and their 'animal spirits'. Entrepreneurs must predict the pattern of the forthcoming effective demand and infer from this the cash outlays they will be required to make in order to pay for the factors of production they will employ, and the outlays required to finance their investment. Once this is done their loan requirements from the banks can be ascertained and their demand for money formulated. The central bank sets the discount rate and commercial banks their interest rates (given banks' uncertain assessment of risk and value of collateral). At this level and structure of interest rates, banks stand ready to provide whatever money the entrepreneurs' requirements for money entail. So an increase in nominal money demand leads to an increase in the existing money stock without necessitating a change in interest rates. It clearly follows that 'interest rates are virtually the sole remaining monetary instrument for achieving monetary control' (Artis and Lewis, 1981, p. 9). This particular proposition is well integrated in the analysis below where the discount rate is supposed to be under the firm control of the monetary authorities (see also Chick, 1986).

This analysis depends heavily on the behaviour of the monetary authorities and it is, therefore, very important to explore at some length their attitude when it appears that they should apply severe constraints on the liquidity of the banking system. Monetary authorities are generally reluctant to apply these constraints; they are accommodating in terms of providing the reserves required by the banking system, at a penal rate if necessary. Commercial banks are then able to pass on the cost of borrowing to their customers. Central banks simply cannot refuse to provide 'last resort' facilities because they cannot afford to jeopardize the solvency of the banking system. For a solvency crisis can easily precipitate a liquidity crisis, given that 'even a rumour of insolvency can lead to a run, and, if not checked, the liquidity crisis could spread even more quickly than the solvent crisis that caused it' (Guttentag and Herring, 1983, p. 4). The central bank's main function as lender of last resort must be preserved religiously and continuously so that the liquidity of financial institutions and markets may be fully guaranteed. Kaldor (1982, p. 47) puts it very succinctly when he argues that the central bank

> cannot *refuse* the discounting of 'eligible bills' rendered to it by the discount houses. If it did ... the Bank would fail in its function as 'lender-of-last-resort' to the banking system which is essential to ensure that the clearing banks do not become insolvent as a result of a lack of liquidity. Precisely because the monetary authorities cannot afford the disastrous consequences of a collapse of the banking system, and the banks in turn cannot allow themselves to get into a position of being 'fully stretched', the 'money supply' in a credit money economy is endogenous.

After all, one rationale for the creation of central banks is to provide an elastic currency supply. Financial assets must possess liquidity which can only be ensured if central banks are prepared to perform the role of lender of last resort. Only in this way can financial assets ultimately be exchanged quickly, easily and cheaply into cash, thus ensuring the liquidity referred to. The commercial banking system is the pillar in the liquidity-creating process. Monetary authorities have an obligation to create and maintain orderly conditions in financial markets in general and in commercial banking in particular.

Monetary authorities must, therefore, accommodate the reserve needs of the financial markets. Wojnilower (1980) offers an excellent example in support of this proposition. Chronicling the 'credit crunches' that occurred in the USA in the 1960s and 1970s, he argues persuasively that when the monetary authorities attempted to squeeze the credit markets they found themselves in a position of having to back off for fear of provoking a scramble for liquidity.[2] Another example in support of the above proposition is the operation of the UK discount market which covers the entire Treasury bill tender. There is a lot of evidence to suggest that discount houses would not bid for the entire tender 'without the assurance that necessary cash would be made available' (Artis and Lewis, 1981, p. 65).

Related to this is the existence of substantial 'unused overdraft facilities' and 'open credit lines' as structural features of the financial system. These facilities,[3] which are not included in monetary aggregates, are reported as having exceeded bank demand deposits in the USA in 1980 (Wojnilower, 1980, p. 289), whilst in 1981 they exceeded the M1 definition of money supply (Moore, 1983, p. 543). In the UK commercial banks rely heavily on previously negotiated overdraft limits. In both the UK and USA 'total bank debt in existence of any time characteristically lies between one-half to two-thirds of the total amount of outstanding lines of credit and overdraft facilities which have been formally committed' (Moore, 1985, p. 25). The utilization of such credit facilities is at the discretion of the banks' borrowers, not the banks themselves. Also of interest is the possibility of foreign banks being able to obtain 'last resort' facilities from head office (although the exchange rate constraint ought to be acknowledged here). Most importantly, though, liability management ensures that even in periods when the monetary authorities wish to initiate credit stringency, commercial banks can still find the required funds in the wholesale financial markets. Commercial banks are able to do this

by building a reputation in the market through lending funds whenever possible so as to be able to borrow funds more easily when the need arises; by developing credit lines with other banks; by diversifying the sources of credit so as not to rely excessively on one credit supplier; and by seeking new sources of funds to appropriate maturities. (Podolski, 1986, p. 161)

So much so that 'corporate bank customers expect a steady supply of funds even during periods of restrictive monetary policy' (ibid.).

This analysis clearly suggests that financial innovations have enabled commercial banks to satisfy the demand for funds through their operations in the wholesale money markets; as a result commercial banks become increasingly immune from central bank control and therefore less dependent upon it as the lender of last resort. Furthermore, when pressures on liquidity are imposed by the monetary authorities, economic agents can and do 'improvise' and 'innovate' very quickly and efficiently on what they use as means of exchange. For example, there might be a switch from banking activities towards non-banking financial activities. Credits between companies could very well be further developed, given that there is already in the UK a flourishing 'inter-company' market (Revell, 1973). Large firms would begin to act as banking institutions. Monetary authorities are, of course, fully aware of these possibilities and as a result they apply flexibility and pursue accommodating monetary policies; for if they did not, they would probably lose whatever control of financial operations is left to them.

With these propositions firmly in mind we proceed to develop the monetary part of our model along with the open economy aspects of it.

8.4 A MODEL OF MONEY, CREDIT AND FINANCE

The ideas expounded so far are formally put together in what follows in this section. In doing so we draw on the UK monetary institutional scene. We begin with the money supply identity:

$$\Delta M = \Delta TD + \Delta SD + \Delta GDC \tag{8.1}$$

where changes in the money supply (ΔM) are equivalent to the sum of changes in time deposits (ΔTD), changes in sight deposits (ΔSD) and changes in deposits of the public sector including currency (ΔGDC). The item ΔGDC is only a small fraction of the total money supply, so we treat it as exogenous for convenience and endogenise the other two elements in (8.1).

In the UK, commercial banks are invariably regarded as oligopolists both in terms of their loans and deposits (Moore and Threadgold, 1980, 1985). They can be thought of as firms with two inputs (their liabilities: retail and wholesale deposits) and two outputs (their assets: retail and wholesale loans). Their behaviour with respect to retail loan and deposit rates is that they set both of these rates in line with the Minimum Lending Rate (or discount rate) and money-market rates, and allow demand conditions to determine the quantity of retail loans and deposits. Any resulting surplus or deficit of funds is met through wholesale deposits and loans which are broadly similar securities such as certificates of deposits (CDs), bankers' acceptances and commercial bills. The wholesale market is thus the source of any surplus or deficit of funds which cause fluctuations in the wholesale rates which are, in turn, reflected in deposit and borrowing rates. It thus follows that commercial banks in the UK are, in fact, price-setters and quantity-takers in terms of their behaviour with respect to retail deposits and loans and price-takers and quantity-setters in the wholesale market (Wills, 1982).

One important implication of this institutional framework is that UK commercial banks have been able to balance their books by issuing wholesale deposits (these are interest-bearing deposits which comprise large fixed-term deposits in general and certificates of deposit in particular, certificates of deposit being wholesale deposits held by the non-bank public for a fixed period, usually three to six months). Whilst in the past imbalances between changes in deposits and loans were financed by changes in marketable securities, local authority debt and gilt-edged bonds (Radcliffe, 1959), the development of the wholesale deposit market since the late 1960s has meant that banks have been able to place large quantities of these liabilities on their own initiative. In other words:

Banks no longer adjusted their assets passively to an (exogenously determined) flow of deposits; instead it became a central, treasury function to adjust their wholesale liabilities, via operations in CDs, in the inter-bank market, and, when allowed by exchange controls, in the global euro-currency market, in order to provide any necessary funds to finance their loan book. (Goodhart, 1986, p. 85)

The adoption of liability management has implied that the banks can more easily accommodate changes in the demand for loans than previously, and that the growth of bank lending has become over the period 'the major driving force in the expansion of the banking system' (Goodhart, 1984, p. 263). It is important to note at this juncture that liability management has taken place not just in the UK but in other industrialized nations as well. In the USA, for example, it was in early 1962 that negotiable certificates of deposit appeared in the financial markets and during the credit crunch of 1966 that their use became widespread (Minsky, 1986b, p. 351). Furthermore, following the 'credit crunch' of August/September 1966 and certainly by 1969 Eurodollar borrowings became another significant market (Wojnilower, 1980; Moore, 1986; Rousseas, 1986). In fact, Goodhart (1986) suggests that commercial banks in the UK began in the early 1970s to apply liability management techniques similar to those already in use in the USA.

This 'liability-side' management aspect means that the aggregate bank balance-sheet identity can be solved for ΔTD. In effect, we assume here that wholesale deposits are entirely time deposits. This may not be an unrealistic assumption to adopt: it is impossible to distinguish between purely retail banks and purely wholesale banks, since all British banks are multiproduct firms. Further, 'the division between retail and wholesale has been broken down by what is termed "intermediate" business, as some companies move between the two markets in response to credit needs' (Artis and Lewis, 1981, p. 90). This, then, allows us to write:

$$\Delta TD = \Delta BLP + \Delta BLG + \Delta BLOS - \Delta SD - \Delta OBD \qquad (8.2)$$

where ΔTD and ΔSD are as above, ΔBLP is changes in bank lending to the public, ΔBLG is changes in bank lending to the government, $\Delta BLOS$ is changes in bank lending to the overseas sector, and ΔOBD is changes in other bank deposits (including changes in net non-deposit liabilities). We treat the variables $\Delta BLOS$ and ΔOBD as exogenously determined.

The other endogenous element in (8.1) is ΔSD. We postulate that its behaviour depends on changes in the level of income (ΔY), reflecting the flow of funds into the banking sector as a result of changes in the level of economic activity. ΔSD is also related to changes in interest rates (ΔR), which is hypothesized to account for possible portfolio effects; ΔR proxies the relative attractiveness of alternative financial assets available to depositors. The ratio (EP/FP) is included in the menu of explanatory variables to register the need for sight deposits, as discretionary expenditures of the personal sector (EP) deviate from discretionary funds of the same sector (FP). In other words, the ratio (EP/FP) reflects the creation of deposits in response to the demand for them. We can, therefore, formally write:

$$\Delta SD = \Delta SD(\Delta Y, \Delta R, EP/FP) \qquad (8.3)$$
$$+ \quad - \quad +$$

with the signs under variables indicating the signs of partial derivatives.

The ideas expounded so far on commercial bank behaviour can be succinctly summarized in Figure 8.1. In it we plot the demand for bank deposits (D_D) as an upward-sloping relationship with respect

Figure 8.1

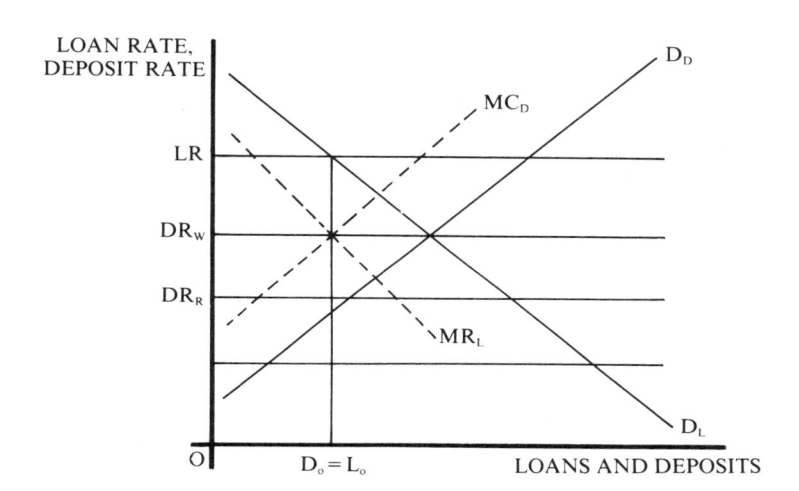

```
LOAN RATE,
DEPOSIT RATE                              D_D
                              MC_D
    LR ─────────────────\────/──────────
                         \  /
   DR_W ─────────────────*───────────────
                        /  \
   DR_R ────────────── /    \ ───────────
                              \  MR_L
                                    \
                                     D_L
     O        D_o = L_o       LOANS AND DEPOSITS
```

Source: Moore (1988)

to the deposit rate, and similarly for the demand for bank loans (D_L), which is drawn as inversely related to the loan rate. The marginal cost of bank funds is determined in the wholesale market where banks are price-takers and quantity-setters. This is represented by DR_W where the upward-sloping marginal cost for deposits (MC_D) intersects the downward-sloping marginal revenue of loans (MR_L) to give equality between deposits and loans at $D_o = L_o$. The retail market is represented by LR and DR_R, the loan rate and retail deposit rate respectively. Once the banks have set both rates, then the straight line emanating from LR is the supply of loans (which is perfectly elastic up to borrowers' allotted credit ceilings) and the one from DR_R is the supply of retail deposits. The difference between LR_R and DR_R represents banks' normal profit mark-up. Thus, since banks are regarded as oligopolists they are assumed to mark-up their average cost of funds when they set their supply price for loans. It is important to note that DR_W depends on the discount rate, and it is through this avenue that interest rate policy can be conducted. An increase in the discount rate, for example, will shift the marginal cost of funds and, with the banking sector trying to maintain the differential $LR - DR_R$, changes in the administered rates will ensue. What will happen to the volume of bank loans and deposits depends crucially on the elasticity of demand for bank loans and deposits in the retail and wholesale markets. Liability management implies that the banking sector ensures the creation of the necessary amount of deposits as required by the demand for bank loans. The moving force, therefore, is bank loans, hence the proposition that loans make deposits. Consequently, the next logical step in our analysis must be a close scrutiny of the variable ΔBLP.

We disaggregate ΔBLP:

$$\Delta BLP = \Delta BLI + \Delta BLC + \Delta BLF \qquad (8.4)$$

where ΔBLI stands for changes in bank lending to industry, ΔBLC for changes in bank lending to consumers, and ΔBLF for changes in bank lending to other (non-commercial bank) financial institutions. This last is treated as exogenous.

Changes in bank lending to industry are hypothesized as being determined by the needs of the industrial sector for working-capital finance (Moore and Threadgold, 1980; Johannsen, 1908; Hagemann and Ruhl, 1990). These needs are determined by the expected level of transactions which can be proxied by two alternative sets of variables: changes in costs and changes in the expected level of demand for the output of the firm (Kalecki, 1971a, ch. 3; Sawyer, 1985, ch. 5; Davidson and Weintraub, 1973). Given the mark-up over historic, actual or normal unit costs hypothesis of price determination (Coutts et al., 1978; Sawyer, 1983) increases in costs will raise the working-capital finance needs of firms until larger receipts from sales are forthcoming as a result of higher mark-up prices. The amount of extra working capital required will depend on the length of time before output prices are raised in response to higher costs and on the time it takes for receipts to materialize. This process is depicted in Figure 8.2: at time t_0 there is a cost increase (for example, trade unions secure a wage rise). Total revenues increase gradually as prices are raised due to the mark-up, as we have just analysed. Until point t_1 is reached additional working capital finance is required which is satisfied through bank borrowing. Clearly, point t_2 depends crucially on the production/sales time interval.

Similarly, changes in expected demand for the firm's output will

Figure 8.2

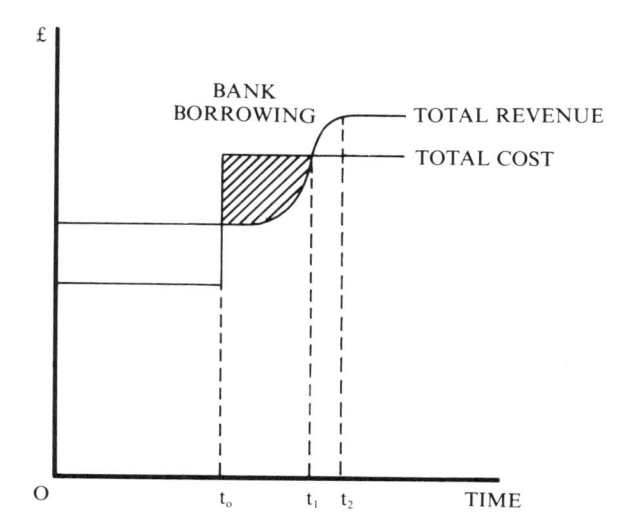

```
£ |
  |         BANK
  |      BORROWING ┌──── TOTAL REVENUE
  |            ┌───┤
  |            │▓▓▓├──── TOTAL COST
  |            │▓▓▓│
  |     ───────┤   │
  |            │   │
  |            │   │
  |            │   │
  |            │   │
  |            │   │
  O ──────────t₀──t₁─t₂─────────── TIME
```

Source: Moore (1983, p. 546)

influence its financial needs. This is so because bank lending can be thought of as facilitating the firm's transactions in view of gaps between expenditures incurred to finance a higher volume of output and revenues received (Figure 8.2 is applicable here too). Bank lending can thus be viewed as performing a 'transactions balance' role here, very similar to Keynes's finance motive (Davidson, 1978; Asimakopulos, 1983), especially when the latter is interpreted as a demand for a *flow of credit* by the industrial sector (and not as a demand for a stock of assets) in its pursuit of profit in the capital accumulation process (Rousseas, 1986, pp. 44–5). We should, therefore, expect a higher demand for bank loans related to a higher expected level of the output of the firm.

Regardless of whether one utilizes cost or transaction elements, the point must be emphasized that in this approach historical time is taken seriously, particularly in the sense that production takes time. Now, whether cost variables or transactions variables are superior is really an empirical question. The evidence here is not very helpful for both variables have been shown to perform satisfactorily at the empirical level (Arestis, 1987/8, Moore and Threadgold, 1980, 1985; Cuthbertson, 1985). We utilize cost variables for the purposes of this book, but the argument would not be affected if transactions variables were to be utilized instead. Three such variables have been shown to be particularly relevant: wage costs in the form of wage bills (WB); costs of raw materials (RM); and tax payments (TP) (see Moore and Threadgold, 1980, 1985; and Moore, 1983, for more details). The variables we have considered so far are related to *expected* changes in the borrowing needs of the industrial sector. Unexpected changes in their borrowing are hypothesized as being captured by the (EI/FI) variable, where EI is this sectors' discretionary expenditure and (FI) the same sector's discretionary funds. The ratio (EI/FI) measures this sector's total external financing requirements and can, therefore, serve as a useful proxy for unexpected changes in borrowing needs (Cuthbertson, 1985, p. 95). We may thus view the cost variables as capturing the *expected* changes whilst the (EI/FI) variable captures *unexpected* financing needs, with both met by bank lending. We can now formally write:

$$\Delta \text{BLI} = \Delta \text{BLI}(\Delta \text{WB}, \Delta \text{RM}, \Delta \text{TP}, \text{EI/FI}) \qquad (8.5)$$
$$\phantom{\Delta \text{BLI} = \Delta \text{BLI}(} + \phantom{\text{WB},} + \phantom{\Delta \text{RM},} + \phantom{\Delta \text{TP},} +$$

An interesting aspect of this relationship is its apparent insensitivity to interest rate variations. Most empirical studies (Arestis, 1987/8; Moore and Threadgold, 1980, 1985; Cuthbertson, 1985) report zero or very low interest elasticities for ΔBLI with respect to an absolute rate of interest. But there are good theoretical reasons to suggest that this is not unexpected. The periods during which the monetary authorities seek to contain bank lending through higher interest rates coincide with increased industrial demands for more finance to meet higher and rising costs. Furthermore, industry uses bank lending as a permanent source of finance: Artis and Lewis (1981) report that bank lending to industry represents over 55 per cent of industry's external borrowing. Most large companies finance stocks, working capital and some initial cash flow for capital projects from bank borrowing. The financing of such expenditure is relatively inflexible unless a change in demand conditions is anticipated. Companies would tend to lose non-price competitiveness, for instance, were they to economize on stocks as interest rates rose, nor is switching to other financial sources, or raising prices, possible in the short run. The balance between increased bank borrowing and a run-down in liquid assets is not a simple function of the level of interest rates. It is, if anything, responsive only to the spread between lending and borrowing rates. For corporate borrowers, however, the spread is at times so low that the sourcing of funds between these categories may be a matter of indifference. An interesting example here is the period since 1979 in the UK. During this period interest rates have been generally high and there has been a considerable squeeze on liquidity. The response of many companies has not been to cut down net expenditure and/or sell some of their assets but, instead, to increase bank borrowing (Gowland, 1984, p. 186). This supports the argument that what matters in terms of the demand for credit by industry is the *availability* of credit, net the *price*.

The way in which we have postulated the determination of ΔBLI casts considerable doubt on the ability of the UK monetary authorities to control not just bank lending to industry via interest rate changes, but also to meet money supply targets. Bank lending to industry is by far the largest component of bank lending to the private sector (two thirds of the movement in bank lending is accounted for by bank lending to industry; see, for example, Kaldor, 1980, para. 95, p. 17; but see Arestis *et al.*, 1992, for recent changes in the UK in this regard), with the latter being both a large and a volatile component of the money stock. Given then the interest inelasticity of the demand for bank lending by industry with respect to an absolute rate of interest, it follows that extremely large interest rate increases would be required to hit a restrictive monetary aggregate target. Clearly, though, large interest rate changes of this magnitude are unlikely to be sanctioned by the Bank of England in view of its function as a pillar of the monetary system, its associated obligation to maintain 'orderly' conditions in the financial markets, and above all its function as lender of last resort (Wills, 1982; Minsky, 1985).

An interest rate effect, though, is more apparent in the ΔBLC equation on purely 'portfolio theory' grounds, as argued above. Furthermore, changes in economic activity (as proxied by ΔY) can be thought of as another major determinant of ΔBLC. For example, as economic activity expands, consumers are prepared to go into debt to finance purchases of durable goods. The ratio (EP/FP) is assumed to influence ΔBLC positively on grounds similar to those that the equivalent variable (EI/FI) affects ΔBLI. We may, therefore, write the ΔBLC relationship as follows:

$$\Delta BLC = \Delta BLC(\Delta R, \Delta Y, EP/FP) \qquad (8.6)$$
$$-++$$

The appearance of the variable (EI/FI) and (EP/FP) in both ΔBLI and ΔBLC respectively has an important implication. Since these two ratios proxy the external borrowing requirements of the private sector, any successful attempt by the authorities to squeeze this sector's cash-flow will increase its borrowing requirement and thus bank lending. There would thus be a growth in the money stock as a result of an endogenous response of the private sector to what was intended to be a severe monetary squeeze. Two conclusions follow from this observation: first, it casts considerable doubt on the wisdom of being concerned with money supply aggregates; secondly, and more importantly, it provides further support to the post-Keynesian argument that attention ought to be paid to credit and its availability rather than to futile monetary aggregates.

In terms of Table 4.1, equations (8.4), (8.5) and (8.6) have been combined into one equation (16) for ease of exposition. In the same table there is another equation, (17): changes in total lending to the public (ΔLP), which is simply the sum of ΔBLP and ΔOLP (that is, changes in other lending to the public). In Equation (16) of Table 4.1 there appears a variable labelled X_i which stands for policy variables which can affect credit directly. This possibility occurs when the demand for bank lending exceeds the 'available' supply, leading to a certain degree of credit-rationing by the authorities. Lavoie (1984, p. 782) discusses the relevant case of commercial banks refusing to lend to more-risky customers who are judged as imprudent in terms of their borrowing behaviour. The ensuing brake on lending expansion implies that there may very well arise a case of conflict of interests between commercial banks and industrial firms in particular (see Gedeon, 1985/6 for more details on this point).

We consider next the ΔBLG variable, which is determined through the government budget constraint identity. This is written as:

$$\Delta BLG = PSBR - \Delta BC + \Delta EF \qquad (8.7)$$

reflecting institutional arrangements in the UK. The banking sector in the UK provides the residual to private finance (ΔBC, which stands for sales of public debt to the non-bank public including currency) and overseas finance (ΔEF, which stands for changes in external flows) of the public sector borrowing requirement (PSBR). The *Bank of England Quarterly Bulletin* (1982, p. 87) is very clear on this particular point: 'Normally, that part of the Government's borrowing requirement which is not financed by the sale of debt outside the banking system is met by the sale of debt – in particular Treasury bills – to the banking system, which thus acts as the residual source of borrowing for the Government'. A very important consideration here concerns the magnitude of the 'bank lending to the government' item. It can plausibly be argued that the higher it is, the greater the possibility of severe constraints being imposed upon the economic policy-makers. This proposition is directly related to the thesis that 'In reality the City's relationship with the state is based on its economic power, and it is principally through economic levers that it acts upon the state' (Fine and Harris, 1985, p. 73). For in this case, the 'City' can dictate policies to suit its own interests, interests which may not necessarily coincide with those of the economic policy-makers. Indeed, 'the City has exercised a dominant position in the determination of economic policy, which is to say that its perceived interests have generally, although not exclusively, been the guiding thread for economic policy. . . . . The City has, in other words, largely set the parameters of economic policy and its interests have generally predominated' (Longstreth, 1979, pp. 160–1). This has been associated with deflationary policies so much favoured by the City, higher interest rates and exchange rates associated with 'money supply targets', and tight monetary policies.

Recent, and not-so-recent, experiences in the UK can be used to demonstrate the point vividly: the return to the Gold Standard in 1925 at an overvalued pound, which prompted the argument that the Chancellor (Churchill) put the interests of the City above that of British industry; the Wilson government's reluctance to devalue the pound in the mid-1960s; the introduction of monetary targets by Chancellor Healey in the mid-1970s; the high interest rates and exchange rates achieved and maintained by the Thatcher administration in the 1980s; and the abolition of foreign exchange and capital controls at the beginning of the Thatcher administration in the early 1980s, all are examples in support of the proposition. They also highlight similar problems and constraints emanating from the considerable magnitude of the item 'overseas finance', as the role of international financiers and multinational companies is central in this context. With their ability to control 'literally immeasurable sums of international money, which they could switch into and out of sterling and into and out of British bills and bonds' (Coakley and Harris, 1983, p. 206), they impose a serious constraint on governmental economic policies and are able to impose their wishes upon the economic policy-makers. Within this perspective, the argument that the City has become allied to international capital (see, for example Longstreth, 1979) provides support to the thesis that the City assumes economic objectives different from those of the national government and that conflict may very well arise between them.

(PSBR) is simply defined as the difference between government expenditure (G) and tax revenues (T) along with other government revenues (OGR), so that:

$$PSBR = G - T - OGR \qquad (8.8)$$

where OGR is treated as exogenous and both G and T are simply related to national income as in Table 4.1. Although ΔCB in (8.7) is treated as exogenous for the purposes of this study, some commentary on the sales of public debt is in order. The demand for debt depends not just on the current rate of interest but on its level in relation to the expected changes in interest rates. The impact on the demand for bonds of a change in interest rates cannot be predicted accurately since expectations can and do vary; they can be *extrapolative* or *regressive*. Extrapolative expectations prevail when investors expect a given change to continue in the same direction, and regressive expectations when investors expect a given change to reverse itself. Investors with extrapolative expectations will sell bonds, while those with regressive expectations will buy bonds following an increase in interest rates. Clearly, then, in such an atmosphere the monetary authorities cannot establish with confidence what the required price change should be to bring about the desired change in the demand for government bonds for, say, monetary control purposes. The greater the instability of interest rates in response to open-market operations designed to establish a target rate for money supply, the greater the uncertainty surrounding the actions of the monetary authorities and, therefore, the higher the probability that the authorities will be unsuccessful in terms of hitting their targets.

Next, we consider interest rates. We argue that, unlike the supply of money, interest rates *can* be set by the monetary authorities. The rate under their control is the discount rate (r), changes of which directly influence changes in the market interest rates (ΔR) via a mark-up. We thus apply Kalecki's (1971a, ch. 5) theory of mark-up pricing to interest rates. In this way, market interest rates are seen as the 'prices' of financial 'goods', with the mark-up being imposed by the individual banks on the banking industry and determined by their degree of monopoly. The mark-up is based on unit variable banking costs which can be proxied by the discount rate administered by the central bank. This particular analysis follows directly from our discussion of the oligopolistic lending and borrowing behaviour of the commercial banking sector. Rousseas (1986, p. 60) offers a very similar analysis which allows him to conclude:

what all this adds up to is that the notion of a market-clearing equilibrium 'interest' rate – whether in the old 'productivity–thrift' theory, or the 'bastard' Keynesian IS-LM approach, or a market-determined short-run rate – is a theoretical fiction used to provide determinate theoretical solutions within arcane models bearing no relation to the real world. In the universe of economics, interest rates are not the equilibrating force of textbooks. They are essentially a markup over competitive prime costs in a broadly conceived financial sector that is bound to exhibit an even greater concentration of economic power, especially in the banking industry.

The corollary to this analysis is that short-term interest rates are a set of politically administered, rather than market-determined, prices. This particular proposition has been given a lot of support recently by none other than the Governor of the Bank of England when he argued: 'There is a popular perception that the monetary authorities dictate the general level of interest rates, and it is of course true that we are able to exert a very considerable influence on it' (Leigh-Pemberton, 1987, p. 11). When the rate of interest is viewed in this way, it becomes a distributional variable that determines the distribution of income between fixed-interest debt holders and the rest of the personal sector.

Furthermore, it is assumed that open-market operations can have an influence on market interest rates, so a second variable influencing ΔR is ΔBC. In the case of open economies such as the UK, changes in external flows can also have an impact on ΔR, reflecting foreign demand for domestic government securities. All these assumptions are incorporated in:

$$\Delta R = \Delta R(\Delta r, \Delta BC, \Delta EF) \qquad (8.9)$$
$$+ \quad\ + \quad\ \ -$$

The other item in Equation (8.7) is the variable that refers to changes in external flows (ΔEF), equal to the sum of current balance (CB) and capital movements (ΔKM), minus changes in overseas lending to the public sector (ΔOLG) and changes in bank lending to the public sector in foreign currencies ($\Delta BLGF$). We can thus write:

$$\Delta EF = CB + \Delta KM - (\Delta OLG + \Delta BLGF) \qquad (8.10)$$

In Table 4.1 we label ($\Delta OLG + \Delta BLGF$) as ΔOEF so that one variable is utilized instead. The justification of Equation (8.10) provides essentially the theoretical background to Block VI. We begin with CB which is hypothesized to behave as indicated by:

$$CB = CB[[(Y-T)_{wi}/(Y-T)_{ci}], Y, WT, [(P/P_x).(ER)]] \qquad (8.11)$$
$$- \phantom{(Y-T)_{wi}/} - \phantom{(Y-T)_{ci}],} + -$$

where the meaning of variables is as before, with the exception of WT which stands for world trade and $(P/P_x.ER)$ which measures competitiveness, P_x being export prices and ER the exchange rate. The expected impact of the variables Y, WT and $(P/P_x. ER)$ are as shown in (8.11) (but see, for example, Arestis, 1989, for more details). What needs to be said, though, is that in all these impacts the income affects outweigh by far the substitution effects in line with the propositions expounded above in the case of household and investment expenditures behaviour. Furthermore, the income variable that registers distributional effects appears in Equation (8.11) in line with the argument that the propensity to import consumer goods varies significantly by class of income (Arestis and Driver, 1987). It is, in fact, analagous with the case that has been made for distinguishing income classes in consumer demand functions as postulated in our discussion of Block I. The influence of income distribution on consumer demand in general, and on demand for consumer importables in particular, can be justified within the framework of Muellbauer (1976) where in an attempt to specify the requirements for community preferences, he derives non-linear Engel curves that imply a behavioural role for income distribution.

A further and more relevant rationale of why imports of consumer goods may be influenced by income distribution is concerned with the composition of imports in consumer expenditure, and refers to the characteristics of the goods *vis-à-vis* domestically produced consumer goods and services. In development theory, for instance, the low income levels of wage workers which restrict their consumption to basic needs, generally met by local production, have often been used to support the argument that balance of payments difficulties are due to excessive imports of luxuries for the managerial or land-owning classes. In the case of industrialized (or post-industrial) economies, those in receipt of wages and salaries as a prime source of income may have a greater propensity to spend their marginal income on imported commodities, such as cars and consumer durables, than do the recipients of unearned income and the self-employed. The latter may be expected to spend more of their marginal income on such items as land, second homes, house improvements, and objects, private health and education or other services, all of which most certainly have a low import content. This hypothesis receives some support from statistics on the share of services in consumption by income bracket. Household consumption figures show that for those on above-average incomes the proportion of income spent on services more than doubles with a doubling of income (Gershuny, 1983). If there is a strong correlation between non-wage incomes and higher incomes and also a strong correlation between services and non-traded activities, these figures provide *prima facie* support for the hypothesis that consumer imports are more affected by a rise in wage income than by non-wage income.

With ΔOEF treated as exogenous we attempt to elaborate on the determinants of ΔKM:

$$\Delta KM = \Delta KM(R/R_f, ER) \qquad (8.12)$$
$$+\ +$$

The ratio of domestic interest rates (R) to foreign interest rates (R_f) is included on the assumption that capital flows are sensitive to returns available internationally (Branson and Hill, 1971). These returns, however, are not captured simply by interest rates but, perhaps more importantly, by expected exchange rate movements, hence the inclusion of the exchange rate (ER). The latter is assumed to be sensitive to the level of domestic interest rates in relation to foreign rates and to the balance of payments on current account. We have, therefore, the relationship:

$$ER = ER\ (R/R_f, CB) \qquad (8.13)$$
$$+\ +$$

There is one implication emanating from (8.13) that is worth exploring at this juncture. So long as the money supply is entirely credit-driven and demand-determined, the exchange rate regime is of absolutely no consequence in determining whether money and credit are endogenous or not (Arestis and Eichner, 1988). The importance of this implication can only be fully appreciated when the analysis pursued in this section is contrasted to the GNS approach. The latter replaces Equation (8.13) by Equation (8.14):

$$ER = ER\ (M/M_f, R/R_f, ...) \qquad (8.14)$$
$$-\ -$$

which determines the exchange rate by combining the monetary approach to the balance of payments with purchasing power parity (PPP) theory and the quantity theory of money. In (8.14) ER is related to the ratio of domestic money supply (M) to foreign or world money supply (M_f) and the ratio of domestic to foreign interest rates. Clearly, other variables should appear in Equation (8.14) but are ignored for simplicity, for their absence does not affect the argument in any way whatsoever. We note that the sign of (R/R_f) in (8.14) is opposite to what one might expect and, indeed, opposite to the positive sign of Equation (8.13). This is because in Equation (8.14) an increase in the rate of interest (R) will raise the demand for money which will necessitate an increase in prices to clear the market. The latter, via the PPP, leads to a depreciation of the currency. More importantly, though, under a flexible exchange rate system, ER changes to clear the money market and M is treated as exogenous. Under a fixed exchange rate system, it is ER that is exogenously determined and M is then endogenous. In terms of the endogeneity of the money supply as presented in this section, it makes no difference what exchange rate regime is in operation: money would always be credit-driven and demand-determined, regardless of the prevailing exchange rate regime.

The relationships postulated in this chapter become Equations 13–26 in Table 4.1 once the variables are transformed in the usual way; that is, when all the variables are taken as differences between actual and secular rates of growth.

8.5 THE POST-KEYNESIAN CONSENSUS ON MONEY, CREDIT AND FINANCE

The model which has just been developed contains certain important elements which are acceptable to most, if not all, post-Keynesians. In this sense, this model can be said to encompass a 'consensus' of views in post-Keynesian thinking on money, credit and finance. There are five aspects to this 'consensus'.

The first aspect refers to the view that money is credit-driven and demand-determined. Loans constitute the majority of money. The determinants of loans as identified above become, therefore, of paramount importance as the ultimate determinants of the money stock. Thus money is created as a by-product of the loans provided by the banking system.

The act of money creation is also an act of expenditure and (therefore) of income creation ... That is all there is to it. Apart from decisions to spend out of income at a certain rate, there is no separate or additional process requiring equilibration between the 'supply' and 'demand' for money. (Godley and Cripps, 1983, pp. 82–3)

In this view, credit money is a requirement of the economic system. It is not a parasite on the system and it certainly is not a veil! It ought to be emphasized here that the foregoing analysis is not just applicable to the UK financial framework. Although the financial institutions of other countries may be different they do, none the less, exhibit the same basic properties identified in this chapter as being responsible for the endogeneity of the money stock. In other European countries firms are indebted permanently to banks and rely on them for the provision of borrowed financial resources (Lavoie, 1985, p. 68). The North American financial system also falls very much within this institutional framework and mould of analysis (Wojnilower, 1980, p. 289).

The second aspect of the 'consensus' is that commercial banks are rarely constrained in terms of their reserves. Once commercial banks have created credit money, they can obtain the reserves required from the central bank. When the commercial banking sector is in need of more reserves it can increase its borrowings from the central bank at the discount rate set by the latter. Commercial banks decide upon the amount of loans they are ready to grant and worry later about their liquidity position. It is impossible for the central bank not to provide the required reserves, albeit at a penalty in the form of a higher discount rate. The increased cost of borrowing for the banks is passed over to their customers who are not expected to reduce their demand for bank loans, given that the demand for credit is not sensitive to changes in interest rates (except, of course, when these changes are so large as to disrupt all financial markets). Thus, money supply is endogenous at the rate of interest fixed by the monetary authorities. Post-Keynesians agree that the central bank cannot directly control the stock of money, this being determined by previously made decisions on credit and loans. It does not make much sense, therefore, to attempt the control of an aggregate which is a consequence rather than a cause. The endogenous character of the money supply implies that there can never be 'an excess supply of money'. The recipients of such an 'excess' would use it to diminish their liabilities so that the 'excess' is extinguished as a result of the repayment of bank debts. This argument explains the post-Keynesian contention that a government deficit and a favourable balance of payments have no direct effect on the creation of money. Any money thus created is completely compensated for by an equivalent reduction in credit money (but see Chick, 1986 and Goodhart, 1989). A very good example here is the 1981 civil service strike in the UK when 'The massive distortions in the monthly flow of cash between the public and private sectors were quite largely offset by opposite fluctuations in bank borrowing by the private sector, primarily by companies' (Goodhart, 1984, p. 264). A further implication here is that since the supply of finance is not normally expected to be a constraint, the emphasis on the 'finance motive' (Davidson, 1978; Asimakopulos, 1983) 'has been greatly exaggerated; that it is much ado about very little' (Rousseas, 1986, p. 44).

The third element of the 'consensus' relates to recent financial innovations, especially the 'liability-management' aspect. It is generally agreed that these innovations have affected the endogeneity of the money supply in two ways. First, banks are now more able to accommodate changes in the demand for loans with less-frequent use of the central bank penal facilities for reserves. Thus, the process of financial innovations has made it increasingly more difficult for the monetary authorities to monitor developments in financial and money markets (Goodhart, 1986; Podolski, 1986). Secondly, the expansion of bank lending has been the predominant force in banking developments, an aspect of considerable importance, given that bank lending constitutes the driving force of the money stock.

The fourth aspect of the 'consensus' is that once it is recognized that money is credit-driven and demand-determined, the prevailing exchange rate regime is of no consequence at all in terms of money supply determination. This is in sharp contrast to the GNS view that under a flexible exchange rate system the money supply is fully controlled by the monetary authorities, whereas under a fixed exchange rate system this control is lost.

The fifth constituent element of the 'consensus' refers to interest rate control. Whilst the money supply is not under the control of the monetary authorities, interest rates *are* controlled by the central bank. This occurs through discount rate adjustments or through the rate of intervention on the open market by the central bank. Rates of interest as they are determined abroad, the exchange rate of its foreign currency reserves or any such external variables, are viewed as important factors which the central bank takes into consideration when it decides to adjust its discount rate to affect market interest rates.

8.6 CONCLUDING REMARKS

This chapter has shown that in post-Keynesian economic analysis money is the outcome of credit creation. It is a residual and as such cannot be the *cause* of changes in any economic magnitudes (Lavoie, 1984; Moore, 1979a, 1979b). Bank lending to the private sector is essentially demand-determined, with the monetary authorities having little means of influencing it. But perhaps more importantly, this chapter has provided theoretical backing to the Kaleckian view that money is primarily credit money, created by the banking system in response to the demand for loans (Kalecki, 1971a; see also Myrdal, 1939).[4] The money supply increases or decreases as the result of increases or decreases in commercial bank lending. In this way, the post-Keynesian position on money, credit and finance is related to the view that sees money as essentially 'command over resources and hence at the root of class division. We see it as capital-money, the possession of which or the access to which is the preliminary condition for starting a private production initiative' (De Vroey, 1984, p. 387).

The discussion in this chapter completes the analysis that underpins the relationships postulated in Table 4.1. What remains to be explained, however, is the contention, touched upon in Chapter 4, that one other aspect of post-Keynesian analysis is its emphasis on dynamics and history in the study of real economic systems. This calls for a detailed discussion of growth dynamics and business cycles, which is what Chapter 9 is designed to provide.

NOTES

1. Minsky's (1982) 'financial instability' hypothesis is firmly based on the premiss elucidated in the text and also on the proposition that 'financial instability is a normal evolutionary outcome of periods of financial and economic tranquility' (Minsky, 1990, p. 393). Dow and Earl (1982, chs 11–12) utilize this hypothesis in an attempt to show how financial crises are produced by the workings of a free financial system and, indeed, how intervention by the monetary authorities can mitigate them.
2. Minsky (1990) refers to a number of incidents in the USA during the 1980s when the monetary authorities offered lender-of-last-resort facilities for precisely the reasons mentioned in the text: to prevent insolvency of the fragile financial system and ensure 'orderly conditions' in financial markets. In this case the authorities were more successful in their function as 'lender of last resort' than as controllers of the money stock.
3. Keynes (1930) was very sceptical about the extent to which these facilities were actually used and whether they were readily available.
4. When Kaleckian monetary theory is viewed in this way, the importance of the tension between the followers of Kalecki and Keynes, referred to by Eichner in Arestis and Skouras (1985, p. xiii), is substantially reduced.

9. Growth Dynamics and Business Cycles Theories

9.1 INTRODUCTION

Post-Keynesian economic analysis is concerned with an economic system that is expanding over time in the context of history. The study of growth dynamics, therefore, is of paramount importance. The study of the cyclical behaviour of the economy is also of immense concern to post-Keynesians and gives rise to the business cycles aspect of post-Keynesian economics. This chapter concentrates on both these aspects.

Growth dynamics in the post-Keynesian mould of analysis is based on Harrod's (1939, 1948) fundamental equation of the rate of growth of national income as modified to incorporate the possibility of varying propensities to save out of different types of income. Business cycles theory in the post-Keynesian tradition, starts from the fundamental assumption that cycles are inherent in capitalist economies. Business cycles are treated as endogenous phenomena, with exogenous shocks viewed as merely accentuating an underlying endogenous instability. Central to both growth and business cycles theories is capital accumulation, expectations and distributional effects. We begin our analysis of these phenomena with growth dynamics and then turn our attention to business cycles.

9.2 GROWTH DYNAMICS

One of the contentions of post-Keynesian economic analysis is the proposition that growth is tightly linked to distribution, pricing and capital accumulation. We have discussed these three aspects of post-Keynesian economics and very obviously the next step should be the study of their relationship with growth dynamics. We begin, however, with Harrod's growth model because post-Keynesian growth models are based on this particular framework.

9.2.1 Harrod's Growth Model

Early contributors to the development of post-Keynesian economics emphasized the fact that Keynesian economics, with its concentration on under-employment conditions, ignored the problems of long-run growth and the role of capital accumulation in this process. Harrod (1939) attempted to fill this gap by placing and extending Keynes's model into a dynamic setting. Harrod propounded the view that, to move from Keynes's static model of analysis to a dynamic situation, income should be growing, which implies that planned investment would be growing and also savings to match it. Harrod's reformulation of Keynes is based on two behavioural relationships.

The first is that net saving during any period of time is a constant proportion of the income received during that period; denoting net savings with the symbol S, we may write:

$$S_t = sY_t \qquad (9.1)$$

It should be noted that this relationship refers to actual rather than intended magnitudes. It relates actual saving as a proportion to actual income. This implies that actual and intended saving are equal and that actual and expected income are equal too. It then follows that any discrepancy between intended saving and investment is due entirely to investment not turning out as planned. Consequently, one has to explain what determines planned investment which requires the second assumption referred to above. It is assumed that planned investment (I) depends on changes in the level of income (ΔY), thus alluding to the accelerator principle of investment behaviour:

$$I_t = v(\Delta Y_t) \qquad (9.2)$$

where v is the capital/output ratio.

Furthermore, when planned investment happens to be equal to actual saving we can have:

$$sY_t = v(\Delta Y_t)$$

Growth Dynamics and Business Cycles Theories 207

from which

$$(\Delta Y_t/Y_t) = (s/v) \qquad (9.3)$$

and since $(\Delta Y_t/Y_t) = G_w$, that is, what Harrod called the 'warranted' rate of growth (to be distinguished from G, the actual growth rate), we derive:

$$G_w = (s/v) \qquad (9.4)$$

Growth in this view will proceed at a 'warranted' rate defined as the ratio of the propensity to save to the required capital/output ratio, since this is the rate at which investment and savings are equal over time. In other words, G_w will be maintained as long as producers find that the increase in output they have planned is exactly matched by an increase in aggregate demand.

There are two observations to be made at this juncture. First, the 'warranted' growth path is unstable, for any discrepancy of the actual growth rate from it would take the economy further away from the 'warranted' growth rate. Consider the case of $G < G_w$ or $s/v_a < s/v$ where v_a is the actual capital/output ratio. In this case $v_a > v$, which means that the actual ratio of capital to output is greater than that which is required; or what amounts to the same thing, the volume of investment actually undertaken to produce the current increase in output is greater than the amount of investment required. Firms will be demanding less equipment and materials than are currently available, and this will have a depressing effect on output through the usual multiplier and accelerator effects. This will make the shortfall of G in relation to G_w still greater, so that the actual growth rate, far from returning to equality with the 'warranted' growth rate, will deviate from it even more. *Mutatis mutandis*, when G exceeds G_w, in which case v_a will be smaller than v, the amount of investment actually undertaken is smaller than the amount required to produce the current increase in output. Firms will now be demanding more equipment and materials than are available. The effort to satisfy this demand will cause output to rise faster than previously. The actual growth rate will deviate even further from G_w. The 'warranted' growth path is fundamentally unstable in the sense that deviations of the actual from the warranted growth rate would not disappear automatically, but would cause even larger disparities.

The second observation requires the notion of the 'natural' rate of growth (G_n). This is defined as that rate which is consistent with full employment of labour, allowing for increases in productivity due to technological improvements. It thus depends crucially on the rate of technological progress and on demographic factors, both of which are seen here as exogenously determined. The 'warranted' rate of growth depends on entirely different factors, as explained above. The two rates, G_n and G_w, therefore cannot be expected to coincide automatically; if they ever do, it would be sheer coincidence. When $G_n > G_w$ an economy will be growing at an ever-increasing rate of unemployment, and when $G_n < G_w$ full employment will prevail but with accelerating inflation. It is clear, then, that the 'warranted' growth rate bears no necessary relation to the 'natural' growth rate (G_n) which would ensure full employment. Consequently, in a free-market capitalist economy there would be no automatic tendency towards a full-employment 'equilibrium' growth path. It is conceivable, however, to incorporate in Harrod's model a government sector whose expenditure and taxes can be manipulated to adjust s in such a way as to keep G_w equal to G_n permanently and a monetary authority which can operate on s and v so that both types of policy could potentially attain full employment and maximum growth as allowed by the productive potential of the economy. It is fair to note at this stage, however, that whilst Harrod acknowledged the logical possibility of this case, he was still sceptical of the extent of such adjustments (Harrod, 1973). Consequently, Harrod's extension of the *General Theory* to account for the case of a 'growing' economy is very much within Keynes's economic analysis.

9.2.2 Early Post-Keynesian Growth Models

Post-Keynesian growth dynamics theory has evolved from Harrod's extension of Keynes's analysis. In order to demonstrate this proposition we may begin with the expression derived above (section 5.4, Equation 5.12):

$$(\pi/Y) = [(1/(1-c_c)](I/Y) \qquad (9.5)$$

which can be rewritten in the following form (letting $1 - c_c = s_c$):

$$(\pi/Y) = (1/s_c)(I/Y) \qquad (9.6)$$

Furthermore, by simple manipulation of this expression we may derive:

$$(\pi/Y) = (1/s_c)(I/Y)(K/K) = (1/s_c)(K/Y)(I/K) \qquad (9.7)$$

In this expression (K/Y) is equal to v in 'equilibrium' circumstances. That is to say, the required capital/output ratio (v) is equal to the actual capital/output in these situations. Also, for long-run 'equilibrium' and with the ratio of capital to labour assumed given, as determined by technological conditions, the capital stock must grow at the same rate as the supply potential of the economy. The rate of growth of capital stock is determined by the level of investment in relation to the existing stock, that is (I/K). Consequently, a necessary condition for steady growth at full employment is that the rate of growth of capital stock (I/K) is equal to the natural rate of growth (G_n).

We can now write the ratio (π/Y) as:

$$(\pi/Y) = (1/s_c)(v)(G_n) \qquad (9.8)$$

Thus, steady-state growth at full employment is linked to distribution and capital accumulation. The distribution of income is determined by the savings propensity of capitalists, the natural growth rate and the required capital/output ratio.

Dividing through by v in the last expression we arrive at:

$$(\pi/K) = (1/s_c)(G_n) \qquad (9.9)$$

which is the steady-state rate of profit. Thus, using the assumption that G_n is exogenously determined, it is clear from this expression that the rate of profit in a state of balanced growth is determined by the propensity to save out of profit income, a result which was noted by Kalecki (1971a), of course. If we assume further that $s_c = 1$, that is, that capitalists do not consume, the last expression collapses to:

$$(\pi/K) = G_n \qquad (9.10)$$

which suggests that the rate of profit is equal to the natural rate of growth.

This analysis proposes that s in $G_n = (s/v)$ is no longer a constant. This is so, since we can rewrite S as follows. First, recall that:

$$S = s_w W + s_c \pi \tag{9.11}$$

or, since $W = Y - \pi$,

$$S = s_w(Y - \pi) + s_c \pi \tag{9.12}$$

or

$$S = (s_c - s_w)\pi + s_w Y \tag{9.13}$$

and dividing through by Y:

$$S/Y = s = (s_c - s_w)(\pi/Y) + s_w \tag{9.14}$$

and if we assume that $s_w = 0$, the last expression becomes:

$$S/Y = s = s_c(\pi/Y) \tag{9.15}$$

Clearly now, there can be a ratio of profits to income (π/Y) which ensures that s is such that equality between G_n and G_w is achieved. Kaldor (1956, p. 97) argues that within certain limits the appropriate value for π/Y can in fact materialize: 'the "warranted" and the "natural" rates of growth are not independent of one another; if profit margins are flexible, the former will adjust itself to the latter through a consequential change in π/Y'. Kalecki, of course, had already anticipated a lot of these arguments in the mid-1930s (see, for example, Kalecki, 1971a, ch. 1).

The expression $(\pi/K) = (1/s_c)G_n$ can be contrasted to the expression derived by Pasinetti (see above, section 5.4); that is, $(\pi/K) = 1/(1 - c_c')G_n$ where $(1 - c_c')$ is the propensity to save by capitalists out of their profit (workers are also assumed to receive profits). The two expressions are very similar, with one very important exception, which is that in the expression $(\pi/K) = (1/s_c)G_n$ the propensity to save out of wages is assumed to be zero. No such assumption is employed in the Pasinetti (1962) expression. The rate of profit depends on the natural rate of growth and on the propensity to save out of capitalists' profits. Most importantly, though, it is independent of the propensity to save out of wages and workers' profits.

Robinson's (1956, 1962a) contributions are very much related to this analysis and since they had a major influence on post-Keynesian growth theory, we refer to them at some length. What is particularly important about this work is the insistence that growth theory, like any other aspect of economics, should be concerned with *real* economies as they operate in actual/historical time, rather than in timeless equilibrium of the GNS type. The analysis so far in this section has concerned itself with the conditions under which long-run steady-state situations can arise. It suggests that changes in income distribution can be so powerful as to produce and maintain full employment in the long run. Robinson's work accepts that distribution along with investment and technical change are important determinants of growth but does not agree with the argument that changes in income distribution would produce full employment. She was very much influenced by the view that 'the rate of growth at a given time is a phenomenon rooted in past economic, social and technological developments ... This is, indeed, very different from the approach of purely mechanistic theories' (Kalecki, 1971a, p. 183). Robinson and Kalecki believed that long-run steady-state situations have no independent entity except as imaginary states of affairs which can be fruitfully utilized as theoretical benchmarks. Of paramount importance for Robinson are the 'determinants of growth', with investment and technical progress being predominant. Of the two, investment is given the leading role. Investment is, in fact, viewed by Robinson as the engine of growth.

To show the importance of investment in this framework we use Figure 9.1. The relationship AA' plots different profit rates for different rates of accumulation which emanate from the relationship which can be deduced from (9.8) where we divide through by v and remember that $G_n = I/K$, to give us:

$$(\pi/K) = (1/s_c)(I/K) \tag{9.16}$$

Note that the slope of AA' depends on the propensity to save by capitalists. Profitability here is influenced by capital accumulation, in that once investment has been undertaken a certain rate of profit will follow. The relationship II' is Robinson's (1962a) 'investment function' which depicts investment 'as a function of the rate of profit that induces it' (p. 48). It can be thought of as being derived from Kalecki's (1971a, p. 6) proposition that 'The volume of investment orders ... at a given time depends on the anticipated net profitability' and that 'The anticipated growth profitability ... may be esti-

Figure 9.1

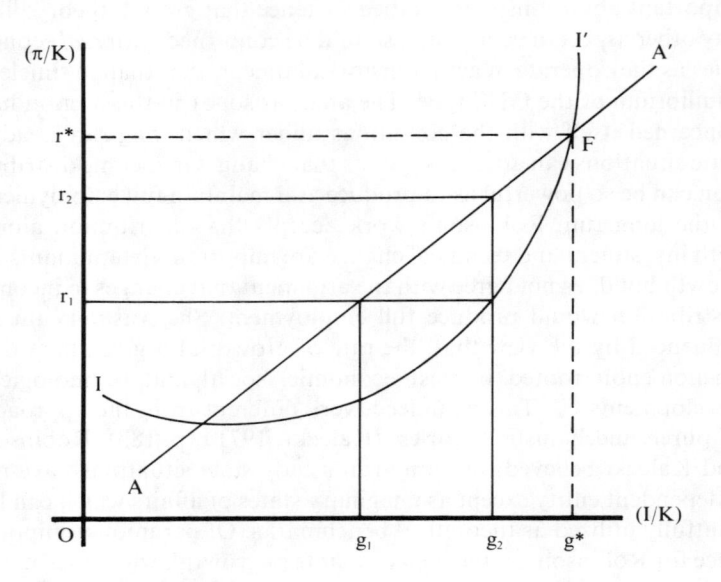

Source: Robinson (1962a)

mated from the actual gross profitability of the existing plant'. We thus have a relationship between accumulation and profitability where the causation is from the latter to the former. The slope of the II' relationship reflects the principle of increasing risk associated with larger levels of investment in relation to total capital. The position of the II' relationship depends on economic as well as non-economic arguments. Robinson (1962a, p. 37) is very clear on this score: 'To attempt to account for what makes the propensity to accumulate high or low we must look into historical, political, and psychological characteristics of the economy'. Keynes's 'animal spirits', of course, are expected to influence the position of this relationship. So the relationship will lie to the left of II' when firms are less active and to the right of II' when firms are more enterprising, given all the other factors which influence the 'investment function'. Financial variables also affect it. Lower interest rates and less-stringent credit conditions would cause the relationship to be to the right of II'; higher interest rates and more stringent conditions would position it to the left of II'. As demonstrated in Chapter 6, private investments are financed to a considerable extent out of retained profits. Their size, therefore, would affect the position of II'. The larger they are the further to the right II' would be; similarly, the relationship would be further to the left the smaller the volume of retained profits (Asimakopulos, 1971, pp. 385–7).

Actual rates of accumulation such as g_1 lead to a realized rate of profit r_1. But this implies expected profitability of r_1 which leads to g_2 rate of capital accumulation. This in turn produces r_2 rate of profitability, so that the economy would tend to move to point F. Similarly, for an initial rate of accumulation which might exceed g^* there would be opposite pressures at work which would take the economy to F. At g^* the economy is in a steady state. If it can be assumed also that full employment prevails, the relationship $(\pi/K) = (1/s_c)(G_n)$ gives us the link between the rate of profit, thriftiness and the natural rate of growth.

The treatment of technical progress in post-Keynesian growth economics follows Robinson (1956) who argues that it is entirely endogenous. Technical change is seen as the result of entrepreneurial initiative and drive to search for cheaper and more efficient methods of production. Kaldor (1960a, 1966) also argues that technical progress is both the cause and the result of economic growth. This analysis is based on the notion of circular causation: a faster rate of growth leads to a higher rate of technical progress which in turn influences the rate of growth too. Cornwall (1979, p. 85) puts it very aptly when he argues: 'Technical progress does not fall like manna from heaven, as in neoclassical analysis, but is the result of deliberate, purposive action induced by economic events at each stage of this sequence.'

A more recent development within post-Keynesian growth economics which is more comprehensive than the cases considered in this chapter is the contribution by Rowthorn (1981), and we turn our attention to it in the next section.

9.2.3 A Recent Post-Keynesian Model

In this section we follow Rowthorn's (1981) model closely, which synthesizes the ideas expounded above along with demand considerations within the confines of a single framework. This model concerns itself with steady-state growth. Production requires labour and capital equipment and there is only one type of good used both for personal consumption and as fixed capital. Marginal costs of production are constant until full capacity is reached, after which they begin to rise. Consequently, the marginal product of labour (MP_L) is also constant up to full capacity, and then starts to rise.

We may let Y stand for gross output that can be produced on available equipment and write:

$$Y = MP_L.E \qquad (9.17)$$

where E stands for employment. We also let Y^m be the maximum output that can be produced by available fixed capital (K) so that:

$$Y^m = (1/k)K \qquad (9.18)$$

where k is the 'capital coefficient' that tells us the amount of fixed capital required per unit of output at full capacity. Furthermore, the ratio CU, defined as:

$$CU = Y/Y^m \qquad (9.19)$$

is used throughout as an index of capacity utilization; clearly, when CU = 1 full capacity is achieved.

Pricing in this model follows the mark-up hypothesis, so that when there is excess capacity we have:

$$P = (1 + \beta)MC \qquad (9.20)$$

where P is the price of output, MC is the marginal cost and β is a constant. Equivalently, we may have:

$$(P - MC)/P = m \qquad (9.21)$$

where $m = \beta/(1 + \beta)$, which is Kalecki's 'degree of monopoly'. This pricing equation is valid up to full capacity, but beyond it the mark-up is assumed to rise to eliminate any excess demand. What is therefore suggested here is that up to full capacity changes in demand would affect output only, and above full capacity prices would be affected. Therefore, above full capacity (9.21) should be replaced by

$$(P - MC)/P \geqslant m \tag{9.22}$$

which is interpreted to mean that at full capacity prices are not determined by the degree of monopoly but by demand conditions.

Furthermore, if workers do not pay taxes and if there are no social security contributions, the real wage is then equal to the real cost of labour to employers. We may, therefore, write MC as:

$$MC = (Pw)/MP_L \tag{9.23}$$

where w is the real product wage rate. We may now substitute (9.23) into (9.21) and rearrange to give us:

$$w = (1 - m) MP_L \tag{9.24}$$

below full capacity; similarly, from (9.22) we may have:

$$w \leqslant (1 - m) MP_L \tag{9.25}$$

at full capacity.

These last two expressions indicate that since MP_L and m are constant, real wages are independent of demand at levels below full capacity. Any change in demand would affect output and not the real wage. At full capacity, since output cannot rise, any increase in demand would be translated into increased prices and lower real wages.

We may now proceed to derive an expression for the rate of profit. Total *net* profits are defined in the usual way, that is:

$$\pi = Y - W - D - T_\pi \tag{9.26}$$

where the variables are as before, with the exception of D which stands for depreciation and T_π, the total amount of tax on profits. We make the following assumptions on D and T_π:

$$D = \delta K \tag{9.27}$$

and

$$T_\pi = t_\pi K \tag{9.28}$$

It is assumed in this way that a constant proportion δ of fixed capital depreciates every year, and the amount of tax on profits is proportional to fixed capital. It can also be assumed that technical progress speeds up depreciation and thus we can write:

$$\delta = d_0 + d_1 \Omega \tag{9.29}$$

where Ω is labour-saving technical progress, and d_1 is the coefficient that shows how much of the existing equipment becomes obsolete due to technical progress.

Combining Equations (9.26)–(9.29) and dividing through by K we arrive at:

$$\pi/K = (Y - W)/K - (d_0 + d_1\Omega) - t_\pi \tag{9.30}$$

where π/K is, of course, the rate of profit. We note that $W = wE$, that is, the total real wage bill which can be substituted in (9.30) to give:

$$\pi/K = (Y - wE)/K - (d_0 + d_1\Omega) - t_\pi \tag{9.31}$$

Making use of (9.17), (9.18) and (9.24), and as long as we concern ourselves with less than full capacity levels of CU, along with the necessary rearrangements in the resulting equation, we can obtain:

$$\pi/K = (m/k)CU - (d_0 + d_1\Omega) - t_\pi \tag{9.32}$$

which is the rate of profit at less than full capacity. At full capacity (9.32) should be written as:

$$\pi/K \geqslant (m/k)CU - (d_0 + d_1\Omega) - t_\pi \tag{9.33}$$

The last two relationships define in Figure 9.2 what Rowthorn (1981, p. 9) has labelled as the 'profits curve'. The 'profits curve' stipulates the amount of net profits created for different levels of capacity utilization. It has a positive slope of (m/k) below full capacity but it is vertical at full capacity. It is, in fact, the mirror-image of the cost curve. Events which result in lowering the cost curve shift the 'profits curve' upwards so that for given levels of capacity utilization the profit rate will be higher. Where exactly the

Figure 9.2

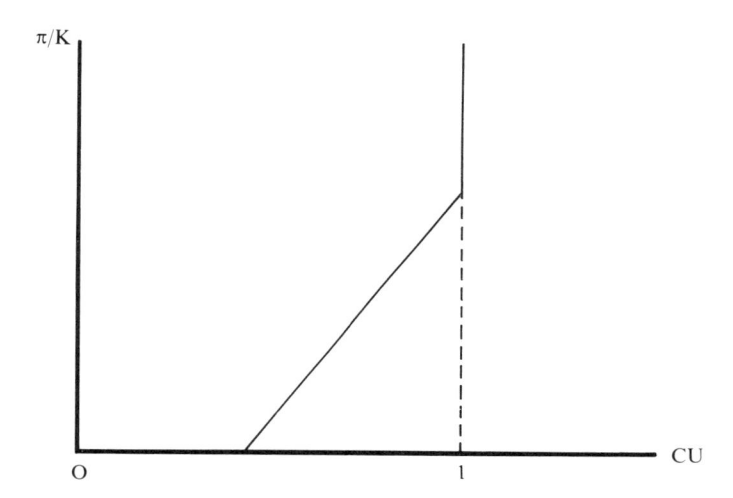

[Figure: Graph with π/K on vertical axis and CU on horizontal axis. A line rises from CU=1 point on the horizontal axis, going up and to the right, then becomes vertical at a point beyond 1.]

Source: Rowthorn (1981)

economy will find itself on this curve depends on the level of demand. Consequently, the next step in the argument is to stipulate how demand is determined.

The determination of demand begins with the condition that investment and savings must be equal, so that profits are actually realized. We thus have:

$$I = S \tag{9.34}$$

An important assumption made at this juncture is that the banking system provides the necessary amount of credit at fixed interest rates determined by the monetary authorities. Investment and savings are completely immune from any interest rate influences. The economy is closed but there is a government sector that borrows funds to finance its own consumption. Furthermore, it is assumed that investment expressed as a fraction of K depends on current profitability, capacity utilization and technical progress. When the relationship is linearized we have:

Figure 9.3

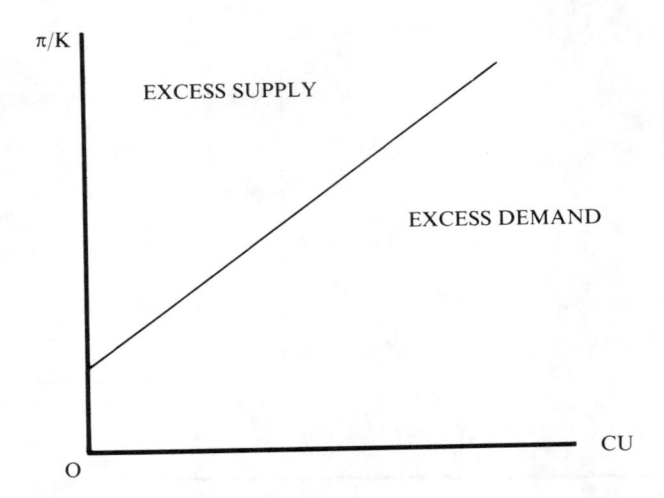

```
π/K
│
│        EXCESS SUPPLY              /
│                                  /
│                                 /
│                                /
│                               /   EXCESS DEMAND
│                              /
│                             /
│                            /
│                           /
│                          /
│                         /
│                        /
│                       /
│_____/_____ CU
O
```

Source: Rowthorn (1981)

$$I/K = i_c(\pi/K) + i_u CU + i_\Omega \Omega \qquad (9.35)$$

It is worth noting at this stage that the coefficient i_Ω registers the impact on investment of technical progress over and above that required for replacement (see Equation 9.29 above). Savings are written as follows:

$$S = s_c \pi - B \qquad (9.36)$$

where the workers do not save and a part, B, of total savings is borrowed by the government. Dividing through (9.36) by K and upon utilizing (9.34) and (9.35) we have:

$$\pi/K = (i_u/s_c - i_c)CU + (B/K)/(s_c - i_c) + i_\Omega \Omega(s_c - i_c) \qquad (9.37)$$

Equation (9.37) now defines what Rowthorn (1981, p. 12) calls the 'realization curve' which would give us the realized rate of profit for given levels of capacity utilization. This relationship is depicted in Figure 9.3. Above the 'realization curve' where for given CUs higher realized profit rates are forthcoming, excess supply is inevitable. Similarly, below the 'realization curve' for given CUs realized profit rates are lower than otherwise, so that excess demand prevails. We note that the slope of the 'realization curve' is positive on the assumption that $s_c > i_c$ – otherwise the slope would be negative when $s_c < i_c$.

When Figures 9.2 and 9.3 are brought together we obtain Figure 9.4. The economy would always be on the profits curve, since the latter portrays the relation between output and costs at different levels of capacity utilization. For profits to be realized the economy must also lie on the realization curve. We portray the excess-capacity case and the full-capacity case in Figures 9.4 (a) and 9.4 (b) respectively, where such realization of profits occurs at points E^a and E^b. These points are stable in that any displacement from them generates forces which take the economy back to them. Any displacement to the right of the two points along the profits curve, for example, implies excess supply which generates more savings than investment and the economy is pulled back to E^a and E^b. Similarly, any downward displacement along the profits curve causes excess demand with more investment than savings being created, so that the economy moves back to the two points of rest where the profit rate is realized. Shifts in the two curves occur for a number of reasons. In the case of the profits curve it would shift to the right if there were a fall in the degree of monopoly, an increase in the amount of capital required to produce a given output, higher taxes or faster depreciation due, for example, to technical progress. The profits curve would shift to the left if these changes were in the opposite directions to the ones just described. The realization curve would shift to the left if there were an increase in i_u (that is to say, a higher volume of investment is forthcoming at any given rate of profit or level of capacity utilization), a reduction in s_c (or the same higher consumption out of profits), or more borrowing from the private sector. Again, a rightward shift in the realization curve would occur if the changes just referred to were to be in the opposite direction.

In an attempt to illustrate the implication of the changes just considered, we examine the case where 'costs' rise, which of course causes the profits curve to shift downwards. Initially, the rate of profit will fall. So long as $s_c > i_c$ the reduction in profits causes savings to decrease more than investment, so that excess demand appears. In Figure 9.5 and in the case of full capacity excess demand

Figure 9.4

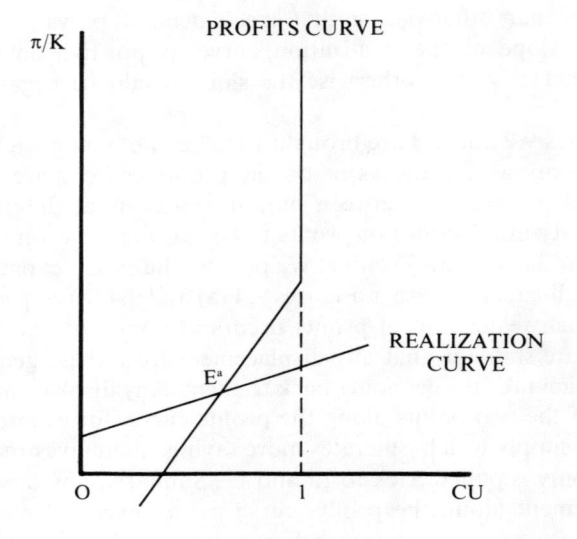

(a) excess capacity

[Graph with axes π/K (vertical) and CU (horizontal), showing PROFITS CURVE (steep, vertical at CU=1) and REALIZATION CURVE (upward sloping), intersecting at point E^a to the left of CU=1]

(b) full capacity

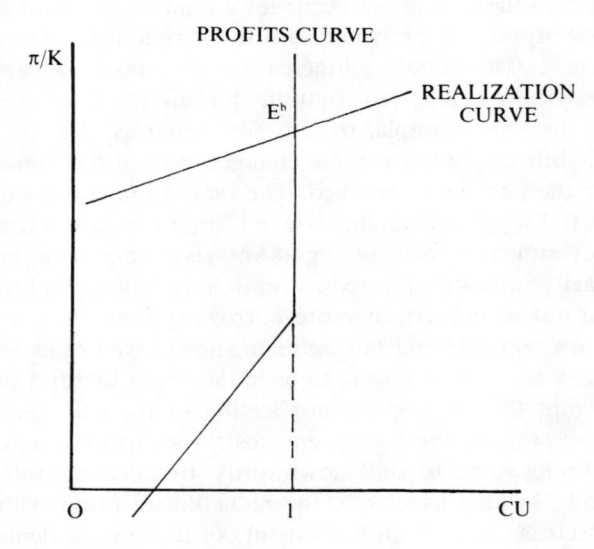

[Graph with axes π/K (vertical) and CU (horizontal), showing PROFITS CURVE (steep, vertical at CU=1) and REALIZATION CURVE (upward sloping), intersecting at point E^b at CU=1]

Source: Rowthorn (1981)

Figure 9.5

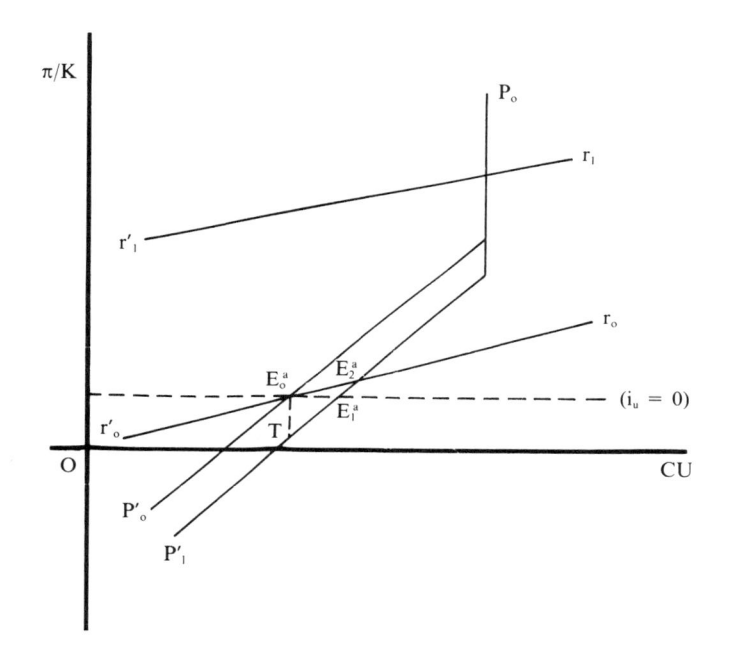

Source: Rowthorn (1981)

will raise prices and increase profits as well as savings and investment which return to their old positions. The rate of profit will be restored to its position prior to the change. In the excess capacity case, excess demand will cause output and profits to rise so that the economy will rest eventually at a point such as E_2^a where the profit rate and CU are higher than what they were at E_0^a before the initial change. The importance of the accelerator effect (i_u) in this sequence of events must be emphasized. It is responsible for the economy settling eventually at a point such as E_2^a where both the rate of profit and capacity utilization are higher than at E_0^a. We may note that if $i_u = 0$, $r_0'r_0$ would be vertical and the rate of profit would be the same before and after the shift in $P_0'P_0$. In all the cases considered above, whenever $i_u > 0$, and as long as the economy is at the excess capacity region, both (π/K) and (CU) would change. When full capacity is reached, shifts in the profits curve would not change anything. Shifts in the realization curve, however, would simply change (π/K) but not, of course, CU.

It is very important to note that higher wages in this model can induce a higher profit rate. We explain how this can come about with the help of Figure 9.5. We begin with E_0^a and assume that real wages increase. This shifts the profits curve from $P_0'P_0$ to $P_1'P_0$ and the economy to point T, where output is the same but the profit rate is lower. Workers' income has increased at the expense of profits. Workers do not save, so that the increase in worker consumption is the same as the capitalist decrease in profits. But since $s_c > i_c$, it follows that the capitalist marginal propensity to spend, that is, $[(1 - s_c) + i_c]$ would always be less than unity. It also follows that the sum of capitalist consumption and investment falls by a smaller amount than the increase in workers' consumption. Thus, total expenditure in the whole of the economy rises and excess demand appears. Output increases and the economy moves towards E_2^a. Capitalist consumption and investment at this point are greater than they are at E_0^a and it is this increase that makes possible the realization of a higher profit rate at E_2^a. Thus higher real wages do not realize profits directly. They facilitate such realization through their impact on economic expansion and through the subsequent increase in capitalist consumption and investment. It is the capitalist expenditure which realizes the profit rate, a point repeatedly made by Kalecki (see, for example, 1971a).

Technical progress shifts both curves. The profits curve shifts to the right because technical progress reduces the rate of profit at given levels of capacity utilization. The realization curve shifts to the left given that technical progress increases the rate of profit that can be realized for given levels of capacity utilization. Induced technical progress implies stronger effects on output and investment than otherwise, and a positive link between real wages and growth. Productivity improvements emanating from technical changes would always ensure that growth, itself the result of technical progress, and real wages move in tandem. Clearly, therefore, the model predicts that greater demand benefits workers in that it induces growth, technical progress, productivity and, inevitably, higher real wages.

It is clear from our discussion in this section that growth is tightly linked to distribution and capital accumulation. Central to the analysis is investment based on profitability which generates savings in the form of retained profits which are vital for the finance of investment. The process of the creation of retained profits, though, cannot be understood without reference to pricing. Thus, within post-Keynesian economics all these aspects are tightly linked and interrelated. They are also linked with the cyclical movements of an economic system. The study of this particular theme requires an understanding of what we referred to earlier in this chapter as the area of *business cycles*. It is to these aspects that we turn our attention next.

9.3 BUSINESS CYCLES

The essential characteristic of post-Keynesian *business cycles* theory is that cycles are self-generating. The functioning of the capitalist system brings into play forces which produce cyclical movements. Relatively high levels of economic activity themselves eventually set in motion forces which produce a downward tendency of the level of economic activity that ultimately reaches relatively low income levels and vice-versa. These forces, such as the size of the propensity to save, shares of factors of production, accumulation/decumulation of capital, that materialize over the cycle are endogenous forces which are inherent in economic processes and are part of the normal functioning of the capitalist system. They are not exogenous forces in the form of external shocks as they are required to be in the case of the GNS theory examined earlier on in the book. The rest of this chapter considers and analyses a number of post-Keynesian models of business cycles, beginning with Kaldor's (1940) model.

9.3.1 Kaldor's Model

Kaldor's (1940) model is one of the most influential post-Keynesian *business cycles* models. It depends on the intersection of the non-linear savings and investment relationships and on their shifts caused by changes in capital stock, which create both stable and unstable 'equilibria'. We depict in Figure 9.6 how this can come about.

The non-linearity of these two relationships can be explained as

Figure 9.6

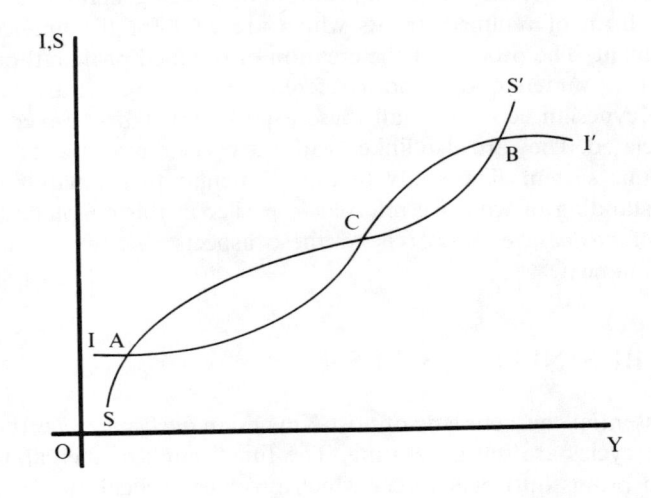

Source: Kaldor (1940)

follows. We may think of the cycle as divided into phases of relatively high, relatively low and 'normal' income. In the case of the investment relationship (II′) for both relatively high and relatively low levels of income it is roughly flat.

For relatively low income levels, investment is insensitive to income changes because of the existence of a great deal of excess capacity, so that an increase in income will scarcely affect investment. For relatively high income levels, the insensitivity of investment to income is due to rising costs of construction, increasing costs of borrowing and shortage of funds. The savings relationship (SS′) depicts a picture which is the reverse of that shown for investment. Savings are sensitive to changes in income at relatively low and high income levels, more so than they are at 'normal' income levels. As income falls to relatively low levels of income in recession, economic agents cut their savings drastically in an attempt to maintain their 'normal' standard of living. *Mutatis mutandis*, in the early stages of recovery economic agents increase their savings sharply to restore previous levels. Similarly, as income reaches high levels economic agents save not only a larger amount but also a larger proportion of their income. For at high levels of income the shift in the distribution of income towards profits and away from wages implies a steepening of the savings function in relation to its slope in the 'normal' range of income.

In Figure 9.6 there are three points where 'equilibrium', in the sense of equality of investment and savings, occurs: A and B, which are 'stable' points and point C which is 'unstable'. In deriving the two relationships in this figure, capital stock is assumed to be given. However, when capital stock is allowed to vary, as it should, the two relationships shift in the following manner. Savings is a direct function of the capital stock so that the higher the volume of capital stock, the higher the amount of saving at given levels of income. Investment, by contrast, is an inverse function of capital stock: for given levels of income, the greater the capital stock, the smaller the amount of investment. Kaldor argued that shifts in investment as a result of changes in capital stock should be expected to dominate. With these assumptions we proceed to explain how business cycles are generated within this model. Figure 9.7 depicts the various stages whereby this can come about.

We begin with Stage I, where it is assumed that the economy is at B; this point represents a level of income that is higher than what might be considered as the average level. Investment is correspondingly high, which causes a more rapid increase in the size of capital stock. A growing capital stock, however, produces a downward shift in the II' relationship and an upward shift in the SS' relationship. This implies that as the two relationships shift in the way just described, points B and C are brought closer together (as shown in Stage II) and eventually the two relationships become tangential at point (B + C), as shown in Stage III. Point (B + C), however, is unstable in a downward direction. As soon as a cyclical contraction is set in motion the level of income falls rapidly until a new stable 'equilibrium' point is reached such as A (Stage IV) which, of course, will be at a relatively low level of income. As with Stage I, forces will be generated to shift the relationships, but this time in the opposite direction. The investment relationship will shift upwards and the savings relationship downwards as in Stage V, bringing points A and C closer. Eventually the two curves become tangential so that in Stage VI, A and C coincide to give point (A + C). This point, though, is unstable in an upward direction. Once the cyclical expan-

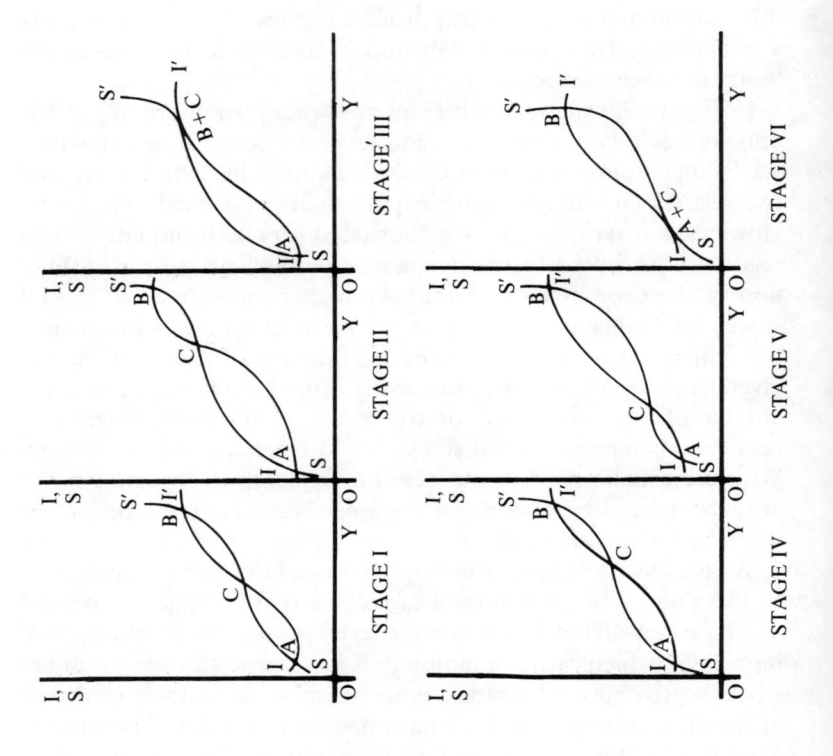

Figure 9.7

Source: Kaldor (1940)

sion commences it will raise the level of income until a new 'equilibrium' is reached at a high level of income, such as B in Stage I. Another cycle will then begin as explained above.

Kaldor's model has been subjected to a number of criticisms. The most obvious is that it relies on non-linearities for its cyclical behaviour. If the investment and savings relationships are linearly homogeneous the model cannot produce an endogenous cyclical pattern. The most important criticism directs attention to its total neglect of the labour market. Since it is built around the product market only, the bargaining position and strength of labour is completely ignored. This is an aspect which is predominant in Goodwin's (1967) theory of business cycles, which we discuss next.

9.3.2 Goodwin's Model

Goodwin's model is another contribution that belongs to the post-Keynesian tradition in that it relies heavily on the distributive shares to capital and labour to explain the economy's cyclical behaviour. Business cycles within this model are also an inherent part of the workings of a capitalist system. The model, however, suffers from the fact that it ignores 'demand' entirely.

There are two factors of production, labour and capital (plant and equipment) which are assumed to be 'homogeneous' and 'non-specific', so that differences in skills are ignored and factors can move from one production area to another without penalty. Output too is 'homogeneous' and 'non-specific'. Price changes are assumed away, so that quantities are taken as 'real' and, where appropriate, 'net' of depreciation. There is steady technical progress in terms of labour productivity due to better capital equipment.

With these assumptions the starting point of the theory is the proposition that the 'reserve army of unemployed' influences inversely the strength of workers. The stronger the working class is, the greater the chance that workers are able to demand and actually gain a higher share of wages in income. But then, the higher the share of wages in income the more of an adverse effect it would have on the rate of accumulation and thus on the employment rate. It is this interaction between the reserve army of unemployed, shares in the income distribution and accumulation that is responsible for the cyclical behaviour of a capitalist economic system.

Figure 9.8

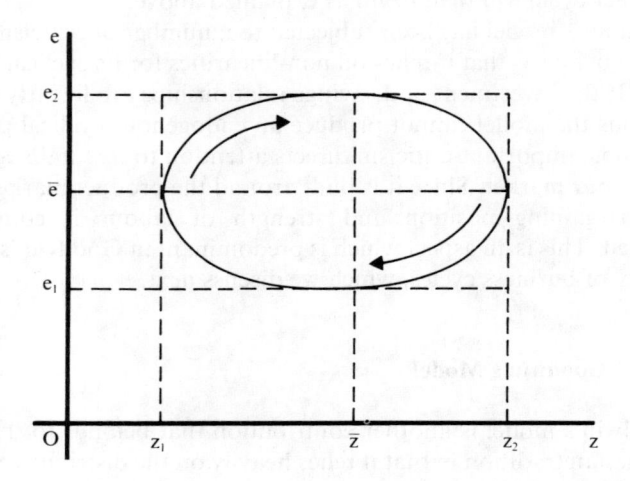

[Figure: A graph with vertical axis e and horizontal axis z. Points marked on vertical axis: e_2, $\bar{e}$, e_1. Points marked on horizontal axis: z_1, $\bar{z}$, z_2. A closed elliptical cycle is shown with arrows indicating counterclockwise motion, centered around $(\bar{z}, \bar{e})$.]

Source: Goodwin (1967) and Gadolfo (1980)

The analysis derives points like $\bar{e}$ (the ratio of labour employed to the labour force) and $\bar{z}$ (the workers' share) in Figure 9.8 which may be thought of as 'equilibrium' points. What is particularly interesting about these points is that they are neither stable or unstable; they are instead *neutral*. There is no tendency to return to them once the equilibrium is disturbed, but neither is there any tendency to depart from the 'equilibrium' position once achieved. The system is one that proceeds along a closed cycle in the e/z plane, returning to its initial position and repeating the cycle indefinitely. The cycles are not perfect circles either; their shape depends critically on the initial values of the two variables in question. Figures 9.8 and 9.9 tell the story very vividly. In Figure 9.8 and at point z_1, the workers' share is relatively low, so the profit share is relatively high. The employment rate is at $\bar{e}$ which is accompanied by a healthy growth rate, so that employment is pushed to point e_2. But at e_2 the workers' share is at $\bar{z}$ and the profit is squeezed. The growth rate deteriorates as a result, with employment falling to $\bar{e}$ and pushing the workers' share to its

Figure 9.9

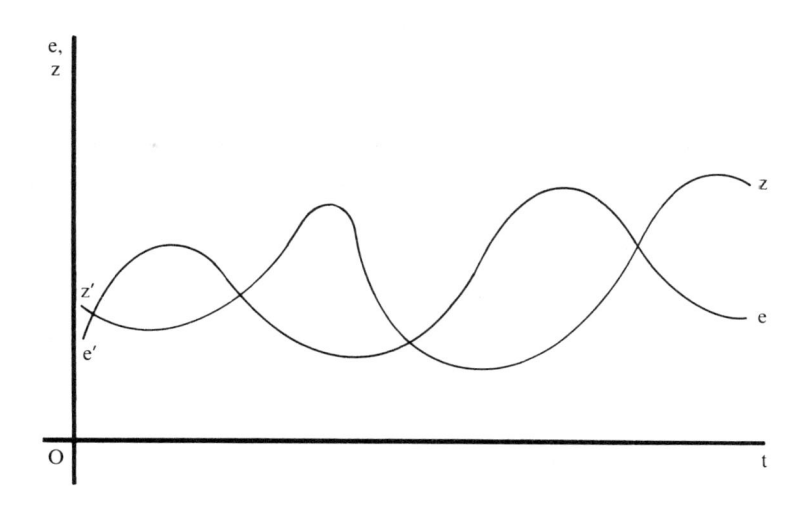

```
e,
z
            z'                                              z
              ⟩⟨                                    
            e'                                              e
O                                                           t
```

Source: Goodwin (1967) and Gadolfo (1980)

maximum z_2. Employment and output fall well below full employment. As they do so, however, productivity begins to rise which helps to improve profitability. A vigorous expansion in output and employment ensues which reduces substantially the reserve army of unemployed and thus strengthens the bargaining power of the labour force. This cyclical process is highlighted in Figure 9.9 which is a direct result of the analysis just outlined.

In Goodwin's model class struggle over distribution is confined exclusively to the labour market. There are no aggregate demand problems to worry about, since investment always adjusts automatically to clear the product market. Both investment and output are passive and accommodating variables. Control over production and investment decisions, which is a powerful weapon in the hands of capital in the class struggle, is entirely absent.[1]. By contrast, Kalecki's model of business cycles concentrates crucially on the behaviour of investment to explain fluctuations in economic activity. We discuss this model in the next section.

9.3.3 Kalecki's Model

Kalecki's (1971a) approach to business cycles is based on the notion that it is the cyclical behaviour of investment expenditures which is the major cause of macroeconomic fluctuations. Consequently, it should not be surprising to find that cycles in investment expenditure are the focus of analysis in Kalecki's theory. The simplifying assumption of a closed economy is maintained, along with the standard Kaleckian assumption that the marginal propensity to save out of wages is zero. The following two familiar expressions (where the symbols are as before):

$$Y_t = W_t + \pi_t \tag{9.38}$$

$$Y_t = C_{ct} + C_{wt} + I_t \tag{9.39}$$

enable us to solve for profits:

$$\pi_t = C_{ct} + I_t \tag{9.40}$$

Capitalist consumption is related to profits with a lag which we may express as:

$$C_{ct} = c_0 + c_1 \pi_{t-h} \tag{9.41}$$

so that by substitution of (9.41) into (9.40) yields:

$$\pi_t = c_0 + c_1 \pi_{t-h} + I_t \tag{9.42}$$

and by successive substitutions we get:

$$\pi_t = c_0 + c_1 c_0 + c_1 c_0^2 + \ldots + I_t + c_1 I_{t-h} + c_1 I_{t-2h} + \ldots \tag{9.43}$$

which is approximated to (see, for example, Sawyer, 1985, p. 55):

$$\pi_t = (I_{t-w} + c_0)/(1 - c_1) \tag{9.44}$$

from which

$$(d\pi_t/dt) = [1/(1 - c_1)] [(dI_{t-w}/dt)] \tag{9.45}$$

Growth Dynamics and Business Cycles Theories 231

What is particularly interesting about (9.44) is that it provides Kalecki's theory of profits. According to this theory the volume of profits is primarily determined by investment decisions taken in the past and the marginal propensity of capitalists to consume. And to quote Kalecki (1971a, p. 113) 'Thus, capitalists, as a whole, determine their own profits by the extent of their investment and personal consumption. In a way they are masters of their own fate.' These observations highlight the importance of the dynamic behaviour of investment in the determination of profits and national income.[2]

We may also derive the following expressions at this stage. Gross output (Q) is equal to Y plus aggregate indirect taxes, that is:

$$Q_t = Y_t + E_t \qquad (9.46)$$

where all the variables are in real terms. Now from the expression (9.38) and upon letting $W_t = w_0 + w_1 Y_t$ we may derive:

$$Y_t = (\pi + w_0)/(1 - w_1) \qquad (9.47)$$

so that by combining (9.47) and (9.46) we have:

$$Q_t = (\pi + w_0)/(1 - w_1) + E_t \qquad (9.48)$$

and

$$(dQ_t/dt) = [1/(1 - w_1)] (d\pi_t/dt) \qquad (9.49)$$

Obviously (9.45) and (9.49) together give us:

$$(dQ/dt) = [1/(1 - w_1)][1/(1 - c_1)](dI_{t-w}/dt) \qquad (9.50)$$

The most important aspect of the theory is, of course, investment. Following on from our discussion in Chapter 5, section 5.3, we recall that Kalecki considers total investment to be the sum of fixed investment (FI) and inventory investment (INI), or

$$I_{t+v} = (FI)_{t+v} + (INI)_{t+v} \qquad (9.51)$$

Fixed investment is essentially determined by three sets of factors: first, the available finance in the form of gross savings out of profits; secondly, the change in profits; and thirdly, the change in capital stock. The change in capital stock is assumed to be equal to gross investment minus depreciation (FI − D). We can then write:

$$FI_{t+r} = aS_t + b(d\pi/dt) - c(FI_t - D) + d \tag{9.52}$$

from which

$$FI_{t+r} + cFI_t = aS_t + b(d\pi/dt) + cD + d \tag{9.53}$$

which Kalecki approximates by:

$$FI_{t+v} = [a/(1 + c)]S_t + [b/(1 + c)](d\pi/dt) + [c/(1 + c)]D + d/(1 + c) \tag{9.54}$$

We may go back to (9.51) and note that since INI is made a function of the change in output, Equation (9.51) can now be written as:

$$I_{t+v} = [a/(1 + c)]S_t + b'(d\pi/dt) + c'D + e(dQ/dt) + d' \tag{9.55}$$

where $b' = b/(1 + c)$, $c' = c/(1 + c)$ and $d' = d/(1 + c)$. We may note that d' could be seen as standing for the rate of technical progress. In Equation (9.55) we have the *level* of economic activity (reflected in S) and *changes* in economic activity (reflected in $d\pi/dt$) affecting investment, where profits are proxying economic activity.

We may now proceed to modify Equation (9.55) as follows: we may add the condition that actual investment and actual savings are equal and also substitute in (9.55) Equations (9.45) and (9.50) to arrive at:

$$I_{t+v} = i_0 + i_1 I_t + i_2(dI_{t-w}/dt) + i_3 D \tag{9.56}$$

where $i_0 = d'$, $i_1 = a/(1 + c)$, $i_2 = [1/(1 - c_1)][b' + e(1 - w_1)]$, and $i_3 = c'$. When the system is at rest, or 'static', we then have $(dI/dt) = O$ and gross investment (I) is equal to depreciation (D). When this is accounted for in (9.56) we have:

$$D = i_0 + i_1 D + i_3 D \tag{9.57}$$

from which a condition on i_0 follows, that is to say:

$$i_o = D[(1 - a)/(1 + c)] \tag{9.58}$$

We may now obtain an equation for net investment by subtracting (9.57) from (9.56):

$$(I_{t+v} - D) = i_1(I_t - D) + i_2[d(I_{t-w} - D)/dt] \quad (9.59)$$

where $d(I_{t-w} - D)/dt = dI_{t-w}/dt$, since D is a constant.

Equation (9.59) is, in fact, a mixed difference-differential equation and is the one that features in Kalecki's attempt to explain the cyclical behaviour of a capitalist system. It is expressed in terms of investment rather than output, which clearly indicates the importance Kalecki ascribes to this variable. It is clear, none the less, that given the multiplier relationship, the path of output would follow the path of investment. We may also note at this juncture that Kalecki did not provide a formal mathematical solution to Equation (9.59) which would have enabled him to discuss the conditions for generating different types of cycles. What he insisted upon in this context was that $i_1 = a/(1 + c)$ was less than unity. With a being less than unity (which Kalecki thought was very likely) and c expected to be positive, it is plausible to argue that i_1 would be less than unity. In this case the i_1 term helps to dampen investment since the impact of the past on current investment is 'moderated' by this term.

We consider Figure 9.10 now in an attempt to explain the genesis of business cycles in Kalecki's model. The process begins at point A where net investment is zero, but with $d(I_{t-w} - D)/dt > 0$, which means, of course, that before point A is reached, at time $t - w$, investment was increasing towards the level of depreciation. From Equation (9.59) it is clear that I_{t+v} is positive so that net investment increases to reach point B. With $i_1 < 1$, $i_1(I_t - D)$ is lower than $(I_t - D)$ which tends to lower $(I_{t+v} - D)$ below $(I_t - D)$. On the other hand, $i_2.d(I_{t-w} - D)/dt$ is such that it tends to raise $(I_{t+v} - D)$ above $(I_t - D)$. What this suggests is that sooner or later the point will be reached where investment comes to a halt. This happens at point C. The system will creep along C to D depending on the length of lag w, and sooner or later, depending on the length of lag v, it will move from D to E. At E $i_2.d(I_{t-w} - D)/dt = 0$ and $i_1.(I_t - D)$ is less than what it was at point C. Investment declines and will continue to do so, given that $i_2.d(I_{t-w} - D)/dt$ becomes negative as the system moves through E. Eventually investment reaches point A' where $I_t = D$. At point A' investment will continue to fall until it comes to a halt at point C'. The process repeats itself as described above to give the upswing.

Figure 9.10

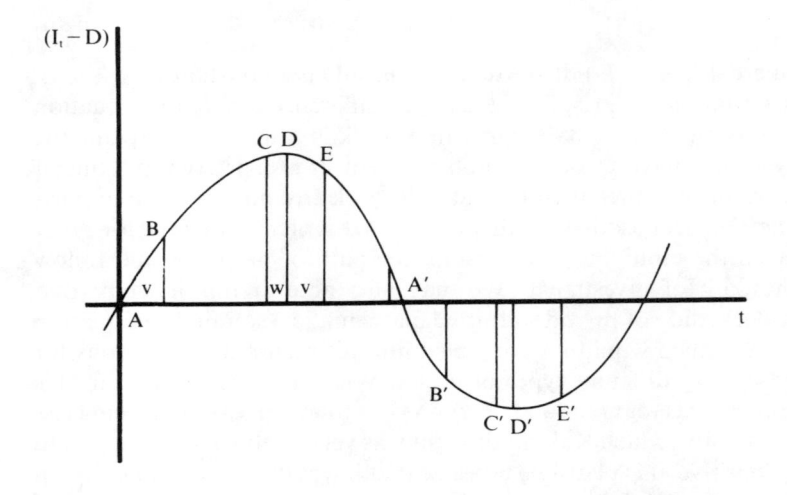

Source: Kalecki (1971a)

There are a number of points that can be made about this analysis. We begin by noting that every time the economy crosses the depreciation level, points A and A' for example, it does not stop at these points. This is so because as the economy goes through these points there are past investment changes which push the economy through these points. Furthermore, when the upward or downward movement in investment comes to a halt, at points C and C', it does not stay at this level. This follows from the assumption that the value of i_1 is less than 1, reflecting the negative influence of changes in capital equipment on investment ($c > 0$) and the incomplete reinvestment of saving ($a < 1$). If savings were fully reinvested ($a = 1$) and if the impact of changes in capital stock on investment were negligible (c being very small), then the system would stay at levels such as C and C'. But Kalecki thought these cases were rather unlikely to materialize. Further, whilst the situation just described is analogous to both booms and slumps, it may not be symmetrical in that the slumps may be more prolonged than the booms because

Growth Dynamics and Business Cycles Theories 235

'destruction' of capital is much weaker than accumulation, given that equipment in the slump would normally be idle in any case. The analysis just undertaken depends entirely upon the values of the coefficients involved in (9.59) as well as the length of the lags v and w. In this sense it is possible to get stable, explosive or damped fluctuations for different values of the coefficients and lags. Kalecki also considered the possibility of 'floors' and 'ceilings' but rejected it on the grounds that there was no evidence to suggest that 'ceilings' would be reached in the boom, whilst in the case of 'floors', disinvestment in inventories did not have the 'floor' assumed for fixed investment. As mentioned earlier, Kalecki's model relies heavily on the real sector to explain cycles, just as Goodwin's model emphasizes the workings of the labour market. But both ignore monetary forces entirely, and the next model attempts to account for them.

9.3.4 Minsky's Model

None of the theories we have considered so far actually relies on financial variables to explain business cycles. By contrast, Minsky's (1982, 1986a) business cycles theoretical framework puts the emphasis on finance and financial crises in explaining cyclical fluctuations. In doing so Minsky draws on Keynes's effective demand and uncertainty, on the Kaleckian theory of distribution, and on the notion of 'debt deflation'. These theoretical constructs when put together provide an endogenous explanation of business cycles.

Minsky begins with the standard income identity:

$$Y = C + I + GDTB \tag{9.60}$$

where the variables are as before, with the exception of GDTB which stands for Government Deficit including the Trade Balance. The Kaleckian dichotomization of consumption into C_c and C_w is alluded to, so that substitution in (9.60) for $C_c = c_c\pi$ and $C_w = W = c_w Y$, where c_w now stands for both the wage-earners' marginal propensity to consume and the wage share, gives us:

$$Y = c_c\pi + c_w Y + I + GDTB \tag{9.61}$$

Clearly, $\pi = Y - c_w Y$ so that:

$$Y = c_c (Y - c_w Y) + c_w Y + I + GDTB \tag{9.62}$$

which can be solved for Y to give us:

$$Y = (I + GDTB)/(1 - c_w)(1 - c_c) \tag{9.63}$$

Using $\pi = (1 - c_w)Y$ we have an expression for profits as follows:

$$\pi = (I + GDTB)/(1 - c_c) \tag{9.64}$$

which is very similar to Kalecki's theory of profits (compare 9.64 with 9.44). Obviously, profits are not determined by technology and production functions as in GNS, but by a host of economic, political, social and psychological variables that help to determine c_c, investment and GDTB.

Expressions (9.63) and (9.64) highlight the importance of the marginal propensities to consume out of wages and profits in the determination of income and profits. But for the purpose of a business cycles theory, just as in Kalecki's theory where investment is the essential determinant of the path of a capitalist economy, so in the case of Minsky's theory it is to the behaviour of investment that we must turn our attention. In Minsky's model investment is determined by the difference between the supply price of a new investment good, P_I, and the demand price of capital assets, P_K. The supply price of the new investment good is the price that results by marking-up on the firm's variable cost. The demand price of capital assets depends upon future profits that these assets are expected to earn and upon the discount of these future profits into a present price, P_K. This stream of profits, none the less, cannot be calculated from a known probability function, and therefore they are subject to substantial revisions. This proposition emanates, very obviously, from Keynes's idea of non-probabilistic uncertainty. Underlying this premiss there is the view that a decision to invest is ultimately about financing the acquisition of capital assets and consequently about the liability structure of the firm.

We may sketch the essentials of this analysis with the help of Figure 9.11. We measure P_K and P_I on the vertical axis and investment along the horizontal axis. There would then be a demand curve for investment (P_K) and a supply curve for investment (P_I). They are both horizontal to the investment axis as long as internal funds are available for investment purposes. Investment can proceed without

Figure 9.11

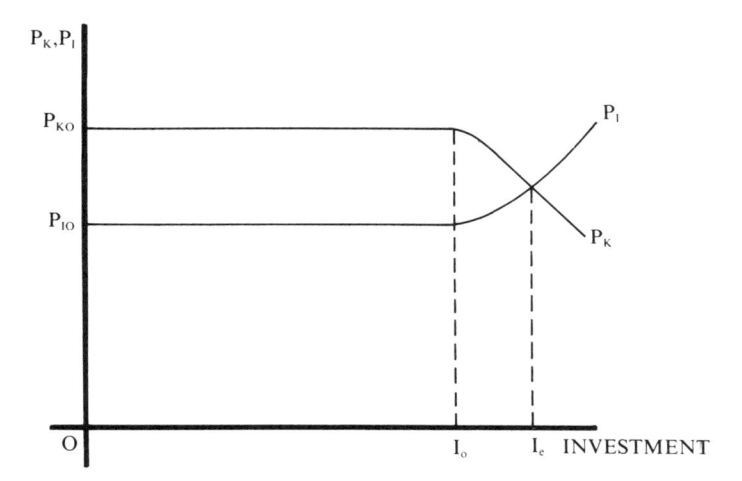

Source: Minsky (1986)

any change in P_I and P_K as long as internally created funds can be generated. In Figure 9.11 it is assumed that at point I_o internal funds are exhausted and external finance is sought. Beyond this point the slope of both relationships changes. P_I begins to rise, since lender's risk raises the cost of finance. P_K, on the other hand, begins to fall, since there is an increase in the borrower's risk. Investment will continue to take place until P_K and P_I are equal to each other at I_e. At this point the OI_o part of investment will be financed internally, leaving $I_o I_e$ to be covered by external finance.

The basis of Minsky's business cycles model can be sought in the connection between investment and finance as depicted in Figure 9.11. We may begin with I_e, which we can consider as the result of a boom. As such this state of affairs is characterized by expectations that are increasingly buoyant causing expansion in debts. Interest rates increase in a climate of inelastic demand for and supply of finance, as one might expect in periods of expansion. These changes produce a situation of financial fragility, in that increases in interest rates make it more difficult for economic agents to meet their debt payments. Profits will fall thus decreasing further the ability of firms to repay their debts, a situation which may force them to sell assets. P_K shifts to the left. The more liquid firms wish to become, the greater the pressure on interest rates to rise and, consequently, the more difficult it becomes to repay debts. At the same time the increasing cost of borrowing shifts the P_I relationship to the left, so that investment begins to increase. We are in the downswing.

The depth of such a decline is determined by the degree of financial fragility, the liquidity and expectations of capitalists and any action the government might initiate. Clearly, the degree of the system's fragility affects the ability of capitalists to respond to changes in the level of investment. Changes in liquidity preference and expectations are important in that they can cause an already fragile situation to deteriorate. As should be obvious from Equations (9.63) and (9.64), GDTB can be helpful in this respect. Government deficit can cause profits to recover and thus ameliorate the crisis. It follows that the more fragile and volatile the system is and the less vigorous government intervention, the higher the risk of a deep crisis.

As the crisis proceeds firms will have relatively fewer debts to worry about, liquidity increases and borrowers' and lenders' risks begin to decrease. When this happens both P_K and P_I relationships shift outward. Investment begins to recover and profitability picks up, thus reinforcing the recovery of investment. The economy is on its way to the upswing.

In Minsky's analysis, therefore, business cycles are a self-reinforcing process where finance and financial crises are at the heart of the explanation of the cyclical process. The crises are essentially caused by risky financial practices during periods of financial tranquility. Effective demand and capitalist expectations are further important variables in the argument. It is in the interaction between financial and real factors that Minsky's theory of business cycles, what he labels as the 'financial instability hypothesis', is based on. However, the impact of changes in the distribution of income on the cyclical behaviour of the economy does not play as predominant a role in this model as it does in some other explanations of the cycles, with the Goodwin model being the obvious example we have considered here.

9.4 CONCLUDING REMARKS

The section on business cycles has highlighted an important aspect of post-Keynesian analysis which, although touched upon earlier in the book, is worth repeating in the context of this chapter. This is that the analysis is based on different post-Keynesian themes, namely, aggregate demand, conflict and financial considerations. Different approaches emphasize different themes with none of the theories encapsulating all of them.[3] Minsky's model contains a significant element worth emphasizing, which is that it highlights the paramount importance of monetary factors in the explanation of the cyclical behaviour of the economy. It also invites the question of the role of monetary policy in particular, and economic policy in general, in ameliorating the amplitude of the cyclical behaviour of the economy. This brings us to the final chapter of this book which is inevitably the economic policy implications of the theoretical framework we have developed here.

NOTES

1. Blatt (1983) offers more details on Goodwin's model. For a brief summary see Skott (1989) and the references cited therein. Skott (1989) offers, actually, an interesting extension of Goodwin's model by incorporating Keynesian elements in it. He shows that the underlying cyclical mechanism of his model implies significant differences between it and Goodwin's model.
2. Kalecki (1971a, ch. 7) generalizes the simplified model discussed in the text to account for foreign trade, a government budget and the possibility of workers' savings.
3. Skott (1989) provides a very interesting exposition which attempts to bring together a number of post-Keynesian themes within an economic growth framework.

10. Economic Policy Implications

10.1 INTRODUCTION

Post-Keynesian economic policy analysis is mindful of the proposition that policy prescriptions cannot be generalized to all situations and experiences. Economic policies of the post-Keynesian type are predicated upon concrete situations where historical experiences and sociological characteristics are of immense importance. In this sense, post-Keynesian economics can be said to be of particular relevance to *real* economic problems and is, consequently, in a good position to analyse and explain current economic problems satisfactorily.

A further position taken by post-Keynesians on economic policies is that they are necessary to reduce the inequalities that exist in a capitalist system and to ensure fuller utilization of resources. It is actually demonstrated that inequality is *structurally inherent* in a capitalist system, in contrast to the GNS position that economic agents participate, at least in principle, on an equal footing. Market forces create many of the inequalities and exacerbate the disparities that are evident in such a system. There is plenty of evidence, too, to suggest the *persistence* of economic disparities and the role of markets in perpetuating inequality (Sawyer, 1989, esp. chs 3 and 12). The capitalist economic system, based on free market principles, is inherently cyclical and unstable. Left to itself it would not achieve, let alone maintain, the full use of existing resources, neither would it promote their equitable distribution. These features of the capitalist system are due mainly to the behaviour of private investment, which is attributed to volatile expectations and business confidence. Under these circumstances, full employment is very difficult to achieve, making it the exception rather than the rule. But even if achieved, it is not likely to be sustained without government intervention. There is, therefore, a potential role for government to initiate and implement economic policies. Central to these policies is management of aggregate demand to achieve the required growth for full utilization of capacity.

We start from the position that growth is surely desirable. However, there are problems associated with it. In particular, not only is poverty not overcome by growth, but absolute poverty is increased by it. Growth requires technical progress which, in its turn, implies more opportunities for educated workers and less for the uneducated; and since 'opportunities to acquire qualifications are kept (with a few exceptions for exceptional talents) for those families who have them already', it follows that 'Absolute misery grows while wealth increases' (Robinson, 1972, p. 7). Full employment cannot be the only objective of post-Keynesian economic policy. Governments should also strive to promote a more equal distribution of market power and, thus, income and wealth. In reality, a completely 'free' market system does not actually exist. Government intervention and appropriate institutions have evolved with the specific aim of reducing the fluctuations that are inherent in a 'free' market system. Despite attempts in certain countries to 'roll back the frontiers of the State' (the UK in the 1980s is the best example; see Arestis and Skuse, 1989), the trend in the twentieth century has been for more government intervention. Sawyer (1989, p. 302, Table 10.1) argues that this trend continued even in the 1980s: on a crude indicator such as public expenditure as a percentage of GDP, it is shown that for a range of developed capitalist countries this ratio has increased in each of the decades since the 1950s and for all countries considered, the ratio being at its highest in the 1980s.

The range of government intervention is wider than merely the passing of laws and the levying of taxes. In modern times there are two further aspects of government intervention which are of immense importance. The first refers to the composition of public services which range from education, public health and pensions to items like income maintenance and housing. Secondly, the emergence of Keynesian economic management policies has meant that the direction of government intervention is towards regulating the operation of the economy. This intervention ranges from facilitating industrial development through subsidies and tax concessions to direct involvement in the process of capital accumulation and public ownership of key industries (Ham and Hill, 1984). Control of the capital accumulation process is seen as one of the most important policy implications of post-Keynesian economics. Another is the planning of incomes.

In what follows in this chapter we attempt to draw and analyse these and other policy implications of the model we have been discussing in this book. We begin, however, with a discussion of the potential obstacles to achieving the goals of economic policy.

10.2 OBSTACLES TO ECONOMIC POLICY

Post-Keynesian economic analysis follows closely Kalecki (1943) to suggest that there are severe obstacles to reaching the goals of economic policy. Political and social pressures, however, are thought to impose significant constraints to the achievement of these objectives. Kalecki (1943) argued very strongly that although governments are able to influence economic magnitudes, this prerogative will not be utilized to its full potential. This is entirely due to the 'power of vested interests' which Kalecki emphasized so much.[1] Much more recently, Kaldor (1983) gave further support to these ideas when attempting to throw some light on the reasons behind the objection to Keynesian economic policies. He contended essentially that the changes in the power structure of society which came about as a result of Keynesian economic policies were responsible for the antagonism towards these ideas.

These constraints on economic policies are viewed by Kalecki (1943) as being rooted in the objections to full employment by the 'industrial leaders', or more to the point, by the oligopolists. In general terms these objections emanate from the oligopolists' dislike of government interference in the private sector. They are based on the following objections. First, there is the objection to government interference in the area of full employment. Such intervention is thought to entail the real possibility of replacing capitalism by considerable state activity and socialism. It is also seen by capitalists as a threat to the health of profitability and investment since government intervention would lead to the crowding out of the 'efficient' and wealth-creating private sector by the 'inefficient' public sector. Secondly, there is the objection to government spending on public investment projects and subsidies on consumption. This dislike is essentially based on arguments such as 'not spending more than one's means', 'the need for sound finance', 'the need to balance the budget' and so on, which are associated with the 'moral principle' that 'The fundamentals of capitalist ethics require that "you shall earn your bread in sweat" – unless you happen to have private means' (Kalecki, 1971a, p. 140). The third objection relates to the social and political changes resulting from the maintenance of full employment. There is the possibility here of workers 'getting out of hand', a situation which the 'captains of industry' would not be prepared to tolerate. Rentiers, too, would not tolerate this situation since they would be disadvantaged by the inflationary pressures which are inevitable at full employment. Kalecki (1971a, p. 144) suggests that under these circumstances there could very well develop

a powerful bloc . . . between big business and the rentiers' interests, and they would probably find more than one economist to declare that the situation was manifestly unsound. The pressure of all these forces, and in particular of big business, would most probably induce the Government to return to the orthodox policy of cutting down the budget deficit.[2]

As an example of the pressures alluded to above, we may also cite Kaldor (1982, p. xxi; 1985, ch. 2) here, who refers to the early postwar cheap-money policies to which the banks and financial institutions in the City objected, calling for a more 'active' monetary policy (see also Cowling, 1982; and Steindl, 1952). But there is another significant element in Kalecki's (1943) analysis. The cutting down of budget deficits near full employment, as a result of the insistence by the powerful industrial and financial interests, leads inevitably to a slump. As the next election approaches, however, pressures to relieve unemployment grow very strong. A period of expansion follows until the economy reaches a near-full-employment stage. Pressures for contraction are now expected as explained above. In this way the business trade cycle is replaced by a political trade cycle, a proposition that prompted Robinson (1972, p. 5) to argue: 'Just now the political trade cycle seems to be taking a more violent form than ever before.'

There are, of course, other economic obstacles to lasting full employment beyond the ones discussed above. At the top of the list one could mention: poor research and development; inadequate excess capacity; poor training of the labour force; lack of high educational standards; and consequently absence of skill and talent and thus innovation which is so vital to boost investment in any economic system. In the case of open economies there is a further awkward problem in that the balance of payments can be a severe constraint in terms of allowing the economy to move to full employment. Expansion of demand is met with severe balance-of-payments deficits and undesirable movements in the country's exchange rate, so that the expansionary policy has to be reversed. This difficulty, of course, may not be unrelated to the other problem just mentioned: the balance-of-payments constraint could very well arise from the inability of the economy to respond to the increased demand well before full employment is reached, due entirely to the obstacles enumerated above.

These views are reinforced by the important contributions of Myrdal (1939, 1957) which have been taken up by others, especially by Kaldor (1970a). As we mentioned briefly in Chapter 3, this view is known as the theory of 'circular and cumulative causation' and is essentially based on the dynamic interplay between investment and productivity growth which reinforces inequalities and *regional disparities*. (Kaldor, 1970a, defines regional disparities as unequal rates of growth in regions.) Consequently, the unequal impact of industrial development is explained by endogenous factors in the process of historical development rather than by the exogenous 'resource endowment' (Kaldor, 1970a, p. 343). Regions which are already developed enjoy competitive advantages so that the growth that takes place generates dynamic economies of scale by attracting more skilled labour (especially the young) and capital which embodies new technology; by taking advantage of expanding markets and the like. All these ingredients cause higher productivity and rates of profits in the faster-growing regions, which makes it progressively harder for the slower regions to compete. This inflow of capital and skilled labour allows still further expansion of production and the reaping of further economies of scale, higher productivity and rate of profit. These 'backwash' effects are modified by certain advantages accruing to the slower regions. These are the 'spread' effects which can accrue, for example, from expanded markets, the transfer of new technology from the advanced regions and so on. These advantages, however, can never be strong enough to outweigh the negative effects emanating from 'cumulative causation'. Even if by chance the 'spread' and 'backwash' effects are in balance, this would not be a stable equilibrium, for any change in the balance of the two forces would be followed by cumulative movements.

The theory predicts that the free movement of capital and labour exacerbates regional disparities. Consequently, the market mechanism reinforces regional disparities and imbalances rather than eliminating them, as the market mechanism underlying the GNS would have us believe. There is, further, the idea that 'cumulative causation' in economic terms generates inequalities in non-economic terms, such as political power, cultural domination and the rest. It is thus expected that those regions which are relatively rich dominate, not just in the economic power sense, but also in terms of their ability to exert political superiority. In this way they are in a position to impose their policies and culture over the less-powerful regions. In this scenario, democratic institutions are under severe threat (Cowling, 1985). The policy implications of such a model are crystal clear: comprehensive intervention at a regional level becomes paramount to reinforce the 'spread' effects and, indeed, counterbalance the impact of market forces.

There are two further views in this context which are worth considering. There is the growth-pole model (Perroux, 1955) which assumes that there are certain 'poles' in the system which, like magnets, attract factors of production at the expense of depressed areas. A new industrial unit could have a very significant effect in a depressed area through the creation of demand-induced growth. Such a 'pole' can create a healthy environment for other firms in the region; it can be the engine of economic growth via its secondary effects in the manufacturing and service sectors. It can, however, have devastating effects on firms outside the region which may find that labour and capital are absorbed by the 'pole'. The available evidence, however, suggests that in view of the need for a satisfactory infrastructure, skilled labour and a suitable environment for management, the tendency is that new industrial units locate their production in areas which are already prosperous, thus accentuating regional disparities. This view is closely related to the centre/periphery argument (for example, Baran, 1957; Frank, 1969), whereby uneven development is the result of the subordination of the needs of the periphery to those of the centre. The financial power of the centre reinforces the relative dependency of the periphery. At the policy level governments should encourage regional development by establishing 'counter'-poles. Essentially this can be promoted through assistance given to companies to locate production in depressed areas and also through financial centres in the form of regional central banking (Chick and Dow, 1988).

The second view is located in the debate between post-Fordist, or what is sometimes called 'flexibility' or 'flexible specialization' theory (Piore and Sabel, 1984; Hirst and Zeitlin, 1989) and neo-Fordist theory, or more aptly labelled as 'regulation' theory (Aglietta, 1979, 1982). This debate is about developments in the capitalist world following the collapse of the Fordist model in the late 1960s to early 1970s.

The Fordist model suggests that mass production and consumption were the result of the needs of economic agents. It was a regime of *monopolistic accumulation* whereby capital was concentrated into large multiple enterprises, taking advantage of economies of scale provided by big markets. The manufacturing sectors were, in this view, the prosperous 'pole' centres. This concentration was relevant both in terms of industrial production and employment and was thought to be remarkable because of its size and consistency in many countries, especially in Europe (Keeble et al., 1983). A historical compromise manifested itself in the relationship between capital and labour. Productivity gains produced steady improvements in workers' real incomes, institutionalized as an 'inflation-plus' norm for wage deals. The Keynesian welfare state at the same time expanded the social wage along with the private wage. Fordism was, therefore, a period of high profits, high growth and rising wages.

Fordism, then, depends on a balanced distribution between wages and profits which can keep mass production and mass consumption growing in tandem. It depends, too, on preventing the inevitable capital intensity from causing a fall in the rate of profit. Wages must move in harmony with increasing returns to scale, the propensity to consume and the relation between investment and demand. Oligopolistic pricing that finances investment is, therefore, most appropriate in a Fordist regime where monopolistic competition plays a key role in accumulation (in this sense, Eichner's 1976 theory is most appropriate). Also, wages are required to be tied to productivity, for if they are not, problems will arise. If wages are too high, profits and investment will fall. If wages are too low relative to productivity, mass consumption will fall short of mass production. Clearly, the institutions of collective bargaining, the relation between banks and industry and the role of the state are central issues in Fordism. Monetary and fiscal policies become central in economic management. Their aim is to keep the balance between mass consumption and mass production.

It is argued, however, that this Fordist era came to an end by the late 1960s when the problems of inflation, over-accumulation and declining rates of profit, the enhanced bargaining power and political weight of the trade unions, the development of the affluent consumer who rejected standardized, mass-produced, commodities, and so on, caused capital to develop new strategies. Traditional industries were forced to restructure or close down, thus deserting whole areas, while new 'high tech' industries and service activities mushroomed in other regions. From about the early 1970s onwards there has been a dramatic change in terms of the organization of production and the development of the service sector. Bade (1986) has argued that this is definitely the case for production-orientated services (such as accountancy, legal services, communication services). The Fordist process reversed itself as a result and has produced what has been labelled the post-Fordist era.

Post-Fordism contends that in response to market changes and technology, more flexible units producing *customized* products of different types (Piore and Sabel, 1984), rather than the inflexible Fordist production unit, have become the dominant engine of growth. The standardized products of Fordism are replaced by the customized products of post-Fordism. The production of the latter is made increasingly cheaper, essentially because of their reliance on microprocessor-based technologies. Examples offered to highlight the distinction between Fordism and post-Fordism include mini steel-mills, chemicals and machine tools, with the car industry being the most notable case: the strategy for a world car has been replaced by a greater emphasis on model differentiation. Unlike Fordism which depends on inflexible, unskilled or semi-skilled labour, subordinated to machines, post-Fordism is strongly based on flexible, skilled' workers who are prepared to learn new skills and move between jobs according to the wishes of the market. Further general characteristics of post-Fordism are the attempts to counteract trade union resistance, the dismantling of the welfare state, and the search for new forms of production based essentially on the neo-liberal accumulation strategy of flexible acceleration. One important implication of this shift of production is that the degree of economies of scale is thought to be weakened, whilst the cost of producing a range of differentiated products is seen as reduced.

Furthermore, post-Fordism is supposed to have created a new polarization of service workers: the high-skilled and the low-skilled sectors. Corresponding to this segmentation of the labour market two cultures can be identified, a new culture whose style of life is based on individualization, the yuppie culture (the high-skilled sector); and the persistence of the yuffies (Young Urban Failures) culture, which represents the low-skilled sector. This unprivileged sector provides the specific services required by the new class in the urban areas. These *structural changes*, then, have produced massive deindustrialization and regional restructuring which hit the old manufacturing sector in particular, thereby causing it to suffer a huge reduction in employment. The growth of the service sector tended to compensate to an extent for the loss of jobs in the manufacturing sector, but it was never sufficient to match it completely. This growth was based entirely in the private sector, unlike previous cases where the public sector provided the platform for increases of this nature.

The development of the service sector, however, entailed an important and interesting dimension which reflected directly women's opportunities in the market place. There has been a conspicuous increase in the involvement of women in the labour market. Economic policies within this new economic climate should aim at providing the necessary training to meet the demands of the newly established service sector, at assisting small firms, and at rejuvenating the urban environment. Conflict between capital and labour is recognized to be still there, but labour is expected to make concessions so that the workforce can bargain flexibly with management. Macro-regulation is, thus, not so crucial. It is regional policies which assume particular importance.

Post-Fordism, however, has not escaped criticism. There is the contention that the power of the transnational corporations, both financial and industrial, does not appear to be declining; if anything, it is growing. Economies of scale do not appear to be waning and the markets for consumer durables adhere to Fordist rather than to post-Fordist characteristics. (For evidence on the failure of the post-Fordist model in the cases of 'Third Italy' and London, see O'Donnell and Nolan, 1989.) It is also questioned whether post-Fordism is actually 'a core development in the economy or merely a highly touted epiphenomenon' (Luria, 1990, p. 129). For example, it is argued that the current extent and efficiency of the small units of production is very unlikely to replace to any considerable degree a substantial share of the big mass-production units. It is further argued that it is very difficult to identify clearly and indisputably cases of industrial structures which are characterized by either mass production or flexible accumulation characteristics. In any case, flexibility at one stage of production may be associated with inflexibility at another stage; a situation which may have always prevailed. As Williams *et al.* (1987, p. 415) rightly note, there are three characteristics, dedicated equipment, product differentiation and length of production run, upon which Fordism and post-Fordism are in extreme opposition to each other. Fordism is characterized by low product-differentiation, high dedicated equipment and long length of production runs. By contrast post-Fordism is a regime with high product-differentiation, low dedicated equipment and short length of production run. It makes it absolutely impossible to identify on all three characteristics each case of a firm or industry as belonging to a specific pole. The inevitable conclusion must be, surely, that mass production and flexible specialization cannot be identified, even at firm or industry level. The argument of post-Fordism is, in any case, based essentially on the notion that Fordism reached a stage of crisis. But then, crises are not unusual in mass-production economic processes. These are regulation crises, however, concerning institutions that are vital to the production and consumption relationship. They are not, thus, crises of the type suggested by post-Fordism which have more to do with technological advances that imply 'flexible' specialization and the end of mass production.

It is precisely on this very important issue that regulation theory comes onto the scene. The core of regulation theory is embedded in three concepts. That of the *regime of accumulation*, which signifies stabilization and change and involves the allocation of the social product between consumption and investment. There are two regimes of accumulation: *extensive* which involves lengthening the working day and expanding the labour force; and *intensive* which takes the form of expanding fixed capital embodying technical progress. Productivity growth and the potential of mass consumption are limited in the case of the *extensive* regime of accumulation. By contrast, in the case of the *intensive* regime of accumulation the potential exists for both productivity and mass production increases.

The *mode of regulation* is the second concept emphasized by this school. This is the existing set of institutions which create and ensure stability in the relation between investment and consumption. These are, of course, contradictory relations which are transformed into stability by the operation of social institutions. There are two modes of regulation corresponding to the two regimes of accumulation. The *competitive regulation* which conforms with the *extensive* regime of accumulation, and the *monopolistic regulation* that goes together with the *intensive* regime of accumulation. Demand and supply regulate activities in the *competitive regulation*. In the *monopolistic* case, regulation by institutional rules, mark-up pricing, productivity-related collective wage bargaining and government intervention, replace the market forces of *competitive regulation* to some considerable extent. For example, the Fordist era is usually described as the period of *intensive* accumulation and *monopolistic regulation*, while the post-Fordist epoch is described as one of *extensive* accumulation and *competitive regulation*.

The third core element of the regulation school is the *mode of production*. Production is at the centre of the economy just as accumulation is at the centre of capitalist development and labour at the centre of social life. Crises occur when the symbiosis of the regime of accumulation and mode of production is disturbed. We have *minor* crises when the mode of regulation temporarily fails to respond sufficiently to the potential and the needs of the regime of accumulation, but ultimately this imbalance is restored. These are the crises referred to as 'crises in regulation' and they are a normal occurrence in capitalist systems. Major crises result when the mode of regulation becomes entirely inadequate to the needs of the regime of accumulation. This is either because for a given mode of regulation, the potential of the regime of accumulation is exhausted, or because the mode of regulation becomes so outdated that it ceases to support the regime of accumulation.

The crisis of the Fordist regime of accumulation in the late 1960s is viewed by the regulation school as the result of *intensive* accumulation which led to the collapse of *productivity* and ultimately *profitability*. Thus Fordism required modification by way of transition from one regime of accumulation and mode of regulation (that is the institutional support) to another. Mass production, mass consumption and monopolistic forms of regulation (Keynesian policies and collective bargaining) combined, produced Fordism. The crisis of Fordism was, then, followed by a *transition* period which was characterized by both new structural tendencies and continuities with the previous regime of accumulation. Mass production and mass consumption were still very much in evidence but in a modified form: there is, now, internationalization of Fordism spread by the activities of transnational banks and multinationals, along with the persistence of monopolistic types of regulation in the form of financial and industrial 'cities of capital'. New types of information and communication technologies emerged along with vertical disintegration in production. This neo-Fordist thesis has been criticized by a number of writers. Nielsen (1991) offers a brief summary of this critique which he finds contradictory on occasions and, on the whole, the thesis difficult to criticize, a problem in itself.

The crisis in Fordism caused by the collapse of profitability is seen by the neo-Fordist school as responsible for an emerging new pattern of capitalist development. Multinationals, in particular, in their attempt to recover their profitability sought refuge in the new industrialized countries, the peripheral countries, where low-wage and high-productivity possibilities existed. This development is precisely what Lipietz (1987) has labelled as 'peripheral Fordism'. It is Fordism in as much as it involves intensive accumulation and mass consumption, especially of consumer durables. And it is peripheral in that the centres of 'skilled manufacturing' and engineering are not located in these countries. The local markets of peripheral Fordism are in consumer durables, where the middle classes are more active than the workers in the Fordist sectors. Exports of cheap manufacturing goods to the centre is the other dimension of the local markets. An obvious difference between peripheral Fordism and Fordism itself is that unlike the latter, the former cannot regulate demand or indeed adjust it to local Fordist branches given that it is world demand that is involved in this case. While in traditional Fordism the link of consumption to productivity was met by monopolistic regulation of wage relations, in peripheral Fordism this came about through increases in the income of the middle classes. Industrialization is achieved through imports from the centre which are paid for by exporting cheap manufacturing goods to the centre. But ultimately peripheral Fordism should only be contemplated 'when growth in the home market for manufactured goods plays a real part in the national regime of accumulation' (Lipietz, 1987, p. 80). The finance of peripheral Fordism has taken the form of borrowing on the international capital and money markets. Such financing in the pre-peripheral Fordist period had been channelled through direct investment. Following the emergence of peripheral Fordism, however, financing through direct investment became inadequate and international bank finance began to replenish the shortfall. This development gave rise to what has been known as the *international credit economy*, with some key 'Capital Cities' around the world being its main centres.

An interesting regulationist current is the 'Social Structure of Accumulation' (SSA) developed by Bowles et al (1984). It emphasizes the social and political conditions necessary to support and reinforce the economic forces which are required to sustain periods of accumulation. Stability in these conditions ensures sustained and rapid capital accumulation, and the balance of these forces is the kernel of the SSA analysis. Major crises can emerge when the balance of the social, political and economic forces is disturbed. A protracted class struggle ensues so that ultimately a *new* SSA is arrived at, the shape of which depends on the balance of forces achieved during the period of crisis and resolution.

The distinctive feature of SSA is that a lot of weight is placed upon shifts in the balance of power and social relations. This emphasis is an important feature of SSA and it distinguishes it from the neo-Fordist model. It also clarifies the object of regulation which is, quite simply, the social structure of accumulation, unlike the neo-Fordist strand of regulation theory which is less clear on the precise definition of what it is to be regulated. A further difference is that while regulation theory considers the impact of modes of regulation on regimes of accumulation and modes of production, in the SSA there are no similar concepts. Instead, the notions of 'stage' or 'phase' of accumulation are utilized. There is still another important difference between the two approaches. Whereas in the regulation theory it is the interaction of regimes of accumulation and modes of regulation that cause crises, within the SSA approach institutional or power relation changes are responsible for crises. (See Jessop, 1990, for further details on these and other differences.)

The SSA is concerned with modes of regulation which extend well beyond the economic sphere. Particular attention is paid to the role of the state (unlike the regulation school approach which is weak on its account of the role of the state) and hegemony in regulation and social relations along with other conventions, habits and institutions. The political geography of accumulation, the urban and rural restructuring are further aspects which are increasingly encapsulated in the analysis of SSA.

The views we have just portrayed clearly indicate that regional inequalities exist as a result of a dynamic process, with a cyclical and evolutionary perspective. Regional inequality is, therefore, a multivariate phenomenon. Regional disparities cannot be subscribed by one single indicator but by a combination of factors. Economic policies, then, are needed to contain, if not entirely eliminate, regional inequalities. However, traditional policies which rely on market forces to cure inequalities may indeed accentuate these problems rather than cure them. Consequently, enhancing regional investment through direct government intervention would have to be the prime objective of any economic policy that hoped to have any impact at all in this respect. Considerable extra investment would have to be directed to the poorer regions, both in infrastructure and in local firms, as a means of creating new permanent jobs. In this context it is important to refer to the contribution by Dow and Chick (1988) who argue for regional central banking. Such a policy of 'financial segmentation' would have to be considered in conjunction with the control of investment at regional level. This decentralization should strengthen the feasibility of regional direct control of investment since finance and industrial capital are made to coexist, a relationship which is expected to enhance local employment substantially.

The implications for economic policy of the discussion in this section are very interesting. First, government intervention is necessary in principle to achieve and maintain full employment. Secondly, the increased power of trade unions and workers at full employment along with the resulting inflationary pressures must be addressed. Planning of incomes together with workers' participation in decision-making would have to be considered seriously. Thirdly, there could arise a serious balance-of-payments constraint well before full employment is reached. Policies to enhance the supply side of the economy may be necessary to alleviate this problem. The underlying theme of this scenario is that demand management may well be able to achieve full employment but cannot sustain it alone. Furthermore, one should mention the mounting deficits and debt accumulation required to keep high levels of investment and employment, and thus marginal firms, afloat, thereby contributing to poor productivity, inefficiencies and a declining rate of profit.

Even if sufficient demand were forthcoming, full employment would still be difficult, if not impossible, to maintain for there is inadequate or unbalanced supply potential. Regional disparities are another potentially very explosive and disturbing problem that would have to be tackled. Consequently, some form of control of investment may be necessary to remove these constraints.

The rest of this chapter will be devoted to demonstrating these *economic* policy implications within the confines of the post-Keynesian model with which we have been concerned. We begin with the assumption of a closed economy, and follow with an open economy case.

10.3 THE CLOSED ECONOMY CASE

We may begin with the standard income identities:

$$Y = C + I + G + X - Q \tag{10.1}$$

$$Y = C + S + T \tag{10.2}$$

where the symbols have their usual meaning, that is, Y = national output or national income, C = consumers' expenditure, I = investment expenditure, G = government expenditure, X = exports, Q = imports, S = savings, T = taxes. Subtracting (10.2) from (10.1) we arrive at the expression:

$$O = (I - S) + (G - T) + (X - Q) \tag{10.3}$$

and since we assume for the time being a closed economy we set $(X - Q) = O$, in which case the analysis can follow closely Eichner's (1979a) model (as, for example, in Arestis and Driver 1983, 1984), as far as the policy issues are concerned. We may then have:

$$(S - I) = (G - T) \tag{10.4}$$

or

$$(S_B - I_B) + (S_O - I_O) = (G - T) \tag{10.5}$$

where $(S - I)$ is split into the business sector $(S_B - I_B)$ and the other sectors $(S_O - I_O)$.

We may now assume that expansion is initiated through an increase in government expenditure to achieve full employment.[3] The deficit faced by the government sector implies a surplus in either the business sector or in the other sectors. This is likely to be particularly important for the oligopolistic business sector: for the high levels of aggregate demand will lead to increasing rates of capacity utilization and a disproportionate increase in cash flow (Eichner 1976, p. 237). This surplus will tend to constrain the growth rate of the economy, a consequence which can only be avoided if the government initiates further deficits. We thus have a situation where the government sector must be prepared to tolerate a mounting deficit and debt, if the economy is to remain on the higher output growth rate, a situation not likely to persist for very long. If, however, the business sector is prepared to increase its investment/output ratio or, indeed, reduce its saving/income ratio or some combination of both, then the higher growth rate could be maintained.

Let us take the possibility of the increase in the investment/output ratio first. One could conceivably argue that higher aggregate demand emanating from higher government deficits, and the attendant effect on the growth rate, could be perceived by the oligopolistic sector as a new, higher, secular rate which would be expected to have a favourable long-lasting effect on their sales. The oligopolistic sector would thus be more inclined to revise their capital spending accordingly. It could therefore be suggested that increases in government deficits themselves, coupled with the beneficial effects on long-term expectations, could potentially engineer an expansionary effect upon business-sector investment. But the success of this sequence of events depends heavily on the assumption that the policy is perceived as being correct (McCallum, 1983). For if the economic agents concerned believe that any increase in government deficit completely crowds out business investment, then, of course, there will simply be no expectations effects, as described above. On the contrary, the effects could be the reverse of those required. What one can suggest at this juncture is that the volatility of the business sector can be contained to a considerable extent by the continuous presence of the government in the sphere of investment, and not by periodic pump-priming action (Keynes, 1936, ch. 24). This is 'both ... the only practicable means of avoiding the destruction of existing economic forms in their entirety and ... the condition of the successful functioning of individual initiative' (Keynes, 1936, p. 380). The need for mounting government deficits could thus be mitigated, but the importance of timing cannot be overemphasized. If the government acts precipitously the economy could very well find itself at the old growth rate.

The surplus in the oligopolistic business sector cannot be expected to disappear entirely, given that savings increase disproportionately (Eichner, 1976, p. 238, for example). The increase in the income growth rate is not as high as the increase in the savings growth rate with the latter being higher than the increase in the rate of growth of investment. This is an observation that needs further elaboration. Investment expenditures which depend essentially on the expected growth rate of industry sales are likely to remain relatively stable, whilst the amount of savings actually realized is probably considerably more variable since it is heavily influenced by the current operating ratio. This is not to suggest that investment expenditures are likely to remain fixed no matter what the current level of sales may be. Rather, it is to point out that the expected growth rate of industry sales, which is derived by extrapolating forward the past trend of industry sales, will be only slightly affected by the sales experienced at any single point in time. To the extent that fluctuations in industry sales are consistent with the anticipated cyclical pattern, they may even occasion no substantial revision of the oligopolistic sector's investment plans. This is in contrast to the considerable variation in the realized corporate levy, and hence in the amount of savings generated by the oligopolistic sector as a result of those same fluctuations in industry sales.

The obvious question to ask is whether there are any policy instruments which could be used to stimulate investment in the oligopolistic sector. The message here is that there is very little policy-makers can do, since investment in this sector is insensitive to policy instruments. Oligopolist investment is immune to monetary policy changes, given the self-financing nature of this sector and also its insensitivity to interest rate movements. Oligopolists will expand their plant and equipment to maintain their market share regardless of the going rate of interest. The capital funds market can be avoided entirely, given that pricing is used to finance investment (although it must be conceded here that high and rising interest rates are bound to have an impact sooner or later; this, however, must be a rather rare occurrence). Fiscal policy is equally ineffective essentially for two reasons: first, there is no necessity for a surplus sector to invest when government expenditure is raised or taxation is lowered; secondly, the power of corporations to shift taxes limits the capacity of taxation increases to absorb surpluses.

We are thus led inevitably to consider the possibility of reducing the saving/income ratio of the oligopolistic sector. We begin by writing the savings relationship of the oligopolistic business sector as follows:

$$S_B = S_B[Y_B, (W_B - Z_B), P_B, t_c] \qquad (10.6)$$
$$+ - + -$$

where S_B = savings of the sector, Y_B = income of the sector, W_B = wage rate of the sector, Z_B = output per worker in the sector, P_B = average price level within the sector, t_c = corporate tax rate, and the signs under the variables stand for partial derivatives. The impact of Y_B on S_B is, of course, expected to be positive. Oligopolists typically fix their prices so as to generate enough funds for investment. The generated funds clearly depend on aggregate demand: the higher the aggregate demand, the more funds will be flowing in; similarly for a lower volume of aggregate demand, generated funds will be slower coming in. In terms of the difference between wages and productivity, as wages in the sector increase given productivity, an increase in the average variable cost and thus a reduction in savings will result. Clearly, the opposite will happen when, with given wages, productivity increases. The price level in oligopolistic situations is set so as to yield a margin above costs sufficient to finance the anticipated level of investment over the current planning period. The revenues thus obtained, over and above the sums set aside to cover costs, constitute the savings of the megacorp in that industry. The higher the price level, *ceteris paribus*, the greater will be the rate at which savings grow. In terms of t_c, a negative relationship is expected to prevail. Increases in corporate taxes reduce the megacorp's average revenue and thus the amount of savings. Similarly, oligopolists will be able to enhance their savings when t_c is lower than would otherwise be the case.

It follows from what we have just argued that for S_B to be reduced, Y_B, Z_B and P_B (in the form of price controls) must decrease or else the wage rate and/or the tax rate should increase. Y_B and Z_B, however, cannot be policy instruments, so we must concentrate on the other three variables. We begin with price controls. Price controls have been objected to as being unworkable and ineffective. The main objection to them is that firms will come, sooner or later, to anticipate policies of controlling price increases to redistribute the surplus, so that unless these policies refer to both incomes and prices they are likely to have an adverse effect on business confidence and investment. Price controls have also been shown to be ineffective in that their impact is shown to be 'temporary' and 'sporadic' (Coutts *et al.*, 1978, p. 24). Equally problematic is the case where the tax instrument is employed to shift the savings curve downward. It has been argued that increases in the tax burden on oligopolists are quickly passed on to the household sector in the form of higher prices (Eichner, 1976, p. 255). The empirical evidence on this score tends to support a great deal of 'shifting' but on the question of full 'tax shifting' the evidence is rather inconclusive. Coutts *et al.* (1978, p. 96) suggest that within roughly three years, two-thirds of direct tax adjustments get passed on to price changes. King (1975) and Beath (1979) argue that the full 'tax shifting' hypothesis is confirmed. Their theoretical framework is that firms in oligopolistic industries set prices so as to maintain a target share of profits after tax.

Similar problems exist in the case of the wage rate. Most crucially, the enigma in this case is how to ascertain that wage rate which would be consistent with an acceptable governmental deficit and business sector surplus as well as with a particular growth rate and price level. There is absolutely no guarantee that such a unique wage rate can be achieved. However, if it does not come about then certain severe problems could very well appear. A too low wage rate would not sustain the desirable growth rate, while a too high wage rate would cause a wage–price inflation spiral. A too high wage rate would leave the oligopolistic business sector short of funds to undertake the necessary amount of investment, in which case P_B will be forced to increase. In addition to the problems this increase itself would create, it would also kick off a wage–price inflation spiral. Such a sequence of events clearly implies that market forces cannot be relied upon to avoid the problems just referred to. It would appear that some form of incomes policy may be necessary, a proposition we return to shortly.

We may turn our attention now to the other sectors and enquire whether $(S_o - I_o)$ can assume values which might help the economy sustain a higher growth rate. On the assumption of no foreign sector, the sectors left to consider are the non-oligopolistic sector, where the GNS proprietorship is the representative firm, and the personal sector.

We begin with the non-oligopolistic sector. The sensitivity of investment and savings to aggregate demand in this sector is rather different from what it is in the oligopolistic business sector. The savings relationship is expected to be less sensitive to fluctuations in the income growth rate than in the oligopolistic case. This is because the savings generated as a result of fluctuations in the income growth rate are likely to be transferred at an increasing rate to the owner(s) of the firm and thus to the household subsector – and perhaps returned to the firm if required. There is no corporate levy. The savings relationship for this sector is thus expected to be practically horizontal. Not so, though, for the investment relationship, which is expected to be more sensitive to changes in the growth rate of output in the non-oligopolist than in the oligopolist case. The rationale for this difference is the single-plant operation that is one of the distinguishing characteristics of the non-oligopolistic sector. The absence of multi-plant operation clearly suggests that any expansion of the growth rate of output must be associated with price-level increases, the implication being that, given total costs, the gap between total revenue and cost widens, thus causing new firms to enter the industry due to the growing profit margin. Total investment in the sector will thus expand, with the result that the non-oligopolistic sector is expected to go through periods of alternating boom and contraction. Any expansion will continue until supply constraints emerge in the capital goods industry, precipitating a collapse of the investment boom. Output is no longer enough to sustain high growth rates and the contraction process sets in, coming to an end when investment reaches zero. This instability, however, is very unlikely to prevail throughout the whole economy given the small fraction of total investment accounted for by the GNS proprietorship firm.

The personal sector, by contrast, is not expected to be 'unstable' in the sense just described. The difficulty with this sector is to define investment in a precise manner. It is identified as consumer durables plus residential construction, but there are problems. There is, first, the question of whether to classify the residential construction element as part of personal investment or as business investment. There is also the difficulty emanating from the fact that the two items just identified as constituting investment of the personal sector are expected to behave in very different ways. These problems notwithstanding, it is important to note that investment of the personal sector is not presumed to be as volatile as savings: for as growth proceeds, the marginal propensity to save is likely to increase thus providing a *prima facie* case for the personal sector being faced with a savings relationship that is more volatile than the investment relationship. But both savings and investment are essentially determined by the growth of income and output. It clearly follows, therefore, that when the government sector sustains a deficit, the personal sector is unlikely to behave in such a way as to alleviate it. The overall conclusion, then, must be that mounting deficits initiated by the government in an attempt to push the economy on to a higher growth rate cannot be alleviated by the behaviour of the non-oligopolistic sector in terms of their $(S_o - I_o)$ behaviour. However, the wage–price inflation spiral referred to above is of paramount importance for the personal sector, for when it sets in it could create a further surplus in this sector on top of the one in the oligopolistic business sector. This takes us straight back to the need for an 'incomes policy', touched upon above.

The 'incomes policy' or 'planned income growth' in this context is not a policy for holding down money wages, in the way incomes policies were applied, for example, in the UK in the 1960s and 1970s. Such a policy would require a lower level of real wages while the policy is implemented. But given the hypothesis on money wage determination adopted in Chapter 7, real wages cannot be held below the desired level (or trend) for long periods (Cripps and Godley, 1976; Smith, 1976; Cuthbertson, 1979). It thus follows that although some modicum of success may be possible in the short term, a permanent or long-run incomes policy is impracticable because in the long run there is a full catching-up effect in the level of money wages (for some evidence see Henry and Ormerod, 1978). Nor is it meant to be a TIP (tax-based incomes policy) whereby incentives to firms are intended to hold money wage increases in line with productivity (Weintraub and Wallich, 1973; Neale, 1986). This is an interesting proposition in that it also provides an inbuilt incentive for growth. By allowing firms to increase prices faster than money wages, TIP provides the environment whereby real wages are dampened so that the mark-up over costs is widened, thus establishing a crucial financial condition for investment growth. Clearly, though, the success of these types of policy crucially depends on whether the growth of money wages is sufficiently contained. This observation raises the important consideration of the income distribution effects of TIP which hit workers particularly hard.[4]

What is intended, by contrast, is an incomes policy designed to apply 'to all forms of household compensation – to dividends and rents as well as to money wages' (Eichner, 1980, p. 58). Further characteristics of this policy are that it must not be imposed but must gain acceptance by all affected by it. What Eichner proposes here is the creation of a *Social and Economic Council* that would consist of representatives of the various economic groups. Thus the eventual policy decided upon would have the support not only of trade unions but of the other economic groups as well. Such a policy, therefore, implies that the non-governmental representatives on the Council would have a substantial role to play in the formation of overall government economic strategy.

But there is still a problem with this particular policy prescription (Arestis and Driver, 1984). The decrease in S_B to achieve full employment dictated by this policy implies that firms would be operating in the peak capacity range. But once firms are convinced that the output growth rate has been raised, they will surely wish to return to a lower rate of capacity utilization so as to maintain entry barriers. Clearly, though, restoring excess capacity will involve a rise in the investment function, which would be difficult to finance, given the fall in the savings function. Furthermore, as growth increases, the incremental capital–output ratio will tend to rise if capital goods are produced with more capital-intensive technology than aggregate output, since the increase in the proportion of capital goods in total output will raise the aggregate incremental capital–output ratio directly. Firms will thus be caught between a decrease in S_B and an increase in I_B, partly caused by the necessity to maintain expenditures aimed at securing market dominance.

It may be, therefore, that planned income growth would be an inadequate instrument to persuade market leaders to raise their investment–output ratios. They may prefer a short period at peak capacity rather than commit themselves to faster secular growth by releasing their surpluses. Initiating fast sustained growth could lose market share for the dominant firms, given the fuller utilization levels it would imply. Caution on the part of the market leaders would be reinforced by the prospect of future governments, perhaps uncommitted to maintaining profitability, being in power during the critical payback period of the investments. The experiences of 1963, 1972 and the late 1980s in the United Kingdom testify to the reluctance of industry to risk responding to consumer-led booms with either sustained capital investment or price restraint. It is doubtful that such behaviour could be changed drastically by a putative incomes agreement. The conclusion, therefore, must be that planned income growth would have to be accompanied by some kind of control of investment if policies aimed at higher growth were to be successful. This is an important issue and we shall return to it shortly.

10.4 THE OPEN ECONOMY CASE

In section 10.2 we tacitly assumed $(X - Q)$ to be zero. We relax this assumption in this section, so that from Equation (10.3) we could easily have:

$$(T - G) + (S - I) = (X - Q) \tag{10.7}$$

which clearly states that the surplus of the public sector plus that of the private sector must be equal to the external sector surplus. We may follow Godley and Cripps (1983) who argue that the surplus of the private sector $(S - I)$ is in general small and its changes are also small and predictable. For brevity we may assume that this surplus is constant, so that we can have:

$$(S - I) = h_o \tag{10.8}$$

in which case (10.7) can now be rewritten as:

$$(T - G) + h_o = (X - Q) \tag{10.9}$$

Furthermore, it is assumed, for the purposes of this section, that since exports are determined by events outside the economy, world trade for example, they, along with government expenditure, are exogenously determined. For taxes and imports the simplifying assumptions:

$T = tY$ (10.10)

$Q = qY$ (10.11)

are adopted. With these assumptions we can solve (10.8)–(10.11) to arrive at:

$Y = (X + G - h_o)/(t+q)$ (10.12)

from which we can derive:

$(dY/dG) = 1/(t + q) > 0$ (10.13)

$(dY/dt) = - (X + G - h_o)/(t + q)^2 < 0$ (10.14)

Clearly, then, fiscal policy can raise output. Equation (10.9), though, is a vivid reminder that a budget deficit will result sooner rather than later in a deficit in the balance of trade. Unless capital inflows are attracted by growth prospects, a balance of payments crisis could very well ensue, which implies that expansionary policies would have to be reversed, producing the familiar scenario of 'stop–go' policies. Consequently, expansionary policies cannot be effective for long unless they are accompanied by policies to tackle the balance of trade deficit. Manipulating the exchange rate for this purpose may be futile since devaluation can raise the level of output, employment and income and lead to a rise in imports that may very well be equal to the increase in exports resulting from devaluation. The view has been forward (Cambridge Economic Policy Group, 1975, 1976; Cripps, 1978; Cripps and Godley, 1978) that the authorities should impose 'import controls' in an environment of 'managed' international trade. This can be achieved by reducing import propensities without reducing imports below the level at which they would otherwise be; and also by introducing as few selective controls as possible in a way which would not promote industrial inefficiency. The strategy envisaged in this view is one which would increase the level of trade and output, not just in the country pursuing it but in the rest of the world as well. The economic policy prescriptions of this thesis are the use of budget deficits and general import controls to achieve the two targets of balance of payments 'equilibrium' and full-employment level of output. These policy prescriptions have not gone uncriticized.

The main attack on this thesis has been directed at the 'controversial' policy prescription of import controls. It has been argued by some economists (see, for example, Scott *et al.*, 1980) that import controls would only make matters worse. There is, to begin with, the question of retaliation by other countries to the imposition of controls on the country's imports, and this would result in a lower volume of foreign trade (Blinder, 1978; see also Hare, 1980). Furthermore, import prices would rise above the level that would result if the exchange rate, for example, were allowed to fall to cure a deficit in the balance of payments. This would come about because the burden of adjustment would fall on one category of imports, namely manufactures. In addition, it is argued that with less foreign trade, consumers would increase their demand for more-expensive or lower-quality substitutes for imports. Producers would be forced to buy more-expensive or lower-quality substitutes for imported raw materials. These latter two effects would inevitably, so the argument goes, reduce consumers' real income. Producers would also lose some economies of scale, since with less foreign trade they would have to rely on the smaller domestic market.

It has been suggested by the proponents of the managed trade thesis, however, that most of these criticisms are ill-founded. Cripps and Godley (1978) and Christodoulakis and Godley (1987), for example, have argued that retaliation and reduction in the volume of international trade need not necessarily occur following import controls. This argument rests on the assumption that if the composition of imports changed in favour of raw materials and away from manufactures, then, since the exports of countries rich in raw materials would increase, they would be able to increase their imports of manufactures from countries that lose trade as a result of the United Kingdom's import controls. Furthermore, prices would not rise above the level that would be achieved if devaluation were implemented instead because, in the case of import controls in the form of tariffs, these are given back to economic agents in the form of tax reliefs so that, initially at least, there would be a tendency for prices to come down, not to increase, as would be the case with devaluation. If, then, foreign trade would not be lower with import controls, and prices would not be higher, the argument that consumers' real income would be reduced and that producers would lose some economies of scale cannot be sustained. The proponents of the thesis have thus been able to suggest that the case against import controls does not rest on well-articulated theoretical propositions and, consequently, that their argument of 'managed' international trade emerges unscathed. However, in view of the recent global and European developments in particular (especially in view of the prospects of the 'one market' after 1992), import controls do not assume the same importance in the menu of economic policies in this thesis. It can be argued, however, that managed international trade can easily be initiated by the whole European Community rather than by a single member-country. Indeed, the supporters of import controls favour the notion that some form of managed international trade should be in place.

Whether or not import controls could be effectively employed without undesirable repercussions, there is still the real possibility of investment not being sufficiently stimulated to sustain full employment. The usual argument is that the manufacturing sector needs some sort of 'sheltering', which would increase productivity and thus investment. However, there is nothing to guarantee that this investment will in fact materialize, particularly given the political uncertainty that would attend any such radical development.

These arguments obviously support and strengthen the policy conclusions arrived at above, namely, that attempts to stimulate the economy through fiscal and monetary policies cannot be successful unless they are accompanied by some form of control of investment. This control is absolutely necessary if the type of constraints identified above are to be removed so that the economy can move to, and sustain, a full-employment level of economic activity. Such policies should also contain strong regional elements both in terms of direct control of investment and 'financial segmentation' to account for the problems and suggestions discussed in section 10.2. Decentralization of this type is of paramount importance if democratic participation is to be taken seriously. A further policy implication is that control of investment by itself may not be effective if co-operation from the trade union movement is not forthcoming. But trade unions would be far more likely to co-operate if they were to be involved in the decision-making mechanism. Consequently, the type of investment control envisaged here is the socialization of investment which would actually involve the trade unions in the process.

Socialization of investment in this context gives active roles not just to governments but also to trade unions. An interesting implication of the principle of socialization of investment is that it involves structural changes in the way the economy is organized and not just a smoothing out in the amplitude of the business cycle. This is required to cure two major defects of capitalism. The first is seen to be the inadequate volume of private investment expenditure to drive the economy to full employment, due to the pervasive nature of investors' uncertainty about future economic performance. The second is its inequitable distribution of income and wealth. The socialization of investment is seen in this context as a way of redistributing income and wealth in a more equitable manner. This is inevitable since the socialization of investment involves trade unions and workers in the process. Redistribution of income and wealth along these lines should go together with attempts through fiscal and monetary policies to redress inequalities.

Wood (1975) argues for a policy of 'profit-sharing' whereby every company would be obliged by law to transfer each year a fixed proportion of its retained profits in the form of ordinary shares into the ownership of its employees. Bowles and Gintis (1989) argue for 'worker-owned and worker-run' firms. This can be achieved by transferring to the workers both ownership and control of firms – with due compensation to the owners for the loss of their assets. The fundamental assumption of this thesis is that workers' performance in the 'democratic' firm would be enhanced due to stronger incentives and motivation on the part of workers. Thus, the 'democratic' firm, in this view, provides a superior mechanism for tackling labour problems and, in general terms, working conditions. The danger with this scheme, though, is that it could potentially create divisions between workers in the oligopolistic and in the competitive sectors and between workers themselves when their performances differ. It might be better, therefore, to consider the possibility of a scheme whereby partial ownership of capital is transferred to an organization representing the political and economic interests of all workers. In this way there is direct involvement of the trade union movement in the process of capital formation.

The socialization of investment was, of course, one of Keynes's (1936) important policy prescriptions. We can see this in his suggestion that 'a somewhat comprehensive socialisation of investment will prove the only means of securing an approximation to full-employment; though this need not exclude all manner of compromises and of devices by which public authority will co-operate with private initiative' (p. 378). At a later date, Keynes (1980, p. 322) made more explicit his notion of socialization when he argued:

If two-thirds or three-quarters of total investment is carried out or can be influenced by public or semi-public bodies, a long-term programme of a stable character should be capable of reducing the potential range of fluctuations to much narrower limits than formerly, when a smaller volume of investment was under public control and when even this part tended to follow, rather than correct, fluctuations of investment in the strictly private sector.

In this way the socialization of investment is seen as filling the gap left by private investors and also as encouraging more private investment by reducing uncertainty through the creation of a more stable environment. The problem with Keynes's notion of the socialization of investment is that it cannot really be effective for it excludes from the socialization process the trade union involvement which is the *sine qua non* of its success.

The socialization of investment alongside trade union participation would also remove the obstacles to achieving full employment that so concerned Kalecki, especially as the dislike of sociopolitical change normally associated with attempts to sustain full employment disappears altogether. Changes of this nature would be welcomed by the trade unions since they strengthen the position of their members, enhancing their industrial muscle. In this environment, trade unions would be more willing to engage in permanent 'incomes planning'; for 'incomes planning' would have to be a permanent feature of the post-Keynesian menu of economic policies. This is because inflation is essentially determined by wage changes and the prices of imported raw materials and commodities. These types of policy, however, would have to be accompanied by an active labour market and manpower policies to encourage labour mobility and thus facilitate labour market adjustments for the unemployed. It is important to note that tackling unemployment would have to be top priority for this set of policies, since if they are not pursued with a firm commitment to full employment, their chances of success are seriously threatened. Rowthorn (1986) argues that unemployment has been lower in those countries (Sweden, Norway and Austria) where commitment to full employment has been part of a broad consensus between trade unions, industry and the state. This consensus has also involved economic restructuring and the 'planning of incomes'.

We may, therefore, suggest that a combination of fiscal and monetary as well as exchange rate policies, permanent 'planning of incomes', commitment to full employment on the part of the policymakers, an active labour market and manpower policies, and the socialization of investment, stand a better chance of success than just the orthodox way of manipulating the economy coupled with emergency 'incomes policies'.[5] A very important implication of this set of policies is that they go a long way towards meeting the Marxist critique of post-Keynesian economics that it 'cannot resolve the struggle over the distribution of factor shares between capital and labour, nor over control of the labour process that gives rise to profits' (Chernomas, 1982, p. 139). It clearly can do so within the parameters set by the socialization of investment process.

10.5 POTENTIAL CONSTRAINTS

This policy menu is by no means problem-free. There is, to begin with, the problem that since the policies rely heavily on social co-operation and social consensus between the state, industry and labour – experiments which failed in the past, especially in the UK – there is nothing to suggest that they will not fail again. The short answer is to say that social co-operation and social consensus would have to be created by involving people in the process itself (Cowling, 1987). There is, of course, the experience of some other countries which have been conspicuously successful with economic policies that relied on consensus (Sweden, Norway, Australia and Austria are the best examples in this respect). Indeed, there exists overwhelming evidence to suggest that increased participation is one of the dominant determinants of productivity (Hodgson, 1984), and that those firms that adopt the 'worker participation' type of policies experience superior sales, growth, profitability and better performance overall than similar firms which do not pursue policies of this nature (see Knight and Sugden, 1989, p. 45, for a short summary).

There is still the problem of the serious constraint imposed on these policies by the operation of transnational corporations and international financial capital. The operations of transnationals in the short run could very well jeopardize expansion, and the UK experience clearly indicates that this possibility is very real. In the long run it is expected that these firms would undertake a greater volume of investment once the economy achieved a sustained expansionary path. In the short run, however, control over the operations of transnational corporations would have to be established. Fiscal measures could be used to promote domestic rather than foreign investment, although the evidence here is that transnationals could easily overcome these types of measure. We should also consider the experience of other countries, which is very revealing indeed. Japan, USA, France, Canada and most notably a number of developing countries have all adopted policies towards transnationals. These policies have ranged from monitoring their activities and taking positive steps to discriminate in favour of domestic firms where there were fears of multinational dominance, to tighter and direct regulation on their activities. Sugden (1989) proposes that the experience of these countries is sufficiently revealing for us to learn a lot from them. In particular, a *transnational unit* is proposed with sufficient muscle to enable it to monitor the activities of transnationals. Most importantly, though, it would scrutinize their investment activity, including both inward and outward investment, whenever it exceeded a specified small size. This monitoring would then become part of an overall strategic planning (Cowling, 1989).

Similarly, policy-makers can and should attempt to have an impact on the sphere of regulation of international financial capital and trade flows. Clearly, the degree of success in this respect for countries like the UK is enhanced when such measures are taken at the European level as part of the European Community's collective measures. None the less, hostility to these types of policy by international financial capital usually lasts for a few months only, after which governments are judged by actions rather than rhetoric. It is interesting to note in this context that Keynes (1980, p. 52) envisages strict capital controls to deal with situations in which the centres of international financial capital become untameable. Indeed, he argued that capital controls, both inward and outward, should be permanent. Also permanent in his view should be the control of the entire financial system. Keynes (1980) even propounded the idea of planning to embrace the whole of the international economic system (see also Crotty, 1983). Hicks (1985) reinforces these views by advocating concerted action by a number of the more 'important' countries. An interesting proposal in this respect has been made recently by Tinbergen (1989) who proposes close co-operation between the European Community and Japan. One wonders, however, whether this would encompass enough of the Continent in view of the recent far-reaching developments in Eastern Europe.

These measures, especially those taken in collaboration with other countries or groups of countries, have assumed even more significance and importance recently in those countries where international capital has taken a new twist. One may refer to the UK as an example to make the point. What has apparently happened in the UK is that a new form of internationalization of the City of Finance Capital has taken place which has coincided with, or was perhaps induced by, the internationalization of British industrial capital. These developments have been taking place over the last ten years or so, at any rate since the abolition of exchange and credit controls initiated at the beginning of the 1980s. The interesting implication of these developments is that any attempt to distinguish between the interests of finance capital and those of industrial capital is a futile exercise. They are so tightly linked that the power of international capital is stronger than it would otherwise have been. The problem of controlling the activities of international capital, both industrial and financial, in the new environment becomes even more awkward when attempted in isolation. The inevitable conclusion emanating from these developments and the analysis pursued in this study is that there may be no alternative to policies being explicitly and firmly 'internationalist' (Radice, 1989).

10.6 CONCLUDING REMARKS

The major policy implication of post-Keynesian thinking as exemplified above would appear to be some form of socialization of investment. But socialization ought to be accompanied by explicit and permanent planning of incomes under the umbrella of a 'social contract' among the three groups, trade unions, industry and state, which are generally recognized as being the three all-important groups in any economic system. In this environment wage pressures that damage profitability and accumulation can be avoided, especially if there is a commitment to full employment by governments. These policies should also be accompanied by appropriate industrial policies which would promote the participation of the workforce in decision-making. In fact, some of these ideas have been successfully implemented in certain 'capitalist' economies. There are in particular two well-documented examples of the socialization of investment: Sweden, which is probably the most well-known example (Arestis, 1986b, 1989), and Austria where a successful form of 'social control' of investment has been implemented (Tichy, 1984). The example of Japan could be added (Cowling, 1987) and, to a lesser extent, those of France and Germany. As it happens, these economies belong to that group of countries which has been doing particularly well in terms of economic performance in the turbulent recent, and not so recent, past. In this sense, the post-Keynesian economic analysis and policy implications explored in this book give credence to the view that the future of post-Keynesian economics looks very promising indeed. It can, and should, become more influential in terms of both economic theory and policy. It appears, therefore, that Keynes (1936, 1980), Kalecki (1971a) and the other influential post-Keynesians were more prophetic than is generally recognized. In fact, one can maintain that they are as relevant to-day as they have ever been; perhaps even more relevant.

We finally conclude this chapter and the book by suggesting that the post-Keynesian analysis and economic policies discussed here are very germane to the points Keynes (1920, p. 17) was making when he argued that the 'remarkable' capitalist system

> depended for its growth on double bluff or deception. On the one hand the labouring classes accepted from ignorance or powerlessness . . . a situation in which they could call their own very little of the cake that they and Nature and the capitalist classes were co-operating to produce. And on the other hand the capitalist classes were allowed to call the best part of the cake theirs and were theoretically free to consume it, on the tacit underlying condition that they consumed very little of it in practice.

They can also contribute to the implementation of the far-reaching changes to the capitalist system that Keynes was proposing in the same passage:

> If only the cake were not cut but was allowed to grow . . . a day might come when there would be enough to go round, and when posterity could enter the enjoyment of our labours. In that day overwork, overcrowding and underfeeding would come to an end, and men, secure of the comforts of the body, could proceed to the nobler exercise of their faculties. (Ibid.)

The ultimate objective of post-Keynesian economics is to achieve precisely this goal.

NOTES

1. There is an interesting contrast here between Kalecki and Keynes. Kalecki's 'power of vested interests' is different from Keynes's faith in the 'power of ideas' (Sawyer, 1985, ch. 9; Reynolds, 1987, p. 226).
2. Sawyer (1985, p. 140) suggests that the group of 'more than one economist' who would support strongly the interests of big business and rentiers is none other than the monetarists, as the experience of the 1980s in the UK and elsewhere clearly testified.
3. The direction of budget deficits should be carefully considered. For merely demonstrating that budget deficits are important without further specifying that there may be undesirable directions for them can lead to peculiar results, to say the least. Robinson (1972, p. 7) puts it very aptly when she argues that :'It was the so-called Keynesians who persuaded successive presidents that there is no harm in a budget deficit and left the military–industrial complex to take advantage of it. So it has come about that Keynes' pleasant daydream was turned into a nightmare of terror.'
4. There are, of course, other omissions of TIP. Appelbaum (1982, p. 555) provides an interesting list: 'differences in market power among firms, the distribution of earned income, the elimination of poverty, the taxation of wealth, the adequacy of childcare facilities or public education or public transportation, the access to quality health care, the provision of cultural and recreational programs, the construction of middle-income housing . . . the level of social security payments', all of which are not discussed in TIP. This long list of omissions was also very characteristic of 'incomes policies' implemented, for example, in postwar Britain, and in Australia in the period 1983–91, which, however, appeared to be more 'successful' than the British.
5. A contribution which is very supportive of the thesis developed in the text in the case of Australia is Groenewegen (1979). Although he paints a rather pessimistic picture of the Australian political economists who are reluctant 'to come to grips with the basic instruments of the State's interrelationships with capitalism' (p. 198), he none the less singles out Australian developments in post-Keynesian economics as providing positive contributions. Indeed, from the economic policy viewpoint Harcourt and Kerr (1979) is seen as the best example of post-Keynesian economic policy analysis in Australia. What is interesting from our perspective is that the economic policies we have discussed in this book are truly within the spirit of Harcourt and Kerr's (1977) analysis and policy recommendations. But what is particularly interesting in this context is Groenewegen's (1979, p. 204) suggestion that these policies should not be seen as implying that state intervention is intended to organize capitalism more efficiently, but as a 'reformist' approach to economic policy. This statement fully justifies the claim that post-Keynesian economics is a 'revolution' in economic analysis and policy.

Bibliography

Adnett, N. (1989), *Labour Market Policy*, London: Longmans.
Aglietta, M. (1979), *A Theory of Capitalist Regulation: The US Experience*, London: Verso.
Aglietta, M. (1982), 'World Capitalism in the Eighties', *New Left Review*, November/December.
Akerlof, G.A. (1979), 'The Case against Conservative Macroeconomics: an Inaugural Lecture', *Economica*, August.
Akerlof, G.A. and Yellen, J.L. (1985a), 'A Near-Rational Model of the Business Cycle with Wage and Price Inertia', *Quarterly Journal of Economics*, Supplement.
Akerlof, G.A. and Yellen, J.L. (1985b), 'Can Small Deviations from Rationality Make Significant Differences to Economic Equilibrium?', *American Economic Review*, September.
Akerlof, G.A. and Yellen, J.L. (1987), 'Rational Models of Irrational Behavior', *American Economic Review*, Papers and Proceedings, May.
Appelbaum, E. (1982), 'The Incomplete Incomes Policy Vision', *Journal of Post Keynesian Economics*, Summer.
Arestis, P. (1986a), 'Wages and Prices in the UK: the Post Keynesian View', *Journal of Post Keynesian Economics*, Spring.
Arestis, P. (1986b), 'Post-Keynesian Economic Policies: the case of Sweden', *Journal of Economic Issues*, August.
Arestis, P. (1987/8), 'The Credit Segment of a UK Post Keynesian Model', *Journal of Post Keynesian Economics*, Winter.
Arestis, P. (ed.) (1988), *Post-Keynesian Monetary Economics: New Approaches to Financial Modelling*, Aldershot: Edward Elgar.
Arestis, P. (1989), 'On the Post Keynesian Challenge to Neoclassical Economics: a Complete Quantitative Macro-Model for the UK Economy', *Journal of Post Keynesian Economics*, Summer.
Arestis, P. (1990), 'Post-Keynesianism: a New Approach to Economics', *Review of Social Economics*, Fall.

Arestis, P. and Biefang-Frisancho Mariscal, I. (1991), 'Hysteresis and Unemployment in Wage Determination', *British Review of Economic Issues*, June.

Arestis, P., Biefang-Frisancho Mariscal, I. and Howells, P. (1992), 'Theoretical and Empirical Reflections on the Endogenous Money Supply', paper delivered at the New Orleans conference of the Union of Radical Political Economics at Allied Social Science Association, January.

Arestis, P. and Dow, S.C. (eds) (1992), *On Money, Method and Keynes: Selected Essays of Victoria Chick*, London: Macmillan.

Arestis, P. and Driver, C. (1980), 'Consumption out of Different Types of Income in the UK', *Bulletin of Economic Research*, November.

Arestis, P. and Driver, C. (1983), 'UK Unemployment and Post-Keynesian Remedies', *Metroeconomica*, October.

Arestis, P. and Driver, C. (1984), 'The Policy Implications of Post-Keynesianism', *Journal of Economic Issues*, December.

Arestis, P. and Driver, C. (1987), 'The Effects of Income Distribution on Consumer Imports', *Journal of Macroeconomics*, Winter.

Arestis, P., Driver, C. and Rooney, J. (1985/6), 'The Real Segment of a UK Post Keynesian Model', *Journal of Post Keynesian Economics*, Winter.

Arestis, P. and Eichner, A.S. (1988), 'The Post-Keynesian and Institutionalist Theory of Money and Credit', *Journal of Economic Issues*, December.

Arestis, P. and Karakitsos, E. (1982), 'Towards a General Theory of Unemployment: Is Leijonhufvud a Keynesian?', *Zeitschrift für Nationalökonomie*, vol. 42, no. 2.

Arestis, P. and Kitromilides, Y. (eds), (1989), *Theory and Policy in Political Economy: Essays in Pricing, Distribution and Growth*, Upleadon, Glos.: Edward Elgar.

Arestis, P. and Skott, P. (forthcoming), 'Conflict, Wage Relativities and Hysteresis in U.K. Wage Determination', *Journal of Post Keynesian Economics*.

Arestis, P. and Skouras, T. (1985), *Post-Keynesian Theory: A Challenge to Neo-Classical Economics*, Brighton, Sussex: Wheatsheaf Books; New York: M.E. Sharpe.

Arestis, P. and Skuse, F.E. (1989), 'Austerity Policies and the New Right: Recent UK Experience', *Economie Appliquée*, vol. 42, no. 1.

Arrow, K.J. (1982), 'Risk Perception in Psychology and Economics', *Economic Enquiry*, January.
Arrow, K.J. and Hahn, F.H. (1971), *General Competitive Analysis*, San Francisco: Holden-Day.
Artis, M.J. and Lewis, M.K. (1981), *Monetary Control in the United Kingdom*, Oxford: Philip Allen.
Asimakopulos, A. (1971), 'The Determination of Investment in Keynes's Model', *Canadian Journal of Economics*, August.
Asimakopulos, A. (1975), 'A Kaleckian Theory of Income Distribution', *Canadian Journal of Economics*, August.
Asimakopulos, A. (1982), 'Keynes's Theory of Effective Demand Revisited', *Australian Economic Papers*, June.
Asimakopulos, A. (1983), 'Kalecki and Keynes on Finance, Investment and Saving', *Cambridge Journal of Economics*, September/December.
Asimakopulos, A. (1988), 'The Theoretical Significance of Keynes's General Theory', *Thames Papers in Political Economy*, Summer; reprinted in Arestis and Kitromilides (1989).
Bade, F. (1986), 'The De-industrialisation of the Federal Republic of Germany and its Spatial Implication', in P. Nijkamp (ed.), *Technological Change, Employment and Spatial Dynamics*, Berlin: Springer.
Baldwin, R. (1989), 'The Growth Effects of 1992', *Economic Policy*, October.
Bank of England Quarterly Bulletin (BEQB) (1982), 'The Role of the Bank of England in the Money Market', March.
Baran, P. (1957), *The Political Economy of Growth*, New York, Monthly Review.
Barro, R.J. (1978), 'Unanticipated Money Output, and the Price Level in the United States', *Journal of Political Economy*, vol. 86, no. 4.
Barro, R.J. and Grossman, H.I. (1976), *Money, Employment and Inflation*, Cambridge: Cambridge University Press.
Barro, R.J. and Hercowitz, Z. (1980), 'Money Stock, Revisions and Unanticipated Money Growth', *Journal of Monetary Economics*, April.
Beath, J. (1979), 'Target Profits, Cost Expectations and Incidence of the Corporate Income Tax', *Review of Economic Studies*, July.
Bharadwaj, K. (1978), 'The Subversion of Classical Analysis: Alfred

Marshall's Early Writings on Value', *Cambridge Journal of Economics*, vol. 2.
Bharadwaj, K. (1983), 'On Effective Demand: Certain Recent Critiques', in J.A. Kregel (ed.), *Distribution, Effective Demand and International Economic Relations*, London: Macmillan.
Bhaskar, V. (1990), 'Wage Relativities and the Natural Range of Unemployment', *Economic Journal*, Supplement.
Blanchard, O.J. (1987), 'Why Does Money Affect Output? A Survey', in B. Friedman and F. Hahn (eds), *Handbook of Monetary Economics*, Amsterdam: North Holland.
Blanchard, O.J. and Diamond, P. (1990), 'Unemployment and Wages: What Have We Learned from the European Experience?' *Employment Institute Pamphlet*, April.
Blanchard, O.J. and Summers, L.H. (1987a), 'Hysteresis in Unemployment', *European Economic Review*, April.
Blanchard, O.J. and Summers, L.H. (1987b), 'Hysteresis and the European Unemployment Problem' in *Macroeconomic Models*, vol. 1, National Bureau of Economic Research, New York.
Blatt, J.M. (1983), *Dynamic Economic Systems: A Post-Keynesian Approach*, New York: M.E. Sharp.
Blaug, M. (1978), *Economic Theory in Retrospect*, 3rd edn, Cambridge: Cambridge University Press.
Blaug, M. (1980), *The Methodology of Economics, or How Economists Think*, Cambridge: Cambridge University Press.
Blinder, A.S. (1978), 'What's New and What's Relevant in "New Cambridge" Keynesianism', in K. Brunner and A.H. Meltzer (eds), *Public Policies in Open Economies*, Carnegie-Rochester Conference Series, no. 9, Amsterdam: North Holland.
Bliss, C. (1983), 'Two Views of Macroeconomics', *Oxford Economic Papers*, March.
Boland, L.A. (1979), 'A Critique of Friedman's Critics', *Journal of Economic Literature*, June; Reprinted in Boland (1982).
Boland, L.A. (1982), *The Foundations of Economic Method*, London: George Allen & Unwin.
Boschen, J. and Grossman, H.I. (1982), 'Tests of Equilibrium Macroeconomics with Contemporaneous Monetary Data', *Journal of Monetary Economics*, November.
Boulding, K.E. (1956), *The Image: Knowledge in Life and Society*, Ann Arbor: University of Michigan Press.
Bowles, S. (1985), 'The Production Process in a Competitive Econ-

omy: Walrasian, Neo-Hobbesian and Marxist Models', *American Economic Review*, March.

Bowles, S. and Gintis, H. (1989), 'The Inefficiency and Competitive Survival of the Capitalist Firm', *Working Paper 1989-6*, Department of Economics, University of Massachusetts.

Bowles, S., Gordon, D.M. and Weisskopf, T.E. (1984), *Beyond the Waste Land: A Democratic Alternative to Economic Decline*, London: Verso.

Branson, W.H. and Hill, D. Jr (1971), 'Capital Movements in the OECD Area: an Econometric Analysis', *OECD Economic Outlook*, December.

Brown, E.K. (1981), 'The Neoclassical and Post-Keynesian Research Programs: the Methodological Issues', *Review of Social Economy*, October.

Buiter, W.H. (1980), 'The Macroeconomics of Dr Pangloss: a Critical Survey of the New Classical Macroeconomics', *Economic Journal*, March.

Burmeister, E. and Taubman, P. (1969), 'Labour and Non-Labour Income Saving Propensities', *Canadian Journal of Economics*, February.

Caldwell, B.J. (1980), 'A Critique of Friedman's Methodological Instrumentalism', *Southern Economic Journal*, October; reprinted in Caldwell (1984).

Caldwell, B.J. (1984), *Appraisal and Criticism in Economics*, London: George Allen & Unwin.

Caldwell, B.J. (1989), 'Post-Keynesian Methodology: an Assessment', *Review of Political Economy*, March.

Cambridge Economic Policy Group (CEPG) (1975), *Economic Policy Review*, no. 1, Department of Applied Economics. Cambridge University.

Cambridge Economic Policy Group (CEPG) (1976), *Economic Policy Review*, no. 2, Department of Applied Economics, Cambridge University.

Canterbery, R. (1979), 'Inflation, Necessities and Distributive Efficiency', in J.H. Gapinsky and C.E. Rockwood Jr (eds), *Essays in Post-Keynesian Inflation*, New York: Ballinger.

Çapoğlu, G. (1991), *Prices, Profits and Financial Structures: A Post-Keynesian Approach to Competition*, Aldershot: Edward Elgar.

Carlin, W. and Soskice, D. (1990), *Macroeconomics and the Wage*

Bargain: A Modern Approach to Employment, Inflation and the Exchange Rate, Oxford: Oxford University Press.
Carvalho, F. (1984/5), 'Alternative Analyses of Short and Long Run in Post Keynesian Economics', Journal of Post Keynesian Economics, Winter.
Carvalho, F. (1990), 'Keynes and the Long Period', Cambridge Economic Journal, vol. 14.
Champernowne, D.G. (1954), 'The Production Function and the Theory of Capital: a Comment', Review of Economic Studies, vol. 21.
Champernowne, D.G. (1963), 'Expectations and the Links between the Economic Future and the Present', in R. Lekachman, Keynes's General Theory: Reports of Three Decades, London: Macmillan.
Chernomas, B. (1982), 'Keynesian, Marxist and Post-Keynesian Policy', Studies in Political Economy, vol. 10.
Chick, V. (1973), 'Financial Counterparts of Saving and Investment and Inconsistency in a Simple Macro Model', Weltwirtschaftliches Archiv, vol. 109, no. 4; reprinted in Arestis and Dow (1992).
Chick, V. (1982), 'Comment on ISLM – an Explanation', Journal of Post Keynesian Economics, Spring; reprinted in Arestis and Dow (1992).
Chick, V. (1983), Macroeconomics After Keynes: A Reconsideration of The General Theory, Cambridge MA: MIT Press.
Chick, V. (1986), 'The Evolution of the Banking System and the Theory of Saving, Investment and Interest', Economies et Sociétés, Cahiers de l'ISMEA, Série Monnaie et Production, no. 3.
Chick, V. and Dow, S.C. (1988), 'A Post-Keynesian Perspective on the Relation Between Banking and Regional Development', in P. Arestis (ed.), Post-Keynesian Monetary Economics: New Approaches to Financial Modelling, Aldershot: Edward Elgar.
Chipman, J.S., Hurwicz, L., Richter, M.K. and Sonnenschein, H.F. (eds) (1971), Preferences, Utility and Demand, New York: Harcourt Brace Jovanovich.
Christodoulakis, N. and Godley, W.A.H. (1987), 'A Dynamic Model for the Analysis of Trade Policy Options', Journal of Policy Modelling, no. 9.
Clark, K.B. and Summers, L.H. (1982), 'Labour Force Participa-

tion: Timing and Persistence', *Review of Economic Studies*, vol. 49, no. 159.
Clower, R.W. (1965), 'The Keynesian Counterrevolution: a Theoretical Appraisal', in F.H. Hahn and F.P.R. Brechling (eds), *The Theory of Interest Rates*, Proceedings of the International Economics Association Conference 1962, New York: St Martin's Press; reprinted in R.W. Clower (ed.) (1969), *Monetary Theory*, London: Penguin.
Coakley, J. and Harris, L. (1983), *The City of Capital: London's Role as a Financial Centre*, Oxford: Basil Blackwell.
Coddington, A. (1976), 'Keynesian Economics: the Search for First Principles', *Journal of Economic Literature*, December.
Cohen, A.J. (1990), 'Does Joan Robinson's Critique of Equilibrium Entail Theoretical Nihilism?', mimeo.
Cornwall, J. (1979), 'Economic Growth: Two Paradigms', *Journal of Post Keynesian Economics*, Spring.
Coutts, K., Godley, W. and Nordhaus, W. (1978), *Industrial Pricing in the United Kingdom*, Cambridge: Cambridge University Press.
Coutts, K., Tarling, R.J. and Wilkinson, S.F. (1976), 'Wage Bargaining and the Inflation Process', *Economic Policy Review*, no. 2, Department of Applied Economics, Cambridge University.
Cowling, K. (1982), *Monopoly Capitalism*, London: Macmillan.
Cowling, K. (1985), 'Economic Obstacles to Democracy', in R.C.O. Matthews (ed)., *Economy and Democracy*, London: Macmillan.
Cowling, K. (1987), 'An Individual Strategy for Britain: The Nature and Role of Planning', *International Review of Applied Economics*, November.
Cowling, K. (1989), 'The Strategic Approach', in Industrial Strategy Group, *Beyond the Review: Perspectives in Labour's Economy and Industrial Strategy*, chapter 1, Edinburgh: University of Edinburgh.
Cowling, K. and Waterson, M. (1976), 'Price-cost Margins and Market Structure', *Economica*, August.
Cripps, T. (1978), 'Causes of Growth and Recession in World Trade', *Cambridge Economic Policy Review*, no. 4, Department of Applied Economics: Cambridge University.
Cripps, T.F. and Godley, W.A.H. (1976), 'A Formal Analysis of the Cambridge Economic Policy Group Model', *Economica*, August.
Cripps, T.F. and Godley, W.A.H. (1978), 'Control of Imports as a

Means to Full Employment and the Expansion of World Trade: the UK's Case', *Cambridge Journal of Economics*, vol. 2.

Cross, R.B. (1988), *Unemployment, Hysteresis and the Natural Rate Hypothesis*, Oxford: Basil Blackwell.

Cross, R.B. and Allen, A. (1988), 'On the History of Hysteresis', in Cross (1988).

Cross, R.B. and Laidler, D.E.W. (1975), 'Inflation, Excess Demand and Expectations in Fixed Exchange Rate Open Economies: Some Preliminary Empirical Results', in J.M. Parkin and G. Zis (eds), *Inflation in the World Economy*, Manchester: Manchester University Press.

Crotty, J.R. (1980), 'Post-Keynesian Economic Theory: an Overview and Evaluation', *American Economic Review*, Papers and Proceedings, May.

Crotty, J.R. (1983), 'On Keynes and Capital Flight', *Journal of Economic Literature*, March.

Crouch, C. (1979), *State and Economy in Contemporary Capitalism*, London: Croom Helm.

Cuthbertson, K. (1979), *Macroeconomic Policy: New Cambridge and Monetarist Controversies*, London: Macmillan.

Cuthbertson, K. (1985), 'Sterling Bank Lending to UK Industrial and Commercial Companies', *Oxford Bulletin of Economics*, May.

Cyert, R.M. and March, J.G. (1963), *A Behavioral Theory of the Firm*, Englewood Cliffs, N.J.: Prentice-Hall.

Dasgupta, P. and Hahn, F.H. (1985), 'To the Defence of Economics', *Nature*, October.

Davidson, P. (1978), *Money and the Real World*, 2nd edn, London: Macmillan.

Davidson, P. (1981), 'Post Keynesian Economics', in D. Bell and I. Kristol (eds), *The Crisis in Economic Theory*, New York: Basic Books.

Davidson, P. (1982), *International Money and the Real World*, London: Macmillan.

Davidson, P. (1988a), 'A Post Keynesian View of Theories and Causes of High Real Interest Rates', in Arestis (ed.) (1988).

Davidson, P. (1988b), 'A Technical Definition of Uncertainty and the Long-run Non-neutrality of Money', *Cambridge Journal of Economics*, vol. 12.

Davidson, P. and Kregel, J.A. (1989), *Macroeconomic Problems and Policies of Income Distribution*, Aldershot: Edward Elgar.

Davidson, P. and Weintraub, S. (1973), 'Money as Cause and Effect', *Economic Journal*, March.

Davidson, P. and Weintraub, S. (1978), 'A Statement of Purposes', *Journal of Post Keynesian Economics*, Fall.

Davies, J.B. (1989), 'Axiomatic General Equilibrium Theory and Referentiality', *Journal of Post Keynesian Economics*, Spring.

De Marchi, N. and Gilbert, C. (eds) (1990), *The History and Methodology of Econometrics*, Oxford: Oxford University Press.

De Vroey, M. (1975), 'The Transition from Classical to Neoclassical Economics: a Scientific Revolution', *Journal of Economic Issues*, September.

De Vroey, M. (1984), 'Inflation: a Non-Monetarist Monetary Interpretation', *Cambridge Journal of Economics*, vol. 8.

Dobb, M. (1973), *Theories of Value and Distribution since Adam Smith*, Cambridge: Cambridge University Press.

Dornbusch, R. (1976), 'Expectations and Exchange Rate Dynamics', *Journal of Political Economy*, vol. 84, no. 6.

Dow, S.C. (1985), *Macroeconomic Thought: A Methodological Approach*, Oxford: Basil Blackwell.

Dow, S.C. (1986/7), 'Post Keynesian Monetary Theory for an Open Economy', *Journal of Post Keynesian Economics*, Winter.

Dow, S.C. (1988), 'Post Keynesian Economics: Conceptual Underpinnings', *British Review of Economic Issues*, Autumn.

Dow, S.C. (1990a), 'Beyond Dualism', *Cambridge Journal of Economics*, vol. 14.

Dow, S.C. (1990b), 'The Post Keynesian School', in D. Mair and A. Miller (eds), *A Modern Guide to Economic Thought*, Aldershot: Edward Elgar.

Dow, S.C. and Chick, V. (1988), 'A Post-Keynesian Perspective on the Relation Between Banking and Regional Development', in Arestis (ed.) (1988).

Dow, S.C. and Earl, P.E. (1982), *Money Matters: A Keynesian Approach to Monetary Economics*, Oxford: Martin Robertson.

Drazen, A. (1980), 'Recent Developments in Macroeconomic Disequilibrium Theory', *Econometrica*, March.

Driver, C.F. (1984), *Investment, Growth and Government Policy in an Economy Characterised by Oligopolistic and Competitive Sectors*,

PhD Dissertation, Council for National Academic Awards; London: Thames Polytechnic.
Duesenberry, J.S. (1949), *Income, Saving and the Theory of Consumer Behavior*, New York: Harvard University Press.
Duesenberry, J.S. (1958), *Business Cycles and Economic Growth*, New York: McGraw Hill.
Earl, P.E. (1989), 'Bounded Rationality, Psychology and Financial Evolution: Some Behavioural Perspectives on Post-Keynesian Analysis', in Pheby (ed.) (1989).
Eatwell, J. (1983), 'Theories of Value, Output and Employment', in Eatwell and Milgate (eds) (1983).
Eatwell, J. and Milgate, M. (eds) (1983), *Keynes's Economics and the Theory of Value and Distribution*, London: Duckworth.
Eckstein, O. and Fromm, G.M. (1968), 'The Price Equation', *American Economic Review*, December.
Eichner, A.S. (1973), 'A Theory of the Determination of the Markup under Oligopoly', *Economic Journal*, December.
Eichner, A.S. (1974), 'Determination of the Mark-up under Oligopoly: a Reply', *Economic Journal*, December.
Eichner, A.S. (1976), *The Megacorp and Oligopoly: Micro Foundations of Macro Dynamics*, Cambridge: Cambridge University Press.
Eichner, A.S. (1979a), 'A Post Keynesian Short-Period Model', *Journal of Post Keynesian Economics*, Summer.
Eichner, A.S. (1979b), *A Guide to Post-Keynesian Economics*, New York: M.E. Sharpe.
Eichner, A.S. (1980), 'A Post-Keynesian Interpretation of Stagflation: Changing Theory to Fit the Reality', *Special Studies on Economic Change: Stagflation*, Joint Education Committee.
Eichner, A.S. (1983a), 'Why Economics is Not yet a Science', in A.S. Eichner (ed.), *Why Economics is Not Yet a Science*, London: Macmillan.
Eichner, A.S. (1983b), 'The Post-Keynesian Paradigm and Macrodynamic Modelling', *Thames Papers in Political Economy*, Summer.
Eichner, A.S. (1985), 'The Lack of Progress in Economics', *Nature*, February.
Eichner, A.S. (1987), *The Macrodynamics of Advanced Market Economies*, New York: M.E. Sharpe.
Eichner, A.S. and Kregel, J.A. (1975), 'An Essay on Post-Keynesian

Theory: a New Paradigm in Economics', *Journal of Economic Literature*, December.
Fine, B. and Harris, L. (1985), *The Peculiarities of the British Economy*, London: Lawrence & Wishart.
Fischer, S. (1977), 'Long-Term Contracts, Rational Expectations, and the Optimal Money Supply Rule', *Journal of Political Economy*, February.
Fischer, S. (1988), 'Recent Developments in Macroeconomics', *Economic Journal*, June.
Fleming, J.S. (1962), 'Domestic Financial Policies under Fixed and under Flexible Exchange Rates', *International Monetary Fund Staff Papers*, vol. 9.
Forman, L. (1980), 'Some Methodological Comments on Estimating the Parameters of a Post-Keynesian Model', Centre for Economic and Anthropogenic Research, Rutgers University, Working Paper no. 3, September.
Forman, L. and Eichner, A.S. (1981), 'A Post Keynesian Short-Period Model: Some Preliminary Econometric Results', *Journal of Post Keynesian Economics*, Fall.
Frank, A.G. (1969), *Capitalism and Underdevelopment in Latin America*, New York: Modern Reader Paperbacks.
Frenkel, J. and Johnson, H.G. (1976), *The Monetary Approach to the Balance of Payments*, London: George Allen & Unwin.
Frey, B.S. and Schneider, F. (1978a), 'A Political Economic Model of the UK', *Economic Journal*, June.
Frey, B.S. and Schneider, F. (1978b), 'An Empirical Study of Politico-economic Interaction in the US', *Review of Economics and Statistics*, May.
Frey, B.S. and Schneider, F. (1978c), 'An Econometric Model with an Endogenous Government Sector', *Public Choice*, no. 33.
Friedman, M. (1953), 'The Methodology of Positive Economics', in his *Essays in Positive Economics*, Chicago: University of Chicago Press.
Friedman, M. (1968), 'The Role of Monetary Policy', *American Economic Review*, April.
Friedman, M. (1975), *Unemployment Versus Inflation: An Evaluation of the Phillips Curve*, IEA Occasional Paper no. 44, London: Institute of Economic Affairs.
Friedman, M. (1977), 'Inflation and Unemployment', *Journal of Political Economy*, June.

Friedman, M. (1979), 'Optional Expectations and the Extreme Information Assumptions of "Rational Expectations" Macro-Models', *Journal of Monetary Economics*, January.

Gadolfo, G. (1980), *Economic Dynamics, Methods and Models*, Amsterdam: North Holland Publishing Company.

Galbraith, J.K. (1973), 'Power and the Useful Economist', *American Economic Review*, March.

Galbraith, J.K. (1978), 'On Post Keynesian Economics', *Journal of Post Keynesian Economics*, Fall.

Garegnani, P. (1978), 'Notes on Consumption, Investment and Effective Demand: I', *Cambridge Journal of Economics*, vol. 2.

Garegnani, P. (1979), 'Notes on Consumption, Investment and Effective Demand: II', *Cambridge Journal of Economics*, vol. 3.

Gedeon, S.J. (1985/6), 'The Post Keynesian Theory of Money: a Summary and an Eastern European Example', *Journal of Post Keynesian Economics*, Winter.

Gershuny, J. (1983), *Social Innovation and the Division of Labour*, Oxford: Oxford University Press.

Gillies, D.A. (forthcoming), *Philosophy of Science in the 20th Century: Three Central Themes*, Oxford: Basil Blackwell.

Godley, W. and Cripps, F. (1983), *Macroeconomics*, Oxford: Fontana.

Goodhart, C.A.E. (1983), 'Comment on A.H. Meltzer's "On Keynes and Monetarism" ', in Worswick and Trevithick (1983).

Goodhart, C.A.E. (1984), *Monetary Theory and Practice: The UK Experience*, London: Macmillan.

Goodhart, C.A.E. (1986), 'Financial Innovation and Monetary Control', *Oxford Review of Economic Policy*, Winter.

Goodhart, C.A.E. (1989), 'Has Moore Become Too Horizontal?', *Journal of Post Keynesian Economics*, Fall.

Goodwin, R.M. (1967), 'A Growth Cycle' in C.H. Feinstein (ed.), *Socialism, Capitalism and Economic Growth*, Cambridge: Cambridge University Press.

Goodwin, R.M. (1972), 'A Growth Cycle', in E.K. Hunt and J.G. Schwartz (eds), *A Critique of Economic Theory*, New York: Penguin Books.

Gordon, R.J. (1982), 'Price Inertia and Policy Ineffectiveness in the United States, 1890–1980', *Journal of Political Economy*, vol. 90, no. 6.

Gordon, R.J. (1990), 'What is New-Keynesian Economics?', *Journal of Economic Literature*, September.
Gowland, D. (1984), *Controlling the Money Supply*, 2nd edn, London: Croom Helm.
Groenewegen, P.D. (1979), 'Radical Economics in Australia: a Survey of the 1970s', in F.H. Gruen (ed.), *Surveys of Australian Economics*, vol. II, Sydney: George Allen & Unwin.
Guttentag, J. and Herring, R. (1983), *The Lender-of-Last-Resort Function in an International Context*, Essays in International Finance, no. 151, Princeton, N.J.: Princeton University Press.
Hacche, G. (1979), *The Theory of Economic Growth*, London: Macmillan.
Hagemann, H. and Ruhl, C. (1990), 'Nicholas Johannsen and Keynes's "Finance Motive" ', *Journal of Institutional and Theoretical Economics*, September.
Hahn, F.H. (1971), *Readings in the Theory of Growth*, London: Weidenfeld & Nicolson.
Hahn, F.H. (1978), 'On Non-Walrasian Equilibria', *Review of Economic Studies*, February.
Hahn, F.H. (1991), 'On Recent Macro-Economic Theory and Policy Debates', *Cyprus Journal of Economics*, June.
Haltiwanger, J. and Waldman, M. (1985), 'Rational Expectations and the Limits of Rationality: an Analysis of Heterogeneity', *American Economic Review*, June.
Ham, C. and Hill, M. (1984), *The Policy Process in the Modern Capitalist State*, Brighton, Sussex: Wheatsheaf Books.
Hamouda, O.F. and Harcourt, G.C. (1988), 'Post Keynesianism: From Criticism to Coherence?', *Bulletin of Economic Research*, January; reprinted in J. Pheby (ed.) (1989).
Harcourt, G.C. (1969a), 'Some Cambridge Controversies in the Theory of Capital', *Journal of Economic Literature*, June.
Harcourt, G.C. (1969b), 'A Teaching Model of the "Keynesian" System', *Keio Economic Studies*, vol. 6.
Harcourt, G.C. (1972), *Some Cambridge Controversies in the Theory of Capital*, Cambridge: Cambridge University Press.
Harcourt, G.C. (1976), 'The Cambridge Controversies: Old Ways and New Horizons – or Dead End?', *Oxford Economic Papers*, vol. 28.
Harcourt, G.C. (ed.) (1977), *The Microeconomic Foundations of Macroeconomics*, London: Macmillan.

Harcourt, G.C. (1984), 'A Post-Keynesian Development of the "Keynesian" Model', in E.J. Nell (ed.), *Growth, Profits, and Property: Essays in the Revival of Political Economy*, Cambridge: Cambridge University Press.

Harcourt, G.C. (1985), 'Post-Keynesianism: Quite Wrong and/or Nothing New?', in Arestis and Skouras (eds) (1985).

Harcourt, G.C. (1989), 'Bastard Keynesianism', in J. Eatwell, M. Milgate and J. Newman (eds), *The New Palgrave*, London: Macmillan Press.

Harcourt, G.C. and Kenyon, P. (1976), 'Pricing and the Investment Decision', *Kyklos*, vol. 29, fasc. 3.

Harcourt, G.C. and Kerr, P.M. (1979), 'The Acceptance of a Mixed Economy', in P. Weller (ed.), *The Australian Labour Party: Past Trends and Future Prospects*, Sydney: Ian Novak.

Hare, P.G. (1980), 'Import Controls and the CEPG Model of the UK Economy', *Scottish Journal of Political Economy*, June.

Hargreaves-Heap, S.P. (1980), 'Choosing the Wrong Natural Rate: Accelerating Inflation or Decelerating Unemployment and Growth', *Economic Journal*, September.

Harris, D.J. (1978), *Capital Accumulation and Income Distribution*, Stanford: Stanford University Press.

Harris, L.H. (1981), *Monetary Theory*, New York: McGraw-Hill.

Harrod, R.F. (1937), 'Mr. Keynes and Traditional Theory', *Econometrica*, January.

Harrod, R.F. (1939), 'An Essay in Dynamic Theory', *Economic Journal*, March.

Harrod, R.F. (1948), *Towards a Dynamic Economics*, London: Macmillan.

Harrod, R.F. (1973), *Economic Dynamics*, London: Macmillan.

Hart, O. (1982), 'A Model of Imperfect Competition with Keynesian Features', *Quarterly Journal of Economics*, February.

Hazeldine, T. (1974), 'Determination of the Mark-up under Oligopoly: a Comment', *Economic Journal*, December.

Heiner, R.A. (1983), 'Origin of Predictable Behavior: Further Modelling and Applications', *American Economic Review*, September.

Heiner, R.A. (1986), 'Uncertainty, Signal-Detection Experiments, and Modelling Behaviour', in Langlois (1986).

Henry, S.G.B. and Ormerod, P. (1978), 'Incomes Policy and Wage

Inflation: Empirical Evidence for the UK, 1961–77', *National Institute Economic Review*, August.
Hey, J.D. (1979), *Uncertainty in Microeconomics*, Oxford: Martin Robertson.
Hicks, J.R. (1937), 'Mr Keynes and the Classics: a Suggested Interpretation', *Econometrica*, April.
Hicks, J.R. (1939), *Value and Capital*, Oxford: Oxford University Press.
Hicks, J.R. (1949), 'Mr Harrod's Dynamic Theory', *Economica*, May.
Hicks, J.R. (1950), *A Contribution to the Theory of Trade Cycle*, Oxford: Oxford University Press.
Hicks, J.R. (1974), *The Crisis in Keynesian Economics*, Oxford: Basil Blackwell.
Hicks, J.R. (1975), 'What is Wrong with Monetarism', *Lloyds Bank Review*, no. 118.
Hicks, J.R. (1980/1), 'IS/LM – an Explanation', *Journal of Post Keynesian Economics*, Winter.
Hicks, J.R. (1982), *Money, Interest and Wages: Collected Essays on Economic Theory*, vol. 2, Oxford: Oxford University Press.
Hicks, J.R. (1985), 'Keynes and the World Economy' in F. Vicarelli (ed.), *Keynes's Relevance Today*, London: Macmillan.
Hirschman, A.O. (1984), 'Against Parsimony: Three Ways of Complicating some Categories of Economic Discourse', *American Economic Review*, May.
Hirst, P. and Zeitlin, J. (1989), 'Flexible Specialisation and Competitive Failure of UK Manufacturing', *Political Quarterly*, vol. 60, no. 3.
Hodgson, G.M. (1984), *The Democratic Economy*, Harmondsworth: Penguin.
Hodgson, G.M. (1988), *Economics and Institutions: A Manifesto for a Modern Institutional Economics*, Cambridge: Polity Press.
Hollis, M. and Nell, E.J. (1975), *Rational Economic Man*, Cambridge: Cambridge University Press.
Hughes, P.R. and Hutchinson, G. (1988), 'Unemployment, Irreversibility and the Long-term Unemployed', in Cross (1988).
Ingrao, B. and Israel, G. (1985), 'General Economic Equilibrium Theory: a History of Ineffectual Paradigmatic Shifts', *Fundamental Scientiae*, vol. 6, nos 1 and 2.

Jarsulic, M. (1985), *Money and Macro Policy*, Boston: Kluwer-Nijhoff.
Jessop, B. (1990), 'Regulation Theories in Retrospect and Prospect', *Economy and Society*, May.
Johanssen, N.A.L.J. (1908), *A Neglected Point in Connection with Crises*, New York: Banker's Publishing Co.
Johnston, J. (1960), *Statistical Cost Analysis*, London: McGraw-Hill.
Kahneman, D. and Tversky, A. (1979), 'Prospect Theory: an Analysis of Decision under Risk', *Econometrica*, vol. 47, no. 2.
Kaldor, N. (1934), 'A Classificatory Note on the Determinateness of Equilibrium', *Review of Economic Studies*, February.
Kaldor, N. (1940), 'A Model of the Trade Cycle', *Economic Journal*, March.
Kaldor, N. (1956), 'Alternative Theories of Distribution', *Review of Economic Studies*, vol. 23, no. 2.
Kaldor, N. (1957), 'A Model of Economic Growth', *Economic Journal*, vol. 67; reprinted in Kaldor (1960a).
Kaldor, N. (1960a), *Essays on Economic Stability and Growth*, London: Duckworth.
Kaldor, N. (1960b), 'A Rejoinder to Mr Atsumi and Professor Tobin', *Review of Economic Studies*, vol. 27.
Kaldor, N. (1961), 'Capital Accumulation and Economic Growth', in F.A. Lutz and D.C. Hague (eds), *The Theory of Capital*, London: Macmillan.
Kaldor, N. (1966), *Causes of the Slow Rate of Economic Growth of the United Kingdom*, Cambridge: Cambridge University Press.
Kaldor, N. (1970a), 'The Case for Regional Policies', *Scottish Journal of Political Economy*, November.
Kaldor, N. (1970b), 'A Model of Distribution', in Sen (1970).
Kaldor, N. (1972), 'The Irrelevance of Equilibrium Economics', *Economic Journal*, December.
Kaldor, N. (1975), 'What is Wrong with Economic Theory', *Quarterly Journal of Economics*, August.
Kaldor, N. (1976), 'Inflation and Recession in the World Economy', *Economic Journal*, December.
Kaldor, N. (1980), *Memoranda on Monetary Policy*, Treasury and Civil Service Committee, HC720-11, July.
Kaldor, N. (1982), *The Scourge of Monetarism*, Oxford: Oxford University Press.

Kaldor, N. (1983), 'Keynesian Economics after Fifty Years', in Worswick and Trevithick (1983).
Kaldor, N. (1985), *Economics without Equilibrium*, Cardiff: University College Cardiff Press.
Kaldor, N. and Mirrlees, J.A. (1962), 'A New Model of Economic Growth', *Review of Economic Studies*, vol. 29; reprinted in Hahn (1971).
Kalecki, M. (1943), 'Political Aspects of Full Employment', *Political Quarterly*, October–December.
Kalecki, M. (1954), *Theory of Economic Dynamics: An Essay on Cyclical and Long-Run Changes in Capitalist Economy*, London: Unwin University Books.
Kalecki, M. (1969), *Studies in the Theory of Business Cycles: 1933–1939*, Oxford: Basil Blackwell.
Kalecki, M. (1970), 'Theories of Growth in Different Social Systems', *Scientia*, vol. 24.
Kalecki, M. (1971a), *Selected Essays on the Dynamics of the Capitalist Economy, 1933–70*, Cambridge: Cambridge University Press.
Kalecki, M. (1971b), 'Class Struggle and Distribution of National Income', *Kyklos*, vol. 24.
Kay, N.M. (1984), *The Emergent Firm: Knowledge, Ignorance and Surprise in Economic Organisation*, London: Macmillan.
Keeble, D., Owens, P. and Thompson, C. (1983), 'The Urban–Rural Manufacturing Shift in the European Community', *Urban Studies*, vol. 20.
Keynes, J.M. (1920), *The Economic Consequences of the Peace*, London: Macmillan.
Keynes, J.M. (1923), *A Tract on Monetary Reform*, London: Macmillan.
Keynes, J.M. (1930), *A Treatise on Money*, London: Macmillan.
Keynes, J.M. (1936), *The General Theory of Employment, Interest and Money*, London: Macmillan.
Keynes, J.M. (1937), 'The General Theory of Employment', *Quarterly Journal of Economics*, February.
Keynes, J.M. (1973), *The General Theory and After, Collected Writings*, vol. XIV, London: Macmillan.
Keynes, J.M. (1980), Activities, 1940–46: *Shaping the Post-War World: Employment, Collected Writings*, vol. XXVII, London: Macmillan.

King, M. (1975), 'The UK Profits Crisis: Myth or Reality?', *Economic Journal*, March.
Knight, B. and Sugden, R. (1989), 'Economic Democracy and a Company Act for the Twenty-First Century', in Industrial Strategy Group *Beyond the Review: Perspectives on Labour's Economic and Industrial Strategy*, chapter 6, Edinburgh: University of Edinburgh.
Knight, F. (1921), *Risks, Uncertainty and Profit*, Boston: Houghton Mifflin.
Kregel, J.A. (1971), *Rate of Profit, Distribution and Growth: Two Views*, London: Macmillan.
Kregel, J.A. (1973), *The Reconstruction of Political Economy: An Introduction to Post-Keynesian Economics*, London: Macmillan.
Kregel, J.A. (1976), 'Economic Methodology in the Face of Uncertainty: the Modelling Methods of Keynes and the Post Keynesians', *Economic Journal*, June.
Kuhn, T.S. (1977), 'Objectivity, Value Judgement and Theory of Choice', in his *The Essential Tension*, Chicago: Chicago University Press.
Laidler, D.E.W. (1990), 'The Legacy of the Monetarist Controversy', *Federal Reserve Bank of St Louis Review*, March/April.
Laidler, D.E.W. and Parkin, J.M. (1975), 'Inflation – a Survey', *Economic Journal*, December.
Lancaster, K. (1973), 'The Dynamic Inefficiency of Capitalism', *Journal of Political Economy*, vol. 81.
Langlois, R.N. (ed.) (1986), *Economics as a Process: Essays in the New Institutional Economics*, Cambridge: Cambridge University Press.
Lavoie, M. (1984), 'The Endogenous Flow of Credit and the Post Keynesian Theory of Money', *Journal of Economic Issues*, September.
Lavoie, M. (1985), 'Credit and Money: the Dynamic Circuit, Overdraft Economies, and Post-Keynesian Economics', in Jarsulic (1985).
Lavoie, M. (1992), 'Towards a New Research Programme for Post-Keynesianism and Neo-Ricardianism', *Review of Political Economy*, January.
Lawson, T. (1983), 'Different Approaches to Economic Modelling', *Cambridge Journal of Economics*, March.
Lawson, T. (1989a), 'Abstraction, Tendencies and Stylised Facts: a

Realist Approach to Economic Analysis', *Cambridge Journal of Economics*, March.
Lawson, T. (1989b), 'Realism and Instrumentalism in the Development of Econometrics', *Oxford Economic Papers*, January; reprinted in De Marchi and Gilbert (eds) (1990).
Lawson, T. (1990), 'Realism, Closed Systems and Expectations', mimeo.
Lawson, T. (forthcoming), 'Realism, Philosophical', in G. Hodgscn, M. Tool and W.J. Samuels, (eds), *Handbook of Evolutionary and Institutional Economics*, Aldershot: Edward Elgar.
Layard, R. and Nickell, S.J. (1986), 'Unemployment in the UK', *Economica*, Supplement, 53.
Leibenstein, H. (1976), *Beyond Economic Man: A New Foundation for Microeconomics*, Cambridge, MA: Harvard University Press.
Leibenstein, H. (1979), 'A Branch of Economics is Missing: Macro–Micro Theory', *Journal of Economic Literature*, June; reprinted in Caldwell (1984).
Leigh-Pemberton, R. (1987), 'The Instruments of Monetary Policy', Seventh Mais Lecture, City University Business School, 13 May.
Leijonhufvud, A. (1968), *On Keynesian Economics and the Economics of Keynes: A Study in Monetary Theory*, London: Oxford University Press.
Leijonhufvud, A. (1969), *Keynes and the Classics*, London: IEA Occasional Papers.
Lekachman, R. (1964), *Keynes's General Theory: Reports of Three Decades*, London: Macmillan.
Leontief, W. (1951), *The Structure of American Economy, 1919–1939*, 2nd edn, New York: Oxford University Press.
Leontief, W., Carter, A.P. and Petri, P.A. (1978), *The Future of the World Economy: A United Nations Study*, Oxford: Oxford University Press.
Lichtenstein, P.M. (1983), *An Introduction to Post-Keynesian and Marxian Theories of Value and Price*, London: Macmillan.
Lindbeck, A. and Snower, D.J. (1986), 'Wage Setting, Unemployment, and Insider–Outsider Relations', *American Economic Review*, Papers and Proceedings, May.
Lindbeck, A. and Snower, D.J. (1987), 'Union Activity, Unemployment Persistence and Wage-employment Ratchets', *European Economic Review*, February/March.
Lindbeck, A. and Snower, D.J. (1988), 'Cooperation, Harassment,

and Involuntary Unemployment: an Insider–Outsider Approach', *American Economic Review*, March.

Lipietz, A. (1987), *Mirages and Miracles*, London: Verso.

Lipsey, R.G. (1960), 'The Relationship between Unemployment and the Rate of Change of Money Wage Rates in the United Kingdom, 1862–1957: a Further Analysis', *Economica*, February.

Lipsey, R.G. (1978), 'The Place of the Phillips Curve in Macroeconomic Models', in A.R. Bergstrom, A.J.L. Catt, M.H. Peston and B.D.J. Silverstone (eds), *Stability and Inflation*, New York: John Wiley.

Longstreth, F. (1979), 'The City, Industry and State', in Crouch (1979).

Lucas, R.E. (1975), 'An Equilibrium Model of the Business Cycle', *Journal of Political Economy*, vol. 83, no. 6; reprinted in Lucas (1981).

Lucas, R.E. (1976), 'Econometric Evaluation: a Critique', in K. Brunner and A.H. Meltzer (eds), *The Phillips Curve and Labour Markets*, Carnegie-Rochester, Conference Series on Public Policy, no. 1, Amsterdam and New York: North-Holland; reprinted in Lucas (1981).

Lucas, R.E. (1977), 'Understanding Business Cycles', in K. Brunner and A.H. Meltzer (eds), *Stabilisation of the Domestic and International Economy*, Carnegie-Rochester Series on Public Policy, no. 5, Amsterdam and New York: North-Holland; reprinted in Lucas and Sargent (1981).

Lucas, R.E. (1981), *Studies in Business Cycle Theory*, Oxford: Basil Blackwell.

Lucas, R.E. and Sargent, T.J. (1978), 'After Keynesian Economics', in Federal Reserve Bank of Boston Conference Series no. 19, *After the Phillips Curve: Persistence of High Inflation and Unemployment*; reprinted in Lucas and Sargent (1981).

Lucas, R.E. and Sargent, T.J. (eds) (1981), *Rational Expectations and Econometric Practice*, London: George Allen & Unwin.

Luria, D. (1990), 'Automation, Markets and Scale: Can Flexible Niching Modernize US Manufacturing?', *International Review of Applied Economics*, June.

MacRae, D. (1977), 'A Political Model of the Business Cycle', *Journal of Political Economy*, April.

MacRae, D. (1981), 'On the Political Business Cycle', in D.A. Hibbs

and H. Fassbender (eds), *Contemporary Political Economy*, Amsterdam and New York: North-Holland.
Mankiw, N.G. (1985), 'Small Menu Costs and Large Business Cycles: a Macroeconomic Model of Monopoly', *Quarterly Journal of Economics*, May.
Mankiw, N.G. (1988), 'Recent Developments in Macroeconomics: a Very Quick Refresher Course', *Journal of Money, Credit and Banking*, Part 2, August.
Mankiw, N.G. (1990), 'A Quick Refresher Course in Macroeconomics', *Journal of Economic Literature*, December.
Marris, R. (1977), 'Book Review of Eichner: "The Megacorp and Oligopoly" ', *Journal of Economic Literature*, vol. 15.
Marshall, A. (1920), *Principles of Economics*, 8th edn, London: Macmillan.
McCallum, J. (1983), 'Policy "Credibility" and Economic Behavior', *Journal of Post Keynesian Economics*, Fall.
McCloskey, D.N. (1983), 'The Rhetoric of Economics', *Journal of Economic Literature*, June.
McDonald, I.M. and Solow, R.M. (1981), 'Wage Bargaining and Employment', *American Economic Review*, December.
Meade, J.E. (1937), 'A Simplified Model of Mr Keynes' System', *Review of Economic Studies*, no. 4.
Minsky, H.P. (1975), *John Maynard Keynes*, New York: Columbia University Press.
Minsky, H.P. (1982), *Can 'It' Happen Again? Essays on Instability and Finance*, New York: M.E. Sharpe.
Minsky, H.P. (1985), 'Money and the Lender of Last Resort', *Challenge*, March/April.
Minsky, H.P. (1986a), *Stabilizing an Unstable Economy*, New Haven and London: Yale University Press.
Minsky, H.P. (1986b), 'The Evolution of Financial Institutions and the Performance of the Economy', *Journal of Economic Issues*, June.
Minsky, H.P. (1990), 'Financial Crises and the Evolution of Capitalism: the Crash of 1987 – What Does It Mean?', in M. Gottdiener and N. Komninos (eds), *Capitalist Development and Crisis Theory: Accumulation, Regulation and Spatial Restructuring*, New York: St Martin's Press.
Mirowski. P. (1989), 'The Probabilistic Counter-Revolution, or

How Stochastic Concepts Came to Neoclassical Economic Theory', *Oxford Economic Papers*, January.

Mishan, E. (1961), 'Theories of Consumers' Behaviour: a Cynical View', *Economica*, February.

Mishkin, F.S. (1982), 'Does Anticipated Monetary Policy Matter? An Econometric Investigation', *Journal of Political Economy*, February.

Mishkin, F.S. (1983), *A Rational Expectations Approach to Macroeconomics*, Chicago: University of Chicago Press.

Mitchell, W.C. (1937), *The Backward Art of Spending Money and Other Essays*, New York: McGraw-Hill.

Modigliani, F. (1944), 'Liquidity Preference and the Theory of Interest and Money', *Econometrica*, January.

Modigliani, F. and Miller, M. (1958), 'The Cost of Capital, Corporation Finance and the Theory of Investment', *American Economic Review*, June.

Moore, B.J. (1979a), 'Monetary Factors', in Eichner (1979b).

Moore, B.J. (1979b), 'The Endogenous Money Supply', *Journal of Post Keynesian Economics*, Autumn.

Moore, B.J. (1983), 'Unpacking the Post Keynesian Black Box: Bank Lending and the Money Supply', *Journal of Post Keynesian Economics*, Summer.

Moore, B.J. (1984), 'Keynes and the Endogeneity of the Money Stock', *Studi Economici*, no. 22.

Moore, B.J. (1985), 'Wages, Bank Lending and the Endogeneity of Credit Money', in Jarsulic (1985).

Moore, B.J. (1986), 'How Credit Drives the Money Supply: the Significance of Institutional Developments', *Journal of Economic Issues*, June.

Moore, B.J. (1988), *Horizontalists and Verticalists: The Macroeconomics of Credit Money*, Cambridge: Cambridge University Press.

Moore, B.J. and Threadgold, A.R. (1980), 'Bank Lending and the Money Supply', *Bank of England Discussion Paper*, no. 10, July.

Moore, B.J. and Threadgold, A.R. (1985), 'Corporate Bank Borrowing in the UK, 1965–1981', *Economica*, February.

Morley, R. (1988), *The Macroeconomics of Open Economics: An Introduction to Aggregate Behaviour and Policy*, Aldershot: Edward Elgar.

Muellbauer, J. (1976), 'Community Preferences and the Representative Consumer', *Econometrica*, September.
Mundell, R.A. (1960), 'The Monetary Dynamics of Adjustment under Fixed and Flexible Exchange Rates', *Quarterly Journal of Economics*, vol. 74.
Mundell, R.A. (1963), 'Capital Mobility and Stabilization Policy under Fixed and Flexible Exchange Rates', *Canadian Journal of Economics and Political Science*, vol. 29.
Muth, J.F. (1961), 'Rational Expectations and the Theory of Price Movements', *Econometrica*, July.
Myrdal, G. (1939), *Monetary Equilibrium*, London: William Hodge.
Myrdal, G. (1957), *Economic Theory and the Underdeveloped Regions*, London: Duckworth.
Neale, W.C. (1986), 'Tax-Based Incomes Policies', *Journal of Economic Issues*, December.
Negishi, T. (1979), *Microeconomic Foundations of Keynesian Macroeconomics*, Amsterdam: North-Holland.
Nell, E.J. (1980), 'The Revival of Political Economy', in E.J. Nell (ed.), *Growth, Profits and Property: Essays in the Revival of Political Economy*, Cambridge: Cambridge University Press.
Nickell, S.J. (1978), *The Investment Decision of Firms*, Cambridge: Cambridge University Press.
Nickell, S.J. (1987), 'Why is Wage Inflation in Britain so High?', *Oxford Bulletin of Economics and Statistics*, no. 1.
Nickell, S.J. (1990), 'Unemployment: a Survey', *Economic Journal*, June.
Nielsen, K. (1991), 'Towards a Flexible Future – Theories and Politics', in B. Jessop, K. Nielsen, H. Kastendick and O.K. Pedersen (eds), *The Politics of Flexibility*, Aldershot: Edward Elgar.
Nordhaus, W.D. (1975), 'The Political Business Cycle', *Review of Economic Studies*, April.
O'Donnell, K. and Nolan, P. (1989), 'Flexible Specialisation and the Cyprus Industrial Strategy', *Cyprus Journal of Economics*, December.
Olson, M. (1984), 'Beyond Keynesianism and Monetarism', *Economic Inquiry*, July.
Oswald, A.J. (1986), 'The Economic Theory of Trade Unions: an Introductory Survey', in L. Calmfers and H. Horn (eds), *Trade Unions, Wage Formation and Macroeconomic Stability*, London: Macmillan.

Paldam, M. (1989), 'A Wage Structure Theory of Inflation, Industrial Conflicts and Trade Unions', *Scandinavian Journal of Economics*, vol. 91, no. 1.

Parkin, J.M., Summer, M.T. and Ward, R. (1976), 'The Effects of Excess Demand, Generalised Expectations and Wage-Price Controls on Wage Inflation in the UK, 1951–1971', in K. Brunner and A.H. Meltzer (eds), *The Economics of Price and Wage Controls*, Carnegie-Rochester Conference Series, no. 7, Amsterdam: North-Holland.

Pasinetti, L.L. (1962), 'Rate of Profit and Income Distribution in Relation to the Rate of Economic Growth', *Review of Economic Studies*, vol. 91, no. 1.

Pasinetti, L.L. (1966), 'Changes in the Rate of Profit and Switches of Technique', *Quarterly Journal of Economics*, vol. 80.

Pasinetti, L.L. (1970), 'Profit and Growth', in Sen (1970).

Pasinetti, L.L. (1974), *Growth and Income Distribution: Essays in Economic Theory*, Cambridge: Cambridge University Press.

Pasinetti, L.L. (1981), *Structural Change and Economic Growth: A Theoretical Essay on the Dynamics of the Wealth of Nations*, Cambridge: Cambridge University Press.

Patinkin, D. (1965), *Money, Interest and Prices*, 2nd edn, London: Harper & Row.

Peel, D.A. and Metcalfe, J.S. (1979), 'Divergent Expectations and the Dynamic Stability of Some Simple Macro Economic Models', *Economic Journal*, December.

Perroux, F. (1955), 'Note on the Concept of Growth Poles', *Economie Appliquée*, nos 1 and 2; reprinted in I. Livingstone (ed.), *Economic Policy for Development*, London: Penguin, 1971.

Pheby, J. (ed.) (1989), *New Directions in Post-Keynesian Economics*, Aldershot: Edward Elgar.

Phelps, E.S. (1968), 'Money-Wage Dynamics and Labour Market Equilibrium', *Journal of Political Economy*, July/August.

Phelps, E.S. (1970), *Macroeconomic Foundations of Employment and Inflation Theory*, New York: W.W. Norton.

Phelps, E.S. (1988), 'Comment on Recent Developments in Macroeconomics: a Very Quick Refresher Course', *Journal of Money, Credit, and Banking*, part 2, August.

Phillips, A.W. (1958), 'The Relation between Unemployment and the Rate of Change of Money Wage Rates in the United Kingdom, 1861–1957, *Economica*, November.

Piore, M.J. (ed.) (1979), *Unemployment and Inflation: Institutionalist and Structuralist Views*, New York: M.E. Sharpe.

Piore, M.J. and Sabel, C. (1984), *The Second Industrial Divide: Possibilities for Prosperity*, New York: Basic Books.

Podolski, T.M. (1986), *Financial Innovations and the Money Supply*, Oxford: Basil Blackwell.

Polanyi, K. (1957), *The Great Transformation*, Boston: Beacon Press.

Popper, K.R. (1959), *The Logic of Scientific Discovery*, London: Harper & Row.

Popper, K.R. (1965), *Conjectures and Refutations: The Growth of Scientific Knowledge*, London: Routledge & Kegan Paul.

Preston, L.E. (1975), 'Corporation and Society: the Search for a Paradigm', *Journal of Economic Literature*, vol. 13.

Radcliffe, Lord (Chairman) (1959), *Committee on the Working of the Monetary System: Report*, London: HMSO, Cmnd 827.

Radice, H. (1989), 'British Capitalism in a Changing Global Economy' in A. MacEwan and N.T. Tabb (eds), *Instability and Change in the World Economy*, New York: Monthly Review Press.

Revell, J. (1973), *The British Financial System*, London: Macmillan.

Reynolds, P.J. (1983), 'Kalecki's Degree of Monopoly', *Journal of Post Keynesian Economics*, Spring.

Reynolds, P.J. (1987), *Political Economy: A Synthesis of Kaleckian and Post Keynesian Economics*, Brighton, Sussex: Wheatsheaf Books.

Reynolds, P.J. (1989), 'Kaleckian and Post-Keynesian Theories of Pricing: Some Extensions and Implications', in Arestis and Kitromilides (1989).

Riach, P.A. (1981), 'Labour-Hiring in Post-Keynesian Economics', mimeo.

Ricardo, D. (1817), 'On the Principles of Political Economy and Taxation', in P. Sraffa (ed.), *The Works and Correspondence of David Ricardo*, vol. 1, Cambridge: Cambridge University Press, 1952.

Robinson, J. (1952), *The Rate of Interest and Other Essays*, London: Macmillan.

Robinson, J. (1954), 'The Production Function and the Theory of Capital', *Review of Economic Studies*, vol. 21.

Robinson, J. (1956), *The Accumulation of Capital*, 1st edn, London: Macmillan.

Robinson, J. (1961), 'The Economics of Disequilibrium Price', *Quarterly Journal of Economics*, May.
Robinson, J. (1962a), *Essays in the Theory of Economic Growth*, London: Macmillan.
Robinson, J. (1962b), 'Review of H.G. Johnson, *Money, Trade and Economic Growth*, 1962', *Economic Journal*, September.
Robinson, J. (1970), 'Quantity Theories Old and New: a Comment', *Journal of Money, Credit and Banking*, November.
Robinson, J. (1972), 'The Second Crisis of Economic Theory', *American Economic Review*, Papers and Proceedings, May.
Robinson, J. (1974), 'History Versus Equilibrium', *Thames Papers in Political Economy*, Autumn.
Robinson, J. (1977), 'What Are the Questions?', *Journal of Economic Literature*, December.
Robinson, J. (1979), *Collected Economic Papers*, vol. 5, Oxford: Basil Blackwell.
Robinson, J. (1980), 'Time in Economic Theory', *Kyklos*, vol. 44, fasc.
Robinson, R. (1974), 'Determination of the Mark-up under Oligopoly: a Comment', *Economic Journal*, December.
Rogers, C. (1989), *Money, Interest and Capital: A Study in the Foundations of Monetary Theory*, Cambridge: Cambridge University Press.
Romer, P. (1986), 'Increasing Returns and Long-run Growth', *Journal of Political Economy*, vol. 94, no. 5.
Roncaglia, A. (1978), *Sraffa and the Theory of Prices*, New York: John Wiley.
Rousseas, S. (1986), *Post-Keynesian Monetary Economics*, London: Macmillan.
Routh, G. (1980), *Occupation and Pay in Great Britain, 1906–79*, London: Macmillan.
Rowthorn, R. (1974), 'Neo-Classicism, Neo-Ricardianism and Marxism', *New Left Review*, July/August.
Rowthorn, R. (1977), 'Conflict, Inflation and Money', *Cambridge Journal of Economics*, vol. 1; reprinted in Rowthorn (1980).
Rowthorn, R. (1980), *Capitalism, Conflict and Inflation*, London: Lawrence & Wishart.
Rowthorn, R. (1981), 'Demand, Real Wages and Economic Growth', *Thames Papers in Political Economy*, Autumn.

Rowthorn, R. (1986), 'Unemployment: a Resistible Force', *Marxism Today*. September.
Salter, W.E.G. (1960), *Productivity and Technical Change*, Cambridge: Cambridge University Press.
Samuels, W.J. (1987), 'Institutional Economics', in J. Eatwell, M. Milgate and J. Newman (eds), *The New Palgrave*, London: Macmillan.
Samuelson, P.A. (1939), 'Interaction between the Multiplier Analysis and the Principle of Accelerator', *Review of Economics and Statistics*, May.
Samuelson, P.A. (1948), *Foundations of Economic Analysis*, Cambridge, MA: Harvard University Press.
Santomero, A.M. and Seater, J.J. (1978), 'The Inflation–Unemployment Trade-Off: a Critique of the Literature', *Journal of Economic Literature*, June.
Sardoni, C. (1987), *Marx and Keynes on Economic Recession: The Theory of Unemployment and Effective Demand*, Brighton, Sussex: Wheatsheaf Books.
Sargent, T.J. (1979), *Macroeconomic Theory*, New York: Academic Press.
Sargent, T.J. and Wallace, N. (1976), 'Rational Expectations and the Theory of Economic Policy', *Journal of Monetary Economics*, April.
Saunders, P.G. and Nobay, A.R. (1972), 'Price Expectations, the Phillips Curve and Incomes Policy', in J.M. Parkin and M.T. Sumner (eds), *Incomes Policy and Inflation*, Manchester: Manchester University Press.
Sawyer, M.C. (1982a), *Macroeconomics in Question: The Keynesian-Monetarist Orthodoxies and the Kaleckian Alternative*, Brighton, Sussex: Wheatsheaf Books.
Sawyer, M.C. (1982b), 'Towards a Post-Kaleckian Macroeconomics', *Thames Papers in Political Economy*, Autumn.
Sawyer, M.C. (1983), *Business Pricing and Inflation*, London: Macmillan.
Sawyer, M.C. (1984), 'The Surprise Supply Function: a Critique', *British Review of Economic Issues*, Autumn.
Sawyer, M.C. (1985), *The Economics of Michal Kalecki*, London: Macmillan.
Sawyer, M.C. (1986), 'Conflict over Aggregate Demand in Post Keynesian Economics: the Problem of Overdeterminacy', mimeo.

Sawyer, M.C. (1989), *The Challenge of Radical Political Economy: An Introduction to the Alternatives to Neo-classical Economics*, Hemel Hempstead, Herts.: Harvester Wheatsheaf.

Schefold, B. (1985), 'Cambridge Price Theory: Special Model or General Theory of Value?', *American Economic Review*, May.

Schumpeter, J.A. (1934), *The Theory of Economic Development*, Cambridge, MA: Harvard University Press.

Scott, M.Fg., Corden, W.M. and Little, I.M.D. (1980), *The Case against General Import Restrictions*, Trade Policy Research Centre: Thames Essay, no. 24.

Sen, A.K. (1970), *Growth Economics*, Harmondsworth, Middx: Penguin.

Sen, A.K. (1979), 'Rational Fools: a Critique of the Behavioural Foundations of Economic Theory', in F. Hahn and M. Hollis (eds), *Philosophy and Economic Theory*, Oxford: Oxford University Press.

Shackle, G.L.S. (1955), *Uncertainty in Economics*, Cambridge: Cambridge University Press.

Shackle, G.L.S. (1967), *The Years of High Theory*, Cambridge: Cambridge University Press.

Shackle, G.L.S. (1970), *Expectation, Enterprise and Profit: The Theory of the Firm*, London: George Allen & Unwin.

Shackle, G.L.S. (1972), *Epistemics and Economics*, Cambridge: Cambridge University Press.

Shapiro, N. (1977), 'The Revolutionary Character of Post-Keynesian Economics', *Journal of Economic Issues*, September.

Sherman, H.J. (1987), 'The Business Cycles of Capitalism', *International Review of Applied Economics*, vol. 1.

Simon, H.A. (1979), 'Rational Decision Making in Business Organizations', *American Economic Review*, September.

Simon, H.A. (1983), *Reason in Human Affairs*, Oxford: Basil Blackwell.

Skott, P. (1989), *Conflict and Effective Demand in Economic Growth*, Cambridge: Cambridge University Press.

Skott, P. (1991), 'Inflation, Unemployment and the Distribution of Income', in B. Amoroso and J. Jespersen (eds), *Macroeconomic Theories and Policies for the 1990s*, London: Macmillan.

Smith, R.P. (1976), 'Demand Management and the "New School" ', *Applied Economics*, September.

Sneessens, H. and Dreze, J. (1986), 'A Discussion of Belgian Unem-

ployment Combining Traditional Concepts of Disequilibrium Econometrics', *Economica*, Supplement, 53.
Solow, R.M. (1956), 'A Contribution to the Theory of Economic Growth', *Quarterly Journal of Economics*, February.
Solow, R.M. (1969), *Price Expectations and the Behaviour of the Price Level*, Manchester: Manchester University Press.
Solow, R.M. (1975), 'Brief Comments', *Quarterly Journal of Economics*, vol. 89.
Solow, R.M. (1991), 'The Sturc Memorial Lecture', *Eighth Annual Memorial Lecture on International Economics*, Johns Hopkins University, 12th November.
Soskice, D. and Carlin, W. (1989), 'Medium-run Keynesianism: Hysteresis and Capital Scrapping', in Davidson and Kregel (1989).
Sraffa, P. (1960), *Production of Commodities by Means of Commodities: Prelude to a Critique of Economic Theory*, Cambridge: Cambridge University Press.
Stanton, D. (1988), 'Hysteresis: Some Policy Implications', in Cross (1988).
Startz, R. (1984), 'Prelude to Macroeconomics', *American Economic Review*, vol. 74.
Stein, H. (1988), 'Comment on Recent Developments in Macroeconomics: a Very Quick Refresher Course', *Journal of Money, Credit, and Banking*, part 2, August.
Steindl, J. (1952), *Maturity and Stagnation in American Capitalism*, Oxford: Oxford University Press.
Steindl, J. (1979), 'Stagnation Theory and Stagnation Policy', *Cambridge Journal of Economics*, vol. 3.
Steindl, J. (1982), 'The Role of Household Saving in the Modern Economy', *Banca Nazionale del Lavoro*, March.
Stigler, G. (1939), 'Production and Distribution in the Short Run', *Journal of Political Economy*, June.
Stiglitz, J.E. (1974), 'The Cambridge–Cambridge Controversy in the Theory of Capital; a View from New Haven: a Review Article', *Journal of Political Economy*, vol. 82.
Sugden, R. (1989), 'The International Economy: Britain at the Mercy of Transnationals', in Industrial Strategy Group, *Beyond the Review: Perspectives on Labour's Economic and Industrial Strategy*, chapter 9, Edinburgh: University of Edinburgh.
Summers, L.H. (1988), 'Relative Wages, Efficiency Wages and

Keynesian Unemployment', *American Economic Review*, Papers and Proceedings, May.
Swan, T.W. (1956), 'Economic Growth and Capital Accumulation', *Economic Record*, November.
Taylor, J. (1980), 'Aggregate Dynamics and Staggered Contracts', *Journal of Political Economy*, February.
Tichy, G. (1984), 'Strategy and Implementation of Employment Policy in Austria: Successful Experiments with Unconventional Assignments of Instruments to Goals', *Kyklos*, vol. 37, no. 3.
Tinbergen, J. (1989), 'How to Reduce Unemployment', *Review of Political Economy*, March.
Tobin, J. (1960), 'Towards a *General* Kaldorian Theory of Distribution', *Review of Economic Studies*, vol. 27.
Tobin, J. (1967), 'Unemployment and Inflation: the Cruel Dilemma', in A. Phillips and O.E. Williamson (eds), *Prices: Issues in Theory, Practice and Public Policy*, Philadelphia: University of Pennsylvania Press.
Tobin, J. (1972), 'Inflation and Unemployment', *American Economic Review*, March.
Toetsch, I. (1988), 'Screening in Labour Markets with Heterogenous Workers', in Cross (1988).
Trevithick, J.A. (1976a), 'Money Wage Inflexibility and the Keynesian Labour Supply Function', *Economic Journal*, June.
Trevithick, J.A. (1976b), 'Inflation, the National Unemployment Rate and the Theory of Economic Policy', *Scottish Journal of Political Economy*, February.
Veblen, T. (1898), 'Why is Economics not an Evolutionary Science?', *Quarterly Journal of Economics*, July; reprinted in T. Veblen, *The Place of Science in Modern Civilisation*, New York: B.W. Huebsch, 1919.
Veblen, T. (1899), *The Theory of the Leisure Class*. New York: Modern Library Edition, 1961.
Walters, A.A. (1963), 'Production and Cost: an Econometric Survey', *Econometrica*, January.
Weeks, J. (1989), *A Critique of Neoclassical Macroeconomics*, London: Macmillan.
Weintraub, S. (1956), 'A Macroeconomic Approach to the Theory of Wages', *American Economic Review*, December.
Weintraub, S. (1959), *A General Theory of the Price Level, Output, Income and Distribution*, Philadelphia: Chilton.

Weintraub, S. (1966), *A Keynesian Theory of Employment, Growth and Income Distribution*, Philadelphia: Chilton.

Weintraub, S. (1973), *Keynes and the Monetarists*, New Brunswick: Rutgers University Press.

Weintraub, S. and Wallich, H. (1973), 'A Tax-Based Incomes Policy', in Weintraub (1973).

Weitzman, M.L. (1982), 'Increasing Returns and the Foundations of Unemployment Theory', *Economic Journal*, December.

Wiles, P. (1956), *Prices, Cost and Output*, Oxford: Basil Blackwell.

Williams, K., Cutler, T., Williams, J. and Haslam, C. (1987), 'The End of Mass Production?', *Economy and Society*, August.

Wills, H.R. (1982), 'The Simple Economics of Bank Regulation', *Economica*, August.

Wilson, T. and Andrews, P.W.S. (1951), *Oxford Studies in the Price Mechanism*, Oxford: Clarendon Press.

Wojnilower, A.M. (1980), 'The Central Role of Credit Crunches in Recent Financial History', *Brookings Papers on Economic Activity*, no. 2.

Wood, A. (1975), *A Theory of Profits*, Cambridge: Cambridge University Press.

Wood, A. (1978), *A Theory of Pay*, Cambridge: Cambridge University Press.

Worswick, D. and Trevithick, J. (eds), (1983), *Keynes and the Modern World*, Cambridge: Cambridge University Press.

Young, A.A. (1928), 'Increasing Returns and Economic Progress', *Economic Journal*, December.

Index

acceleration principle 49–54, 130, 133, 206, 207, 221
adaptive expectations *see* expectations
advertising 68, 125
Aglietta, M. 246
Akerlof, G.A. 36
Allen, A. 170
Arestis, P. ix, xii, 63, 83, 86, 87, 100, 110, 113, 125, 159, 160, 163, 164, 173, 182, 192, 193, 198, 200, 241, 254, 261, 271
Arrow, K.J. 69, 106
Artis, M.J. 183, 185, 188, 192
Asimakopulos, A. 127, 129, 142, 191, 202, 213
asocial nature of GNS 64–5
atomistic nature of GNS 61–2
Austria
  socialization of investment in 271
average costs 140–42, 145–7, 150–51, 159–60, 161, 257
  of bank funds 189
average propensity to save *see* propensity to save

Babylonian approach 87, 95
Bade, F. 247
balance of payments 37–41, 109, 112–13, 181, 198, 200, 202, 244, 253, 263, 264
balance of trade 263
Baldwin, R. 49
bank deposit multiplier 182
banking development, stages of 181–2
banks *see* banking development, stages of; central banks; commercial banks
Baran, P. 245
Barro, R.J. 30–31, 75–6
Beath, J. 258
Bharadwaj, K. 91, 107
Bhaskar, V. 163
Biefang-Frisancho Mariscal, I. 173
Blanchard, O.J. xii, 170, 172, 173, 174
Blatt, J.M. 72–3
Blaug, M. 4, 70, 80, 81, 82
Blinder, A.S. 264
Bliss, C. 58
Boland, L.A. 77
Boschen, J. 76
Boulding, K.E. 69
bounded rationality 69, 99
Bowles, S. 168, 175, 176, 177, 252, 266
Branson, W.H. 199
Brown, E.K. 87
budget constraint 10–12
budget deficits
  and balance of payments 263
  financing of 10–12
  and growth 255–6, 258, 260
Buiter, W.H. 30, 73
Burmeister, E. 125
business cycles
  endogeneity of 105, 107
  in GNS 49–54
  Goodwin's model 105, 107, 227–9
  income distribution and 227–9, 238
  investment and 49–50, 53, 107–8,

305

127, 131, 133, 137, 223–7, 230–35, 236–8
Kaldor's model 107, 223–7
Kalecki's model 56, 105, 107, 230–35
labour market and 227–9
Minsky's model (financial instability hypothesis) 235–8, 239
political 56–7, 243
profits and 108
real 54–6
savings and 223–7

Caldwell, B.J. 77, 79, 85, 96
Cambridge Economic Policy Group 263
capacity scrapping theory 170, 174
capacity utilization 130, 131, 132–3, 145–7, 176, 214–22, 255, 261
capacity scrapping theory and 170, 174
capital, international *see* international capital
capital, measurement of 65–8, 82, 117–19
capital account monetary model 42–3
capital/labour ratio 65, 66
capital movements 198, 199
capital/output ratio 46–7, 49–50, 53, 104, 206–7, 209, 261
capital-reversing 66
capital stock 223–7, 234
Çapoğlu, G. 158
Carlin, W. 170, 174
Cartesian fallacy 84–5
Carvalho, F. 106, 107
central banks 90, 94, 182, 183, 184, 185, 193, 197, 201–2, 203
 regional 246, 253
centre/periphery argument 245
Champernowne, D.G. 66, 100
Chernomas, B. 268
Chick, V. 83, 181, 183, 202, 246, 253
Chipman, J.S. 69
choice, consumer 97–8

choice theoretic explanation of slow adjustments 36–7
Christodoulakis, N. 264
circular and cumulative causation, theory of *see* cumulative causation, theory of
Clark, K.B. 170, 172
classes, social 64–5, 68, 89, 98, 99–100, 101–3, 109, 125, 153, 203, 227–9, 252, 271
closed deterministic models 70–71, 158
Clower, R.W. 2, 30, 36
Coakley, J. 196
Cobb–Douglas production function 44–8
Coddington, A. 3, 37
Cohen, A.J. 71
coherence tests 79, 84
commercial banks 183–203
 loans to consumers 190, 193–4
 loans to governments 188, 194–6
 loans to industry 93, 182–3, 190–93, 194, 201, 246
comprehensiveness tests 79–80, 81
confirmability of GNS theory 78–9
conflict theories 63–4, 89, 94, 101–3, 108–9, 163–9, 173, 176, 177, 248
conjectural equilibrium 36
consumption
 GNS consumption function 3–4, 7–8, 49–50, 53, 58
 by income bracket 198–9
 and income distribution 134–7
 and relative income hypothesis 124–5
 see also propensity to consume
contingency models 36
Cornwall, J. 213
corporate levy 144, 145–6, 147, 151, 153, 154, 256, 259
correspondence tests 79–81, 82, 84
Coutts, K. 81, 190, 258
Cowling, K. 72, 142–3, 151, 268, 269, 271
credit, supply and demand for 93–4, 108, 109, 111–13, 126, Ch.8

post-Keynesian model of
  money, credit and finance
  186–200
credit misallocation 180
credit rationing 194
Cripps, F. 201, 260, 262, 263, 264
crises in regulation 250
Cross, R.B. 164, 170
Crotty, J.R. 269
cumulative causation, theory of 72,
  81, 244–5
current account monetary model
  41–2
Cuthbertson, K. 192, 260
Cyert, R.M. 69

Dasgupta, P. 82
Davidson, P. 88, 91, 93, 180, 190,
  191, 202
Davies, J.B. 95
deficits *see* budget deficits
demand, aggregate
  defined 25–7
depreciation, capital 45, 53–4, 129–
  30, 215–16, 232–5
De Vroey, M. 60, 203
Diamond, P. 170, 172
discount rate 109, 183, 186, 189,
  197–8, 201–2, 203
discretionary expenditure 110–13,
  122–4, 133, 137, 188, 192,
  193–4
discretionary funds 110–13, 123–4,
  137, 188, 192, 193–4
distribution theory *see* income
  distribution
Dornbusch, R. 42
Dow, S.C. 86, 87, 95, 97, 181, 246,
  253
Drazen, A. 36
Dreze, J. 170
Driver, C. 110, 125, 254, 261
dualistic fallacy 84
Duesenberry, J.S. 124, 151
Duhem–Quine thesis 78
duration theory 170–72, 174

Earl, P.E. 99

Eatwell, J. 99, 106
Eckstein, O. 81
econometric modelling 96–7
economic policy, GNS 9–13
economic policy, post-Keynesian
  Ch.10
  in closed economies 254–62
  constraints on 195–6, 242–54,
    268–70
  in open economies 262–8
economies of scale 49, 244, 246,
  247, 248, 264
effective demand 88, 97–100
  passim, 238
efficiency wage theory 35, 175–6
Eichner, A.S.
  on consumer choice 98
  on discretionary expenditure 123
  on economic policy 254, 258, 261
  on economic theory ix, xi, xii, 21,
    87–8, 95
  epistemological rules of science
    79–85
  on growth 105
  institutionalist approach of 100
  on Leontief model 117–18
  on money 182, 200
  pricing theory 103, 104, 139,
    143–54, 158, 159, 246
  see also megacorps
elasticity of substitution 44
employment *see* full employment,
  commitment to; labour, supply
  and demand for
see also unemployment
endogeneity of money 179, 180–82,
  184, 186, 200–203
entry barriers 143, 148–50, 151, 261
epistemological rules of science 79–
  85
equilibrium
  in GNS economics 1–2, 4–9
  passim, 25–7, 38–43, 46–7,
  58, 90
  critique of 69, 70–72, 83–4, 92
  growth path 46–7, 208
  interest rate 197
  in open economies 38–43

short-period and long-period
105–7
short-run and long-run xi, 105–7
unemployment rate 169–70, 174
see also market clearing
Euler's theorem 44
European Economic Community
(EEC) 265, 269–70
exchange rates 37–43, 109, 112,
113, 160, 161, 177, 181, 185,
198, 199–200, 203, 244, 263,
264, 268
expectations
adaptive 74
of exchange rate movements 199
extrapolative 196
formation of 100
importance of, in post-Keynesian
economics 88, 98
of income 126
of interest rate changes 196
of monetary changes 75–6
price/wage 8, 17–21, 28–30, 41–2,
56, 89, 108–9, 165, 166, 168–9
of profitability 103, 108, 127–8,
132, 133, 142, 167, 168–9,
211–13, 236–8
rational 6, 21–3, 27, 29, 30, 35,
42, 54–5, 73–4
regressive 196
of sales 103–4, 132, 255, 256
of transactions 190–92
exports 110, 113, 122, 198, 251, 262
extrapolative expectations 196

falsifiability of GNS theory 78–9
finance frontiers 155, 156–8
finance motive 202
financial instability hypothesis
(Minsky) 235–8, 239
Fine, B. 195
fiscal policy *see* taxation
Fischer, S. 35, 73
fixed-coefficient models 67, 116,
137, 145
see also Leontief model
fixed investment 231–2

Fleming, J.S. 37
flexibility theory *see* post-Fordism
flexible specialization theory *see*
post-Fordism
Fordism 246–7, 249, 250–51
foreign sector *see* open economies
Forman, L. 83
Frank, A.G. 245
Frenkel, J. 41
Friedman, M. 17, 71, 73, 77
Fromm, G.M. 81
full employment, commitment to
economic policy and 242–4,
253, 255, 261, 263, 265,
266–8, 270
see also equilibrium

Galbraith. J.K. xiii–xiv, 63, 64, 90
Garegnani, P. 106
gearing ratio 131, 154
Gedeon, S.J. 194
Gershuny, J. 199
Gillies, D.A. 78
Gintis, H. 266
Godley, W. 201, 260, 262, 263, 264
Goodhart, C.A.E. 179, 182, 187,
202
Goodwin, R.M.
business cycles model 105, 107,
227–9
Gordon, R.J. xii, 35, 75, 175
Government Deficit including
Trade Balance (GDTB) 235–6,
238
government deficits *see* budget
deficits
government expenditure 3–4, 7, 9–
12, 110, 196, 208, 255–6
Gowland, D. 193
gravity centres 106
Grossman, H.I. 30–31, 76
growth, cyclical *see* business cycles
growth dynamics, post-Keynesian
104–5
early post-Keynesian models
208–13
economic policy and Ch.10

Harrod model 104, 106, 123, 206–8
 income distribution and 104–5, 205, 208–10, 222–3
 and inequalities 241
 investment and 45, 72, 98, 99, 104, 132–3, 137, 205, 206–7, 209, 211–13, 215–23, 255–62 *passim*
 pricing and 205, 257–8
 Rowthorn model 213–23
 savings and 47, 49, 255–61 *passim*
 wages and 222, 257, 258, 260–62
 see also business cycles growth model, GNS
growth-pole model 245–6
Guttentag, J. 184

Hagemann, H. 190
Hahn, F.H. 36, 74, 82, 106
Haltiwanger, J. 74
Ham, C. 241
Hamouda, O.F. xii, 86, 87, 99
Harcourt, G.C. xii, xiii, 3, 82, 86, 87, 99, 106, 139, 150, 158
Hare, P.G. 264
Hargreaves-Heap, S.P. 170
harmony-of-interest, assumption of, in GNS economics 62–3
Harris, D.J. 159
Harris, L. 195, 196
Harris, L.H. 4
Harrod, R.F. 3
 growth model 104, 106, 123, 206–8
Hart. O. 36
Hazeldine, T. 154
Heiner, R.A. 69
Henry, S.G.B. 260
Hercowitz, Z. 75
Herfindahl index 142–3
Herring, R. 184
Hey, J.D. 69
Hicks. J.R. ix, 3, 8, 51, 83–4, 91, 92, 163, 164, 165, 269
high-level theories 78–9
Hill, D. Jr 199

Hill, M. 241
Hirschman, A.O. 62
Hirst, P. 246
Hodgson, G.M. 70, 76, 100
homogeneity of economic units 2
household demand theory 124–6
Hughes, P.R. 172
Hutchinson, G. 172
hydraulic aspects of GNS macro-economy 3
hysteresis effects 164, 169–77

imperfect competition 30, 58, 89, 97
implicit interest rate 147–54 *passim*
imports 109–10, 113, 198–9, 251, 262–3
 import controls 263–5
income distribution
 and business cycles 227–9, 238
 and demand for consumer importables 198
 in GNS economics 64, 65–8
 and growth 104–5, 205, 208–10, 222–3
 investment and x–xi, 104, 132–7
 socialization of investment and 266, 268
 post-Keynesian theory of 110–13, 125–6, 133–7
 pricing and 89–90, 141–2
 tax-based incomes policies (TIPs) and 261
 and wage determination 163–4, 168–9
income effects 98, 124, 126, 132, 161, 198
income elasticities 125
incomes planning 258, 260–62, 267–8, 270
indifference curves
 and epistomological rules of science 80
industrial concentration *see* monopoly, degree of
inflation 159–61, 258, 260
 see also expectations; mark-up pricing; prices; wages

Ingrao, B. 71
input–output models 116
  see also Leontief model
institutions
  in post-Keynesian economics 64, 88–90, 97, 98, 100, 249–50, 252
  see also megacorps; trade unions
interest rates
  and financial markets 109, 183, 186–90, 192–200 passim, 202, 203
  in GNS economics ix, 3–5, 6, 7, 10, 82–3
  in open economies 38, 39–41
  implicit 147–54 passim
  and investment ix, 7, 10, 82–3, 103–4, 127, 128, 129, 130, 131, 132, 147, 148–50, 151–3, 154, 212–13, 217, 237–8, 256
  in post-Keynesian model 111–13
international capital 196, 268, 269–70
international credit economy 252
international monetarist model see current account monetary model
inventory investment 231–2
investment
  and business cycles 49–50, 53, 107–8, 127, 131, 133, 137, 223–7, 230–35, 236–8
  and financial practices 236–8, 252, 256
  in GNS economics 3–4
  and growth 45, 72, 98, 99, 104, 132–3, 137, 205, 206–7, 209, 211–13, 215–23, 255–62 passim
  and income distribution x–xi, 104, 133–7, 266, 268
  interest rates and ix, 7, 10, 82–3, 103–4, 127, 128, 129, 130, 131, 132, 147, 148–50, 151–3, 154, 212–13, 217, 237–8, 256
  Keynesian investment function 126–9
  non-linearity of 223–7

post-Keynesian theories of 126–33, 137
pricing and 142, 145, 147, 148–53, 161, 246, 256, 257, 260–61
and productivity 244, 249, 250
profitability and 129–30, 132, 133, 154–9, 211–13, 215–23, 230–32, 235–6
savings and x, 45, 72, 123, 206–7, 217–27, 232, 234, 256
socialization of 265–8, 270–71
technical progress and 133
wages and 176–7, 246
investment/output ratio
  in non-oligopolistic sector 259
  in oligopolistic sector 255–7, 261–2
  in personal sector 259–60
irreversible time 92
IS curves see IS/LM curves
IS/LM curves 3, 4–9, 13–15, 25–30, 31–5, 37–41, 58
  and epistemological rules of science 80, 82–4
isoquant curves 80–81, 121
Israel, G. 71

Japan
  socialization of investment in 271
Jessop, B. 252
Johannsen, N.A.L.J. 190
Johnson, H.G. 41
Johnston, J. 81

Kahneman, D. 73
Kaldor, N.
  business cycles model 107, 223–7
  and critique of GNS 67, 70, 72, 81
  on growth 106, 210, 213
  on income distribution 125
  on monetary policy 90, 184, 193, 243
  on regional disparities 244
Kalecki, M.
  business cycles model 56, 105, 107, 230–35

on conflict 58, 63, 99, 101
on economic policy 242–3
on growth 105, 106, 210, 211, 222
investment theory 126, 129–32, 137
on market structure 58, 89
on money 190, 203
pricing theory 109, 139, 140–43, 151, 153, 159, 197
principle of effective demand 88
profits theory 230–31
on risk 158
on wage determination 94
Kay, N.M. 60
Keeble, D. 246
Kenyon, P. 139, 150, 158
Keynes, J.M.
on capital controls 269
on capitalism 271
on demand for assets 100
on economic policy 255–6, 266–7
on economic theory 96
on equilibrium 70
General Theory 3, 13, 30, 83, 88, 99, 100, 126–9, 179–80, 208, 256
on growth 107, 208
on investment 126–9, 137, 266–7
on irreversible time 92
on money 93, 99, 179–80
on uncertainty 91, 92, 95
on wages 166
King, M. 258
Knight, B. 268
Knight, F. 91
Kregel, J.A. ix, xi, xii, 70, 87–8, 95, 104, 105, 136–7, 182
Kuhn, T.S. 78

labour, supply and demand for
and business cycles 227–9
in GNS economics 3–5, 26–7, 74
in Leontief model 117, 122
in New Classical model 28–9
notional and effective 31–5
in post-Keynesian model 94, 110–13 *passim*

see also unemployment
Laidler, D.E.W. 76
Lancaster, K. 63
large corporations *see* megacorps
'last resort' facilities 90, 182, 184, 185, 193, 201–2
Lavoie, M. 86, 87, 194, 201, 203
Lawson, T. 95–7
Layard, R. 170
Leibenstein, H. 69
Leigh-Pemberton, R. 197
Leijonhufvud, A. 2, 30, 36
Leontief, W. 81, 116, 122
see also Leontief model
Leontief model 116, 117–22, 138
Lewis, M.K. 183, 185, 188, 192
liability management 182, 187–90, 202–3
Lindbeck, A. 170, 172, 173, 175
Lipietz, A. 251
Lipsey, R.G. 13, 14, 15, 16
liquidity, constraints on 183–6, 192–3, 201–2
liquidity preference 238
liquidity trap ix, 7, 10
LM curves *see* IS/LM curves
long-period analysis *see* periods
long-run analysis *see* runs
Longstreth, F. 195, 196
low-level theories 78
Lucas, R.E. 12–13, 55–6
Lucas Critique 13
Lucas supply function 29–30, 54–6
Luria, D. 248

MacRae, D. 56
managed international trade 263–5
Mankiw, N.G. xii, 36, 76
manpower policies 267–8
March, J.G. 69
marginal costs 143, 144, 146–7, 150, 214–15
of bank funds 189
marginal efficiency of capital *see* marginal efficiency of investment (MEI)
marginal efficiency of investment

(MEI) 103–4, 126–32, 150–51, 158
marginal productivity theory 43–4, 48, 62, 64, 67–8, 82, 214–15
marginal propensity to consume *see* propensity to consume
marginal propensity to import *see* propensity to import
marginal propensity to save *see* propensity to save
marginal rate of substitution 48, 121
market clearing 2, 6, 21, 23, 27, 29, 34–5, 54–5, 58, 73, 74–5, 175, 197
mark-up pricing x–xi, 31, 34, 35, 94, 103, 109, 136, Ch.6, 190, 214, 236, 246, 250, 257, 258, 260
in financial markets 189, 197
Marris, R. 154
Marshall, A. 99, 107
mass consumption 246–7, 249, 250, 251
mass production 246–7, 249, 250, 251
maturity thesis 131
McCallum, J. 225
McCloskey, D.N. 80
McDonald, I.M. 36
Meade, J.E. 3
megacorps 63–4, 89–90, 103, 132, 136–7, 143–54, 257
membership theory 170, 172–3, 174
Metcalf, J.S. 73
methodologies
of GNS 77–85
of post-Keynesian economics 94–100
Miller, M. 151
Minsky, H.P. 187
financial instability hypothesis 235–8, 239
Mirowski, P. 61
Mishan, E. 80
Mishkin, F.S. 75
modes of production 250, 253
modes of regulation 249–50, 253

Modigliani, F. 8, 151
money, supply and demand for
in GNS economics ix, 3–5, 7, 9–12, 57–8, 63–4
and flexible exchange rates 39–43
and liquidity trap ix, 7, 10
and output 75–6
and rational expectations 23
in post-Keynesian economics 90, 92–4, 99, 109, 111–13, 126, Ch.8
endogeneity of 179, 180–82, 184, 186, 200–203
model of money, credit and finance 186–200
see also interest rates; IS/LM curves
monopoly, degree of 58, 139, 140, 142–3, 151–3, 159, 197, 214–15
monopsonies 17
Moore, B.J. 86, 93, 94, 180, 185, 186, 187, 190, 191, 192, 203
Morley, R. 37
Muellbauer, J. 198
multinationals *see* transnational corporations
multipliers 9–13, 133, 233
multiplier–accelerator model 49–54, 131, 133, 206, 207, 221
Mundell, R.A. 37
Muth, J.F. 22, 57
Myrdal, G. 72, 81, 203, 244

natural rate of growth 208, 209–10, 213
natural rate of output 27–30, 33–4
natural resources 122
Negishi, T. 36
neo-Fordism 246, 249–52
Nickell, S.J. 83, 170, 172
Nielsen, K. 251
Nolan, P. 248
non-optimizing behaviour 99
Nordhaus, W.D. 56

O'Donnell, K. 248
oligopolies x, 58, 89, 98, 103, 145, 242, 246, 255–8, 261–2

Index

commercial banks as 186–7, 189, 197
see also megacorps
Olson, M. 75
open credit lines 185
open economies
  economic policy in 262–8
  and financial markets 177, 181, 187, 188, 194–5, 197–200
  full employment in 244
  in GNS economics 3, 37–43, 58
  in post-Keynesian model 109–13
  see also exports; imports
open historical models 71, 88, 95–6, 158, 191, 211
open-market operations 180, 194–5, 196, 197–8, 203
open systems *see* open historical models
opportunity frontiers 155–8
optimizing behaviour 69–70
  see also non-optimizing behaviour; profit maximization; utility maximization
Ormerod, P. 260
Oswald, A.J. 36
output, natural rate of 27–30, 33–4

Paldam, M. 163
Parkin, J.M. 17
parsimony tests 80, 81
Pasinetti, L.L. 66, 87, 98, 104, 106, 116, 122, 125, 135–6, 210
Pasinetti paradox 136
Patinkin, D. 30
Peel, D.A. 73
perfect competition, assumption of, in GNS economics 1, 2, 6, 17, 43, 55, 58, 67, 74, 89
perfect information, assumption of, in GNS economics 74
periods
  defined 105–7
peripheral Fordism 251–2
Perroux, F. 245
Phelps, E.S. 17, 20
Phillips, A.W. 15

see also Phillips curve
Phillips curve 13–21, 63, 78, 80, 84
Pigou effect 7–8, 10–12, 30
Piore, M.J. 246, 247
Podolski, T.M. 185, 202
Polanyi, K. 64
Popper, K.R. 77–8, 79
post-Fordism 246, 247–9, 250
post-Keynesian model
  equations of 110–13
  flow diagram of 114
  predictive power of GNS theory 77–9
present values 127
Preston, L.E. 62
price controls 257–8
price elasticities 125, 142–3, 144, 145, 147, 148, 150
price leaders 142, 143, 145–7, 153
prices
  Eichner's pricing theory 103, 104, 139, 143–54, 158, 159, 246
  and growth 205, 257–8
  and income distribution 89–90, 141–2
  and inflation 159–61, 258, 260
  and investment 142, 145, 147, 148–53, 161, 246, 256, 257, 260–61
  Kalecki's pricing theory 109, 139, 140–43, 151, 153, 159, 197
  in Leontief model 121, 139
  Phillips curve and 13–14
  rigidities in ix–x, 7, 31–7, 73, 74, 75
  Wood's pricing theory 103, 139, 154–9
  see also expectations; mark-up pricing; value, theory of
product differentiation 247, 249
production functions 3–5, 27, 43–8, 62, 81, 82
production theory, post-Keynesian 117–22, 137
productivity, labour
  investment and 244, 249, 250

wages and 170–71, 173, 175, 176–7, 246, 250, 260
worker participation and 268
profit maximization 2, 35, 58, 61–2, 69, 75, 81, 142–3
  see also optimizing behaviour
profits
  and business cycles 108
  and investment 103–4, 129–30, 132, 133, 154–9, 211–13, 215–23, 230–32, 235–6
  neglected in GNS economics 65–6, 68
profits curve 216–17, 219–22
profit-sharing 266
  see also income distribution
propensity to consume 104, 134–7, 230–34, 235–6, 246
propensity to import 110, 198–9, 263
propensity to save 47, 49, 68, 104–5, 206–10, 211, 218, 219, 222, 224–5, 230, 260
  see also savings/income ratio
public debt, sales of see open-market operations
public sector borrowing requirement (PSBR) 194–5, 196
purchasing power parity theory 200

quantity theory of money 200

Radcliffe, Lord 187
Radice, H. 270
rational expectations see expectations
rationality, assumption of, in GNS economics 62, 69–70, 92
  bounded 69, 99
realism
  emphasis on, in post-Keynesian economics 94–100
realization curve 218–22
regimes of accumulation 249, 250, 251, 253
regional disparities 244–6, 253, 254, 265

regressive expectations 196
regulation theory see neo-Fordism; Social Structure of Accumulation (SSA)
relative income hypothesis 124–5
rentiers 243
reservation wage 20, 170, 173
reswitching 66
Revell, J. 186
Reynolds, P.J. 153
Riach, P.A. 94
Ricardo, D. 66–7
risk 70, 91–2, 126, 128, 129, 154, 212, 237, 238
Robinson, J. xiii, 65–6, 70–71, 87–8, 92, 98, 100, 105, 106, 180, 183, 210–13, 241, 243
Robinson, R. 154
Rogers, C. 93, 95
Romer, P. 49
Roncaglia, A. 91
Rousseas, S. 187, 191, 197, 202
Routh, G. 164
Rowthorn, R. 21, 63, 64, 87, 163, 168, 267
  growth model 213–23
Ruhl, C. 190
runs
  defined 105–7
Ruth Cohen Curiosum 66

Sabel, C. 246, 247
sales growth rates 103–4, 132, 154, 155–8, 255, 256
Samuels, W.J. 100
Samuelson, P.A. ix, 49
Santomero, A.M. 17, 20
Sardoni, C. 93
Sargent, T.J. 22, 55
savings
  and business cycles 223–7
  and growth 47, 49, 255–61
    passim
  and investment x, 45, 72, 123, 206–7, 217–27, 232, 234, 256
  non-linearity of 223–7
  see also propensity to save
savings/income ratio

in non-oligopolistic sector 259
in oligopolistic sector 255, 256, 257–8, 261
in personal sector 260
see also propensity to save
Sawyer, M.C. 17, 30, 68, 81, 84, 88, 163, 167, 190, 240, 241
Say's Law ix
Schefold, B. 87
Schumpeter, J.A. 164
Scott, M.Fg. 264
Seater, J.J. 17, 20
Sen, A.K. 62
service sector, development of 248
Shackle, G.L.S. 69, 126, 129
Shapiro, N. 127
short-period analyses see periods
short-run analyses see runs
Simon, H.A. 69
skills, labour 117, 241, 244, 245, 247, 248
Skott, P. 163, 164, 166
Skouras, T. xii
Skuse, F.E. 241
Smith, R.P. 260
Sneessens, H. 170
Snower, D.J. 170, 172, 173, 175
social contracts 270
Social Structure of Accumulation (SSA) 252–3
socialization of investment 265–8, 270–71
solipsistic fallacy 84
Solow, R.M. xi, 36, 49, 66
Soskice, D. 170, 174
Sraffa, P. 66, 73, 100, 106, 116, 122
Stanton, D. 172
Startz, R. 60
Steindl, J. 131
Stigler, G. 67
Stiglitz, J.E. 66
strikes 167, 175
substitution effects 98, 124, 126, 132, 147–50, 151, 153, 161, 198
Sugden, R. 268, 269
Summers, L.H. 36, 170, 172, 173, 174
supply, aggregate

defined 25–7
supply curves, positively sloped 34
and epistemological rules of science 80, 81, 82
Swan, T.W. xi
Sweden
socialization of investment in 271
system framework, post-Keynesian 90

target real wages 163–9, 175, 176, 177
Taubman, P. 125
taxation 3, 7, 9–12, 38, 39–40, 57–8, 63–4, 110, 180, 181, 196, 208, 254, 256–7, 262–3
tax shifting 258
tax-based incomes policies (TIPs) 260–61
Taylor, J. 35
technical progress 47–9, 107, 122, 132–3, 208, 211, 213, 216, 217–18, 222, 227, 232, 241, 249
Threadgold, A.R. 186, 190, 192
Ticky, G. 271
Tinbergen, J. 269
TIPs see tax-based incomes policies (TIPs)
Tobin, J. 16, 20, 21, 67
Toetsch, I. 171
total costs
and bank lending to industry 190–92
trade unions xi, 6, 8, 62–4 passim, 89–90, 108, 140, 153, 164–9, 246–7, 253, 261, 265–7, 270
see also wage bargaining
transactions, expected 190–92
transnational corporations 196, 251, 268–9
Treasury bills 195
Trevethick, J.A. 163
turnover costs 172–3, 175
Tversky, A. 73

uncertainty 70, 90–92, 93, 95, 99, 126, 127–8, 132, 153, 180, 236, 266, 267

unemployment
  as a disequilibrium problem 36–7
  hysteresis effects and 164, 169–75
  and market clearing 74–5
  natural rate of 16–21, 27, 57
  search theories of 20–21, 170, 171, 172
  and wages 7, 8, 15–21, 63, 84, 94, 109, 166–7, 170–73, 174, 227–9
  see also labour, supply and demand for
unused overdraft facilities 185
utility maximization 2, 7, 56, 58, 61–2, 75, 167
  see also optimizing behaviour

value, theory of 102–3, 122
value added 118, 120–21
Veblen, T. 63, 79, 100

wage bargaining 89–90, 94, 108–9, 163, 165–9, 172–3, 175, 176, 177, 227–9, 246–7, 248, 250
  see also trade unions
wage determination, theory of 108–9, 160, 161, Ch.7, 260
wage relativities 163–9, 177
wages
  and growth 222, 257, 258, 260–62
  and inflation 159–61, 258, 260
  and investment 176–7, 246
  and productivity 170–71, 173, 175, 176–7, 246, 250, 257, 260
  rigidities in ix–x, 7, 8, 31–7, 74, 75, 163, 165–6
  and unemployment 7, 8, 15–21, 63, 84, 94, 109, 166–7, 170–73, 174, 227–9
  see also wage bargaining; wage determination, theory of
Waldman, M. 74
Wallace, N. 22
Wallich, H. 260
Walters, A.A. 81
warranted rate of growth 105, 106, 207–8, 210
Waterson, M. 143
wealth, real see Pigou effect
Weintraub, S. 190, 260
Weitzman, M.L. 36
wholesale financial markets 185–8, 189
Wills, H.R. 187
Wojnilower, A.M. 184, 185, 187, 201
women, employment of 248
Wood, A.
  pricing theory 103, 139, 154–9
  on profit-sharing 266
  on wage determination 163, 166
  worker participation 268, 270
  see also socialization of investment
world trade, volume of 112, 160, 161, 198, 262

X-inefficiencies 69

Yellen, J.L. 36
Young, A.A. 81

Zeitlin, J. 246